Macroeconomics

BRIEF EDITION, FIRST EDITION

Campbell R. McConnell

University of Nebraska

Stanley L. Brue

Pacific Lutheran University

Sean M. Flynn

Vassar College

With the special assistance of

Randy R. Grant

Linfield College

McGraw-Hill
Irwin

Boston   Burr Ridge, IL   Dubuque, IA   New York   San Francisco   St. Louis
Bangkok   Bogotá   Caracas   Kuala Lumpur   Lisbon   London   Madrid   Mexico City
Milan   Montreal   New Delhi   Santiago   Seoul   Singapore   Sydney   Taipei   Toronto

The McGraw-Hill
Series Economics

ESSENTIALS OF ECONOMICS

Brue, McConnell, and Flynn
Essentials of Economics
Second Edition

Mandel
Economics: The Basics
First Edition

Schiller
Essentials of Economics
Seventh Edition

PRINCIPLES OF ECONOMICS

Colander
Economics, Microeconomics, and Macroeconomics
Seventh Edition

Frank and Bernanke
Principles of Economics, Principles of Microeconomics, Principles of Macroeconomics
Fourth Edition

Frank and Bernanke
Brief Editions: Principles of Economics, Principles of Microeconomics, Principles of Macroeconomics
First Edition

McConnell, Brue, and Flynn
Economics, Microeconomics, and Macroeconomics
Eighteenth Edition

McConnell, Brue, and Flynn
Brief Editions: Microeconomics and Macroeconomics
First Edition

Miller
Principles of Microeconomics
First Edition

Samuelson and Nordhaus
Economics, Microeconomics, and Macroeconomics
Nineteenth Edition

Schiller
The Economy Today, The Micro Economy Today, and The Macro Economy Today
Eleventh Edition

Slavin
Economics, Microeconomics, and Macroeconomics
Ninth Edition

ECONOMICS OF SOCIAL ISSUES

Guell
Issues in Economics Today
Fourth Edition

Sharp, Register, and Grimes
Economics of Social Issues
Eighteenth Edition

ECONOMETRICS

Gujarati and Porter
Basic Econometrics
Fifth Edition

Gujarati and Porter
Essentials of Econometrics
Fourth Edition

MANAGERIAL ECONOMICS

Baye
Managerial Economics and Business Strategy
Sixth Edition

Brickley, Smith, and Zimmerman
Managerial Economics and Organizational Architecture
Fifth Edition

Thomas and Maurice
Managerial Economics
Ninth Edition

INTERMEDIATE ECONOMICS

Bernheim and Whinston
Microeconomics
First Edition

Dornbusch, Fischer, and Startz
Macroeconomics
Tenth Edition

Frank
Microeconomics and Behavior
Seventh Edition

ADVANCED ECONOMICS

Romer
Advanced Macroeconomics
Third Edition

MONEY AND BANKING

Cecchetti
Money, Banking, and Financial Markets
Second Edition

URBAN ECONOMICS

O'Sullivan
Urban Economics
Seventh Edition

LABOR ECONOMICS

Borjas
Labor Economics
Fifth Edition

McConnell, Brue, and Macpherson
Contemporary Labor Economics
Eighth Edition

PUBLIC FINANCE

Rosen and Gayer
Public Finance
Eighth Edition

Seidman
Public Finance
First Edition

ENVIRONMENTAL ECONOMICS

Field and Field
Environmental Economics: An Introduction
Fifth Edition

INTERNATIONAL ECONOMICS

Appleyard, Field, and Cobb
International Economics
Sixth Edition

King and King
International Economics, Globalization, and Policy: A Reader
Fifth Edition

Pugel
International Economics
Fourteenth Edition

Rediscover the market-leading principles text: McConnell, Brue, and Flynn's *Economics*, 18e.

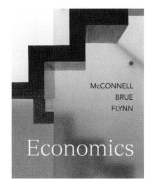 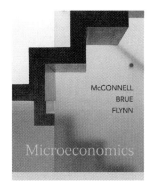 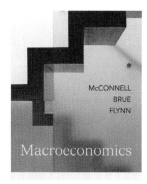

Go to **www.mcconnell18e.com** for sample chapters, the text preface, and more information.

For instructors teaching a one-semester Micro-Macro survey course, we offer *Essentials of Economics*, 2e.

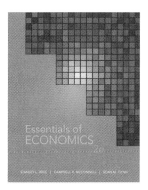

Go to **www.brue2e.com** for sample chapters, the text preface, and more information.

MACROECONOMICS: BRIEF EDITION

Published by McGraw-Hill/Irwin, a business unit of The McGraw-Hill Companies, Inc., 1221 Avenue of the Americas, New York, NY, 10020. Copyright © 2010 by The McGraw-Hill Companies, Inc. All rights reserved. No part of this publication may be reproduced or distributed in any form or by any means, or stored in a database or retrieval system, without the prior written consent of The McGraw-Hill Companies, Inc., including, but not limited to, in any network or other electronic storage or transmission, or broadcast for distance learning.

Some ancillaries, including electronic and print components, may not be available to customers outside the United States.

This book is printed on acid-free paper.

1 2 3 4 5 6 7 8 9 0 CCI/CCI 0 9

ISBN   978-0-07-723097-5
MHID   0-07-723097-3

Publisher: *Douglas Reiner*
Developmental editor: *Anne E. Hilbert*
Developmental editor: *Elizabeth Clevenger*
Editorial coordinator: *Noelle Fox*
Senior marketing manager: *Melissa Larmon*
Senior marketing manager: *Jennifer Lambert*
Senior project manager: *Harvey Yep*
Lead production supervisor: *Michael R. McCormick*
Interior designer: *Cara Hawthorne*

Senior photo research coordinator: *Lori Kramer*
Photo researcher: *Keri Johnson*
Senior media project manager: *Kerry Bowler*
Cover design: *Cara Hawthorne*
Cover image: *© David Churchill/Arcaid/Corbis*
Typeface: *10/12 Janson Text 55 Roman*
Compositor: *Aptara, Inc.*
Printer: *Courier Kendallville*

Library of Congress Cataloging-in-Publication Data

McConnell, Campbell R.
    Macroeconomics : brief edition / Campbell R. McConnell, Stanley L. Brue, Sean M. Flynn. — 1st ed.
        p. cm. — (The McGraw-Hill series economics)
    Includes index.
    ISBN-13: 978-0-07-723097-5 (alk. paper)
    ISBN-10: 0-07-723097-3 (alk. paper)
    1. Macroeconomics. I. Brue, Stanley L., 1945- II. Flynn, Sean Masaki. III. Title.
HB172.5.M3742 2010
339—dc22
                                        2009000129

Dedication

To **Mem,** to **Terri** and **Craig,** and to **past instructors**

About the Authors

Campbell R. McConnell earned his Ph.D. from the University of Iowa after receiving degrees from Cornell College and the University of Illinois. He taught at the University of Nebraska–Lincoln from 1953 until his retirement in 1990. He is coauthor of *Economics*, eighteenth edition (McGraw-Hill/Irwin); *Contemporary Labor Economics*, eighth edition (McGraw-Hill/Irwin); and *Essentials of Economics*, second edition (McGraw-Hill/Irwin) and has edited readers for the principles and labor economics courses. He is a recipient of both the University of Nebraska Distinguished Teaching Award and the James A. Lake Academic Freedom Award and is past president of the Midwest Economics Association. Professor McConnell was awarded an honorary Doctor of Laws degree from Cornell College in 1973 and received its Distinguished Achievement Award in 1994. His primary areas of interest are labor economics and economic education. He has an extensive collection of jazz recordings and enjoys reading jazz history.

Stanley L. Brue did his undergraduate work at Augustana College (S.D.) and received its Distinguished Achievement Award in 1991. He received his Ph.D. from the University of Nebraska–Lincoln. He is a professor at Pacific Lutheran University, where he has been honored as a recipient of the Burlington Northern Faculty Achievement Award. Professor Brue has also received the national Leavey Award for excellence in economic education. He has served as national president and chair of the Board of Trustees of Omicron Delta Epsilon International Economics Honorary. He is coauthor of *Economics*, eighteenth edition (McGraw-Hill/Irwin); *Economic Scenes*, fifth edition (Prentice-Hall); *Contemporary Labor Economics*, eighth edition (McGraw-Hill/Irwin); *Essentials of Economics*, second edition (McGraw-Hill/Irwin); and *The Evolution of Economic Thought*, seventh edition (South-Western). For relaxation, he enjoys international travel, attending sporting events, and skiing with family and friends.

 **Sean M. Flynn** did his undergraduate work at the University of Southern California before completing his Ph.D. at U.C. Berkeley, where he served as the Head Graduate Student Instructor for the Department of Economics after receiving the Outstanding Graduate Student Instructor Award. He teaches at Vassar College in Poughkeepsie, New York and is also the author of *Economics for Dummies* (Wiley) and co-author of *Economics*, eighteenth edition (McGraw-Hill/Irwin) and *Essentials of Economics*, second edition (McGraw-Hill/Irwin). His research interests include finance and behavioral economics. An accomplished martial artist, he has represented the United States in international aikido tournaments and is the author of *Understanding Shodokan Aikido* (Shodokan Press). Other hobbies include running, traveling, and enjoying ethnic food.

Welcome a New Text and a New Author

Welcome to *Macroeconomics, Brief Edition*, 1e, the new trimmed and edited version of *Economics*, 18e, the nation's best-selling economics textbook. In the tradition of the market-leading text *Economics: Problems, Principles, and Policies*, the cover for the *Brief Edition* includes a photograph of steps. The photo is a metaphor for the step-by-step approach that we use to present basic economic principles. It also represents the simplicity, beauty, and power of basic economic models. We have chosen a highly modern photo to reflect the addition of our new coauthor, Sean M. Flynn, who has helped modernize the content of the book from cover to cover. Sean did his undergraduate work at USC, received his Ph.D. from U.C. Berkeley (in 2002), teaches principles at Vassar, and is the author of *Economics for Dummies*. We are greatly pleased to have Sean working on the text, since he shares our commitment to present economics in a way that is understandable to all.

Fundamental Objectives

We have three main goals for *Macroeconomics, Brief Edition*:

- Help the beginning student master the principles essential for understanding the economizing problem, specific economic issues, and the policy alternatives.
- Help the student understand and apply the economic perspective and reason accurately and objectively about economic matters.
- Promote a lasting student interest in economics and the economy.

Integrated, Distinct Book

Although *Macroeconomics, Brief Edition* is a spin-off of *Macroeconomics*, 18e, it is not a cut-and-paste book that simply eliminates several chapters of *Macroeconomics*, 18e and reorders and renumbers the retained content. We can prepare such books via custom publication. Instead, the *Brief Edition* is a very concise, highly integrated macroeconomics textbook that is distinct in purpose, style, and coverage from *Economics*, 18e and its Micro and Macro splits.

Distinguishing Features

Macroeconomics, Brief Edition includes several features that encourage students to read and retain the content.

State-of-the-Art Design and Pedagogy

The *Brief Edition* incorporates a single-column design with a host of pedagogical aids, including a strategically placed "To the Student" statement, chapter opening objectives, definitions in the margins, combined tables and graphs, complete chapter summaries, lists of key terms, carefully constructed study questions, connections to our Web site, an appendix on graphs and a Web appendix on additional examples of demand and supply, and an extensive glossary.

Focus on Core Models

Macroeconomics, Brief Edition shortens and simplifies explanations where appropriate but stresses the importance of the economic perspective, including explaining and applying core economic models. Our strategy is to develop a limited set of essential models, illustrate them with analogies or anecdotes, explain them thoroughly, and apply them to real-world situations. Eliminating unnecessary graphs and elaborations makes perfect sense in a brief edition, but cutting explanations of the truly fundamental graphs does not. In dealing with the basics, brevity at the expense of clarity is false economy.

We created a student-oriented textbook that draws on the methodological strengths of the discipline and helps students improve their analytical reasoning skills. Regardless of students' eventual occupations, they will discover that such skills are highly valuable in their workplaces.

Illustrating the Idea

Numerous analogies, examples, and anecdotes are included throughout the book to help drive home central economic ideas in a lively, colorful, and easy-to-remember way. For instance, a piece on Bill Gates, Oprah Winfrey, and Alex Rodriquez illustrates the importance of opportunity costs in decision-making. Art in the public square brings clarity to public goods and the free-rider problem. A discussion of credit cards helps explain what money is and is not. The practices of sixteenth century goldsmiths demonstrate fractional reserve banking, and a story about a CPA and a painter walks students through the idea of comparative advantage. These brief vignettes flow directly from the preceding content and segue to the content that follows, rather than being "boxed off" away from the flow and therefore easily overlooked.

Applying the Analysis

A glance though this book's pages will demonstrate that this is an application-oriented textbook. *Applying the Analysis* pieces immediately follow the development of economic analysis and are part of the flow of the chapters, rather than segregated from the main body discussion in a traditional boxed format. For example, the basics of the economic perspective are applied to why customers choose the shortest checkout lines. McDonald's sandwich "McHits" and "McMisses" over the years apply the concept of consumer sovereignty. The idea of inflation is reinforced with an application to historical episodes of hyperinflation, the graphics of fiscal policy are followed by a discussion of recent fiscal policy, and the Federal Reserve's role in the economy is demonstrated through an application of its responses to the mortgage debt crisis and the slowdown of the economy. These and many other applications clearly demonstrate the relevance and usefulness of mastering the basic economic principles and models to beginning students.

Photo Ops

Photo sets under the title *Photo Op* are included throughout the book to add visual interest, break up the density, and highlight important distinctions. Just a few of the many examples are sets of photos to illustrate the various types of economic resources; photos of durable goods, nondurable goods, and services to distinguish types of consumer spending; and photos of lumber and newly constructed homes to drive home the difference between intermediate and final goods. Other photo sets illustrate normal versus inferior goods, complements versus substitutes in consumption, public versus private investment, and more.

Web Buttons

The in-text Web buttons (or indicators) merit special mention. Three differing colors of rectangular indicators appear throughout the book, informing readers that complementary content on a subject can be found at our Web site, **www.mcconnellbriefmacro1e.com**. Scattered throughout the text you'll see:

Worked Problems Written by Norris Peterson of Pacific Lutheran University, these pieces consist of side-by-side computational questions and computational procedures used to derive the answers. From a student perspective, they provide "cookbook" help for problem solving.

WORKED PROBLEMS
W 1.1
Budget Lines

Interactive Graphs These pieces (developed under the supervision of Norris Peterson) depict major graphs and instruct students to shift the curves, observe the outcomes, and derive relevant generalizations. This hands-on graph work will greatly reinforce the main graphs and their meaning.

INTERACTIVE GRAPHS
G 3.1
Supply and Demand

Origin of the Ideas These brief histories, written by Randy Grant of Linfield College (OR), examine the origins of major ideas identified in the book. Students will find it interesting to learn about the economists who first developed such ideas as opportunity costs, equilibrium price, elasticity, creative destruction, and comparative advantage.

ORIGIN OF THE IDEA
O 2.2
Specialization/division of labor

Global Snapshots

Global Snapshot pieces show bar charts and line graphs that compare data for a particular year or other time period among selected nations. Examples of these lists and comparisons include income per capita, the index of economic freedom, the differing economic status of North Korea and South Korea, annual growth rates of selected nations, publicly held debt as percentages of GDP, comparative exports, and so forth. These *Global Snapshots* join other significant international content to help convey that the United States operates in a global economy.

Supplements for Students

Online Learning Center

At **www.mcconnellbriefmacro1e.com** students have access to several learning aids. Along with the Interactive Graphs, Worked Problems, and Origin of the Idea pieces, the student portion of the Web site includes Web-based study questions, self-grading quizzes, and PowerPoint presentations. For math-minded students, there is a "See the Math" section, written by Norris Peterson, where the mathematical details of the concepts in the text can be explored.

Premium Content

The Premium Content, available at the Online Learning Center, offers a range of dynamic study aids to the student. Premium Content enables students to study and self-test on their computer or on the go.

- One of the world's leading experts on economic education—William Walstad of the University of Nebraska at Lincoln—has prepared the *Study Guide*. Each chapter contains an introductory statement, a checklist of behavioral objectives, an outline, a list of important terms, fill-in questions, problems and projects, objective questions, and discussion questions. The text's glossary is repeated in the *Study Guide* so that the student does not have to go back and forth between books. Many students will find this "digital tutor" indispensable.

- Narrated PowerPoint presentations enable students to see key concepts and hear the explanation simultaneously.
- The Solman Videos, a set of more than 250 minutes of video created by Paul Solman of *The News Hour with Jim Lehrer*; cover core economic concepts such as elasticity, deregulation, and perfect competition.
- Chapter quizzes can be purchased and downloaded to an iPod, mp3 player, or desktop computer.

McGraw-Hill Connect Economics

Connect Economics is a complete, online supplement system that duplicates and expands upon the textbook's end-of chapter material and test banks. Nearly all the questions from the text, including the numerous graphing exercises, are presented in an autogradable format and tied to the text's learning objectives. Instructors may edit existing questions and author entirely new problems. Connect Economics can be used for student practice, homework, quizzes, and formal examinations. Detailed grade reports enable instructors to see how each student performs on a particular problem, a full assignment, and in the context of the overall class. The Connect Economics grade reports can be easily integrated with WebCT and Blackboard. Connect Economics is also available with an integrated online version of the textbook. With a single access code, students can read the eBook, work through practice problems, do homework, and take exams.

 **CourseSmart eTextbook** For roughly half the cost of a print book you can reduce your impact on the environment by buying McConnell, Brue, and Flynn's *Macroeconomics, Brief Edition* eText. CourseSmart eTextbooks, available in a standard online reader, retain the exact content and look of the print text, plus offer the advantage of digital navigation, to which students are accustomed. Students can search the text, highlight, take notes, and use e-mail tools to share notes with their classmates. CourseSmart also includes tech support in case help is ever needed. To buy *Macroeconomics, Brief Edition* as an eText or learn more about this digital solution, visit **www.CourseSmart.com** and search by title, author, or ISBN.

Supplements for Instructors

Instructor's Manual

Darlene De Vera of De Anza College has prepared the Instructor's Manual. It includes chapter learning objectives, outlines, and summaries; numerous teaching suggestions; discussions of "student stumbling blocks;" listings of data and visual aid sources with suggestions for classroom use; and answers to the end-of-chapter study questions. Available in MS Word on the instructor's side of the Web site and on the Instructor's Resource CD, the manual enables instructors to print portions of the contents, complete with their own additions and alterations, for use as student handouts or in whatever ways they wish. This capability includes printing answers to the end-of-chapter questions.

Test Bank

The *Macroeconomics, Brief Edition* Test Bank, originally written by William Walstad and newly compiled and updated by Mohammad Bajwa of Northampton Community College, contains multiple choice and true-false questions. Each question is tied to a learning objective, topic, and AACSB Assurance of Learning and Bloom's Taxonomy guidelines. While crafting tests in EZ Test Online, instructors can use the whole chapter, scramble questions, and narrow the group by selecting the criteria. The Test Bank is also available in MS Word on the instructor's side of the Web site.

PowerPoints

Galina Hale, Economist, Federal Reserve Bank of San Francisco, created these in-depth slides to accompany lectures. The slides highlight all the main points of each chapter and include key figures and tables from the text. Each slide is tied to a learning objective.

Digital Image Library

Every graph and table in the text is available on the Web site. These figures allow instructors to create their own PowerPoint presentations and lecture materials.

Online Learning Center

The password-protected instructor's side of the Online Learning Center, **www.mcconnellbriefmacro1e.com,** holds all of the instructor resource materials. There, instructors may find the Instructor's Manual, Test Bank, PowerPoint presentations, Digital Image Library, and information on CPS by eInstruction or the "clicker" system.

Acknowledgments

We give special thanks to Randy Grant of Linfield College, who not only wrote the Origin of the Idea pieces on our Web site but also served as the content coordinator for *Macroeconomics, Brief Edition*. Professor Grant modified and seamlessly incorporated appropriate new content and revisions that the authors made in the eighteenth edition of *Economics* into this first edition of the *Brief Edition*. He also updated the tables and other information in *Macroeconomics, Brief Edition* and made various improvements that he deemed helpful or were suggested to him by the authors, reviewers, and publisher.

We also want to acknowledge Norris Peterson of Pacific Lutheran University, who created the See the Math pieces and the new Worked Problem pieces on our Web site. Professor Peterson also oversaw the development of the Interactive Graph pieces that are on the site. Finally, we wish to acknowledge William Walstad and Tom Barbiero (the coauthor of the Canadian edition of *Economics*) for their ongoing ideas and insights.

We are greatly indebted to an all-star group of professionals at McGraw-Hill—in particular Douglas Reiner, Elizabeth Clevenger, Anne Hilbert, Noelle Fox, Harvey Yep, Melissa Larmon, and Brent Gordon for their publishing and marketing expertise. We thank Keri Johnson for her selection of Photo Op images. Cara Hawthorne provided the vibrant interior design and cover.

Stanley L. Brue
Sean M. Flynn
Campbell R. McConnell

Brief Contents

Contents

PART FOUR
Money, Banking, and Monetary Policy

PART ONE

Introduction

To the Student

This book and its ancillaries contain several features designed to help you learn economics:

- *Icons in the margins* A glance through the book reveals many pages with Web buttons in the margins. Three differing colored rectangular indicators appear throughout the book, alerting you when complementary content on a subject can be found at our Online Learning Center, **www.mcconnellbriefmacro1e.com.** The **Worked Problems** serve as your "cookbook" for problem solving. Numeric problems are presented and then solved, side-by-side, step-by-step. Seeing how the problems are worked will help you solve similar problems on quizzes and exams. Practice hands-on graph work with the **Interactive Graphs** exercises. Manipulate the graphs by clicking on a specific curve and dragging it to a new location. This interaction will enhance your understanding of the underlying concepts. The **Origin of the Ideas** pieces trace a particular idea to the person or persons who first developed it.

WORKED PROBLEMS	INTERACTIVE GRAPHS	ORIGIN OF THE IDEA
W 1.1	**G 3.1**	**O 2.2**
Budget lines	Supply and demand	Specialization/division of labor

- *Other Internet aids* Our Internet site contains many other aids. In the student section at the Online Learning Center, you will find self-testing multiple-choice quizzes, PowerPoint slides, and much more.
- *Appendix on graphs* To understand the content in this book, you will need to be comfortable with basic graphical analysis and a few quantitative concepts. The appendix (pages 24–29) at the end of Chapter 1 reviews graphing and slopes of curves. Be sure not to skip it.
- *Key terms* Key terms are set in boldface type within the chapters, defined in the margins, listed at the end of each chapter, and again defined in the Glossary toward the end of the book.
- *"Illustrating the Idea" and "Applying the Analysis"* These sections flow logically and smoothly from the content that precedes them. They are part and parcel of the development of the ideas and cannot be skipped.
- *Questions* Each "Illustrating the Idea" and "Applying the Analysis" section is followed by a question. A comprehensive list of study questions is located at the end of each chapter. Each question is keyed to a particular learning objective (LO) in the list of LOs at the beginning of the chapter. At the Internet site, there are multiple-choice quizzes and one or more Web-based questions that require you to find information at specified Web sites to formulate answers.
- *Study Guide* We enthusiastically recommend the *Study Guide* accompanying this text. This "portable tutor" contains not only a broad sampling of various kinds of questions but a host of useful learning aids.

Our two main goals are to help you understand and apply economics and help you improve your analytical skills. An understanding of economics will enable you to comprehend a whole range of economic, social, and political problems that otherwise would seem puzzling and perplexing. Also, your study will enhance reasoning skills that are highly prized in the workplace.

Good luck with your study. We think it will be well worth your time and effort.

Limits, Alternatives, and Choices

(An appendix *on understanding graphs follows this chapter. If you need a quick review of this mathematical tool, you might benefit by reading the appendix first.)*

Economics is about wants and means. Biologically, people need only air, water, food, clothing, and shelter. But in modern society people also desire goods and services that provide a more comfortable or affluent standard of living. We want bottled water, soft drinks, and fruit juices, not just water from the creek. We want salads, burgers, and pizzas, not just berries and nuts. We want jeans, suits, and coats, not just woven reeds. We want apartments, condominiums, or houses, not just mud huts. And, as the saying goes, "that is not the half of it." We also want flat-panel TVs, Internet service, education, homeland security, cell phones, and much more.

Fortunately, society possesses productive resources such as labor and managerial talent, tools and machinery, and land and mineral deposits. These resources, employed in the economic system (or simply the economy), help us produce goods and services that satisfy many of our economic wants. But the blunt reality is that our economic wants far exceed the productive capacity of our scarce (limited) resources. We are forced to make choices. This unyielding truth underlies the definition of **economics,** which is the social science concerned with how individuals, institutions, and society make choices under conditions of scarcity.

The Economic Perspective

Economists view things through a particular perspective. This **economic perspective,** or economic way of thinking, has several critical and closely interrelated features.

Scarcity and Choice

From our definition of economics, it is easy to see why economists view the world through the lens of scarcity. Scarce economic resources mean limited goods and services. Scarcity restricts options and demands choices. Because we "can't have it all," we must decide what we will have and what we must forgo.

At the core of economics is the idea that "there is no free lunch." You may be treated to lunch, making it "free" to you, but someone bears a cost. Because all resources are either privately or collectively owned by members of society, ultimately, scarce inputs of land, equipment, farm labor, the labor of cooks and waiters, and managerial talent are required. Because these resources could have been used to produce something else, society sacrifices those other goods and services in making the lunch available. Economists call such sacrifices **opportunity costs:** To obtain more of one thing, society forgoes the opportunity of getting the next best thing. That sacrifice is the opportunity cost of the choice.

economics
The study of how people, institutions, and society make economic choices under conditions of scarcity.

economic perspective
A viewpoint that envisions individuals and institutions making rational decisions by comparing the marginal benefits and marginal costs of their actions.

opportunity cost
The value of the good, service, or time forgone to obtain something else.

Did Gates, Winfrey, and Rodriguez Make Bad Choices?

The importance of opportunity costs in decision making is illustrated by different choices people make with respect to college. College graduates usually earn about 50% more during their lifetimes than persons with just high school diplomas. For most capable students, "Go to college, stay in college, and earn a degree" is very sound advice.

Yet Microsoft cofounder Bill Gates and talk-show host Oprah Winfrey* both dropped out of college, and baseball star Alex Rodriguez ("A-Rod") never even bothered to enroll. What were they thinking? Unlike most students, Gates faced enormous opportunity costs for staying in college. He had a vision for his company, and his starting work young helped ensure Microsoft's success. Similarly,

Winfrey landed a spot in local television news when she was a teenager, eventually producing and starring in the *Oprah Winfrey Show* when she was 32 years old. Getting a degree in her twenties might have interrupted the string of successes that made her famous talk show possible. And Rodriguez knew that professional athletes have short careers. Therefore, going to college directly after high school would have taken away 4 years of his peak earning potential.

So Gates, Winfrey, and Rodriguez understood opportunity costs and made their choices accordingly. The size of opportunity costs greatly matters in making individual decisions.

Question:
Professional athletes sometimes return to college after they retire from professional sports. How does that college decision relate to opportunity costs?

* Winfrey eventually went back to school and earned a degree from Tennessee State University when she was in her thirties.

Purposeful Behavior

Economics assumes that human behavior reflects "rational self-interest." Individuals look for and pursue opportunities to increase their **utility:** pleasure, happiness, or satisfaction. They allocate their time, energy, and money to maximize their satisfaction. Because they weigh costs and benefits, their decisions are "purposeful" or "rational," not "random" or "chaotic."

Consumers are purposeful in deciding what goods and services to buy. Business firms are purposeful in deciding what products to produce and how to produce them. Government entities are purposeful in deciding what public services to provide and how to finance them.

"Purposeful behavior" does not assume that people and institutions are immune from faulty logic and therefore are perfect decision makers. They sometimes make mistakes. Nor does it mean that people's decisions are unaffected by emotion or the decisions of those around them. "Purposeful behavior" simply means that people make decisions with some desired outcome in mind.

Nor is rational self-interest the same as selfishness. We will find that increasing one's own wage, rent, interest, or profit normally requires identifying and satisfying somebody else's want. Also, many people make personal sacrifices to others without expecting any monetary reward. They contribute time and money to charities because they derive pleasure from doing so. Parents help pay for their children's education for the same reason. These self-interested, but unselfish, acts help maximize the givers' satisfaction as much as any personal purchase of goods or services. Self-interested behavior is simply behavior designed to increase personal satisfaction, however it may be derived.

utility
The satisfaction obtained from consuming a good or service.

ORIGIN OF THE IDEA

O 1.2

Utility

Marginalism: Benefits and Costs

The economic perspective focuses largely on **marginal analysis**—comparisons of marginal benefits and marginal costs. To economists, "marginal" means "extra," "additional," or "a change in." Most choices or decisions involve changes in the status quo, meaning the existing state of affairs.

Should you attend school for another year? Should you study an extra hour for an exam? Should you supersize your fries? Similarly, should a business expand or reduce its output? Should government increase or decrease its funding for a missile defense system?

Each option involves marginal benefits and, because of scarce resources, marginal costs. In making choices rationally, the decision maker must compare those two

marginal analysis
The comparison of marginal ("extra" or "additional") benefits and marginal costs, usually for decision making.

amounts. Example: You and your fiancée are shopping for an engagement ring. Should you buy a 1/2-carat diamond, a 5/8-carat diamond, a 3/4-carat diamond, a 1-carat diamond, or something even larger? The marginal cost of a larger-size diamond is the added expense beyond the cost of the smaller-size diamond. The marginal benefit is the perceived greater lifetime pleasure (utility) from the larger-size stone. If the marginal benefit of the larger diamond exceeds its marginal cost (and you can afford it), buy the larger stone. But if the marginal cost is more than the marginal benefit, buy the smaller diamond instead, even if you can afford the larger stone!

In a world of scarcity, the decision to obtain the marginal benefit associated with some specific option always includes the marginal cost of forgoing something else. The money spent on the larger-size diamond means forgoing some other product. An opportunity cost, the value of the next best thing forgone, is always present whenever a choice is made.

APPLYING THE ANALYSIS

Fast-Food Lines

The economic perspective is useful in analyzing all sorts of behaviors. Consider an everyday example: the behavior of fast-food customers. When customers enter the restaurant, they go to the shortest line, believing that line will minimize their time cost of obtaining food. They are acting purposefully; time is limited, and people prefer using it in some way other than standing in a long line.

If one fast-food line is temporarily shorter than other lines, some people will move to that line. These movers apparently view the time saving from the shorter line (marginal benefit) as exceeding the cost of moving from their present line (marginal cost). The line switching tends to equalize line lengths. No further movement of customers between lines occurs once all lines are about equal.

Fast-food customers face another cost-benefit decision when a clerk opens a new station at the counter. Should they move to the new station or stay put? Those who shift to the new line decide that the time saving from the move exceeds the extra cost of physically moving. In so deciding, customers must also consider just how quickly they can get to the new station compared with others who may be contemplating the same move. (Those who hesitate in this situation are lost!)

Customers at the fast-food establishment do not have perfect information when they select lines. Thus, not all decisions turn out as expected. For example, you might enter a short line and find someone in front of you is ordering hamburgers and fries for 40 people in the Greyhound bus parked out back (and the employee is a trainee)! Nevertheless, at the time you made your decision, you thought it was optimal.

Finally, customers must decide what food to order when they arrive at the counter. In making their choices, they again compare marginal costs and marginal benefits in attempting to obtain the greatest personal satisfaction for their expenditure.

Economists believe that what is true for the behavior of customers at fast-food restaurants is true for economic behavior in general. Faced with an array of choices, consumers, workers, and businesses rationally compare marginal costs and marginal benefits in making decisions.

Question:
Have you ever gone to a fast-food restaurant only to observe long lines and then leave? Use the economic perspective to explain your behavior.

Theories, Principles, and Models

Like the physical and life sciences, as well as other social sciences, economics relies on the **scientific method.** That procedure consists of several elements:

- Observing real-world behavior and outcomes.
- Based on those observations, formulating a possible explanation of cause and effect (hypothesis).
- Testing this explanation by comparing the outcomes of specific events to the outcome predicted by the hypothesis.
- Accepting, rejecting, or modifying the hypothesis, based on these comparisons.
- Continuing to test the hypothesis against the facts. As favorable results accumulate, the hypothesis evolves into a *theory.* A very well-tested and widely accepted theory is referred to as a *law* or *principle.* Combinations of such laws or principles are incorporated into *models,* which are simplified representations of how something works, such as a market or segment of the economy.

Economists develop theories of the behavior of individuals (consumers, workers) and institutions (businesses, governments) engaged in the production, exchange, and consumption of goods and services. Economic theories and **principles** are statements about economic behavior or the economy that enable prediction of the probable effects of certain actions. They are "purposeful simplifications." The full scope of economic reality itself is too complex and bewildering to be understood as a whole. In developing theories and principles, economists remove the clutter and simplify.

Economic principles and models are highly useful in analyzing economic behavior and understanding how the economy operates. They are the tools for ascertaining cause and effect (or action and outcome) within the economic system. Good theories do a good job of explaining and predicting. They are supported by facts concerning how individuals and institutions actually behave in producing, exchanging, and consuming goods and services.

There are some other things you should know about economic principles:

- ***Generalizations*** Economic principles are *generalizations* relating to economic behavior or to the economy itself. Economic principles are expressed as the tendencies of typical or average consumers, workers, or business firms. For example, economists say that consumers buy more of a particular product when its price falls. Economists recognize that some consumers may increase their purchases by a large amount, others by a small amount, and a few not at all. This "price-quantity" principle, however, holds for the typical consumer and for consumers as a group.
- ***Other-things-equal assumption*** Like other scientists, economists use the *ceteris paribus* or **other-things-equal assumption** to construct their theories. They assume that all variables except those under immediate consideration are held constant for a particular analysis. For example, consider the relationship between the price of Pepsi and the amount of it purchased. It helps to assume that, of all the factors that might influence the amount of Pepsi purchased (for example, the price of Pepsi, the price of Coca-Cola, and consumer incomes and preferences), only the price of Pepsi varies. The economist can then focus on the relationship between the price of Pepsi and purchases of Pepsi in isolation without being confused by changes in other variables.
- ***Graphical expression*** Many economic models are expressed graphically. Be sure to read the special appendix at the end of this chapter as a review of graphs.

scientific method
The systematic pursuit of knowledge by observing facts and formulating and testing hypotheses to obtain theories, principles, and laws.

principles
Statements about economic behavior that enable prediction of the probable effects of certain actions.

other-things-equal assumption
The assumption that factors other than those being considered do not change.

ORIGIN OF THE IDEA
O 1.4
Ceteris paribus

Microeconomics and Macroeconomics

Economists develop economic principles and models at two levels.

Microeconomics

microeconomics
The part of economics concerned with individual decision-making units, such as a consumer, a worker, or a business firm.

Microeconomics is the part of economics concerned with individual units such as a person, a household, a firm, or an industry. At this level of analysis, the economist observes the details of an economic unit, or very small segment of the economy, under a figurative microscope. In microeconomics we look at the decision making by individual consumers, households, and business firms. We measure the price of a specific product, the number of workers employed by a single firm, the revenue or income of a particular firm or household, or the expenditures of a specific firm, government entity, or family.

Macroeconomics

macroeconomics
The part of economics concerned with the economy as a whole or major components of the economy.

aggregate
A collection of specific economic units treated as if they were one unit.

Macroeconomics examines either the economy as a whole or its basic subdivisions or aggregates, such as the government, household, and business sectors. An **aggregate** is a collection of specific economic units treated as if they were one unit. Therefore, we might lump together the millions of consumers in the U.S. economy and treat them as if they were one huge unit called "consumers."

In using aggregates, macroeconomics seeks to obtain an overview, or general outline, of the structure of the economy and the relationships of its major aggregates. Macroeconomics speaks of such economic measures as total output, total employment, total income, aggregate expenditures, and the general level of prices in analyzing various economic problems. No or very little attention is given to specific units making up the various aggregates.

© Robert Holmes/CORBIS

Photo Op Micro versus Macro

Figuratively, microeconomics examines the sand, rock, and shells, not the beach; in contrast, macroeconomics examines the beach, not the sand, rocks, and shells.

Individual's Economic Problem

economic problem
The need for individuals and society to make choices because wants exceed means.

It is clear from our previous discussion that both individuals and society face an **economic problem:** They need to make choices because economic wants are unlimited but the means (income, time, resources) for satisfying those wants are limited. Let's first look at the economic problem faced by individuals. To explain the idea, we will construct a very simple microeconomic model.

Limited Income

We all have a finite amount of income, even the wealthiest among us. Sure Bill Gates earns a bit more than the rest of us, but he still has to decide how to spend his money! And the majority of us have much more limited means. Our income comes to us in the form of wages, interest, rent, and profit, although we may also receive money from government programs or family members. As Global Snapshot 1.1 shows, the average income of Americans in 2006 was $44,970. In the poorest nations, it was less than $500.

Unlimited Wants

For better or worse, most people have virtually unlimited wants. We desire various goods and services that provide utility. Our wants extend over a wide range of products, from *necessities* (food, shelter, clothing) to *luxuries* (perfumes, yachts, sports cars). Some wants such as basic food, clothing, and shelter have biological roots. Other wants, for example, specific kinds of food, clothing, and shelter, arise from the conventions and customs of society.

Over time, economic wants tend to change and multiply, fueled by new and improved products. Only recently have people wanted iPods, Internet service, digital cameras, or camera phones because those products did not exist a few decades ago. Also, the satisfaction of certain wants may trigger others: The acquisition of a Ford Focus or a Honda Civic has been known to whet the appetite for a Lexus or a Mercedes.

GLOBAL SNAPSHOT 1.1

Average Income, Selected Nations

Average income (total income/population) and therefore typical budget constraints vary greatly among nations.

Country	Per Capita Income, 2006*
Switzerland	$57,230
United States	44,970
Japan	38,410
France	36,550
South Korea	17,690
Mexico	7,870
Brazil	4,730
China	2,010
Pakistan	770
Nigeria	640
Rwanda	250
Liberia	140

* U.S. dollars.
Source: World Bank, **www.worldbank.org**.

© Bill Aron/PhotoEdit

© F. Schussler/PhotoLink/Getty Images

Photo Op Necessities versus Luxuries

Economic wants include both necessities and luxuries. Each type of item provides utility to the buyer.

Services, as well as goods, satisfy our wants. Car repair work, the removal of an inflamed appendix, legal and accounting advice, and haircuts all satisfy human wants. Actually, we buy many goods, such as automobiles and washing machines, for the services they render. The differences between goods and services are often smaller than they appear to be.

For most people, the desires for goods and services cannot be fully satisfied. Bill Gates may have all that he wants for himself, but his massive charitable giving suggests that he keenly wants better health care for the world's poor. Our desires for a *particular* good or service can be satisfied; over a short period of time we can surely obtain enough toothpaste or pasta. And one appendectomy is plenty. But our broader desire for more goods and services and higher-quality goods and services seems to be another story.

Because we have only limited income but seemingly insatiable wants, it is in our self-interest to economize: to pick and choose goods and services that maximize our satisfaction.

A Budget Line

budget line
A line that shows various combinations of two products a consumer can purchase with a specific money income, given the products' prices.

The economic problem facing individuals can be depicted as a **budget line** (or, more technically, *budget constraint*). It is a schedule or curve that shows various combinations of two products a consumer can purchase with a specific money income.

To understand this idea, suppose that you received a Barnes & Noble (or Borders) gift card as a birthday present. The $120 card is soon to expire. You take the card to the store and confine your purchase decisions to two alternatives: DVDs and paperback

FIGURE 1.1 **A consumer's budget line.** The budget line (or budget constraint) shows all the combinations of any two products that can be purchased, given the prices of the products and the consumer's money income.

The Budget Line: Whole-Unit Combinations of DVDs and Paperback Books Attainable with an Income of $120		
Units of DVDs (Price = $20)	Units of Books (Price = $10)	Total Expenditure
6	0	($120 = $120 + $0)
5	2	($120 = $100 + $20)
4	4	($120 = $80 + $40)
3	6	($120 = $60 + $60)
2	8	($120 = $40 + $80)
1	10	($120 = $20 + $100)
0	12	($120 = $0 + $120)

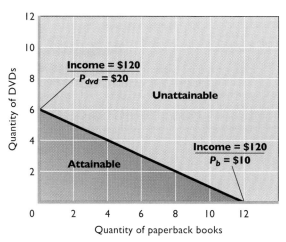

books. DVDs are $20 each, and paperback books are $10 each. Your purchase options are shown in the table in Figure 1.1.

At one extreme, you might spend all of your $120 "income" on 6 DVDs at $20 each and have nothing left to spend on books. Or, by giving up 2 DVDs and thereby gaining $40, you can have 4 DVDs at $20 each, and 4 books at $10 each. And so on to the other extreme, at which you could buy 12 books at $10 each, spending your entire gift card on books with nothing left to spend on DVDs.

The graph in Figure 1.1 shows the budget line. Note that the graph is not restricted to whole units of DVDs and books as is the table. Every point on the graph represents a possible combination of DVDs and books, including fractional quantities. The slope of the graphed budget line measures the ratio of the price of books (P_b) to the price of DVDs (P_{dvd}); more precisely, the slope is $P_b/P_{dvd} - \$-10/\$ + 20 = -1/2$ or $-.5$. So you must forgo 1 DVD (measured on the vertical axis) to buy 2 books (measured on the horizontal axis). This yields a slope of $-1/2$ or $-.5$.

The budget line illustrates several ideas.

Attainable and Unattainable Combinations All the combinations of DVDs and books on or inside the budget line are *attainable* from the $120 of money income. You can afford to buy, for example, 3 DVDs at $20 each and 6 books at $10 each. You also can obviously afford to buy 2 DVDs and 5 books, if so desired, and not use up the value on the gift card. But to achieve maximum utility you will want to spend the full $120.

In contrast, all combinations beyond the budget line are *unattainable*. The $120 limit simply does not allow you to purchase, for example, 5 DVDs at $20 each and 5 books at $10 each. That $150 expenditure would clearly exceed the $120 limit. In Figure 1.1 the attainable combinations are on and within the budget line; the unattainable combinations are beyond the budget line.

Trade-Offs and Opportunity Costs The budget line in Figure 1.1 illustrates the idea of trade-offs arising from limited income. To obtain more DVDs, you

ORIGIN OF THE IDEA

O 1.5

Opportunity cost

have to give up some books. For example, to acquire the first DVD, you trade off 2 books. So the opportunity cost of the first DVD is 2 books. To obtain the second DVD, the opportunity cost is also 2 books. The straight-line budget constraint, with its constant slope, indicates **constant opportunity cost.** That is, the opportunity cost of 1 extra DVD remains the same (= 2 books) as more DVDs are purchased. And, in reverse, the opportunity cost of 1 extra book does not change (= 1/2 DVD) as more books are bought.

constant opportunity cost
An opportunity cost that remains the same as consumers shift purchases from one product to another along a straight-line budget line.

Choice Limited income forces people to choose what to buy and what to forgo to fulfill wants. You will select the combination of DVDs and paperback books that you think is "best." That is, you will evaluate your marginal benefits and your marginal costs (here, product price) to make choices that maximize your satisfaction. Other people, with the same $120 gift card, would undoubtedly make different choices.

WORKED PROBLEMS

W 1.1
Budget lines

Income Changes The location of the budget line varies with money income. An increase in money income shifts the budget line to the right; a decrease in money income shifts it to the left. To verify this, recalculate the table in Figure 1.1, assuming the card value (income) is (a) $240 and (b) $60, and plot the new budget lines in the graph. No wonder people like to have more income: That shifts their budget lines outward and enables them to buy more goods and services. But even with more income, people will still face spending trade-offs, choices, and opportunity costs.

Society's Economic Problem

Society must also make choices under conditions of scarcity. It, too, faces an economic problem. Should it devote more of its limited resources to the criminal justice system (police, courts, and prisons) or to education (teachers, books, and schools)? If it decides to devote more resources to both, what other goods and services does it forgo? Health care? Homeland security? Energy development?

Scarce Resources

economic resources
The land, labor, capital, and entrepreneurial ability used in the production of goods and services.

Society's economic resources are limited or scarce. By **economic resources** we mean all natural, human, and manufactured resources that go into the production of goods and services. That includes the entire set of factory and farm buildings and all the equipment, tools, and machinery used to produce manufactured goods and agricultural products; all transportation and communication facilities; all types of labor; and land and mineral resources.

Resource Categories

Economists classify economic resources into four general categories.

land
Natural resources ("gifts of nature") used to produce goods and services.

Land Land means much more to the economist than it does to most people. To the economist **land** includes all natural resources ("gifts of nature") used in the production process, such as arable land, forests, mineral and oil deposits, and water resources.

labor
The physical and mental talents and efforts of people used to produce goods and services.

Labor The resource **labor** consists of the physical and mental talents of individuals used in producing goods and services. The services of a logger, retail clerk, machinist, teacher, professional football player, and nuclear physicist all fall under the general heading "labor."

Capital
For economists, **capital** (or *capital goods*) includes all manufactured aids used in producing consumer goods and services. Included are all factory, storage, transportation, and distribution facilities, as well as all tools and machinery. Economists refer to the purchase of capital goods as **investment.**

Capital goods differ from consumer goods because consumer goods satisfy wants directly, while capital goods do so indirectly by aiding the production of consumer goods. Note that the term "capital" as used by economists refers not to money but to tools, machinery, and other productive equipment. Because money produces nothing, economists do not include it as an economic resource. Money (or money capital or financial capital) is simply a means for purchasing real capital.

Entrepreneurial Ability
Finally, there is the special human resource, distinct from labor, called **entrepreneurial ability.** The entrepreneur performs several functions:

- The entrepreneur takes the initiative in combining the resources of land, labor, and capital to produce a good or a service. Both a spark plug and a catalyst, the entrepreneur is the driving force behind production and the agent who combines the other resources in what is hoped will be a successful business venture.
- The entrepreneur makes the strategic business decisions that set the course of an enterprise.
- The entrepreneur is an innovator. He or she commercializes new products, new production techniques, or even new forms of business organization.
- The entrepreneur is a risk bearer. The entrepreneur has no guarantee of profit. The reward for the entrepreneur's time, efforts, and abilities may be profits or losses. The entrepreneur risks not only his or her invested funds but those of associates and stockholders as well.

capital
Human-made resources (buildings, machinery, and equipment) used to produce goods and services.

investment
The purchase of capital resources.

entrepreneurial ability
The human talent that combines the other resources to produce a product, make strategic decisions, and bear risks.

factors of production
Economic resources: land, labor, capital, and entrepreneurial ability.

© Lester Lefkowitz/ CORBIS   © Lance Nelson/Stock Photos/zefa/CORBIS   © Creatas/PunchStock   © Neville Elder/Corbis

Photo Op Economic Resources

Land, labor, capital, and entrepreneurial ability all contribute to producing goods and services.

Because land, labor, capital, and entrepreneurial ability are combined to produce goods and services, they are called the **factors of production** or simply inputs.

Production Possibilities Model

Society uses its scarce resources to produce goods and services. The alternatives and choices it faces can best be understood through a macroeconomic model of production possibilities. To keep things simple, we assume:

- **Full employment**   The economy is employing all its available resources.
- **Fixed resources**   The quantity and quality of the factors of production are fixed.
- **Fixed technology**   The state of technology (the methods used to produce output) is constant.
- **Two goods**   The economy is producing only two goods: food products and manufacturing equipment. Food products symbolize **consumer goods,** products that satisfy our wants directly; manufacturing equipment symbolizes **capital goods,** products that satisfy our wants indirectly by making possible more efficient production of consumer goods.

consumer goods
Products and services that directly satisfy consumer wants.

capital goods
Items that are used to produce other goods and therefore do not directly satisfy consumer wants.

Production Possibilities Table

A production possibilities table lists the different combinations of two products that can be produced with a specific set of resources, assuming full employment. Figure 1.2 contains such a table for a simple economy that is producing food products and manufacturing equipment; the data are, of course, hypothetical. At alternative A, this economy would be devoting all its available resources to the production of manufacturing equipment (capital goods); at alternative E, all resources would go to food-product production (consumer goods). Those alternatives are unrealistic extremes; an economy typically produces both capital goods and consumer goods, as in B, C, and D. As we move from alternative A to E, we increase the production of food products at the expense of the production of manufacturing equipment.

Because consumer goods satisfy our wants directly, any movement toward E looks tempting. In producing more food products, society increases the current satisfaction

FIGURE 1.2 The production possibilities curve. Each point on the production possibilities curve represents some maximum combination of two products that can be produced if resources are fully and efficiently employed. When an economy is operating on the curve, more manufacturing equipment means less food products, and vice versa. Limited resources and a fixed technology make any combination of manufacturing equipment and food products lying outside the curve (such as at *W*) unattainable. Points inside the curve are attainable, but they indicate that full employment is not being realized.

Type of Product	Production Alternatives				
	A	B	C	D	E
Food products (hundred thousands)	0	1	2	3	4
Manufacturing equipment (thousands)	10	9	7	4	0

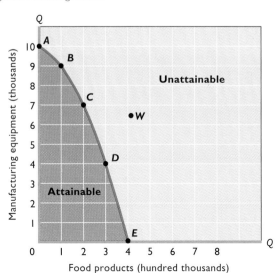

of its wants. But there is a cost: More food products mean less manufacturing equipment. This shift of resources to consumer goods catches up with society over time because the stock of capital goods does not expand at the current rate, with the result that some potential for greater future production is lost. By moving toward alternative E, society chooses "more now" at the expense of "much more later."

By moving toward A, society chooses to forgo current consumption, thereby freeing up resources that can be used to increase the production of capital goods. By building up its stock of capital this way, society will have greater future production and, therefore, greater future consumption. By moving toward A, society is choosing "more later" at the cost of "less now."

Generalization: At any point in time, a fully employed economy must sacrifice some of one good to obtain more of another good. Scarce resources prohibit such an economy from having more of both goods. Society must choose among alternatives. There is no such thing as a free bag of groceries or a free manufacturing machine. Having more of one thing means having less of something else.

Production Possibilities Curve

The data presented in a production possibilities table can also be shown graphically. We arbitrarily represent the economy's output of capital goods (here, manufacturing equipment) on the vertical axis and the output of consumer goods (here, food products) on the horizontal axis, as shown in Figure 1.2.

Each point on the **production possibilities curve** represents some maximum output of the two products. The curve is a "constraint" because it shows the limit of attainable outputs. Points on the curve are attainable as long as the economy uses all its available resources. Points lying inside the curve are also attainable, but they reflect less total output and therefore are not as desirable as points on the curve. Points inside the curve imply that the economy could have more of both manufacturing equipment and food products if it achieved full employment. Points lying beyond the production possibilities curve, like *W*, would represent a greater output than the output at any point on the curve. Such points, however, are unattainable with the current availability of resources and technology.

Law of Increasing Opportunity Costs

Figure 1.2 clearly shows that more food products mean less manufacturing equipment. The number of units of manufacturing equipment that must be given up to obtain another unit of food products, of course, is the opportunity cost of that unit of food products.

In moving from alternative A to alternative B in the table in Figure 1.2, the cost of 1 additional unit of food products is 1 less unit of manufacturing equipment. But when additional units are considered—B to C, C to D, and D to E—an important economic principle is revealed: The opportunity cost of each additional unit of food products is greater than the opportunity cost of the preceding one. When we move from A to B, just 1 unit of manufacturing equipment is sacrificed for 1 more unit of food products; but in going from B to C, we sacrifice 2 additional units of manufacturing equipment for 1 more unit of food products; then 3 more of manufacturing equipment for 1 more of food products; and finally 4 for 1. Conversely, confirm that as we move from E to A, the cost of an additional unit of manufacturing equipment (on average) is 1/4, 1/3, 1/2, and 1 unit of food products, respectively, for the four successive moves.

Our example illustrates the **law of increasing opportunity costs:** The more of a product that society produces, the greater is the opportunity cost of obtaining an extra unit.

INTERACTIVE GRAPHS

G 1.1

Production possibilities curve

production possibilities curve
A curve showing the different combinations of goods and services that can be produced in a fully employed economy, assuming the available supplies of resources and technology are fixed.

law of increasing opportunity costs
The principle that as the production of a good increases, the opportunity cost of producing an additional unit rises.

Shape of the Curve   The law of increasing opportunity costs is reflected in the shape of the production possibilities curve: The curve is bowed out from the origin of the graph. Figure 1.2 shows that when the economy moves from *A* to *E*, it must give up successively larger amounts of manufacturing equipment (1, 2, 3, and 4) to acquire equal increments of food products (1, 1, 1, and 1). This is shown in the slope of the production possibilities curve, which becomes steeper as we move from *A* to *E*.

Economic Rationale   The economic rationale for the law of increasing opportunity costs is that economic resources are not completely adaptable to alternative uses. Many resources are better at producing one type of good than at producing others. Some land is highly suited to growing the ingredients necessary for pizza production, but as pizza production expands, society has to start using land that is less bountiful for farming. Other land is rich in mineral deposits and therefore well-suited to producing the materials needed to make manufacturing equipment. As society steps up the production of manufacturing equipment, it must push resources that are less and less adaptable to making that equipment into its production.

If we start at *A* and move to *B* in Figure 1.2, we can shift resources whose productivity is relatively high in food production and low in manufacturing equipment. But as we move from *B* to *C*, *C* to *D*, and so on, resources highly productive of food products become increasingly scarce. To get more food products, resources whose productivity in manufacturing equipment is relatively great will be needed. It will take increasingly more of such resources, and hence greater sacrifices of manufacturing equipment, to achieve each 1-unit increase in food products. This lack of perfect flexibility, or interchangeability, on the part of resources is the cause of increasing opportunity costs for society.

Optimal Allocation

Of all the attainable combinations of food products and manufacturing equipment on the curve in Figure 1.2, which is optimal (best)? That is, what specific quantities of resources should be allocated to food products and what specific quantities to manufacturing equipment in order to maximize satisfaction?

Recall that economic decisions center on comparisons of marginal benefits (MB) and marginal costs (MC). Any economic activity should be expanded as long as marginal benefit exceeds marginal cost and should be reduced if marginal cost exceeds marginal benefit. The optimal amount of the activity occurs where MB = MC. Society needs to make a similar assessment about its production decision.

Consider food products. We already know from the law of increasing opportunity costs that the marginal costs of additional units of food products will rise as more units are produced. At the same time, we need to recognize that the extra or marginal benefits that come from producing and consuming food products decline with each successive unit of food products. Consequently, each successive unit of food products brings with it both increasing marginal costs and decreasing marginal benefits.

The optimal quantity of food production is indicated by the intersection of the MB and MC curves: 200,000 units in Figure 1.3. Why is this amount the optimal quantity? If only 100,000 units of food products were produced, the marginal benefit of an extra unit of them would exceed its marginal cost. In money terms, MB is $15, while MC is only $5. When society gains something worth $15 at a marginal cost of only $5, it is better off. In Figure 1.3, net gains of decreasing amounts can be realized until food-product production has been increased to 200,000.

In contrast, the production of 300,000 units of food products is excessive. There the MC of an added unit is $15 and its MB is only $5. This means that 1 unit of food

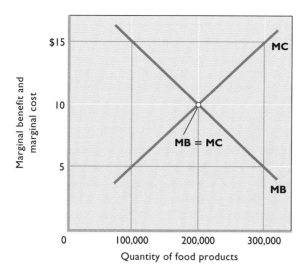

FIGURE 1.3 Optimal output: MB = MC. Achieving the optimal output requires the expansion of a good's output until its marginal benefit (MB) and marginal cost (MC) are equal. No resources beyond that point should be allocated to the product. Here, optimal output occurs when 200,000 units of food products are produced.

products is worth only $5 to society but costs it $15 to obtain. This is a losing proposition for society!

So resources are being efficiently allocated to any product when the marginal benefit and marginal cost of its output are equal (MB = MC). Suppose that by applying the above analysis to manufacturing equipment, we find its optimal (MB = MC) output is 7000. This would mean that alternative *C* (200,000 units of food products and 7000 units of manufacturing equipment) on the production possibilities curve in Figure 1.2 would be optimal for this economy.

The Economics of War

Production possibilities analysis is helpful in assessing the costs and benefits of waging the war on terrorism, including the wars in Afghanistan and Iraq. At the end of 2007, the estimated cost of these efforts exceeded $400 billion.

If we categorize all of U.S. production as either "defense goods" or "civilian goods," we can measure them on the axes of a production possibilities diagram such as that shown in Figure 1.2. The opportunity cost of using more resources for defense goods is the civilian goods sacrificed. In a fully employed economy, more defense goods are achieved at the opportunity cost of fewer civilian goods—health care, education, pollution control, personal computers, houses, and so on. The cost of waging war is the other goods forgone. The benefits of these activities are numerous and diverse but clearly include the gains from protecting against future loss of American lives, assets, income, and well-being.

Society must assess the marginal benefit (MB) and marginal cost (MC) of additional defense goods to determine their optimal amounts—where to locate on the defense goods–civilian goods production possibilities curve. Although estimating marginal benefits and marginal costs is an imprecise art, the MB-MC framework is a useful way of approaching choices. Allocative efficiency requires that society expand production of defense goods until MB = MC.

The events of September 11, 2001, and the future threats they posed increased the perceived marginal benefits of defense goods. If we label the horizontal axis in Figure 1.3 "defense goods," and draw in a rightward shift of the MB curve, you will see that the optimal quantity of defense goods rises. In view of the concerns relating to September 11, the United States allocated more of its resources to defense. But the MB-MC analysis also reminds us we can spend too much on defense, as well as too little. The United States should not expand defense goods beyond the point where MB = MC. If it does, it will be sacrificing civilian goods of greater value than the defense goods obtained.

Question:
Would society's costs of war be lower if it drafted soldiers at low pay rather than attracted them voluntarily to the military through market pay?

Unemployment, Growth, and the Future

In the depths of the Great Depression of the 1930s, one-quarter of U.S. workers were unemployed and one-third of U.S. production capacity was idle. The United States has suffered a number of much milder downturns since then, the latest beginning in December 2007 and still occurring (as of the end of 2008).

Almost all nations have experienced widespread unemployment and unused production capacity from business downturns at one time or another. Since 1995, for example, several nations—including Argentina, Japan, Mexico, Germany, and South Korea—have had economic downturns and unemployment.

How do these realities relate to the production possibilities model? Our analysis and conclusions change if we relax the assumption that all available resources are fully employed. The five alternatives in the table of Figure 1.2 represent maximum outputs; they illustrate the combinations of food products and manufacturing equipment that can be produced when the economy is operating at full employment. With unemployment, this economy would produce less than each alternative shown in the table.

Graphically, we represent situations of unemployment by points inside the original production possibilities curve (reproduced in Figure 1.4). Point *U* is one such point. Here the economy is falling short of the various maximum combinations of food products and manufacturing equipment represented by the points on the production possibilities curve. The arrows in Figure 1.4 indicate three possible paths back to full employment. A move toward full employment would yield a greater output of one or both products.

A Growing Economy

When we drop the assumptions that the quantity and quality of resources and technology are fixed, the production possibilities curve shifts positions, and the potential maximum output of the economy changes.

Increases in Resource Supplies
Although resource supplies are fixed at any specific moment, they change over time. For example, a nation's growing population brings about increases in the supplies of labor and entrepreneurial ability. Also, labor

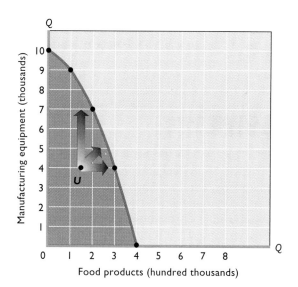

FIGURE 1.4 **Unemployment and the production possibilities curve.** Any point inside the production possibilities curve, such as *U*, represents unemployment or a failure to achieve full employment. The arrows indicate that, by realizing full employment, the economy could operate on the curve. This means it could produce more of one or both products than it is producing at point *U*.

quality usually improves over time. Historically, the economy's stock of capital has increased at a significant, though unsteady, rate. And although some of our energy and mineral resources are being depleted, new sources are also being discovered. The development of irrigation programs, for example, adds to the supply of arable land.

The net result of these increased supplies of the factors of production is the ability to produce more of both consumer goods and capital goods. Thus 20 years from now, the production possibilities in Figure 1.5 may supersede those shown in Figure 1.2. The

FIGURE 1.5 **Economic growth and the production possibilities curve.** The increase in supplies of resources, the improvements in resource quality, and the technological advances that occur in a dynamic economy move the production possibilities curve outward and to the right, allowing the economy to have larger quantities of both types of goods.

Type of Product	Production Alternatives				
	A′	**B′**	**C′**	**D′**	**E′**
Food products (hundred thousands)	0	2	4	6	8
Manufacturing equipment (thousands)	14	12	9	5	0

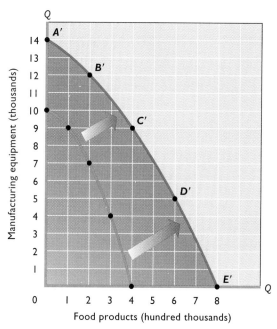

greater abundance of resources will result in a greater potential output of one or both products at each alternative. The economy will have achieved economic growth in the form of expanded potential output. Thus, when an increase in the quantity or quality of resources occurs, the production possibilities curve shifts outward and to the right, as illustrated by the move from the inner curve to curve $A'\ B'\ C'\ D'\ E'$ in Figure 1.5. This sort of shift represents growth of economic capacity, which, when used, means **economic growth:** a larger total output.

economic growth
An outward shift of the production possibilities curve that results from an increase in resource supplies or quality or an improvement in technology.

Advances in Technology
An advancing technology brings both new and better goods and improved ways of producing them. For now, let's think of technological advance as being only improvements in the methods of production, for example, the introduction of computerized systems to manage inventories and schedule production. These advances alter our previous discussion of the economic problem by allowing society to produce more goods with available resources. As with increases in resource supplies, technological advances make possible the production of more manufacturing equipment and more food products.

APPLYING THE ANALYSIS

Information Technology and Biotechnology

A real-world example of improved technology is the recent surge of new technologies relating to computers, communications, and biotechnology. Technological advances have dropped the prices of computers and greatly increased their speed. Improved software has greatly increased the everyday usefulness of computers. Cellular phones and the Internet have increased communications capacity, enhancing production and improving the efficiency of markets. Advances in biotechnology have resulted in important agricultural and medical discoveries. These and other new and improved technologies have contributed to U.S. economic growth (outward shifts of the nation's production possibilities curve).

Question:
How have technological advances in medicine helped expand production possibilities in the United States?

Conclusion: Economic growth is the result of (1) increases in supplies of resources, (2) improvements in resource quality, and (3) technological advances. The consequence of growth is that a full-employment economy can enjoy a greater output of both consumption goods and capital goods. While static, no-growth economies must sacrifice some of one good to obtain more of another, dynamic, growing economies can have larger quantities of both goods.

Present Choices and Future Possibilities
An economy's current choice of positions on its production possibilities curve helps determine the future location of that curve. Let's designate the two axes of the production possibilities curve as "goods for the future" and "goods for the present," as in Figure 1.6. Goods for the future are such things as capital goods, research and education, and

FIGURE 1.6 **Present choices and future locations of production possibilities curves.** A nation's current choice favoring "present goods," as made by Presentville in (a), will cause a modest outward shift of the production possibilities curve in the future. A nation's current choice favoring "future goods," as made by Futureville in (b), will result in a greater outward shift of the curve in the future.

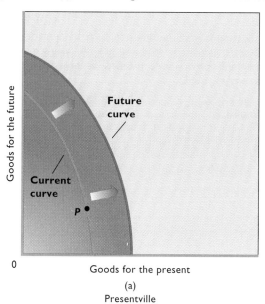

(a)
Presentville

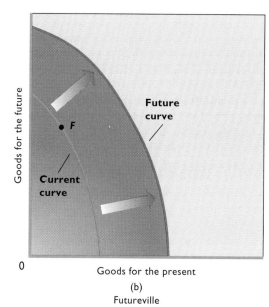

(b)
Futureville

preventive medicine. They increase the quantity and quality of property resources, enlarge the stock of technological information, and improve the quality of human resources. As we have already seen, goods for the future, such as capital goods, are the ingredients of economic growth. Goods for the present are consumer goods such as food, clothing, and entertainment.

Now suppose there are two hypothetical economies, Presentville and Futureville, which are initially identical in every respect except one: Presentville's current choice of positions on its production possibilities curve strongly favors present goods over future goods. Point *P* in Figure 1.6a indicates that choice. It is located quite far down the curve to the right, indicating a high priority for goods for the present, at the expense of fewer goods for the future. Futureville, in contrast, makes a current choice that stresses larger amounts of future goods and smaller amounts of present goods, as shown by point *F* in Figure 1.6b.

Now, other things equal, we can expect the future production possibilities curve of Futureville to be farther to the right than Presentville's curve. By currently choosing an output more favorable to technological advances and to increases in the quantity and quality of resources, Futureville will achieve greater economic growth than Presentville. In terms of capital goods, Futureville is choosing to make larger current additions to its "national factory" by devoting more of its current output to capital than Presentville. The payoff from this choice for Futureville is greater future production capacity and economic growth. The opportunity cost is fewer consumer goods in the present for Futureville to enjoy.

Is Futureville's choice thus necessarily "better" than Presentville's? That, we cannot say. The different outcomes simply reflect different preferences and priorities in the two countries. But each country will have to live with the consequences of its choice.

INTERACTIVE GRAPHS

G 1.2

Present choices and future possibilities

Summary

1. Economics is the social science that studies how people, institutions, and society make choices under conditions of scarcity. Central to economics is the idea of opportunity cost: the value of the good, service, or time forgone to obtain something else.

2. The economic perspective includes three elements: scarcity and choice, purposeful behavior, and marginalism. It sees individuals and institutions making rational decisions based on comparisons of marginal costs and marginal benefits.

3. Economists employ the scientific method, in which they form and test hypotheses of cause-and-effect relationships to generate theories, laws, and principles. Economists often combine theories into representations called models.

4. Microeconomics examines the decision making of specific economic units or institutions. Macroeconomics looks at the economy as a whole or its major aggregates.

5. Individuals face an economic problem. Because their wants exceed their incomes, they must decide what to purchase and what to forgo. Society also faces an economic problem. Societal wants exceed the available resources necessary to fulfill them. Society therefore must decide what to produce and what to forgo.

6. Graphically, a budget line (or budget constraint) illustrates the economic problem for individuals. The line shows the various combinations of two products that a consumer can purchase with a specific money income, given the prices of the two products.

7. Economic resources are inputs into the production process and can be classified as land, labor, capital, and entrepreneurial ability. Economic resources are also known as factors of production or inputs.

8. Society's economic problem can be illustrated through production possibilities analysis. Production possibilities tables and curves show the different combinations of goods and services that can be produced in a fully employed economy, assuming that resource quantity, resource quality, and technology are fixed.

9. An economy that is fully employed and thus operating on its production possibilities curve must sacrifice the output of some types of goods and services to increase the production of others. The gain of one type of good or service is always accompanied by an opportunity cost in the form of the loss of some of the other type.

10. Because resources are not equally productive in all possible uses, shifting resources from one use to another results in increasing opportunity costs. The production of additional units of one product requires the sacrifice of increasing amounts of the other product.

11. The optimal point on the production possibilities curve represents the most desirable mix of goods and is determined by expanding the production of each good until its marginal benefit (MB) equals its marginal cost (MC).

12. Over time, technological advances and increases in the quantity and quality of resources enable the economy to produce more of all goods and services, that is, to experience economic growth. Society's choice as to the mix of consumer goods and capital goods in current output is a major determinant of the future location of the production possibilities curve and thus of the extent of economic growth.

Terms and Concepts

economics	macroeconomics	investment
economic perspective	aggregate	entrepreneurial ability
opportunity cost	economic problem	factors of production
utility	budget line	consumer goods
marginal analysis	constant opportunity cost	capital goods
scientific method	economic resources	production possibilities curve
principles	land	law of increasing opportunity costs
other-things-equal assumption	labor	economic growth
microeconomics	capital	

Study Questions

1. Ralph Waldo Emerson once wrote: "Want is a growing giant whom the coat of have was never large enough to cover." How does this statement relate to the definition of economics? **LO1**

2. "Buy 2, get 1 free." Explain why the "1 free" is free to the buyer but not to society. **LO1**

3. Which of the following decisions would entail the greater opportunity cost: allocating a square block in the heart of

New York City for a surface parking lot or allocating a square block at the edge of a typical suburb for such a lot? Explain. **LO1**

4. What is meant by the term "utility," and how does it relate to purposeful behavior? **LO1**

5. Cite three examples of recent decisions that you made in which you, at least implicitly, weighed marginal cost and marginal benefit. **LO1**

6. Indicate whether each of the following statements applies to microeconomics or macroeconomics: **LO3**

   a. The unemployment rate in the United States was 5.0% in April 2008.

   b. A U.S. software firm discharged 15 workers last month and transferred the work to India.

   c. An unexpected freeze in central Florida reduced the citrus crop and caused the price of oranges to rise.

   d. U.S. output, adjusted for inflation, grew by 2.2% in 2007.

   e. Last week Wells Fargo Bank lowered its interest rate on business loans by one-half of 1 percentage point.

   f. The consumer price index rose by 2.8% in 2007.

7. Suppose you won $15 on a lotto ticket at the local 7-Eleven and decided to spend all the winnings on candy bars and bags of peanuts. The price of candy bars is $.75 and the price of peanuts is $1.50. **LO4**

   a. Construct a table showing the alternative combinations of the two products that are available.

   b. Plot the data in your table as a budget line in a graph. What is the slope of the budget line? What is the opportunity cost of one more candy bar? Of one more bag of peanuts? Do these opportunity costs rise, fall, or remain constant as each additional unit of the product is purchased?

   c. How, in general, would you decide which of the available combinations of candy bars and bags of peanuts to buy?

   d. Suppose that you had won $30 on your ticket, not $15. Show the $30 budget line in your diagram. Why would this budget line be preferable to the old one?

8. What are economic resources? What categories do economists use to classify them? Why are resources also called factors of production? Why are they called inputs? **LO4**

9. Why isn't money considered a capital resource in economics? Why is entrepreneurial ability considered a category of economic resource, distinct from labor? What are the major functions of the entrepreneur? **LO4**

10. Below is a production possibilities table for consumer goods (automobiles) and capital goods (forklifts): **LO5**

Type of Production	Production Alternatives				
	A	B	C	D	E
Automobiles	0	2	4	6	8
Forklifts	30	27	21	12	0

   a. Show these data graphically. Upon what specific assumptions is this production possibilities curve based?

   b. If the economy is at point *C*, what is the cost of one more automobile? Of one more forklift? Explain how the production possibilities curve reflects the law of increasing opportunity costs.

   c. If the economy characterized by this production possibilities table and curve were producing 3 automobiles and 20 forklifts, what could you conclude about its use of its available resources?

   d. What would production at a point outside the production possibilities curve indicate? What must occur before the economy can attain such a level of production?

   e. Suppose improvement occurs in the technology of producing forklifts but not in the technology of producing automobiles. Draw the new production possibilities curve. Now assume that a technological advance occurs in producing automobiles but not in producing forklifts. Draw the new production possibilities curve. Now draw a production possibilities curve that reflects technological improvement in the production of both goods.

11. Specify and explain the typical shapes of marginal-benefit and marginal-cost curves. How are these curves used to determine the optimal allocation of resources to a particular product? If current output is such that marginal cost exceeds marginal benefit, should more or fewer resources be allocated to this product? Explain. **LO5**

12. Explain how (if at all) each of the following events affects the location of a country's production possibilities curve: **LO5**

   a. The quality of education increases.

   b. The number of unemployed workers increases.

   c. A new technique improves the efficiency of extracting copper from ore.

   d. A devastating earthquake destroys numerous production facilities.

FURTHER TEST YOUR KNOWLEDGE AT
www.mcconnellbriefmacro1e.com

Web-Based Questions

At the text's Online Learning Center, **www.mcconnellbriefmacro 1e.com,** you will find a multiple-choice quiz on this chapter's content. We encourage you to take the quiz to see how you do.

Also, you will find one or more Web-based questions that require information from the Internet to answer.

Chapter One Appendix

Graphs and Their Meaning

If you glance quickly through this text, you will find many graphs. These graphs are included to help you visualize and understand economic relationships. Most of our principles or models explain relationships between just two sets of economic data, which can be conveniently represented with two-dimensional graphs.

Construction of a Graph

A graph is a visual representation of the relationship between two variables. The table in Figure 1 is a hypothetical illustration showing the relationship between income and consumption for the economy as a whole. Because people tend to buy more goods and services when their incomes go up, it is not surprising to find in the table that total consumption in the economy increases as total income increases.

The information in the table is also expressed graphically in Figure 1. Here is how it is done: We want to show visually or graphically how consumption changes as income changes. Since income is the determining factor, we follow mathematical custom and represent it on the horizontal axis of the graph. And because consumption depends on income, it is represented on the vertical axis of the graph.

The vertical and horizontal scales of the graph reflect the ranges of values of consumption and income, marked in convenient increments. As you can see, the values on the scales cover all the values in the table.

Because the graph has two dimensions, each point within it represents an income value and its associated consumption value. To find a point that represents one of the five income-consumption combinations in the table, we draw lines from the appropriate values on the vertical and horizontal axes. For example, to plot point *c* (the $200 income–$150 consumption point), lines are drawn up from the horizontal (income) axis at $200 and across from the vertical (consumption) axis at $150. These lines intersect at point *c*, which represents this particular income-consumption combination. You should verify that the other income-consumption combinations shown in the table in Figure 1 are properly located in the graph that is there.

Finally, by assuming that the same general relationship between income and consumption prevails for all other incomes, we draw a line or smooth curve to connect these points. That line or curve represents the income-consumption relationship.

If the graph is a straight line, as in Figure 1, the relationship is said to be *linear*.

Direct and Inverse Relationships

The line in Figure 1 slopes upward to the right, so it depicts a **direct relationship** between income and consumption. A direct relationship, or positive relationship, means that two variables (here, consumption and income) change in the same direction. An increase in consump-

direct relationship The (positive) relationship between two variables that change in the same direction.

FIGURE 1 **Graphing the direct relationship between consumption and income.** Two sets of data that are positively or directly related, such as consumption and income, graph as an upsloping line.

Income per Week	Consumption per Week	Point
$ 0	$ 50	a
100	100	b
200	150	c
300	200	d
400	250	e

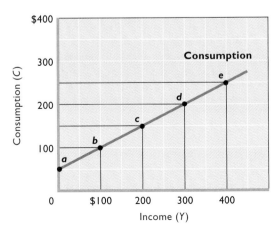

tion is associated with an increase in income; a decrease in consumption accompanies a decrease in income. When two sets of data are positively or directly related, they always graph as an upsloping line, as in Figure 1.

In contrast, two sets of data may be inversely related. Consider the table in Figure 2, which shows the relationship between the price of basketball tickets and game attendance for Big Time University (BTU). Here there is an **inverse relationship,** or negative relationship, because the two variables change in opposite directions. When ticket prices for the games decrease, attendance increases. When ticket prices increase, attendance decreases. The six data points in the table are plotted in the graph in Figure 2. This inverse relationship graphs as a downsloping line.

inverse relationship The (negative) relationship between two variables that change in opposite directions.

Dependent and Independent Variables

Economists seek to determine which variable is the "cause" and which the "effect." Or, more formally, they seek the independent variable and the dependent variable. The **independent variable** is the cause or source; it is the variable that changes first. The **depndent variable** is the effect or outcome; it is the variable that changes because of the change in the independent variable. As in our income-consumption exam-

independent variable The variable causing a change in some other (dependent) variable; the "causal variable."

ple, income generally is the independent variable and consumption the dependent variable. Income causes consumption to be what it is rather than the other way around. Similarly, ticket prices (set in advance of the season and printed on the ticket) determine attendance at BTU basketball games; attendance at games does not determine the printed ticket prices for those games. Ticket price is the independent variable, and the quantity of tickets purchased is the dependent variable.

Mathematicians always put the independent variable (cause) on the horizontal axis and the dependent variable (effect) on the vertical axis. Economists are less tidy; their graphing of independent and dependent variables is more arbitrary. Their conventional graphing of the income-consumption relationship is consistent with mathematical presentation, but economists historically put price and cost data on the vertical axis of their graphs. Contemporary economists have followed the tradition. So economists' graphing of BTU's ticket price–attendance data differs from normal mathematical procedure. This does not present a problem, but we want you to be aware of this fact to avoid possible confusion.

dependent variable The variable that changes as a result of a change in some other (independent) variable; the "outcome variable."

Other Things Equal

Our simple two-variable graphs purposely ignore many other factors that might affect the amount of consumption

FIGURE 2 **Graphing the inverse relationship between ticket prices and game attendance.** Two sets of data that are negatively or inversely related, such as ticket price and the attendance at basketball games, graph as a downsloping line.

Ticket Price	Attendance, Thousands	Point
$50	0	a
40	4	b
30	8	c
20	12	d
10	16	e
0	20	f

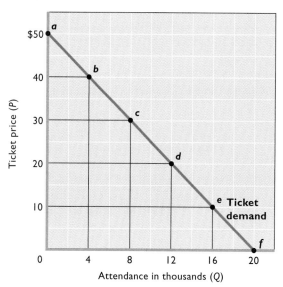

occurring at each income level or the number of people who attend BTU basketball games at each possible ticket price. When economists plot the relationship between any two variables, they employ the *ceteris paribus* (other-things-equal) assumption. Thus, in Figure 1 all factors other than income that might affect the amount of consumption are presumed to be constant or unchanged. Similarly, in Figure 2 all factors other than ticket price that might influence attendance at BTU basketball games are assumed constant. In reality, "other things" are not equal; they often change, and when they do, the relationship represented in our two tables and graphs will change. Specifically, the lines we have plotted would shift to new locations.

Consider a stock market "crash." The dramatic drop in the value of stocks might cause people to feel less wealthy and therefore less willing to consume at each level of income. The result might be a downward shift of the consumption line. To see this, you should plot a new consumption line in Figure 1, assuming that consumption is, say, $20 less at each income level. Note that the relationship remains direct; the line merely shifts downward to reflect less consumption spending at each income level.

Similarly, factors other than ticket prices might affect BTU game attendance. If BTU loses most of its games, attendance at BTU games might be less at each ticket price. To see this, redraw Figure 2, assuming that 2000 fewer fans attend BTU games at each ticket price.

Slope of a Line

Lines can be described in terms of their slopes. The **slope of a straight line** is the ratio of the vertical change (the rise or drop) to the horizontal change (the run) between any two points of the line.

slope of a straight line
The ratio of the vertical change (the rise or fall) to the horizontal change (the run) between any two points on a line.

Positive Slope Between point *b* and point *c* in the graph in Figure 1, the rise or vertical change (the change in consumption) is +$50 and the run or horizontal change (the change in income) is +$100. Therefore:

$$\text{Slope} = \frac{\text{vertical change}}{\text{horizontal change}} = \frac{+50}{+100} = \frac{1}{2} = .5$$

Note that our slope of $\frac{1}{2}$ or .5 is positive because consumption and income change in the same direction; that is, consumption and income are directly or positively related.

Negative Slope Between any two of the identified points in the graph of Figure 2, say, point *c* and point *d*, the

vertical change is -10 (the drop) and the horizontal change is $+4$ (the run). Therefore:

$$\text{Slope} = \frac{\text{vertical change}}{\text{horizontal change}} = \frac{-10}{+4} = -2\frac{1}{2} = -2.5$$

This slope is negative because ticket price and attendance have an inverse relationship.

Slopes and Marginal Analysis Economists are largely concerned with changes in values. The concept of slope is important in economics because it reflects marginal changes—those involving 1 more (or 1 less) unit. For example, in Figure 1 the .5 slope shows that $.50 of extra or marginal consumption is associated with each $1 change in income. In this example, people collectively will consume $.50 of any $1 increase in their incomes and reduce their consumption by $.50 for each $1 decline in income. Careful inspection of Figure 2 reveals that every $1 increase in ticket price for BTU games will decrease game attendance by 400 people and every $1 decrease in ticket price will increase game attendance by 400 people.

Infinite and Zero Slopes Many variables are unrelated or independent of one another. For example, the quantity of wristwatches purchased is not related to the price of bananas. In Figure 3a the price of bananas is measured on the vertical axis and the quantity of watches demanded on the horizontal axis. The graph of their relationship is the line parallel to the vertical axis, indicating that the same quantity of watches is purchased no matter what the price of bananas. The slope of such a line is infinite.

Similarly, aggregate consumption is completely unrelated to the nation's divorce rate. In Figure 3b we put consumption on the vertical axis and the divorce rate on the horizontal axis. The line parallel to the horizontal axis represents this lack of relatedness. This line has a slope of zero.

Slope of a Nonlinear Curve We now move from the simple world of linear relationships (straight lines) to the somewhat more complex world of nonlinear relationships. The slope of a straight line is the same at all its points. The slope of a line representing a nonlinear relationship changes from one point to another. Such lines are always referred to as *curves*.

Consider the downsloping curve in Figure 4. Its slope is negative throughout, but the curve flattens as we move down along it. Thus, its slope constantly changes; the curve has a different slope at each point.

FIGURE 3 **Infinite and zero slopes.** (a) A line parallel to the vertical axis has an infinite slope. Here, purchases of watches remain the same no matter what happens to the price of bananas. (b) A line parallel to the horizontal axis has a slope of zero. In this case, total consumption remains the same no matter what happens to the divorce rate. In both (a) and (b), the two variables are totally unrelated to one another.

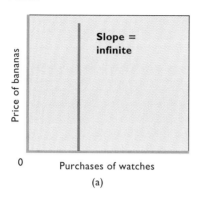

(a)

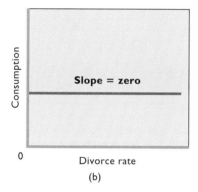

(b)

FIGURE 4 **Determining the slopes of curves.** The slope of a nonlinear curve changes from point to point on the curve. The slope at any point (say, B) can be determined by drawing a straight line that is tangent to that point (line bb) and calculating the slope of that line.

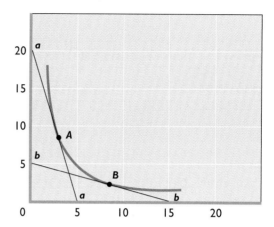

To measure the slope at a specific point, we draw a straight line tangent to the curve at that point. A line is tangent at a point if it touches, but does not intersect, the curve at that point. So line aa is tangent to the curve in Figure 4 at point A. The slope of the curve at that point is equal to the slope of the tangent line. Specifically, the total vertical change (drop) in the tangent line aa is -20 and the total horizontal change (run) is $+5$. Because the slope of the tangent line aa is $-20/+5$, or -4, the slope of the curve at point A is also -4.

Line bb in Figure 4 is tangent to the curve at point B. Using the same procedure, we find the slope at B to be $-5/+15$, or $-\frac{1}{3}$. Thus, in this flatter part of the curve, the slope is less negative.

Several of the Appendix questions are of a "workbook" variety, and we urge you to go through them carefully to check your understanding of graphs and slopes.

Appendix Summary

1. Graphs are a convenient and revealing way to represent economic relationships.

2. Two variables are positively or directly related when their values change in the same direction. The line (curve) representing two directly related variables slopes upward.

3. Two variables are negatively or inversely related when their values change in opposite directions. The curve representing two inversely related variables slopes downward.

4. The value of the dependent variable (the "effect") is determined by the value of the independent variable (the "cause").

5. When the "other factors" that might affect a two-variable relationship are allowed to change, the graph of the relationship will likely shift to a new location.

6. The slope of a straight line is the ratio of the vertical change to the horizontal change between any two points. The slope of an upsloping line is positive; the slope of a downsloping line is negative.

7. The slope of a line or curve is especially relevant for economics because it measures marginal changes.

8. The slope of a horizontal line is zero; the slope of a vertical line is infinite.

9. The slope of a curve at any point is determined by calculating the slope of a straight line tangent to the curve at that point.

Appendix Terms and Concepts

direct relationship

inverse relationship

independent variable

dependent variable

slope of a straight line

Appendix Study Questions

1. Briefly explain the use of graphs as a way to represent economic relationships. What is an inverse relationship? How does it graph? What is a direct relationship? How does it graph? Graph and explain the relationships (other things equal) you would expect to find between (a) the number of inches of rainfall per month and the sale of umbrellas, (b) the price of bottled water and the number of bottles sold per year, and (c) the popularity of an entertainer and the price of her concert tickets.

   In each case cite and explain how variables other than those specifically mentioned might upset the expected relationship. Is your graph in part *b*, above, consistent with the fact that, historically, the quantity and price of bottled water have both increased? If not, explain any difference. **LO6**

2. Indicate how each of the following might affect the data shown in the table and graph in Figure 2 of this appendix: **LO6**

   a. BTU's athletic director hires away the coach from a perennial champion.

   b. An NBA team locates in the city where BTU plays.

   c. BTU contracts to have all its home games televised.

3. The following table contains data on the relationship between saving and income. Rearrange these data into a meaningful order and graph them on the accompanying grid. What is the slope of the line? Interpret the meaning of the slope. What would you predict saving to be at the $12,500 level of income? **LO6**

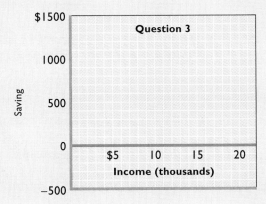

Income per Year	Saving per Year
$15,000	$1,000
0	−500
10,000	500
5,000	0
20,000	1,500

4. Construct a table from the data shown on the graph below. Which is the dependent variable and which the independent variable? **LO6**

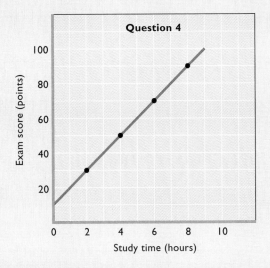

5. Suppose that when the price of gold is $100 an ounce, gold producers find it unprofitable to sell gold. However, when the price is $200 an ounce, 5000 ounces of output (production) is

profitable. At $300, a total of 10,000 ounces of output is profitable. Similarly, total production increases by 5000 ounces for each successive $100 increase in the price of gold. Describe the relevant relationship between the price of gold and the production of gold in words, in a table, and on a graph. Put the price of gold on the vertical axis and the output of gold on the horizontal axis. Comment on the advantages and disadvantages of the verbal, tabular, and graphical forms of description. **LO6**

6. The accompanying graph shows curve XX' and tangents to the curve at points A, B, and C. Calculate the slope of the curve at each of these three points. **LO6**

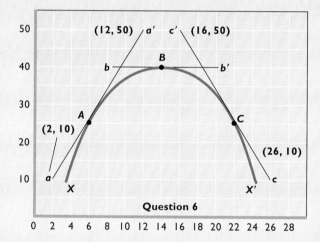

Question 6

7. In the accompanying graph, is the slope of curve AA' positive or negative? Does the slope increase or decrease as we move along the curve from A to A'? Answer the same two questions for curve BB'. **LO6**

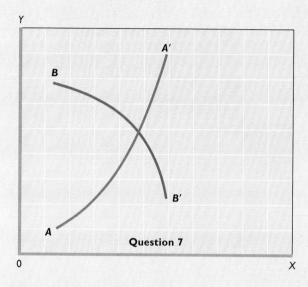

Question 7

2

IN THIS CHAPTER YOU WILL LEARN:

1 The difference between a command system and a market system.

2 The main characteristics of the market system.

3 How the market system answers four fundamental questions.

4 How the market system adjusts to change and promotes progress.

5 The mechanics of the circular flow model.

The Market System and the Circular Flow

You are at the mall. Suppose you were assigned to compile a list of all the individual goods and services there, including the different brands and variations of each type of product. That task would be daunting and the list would be long! And even though a single shopping mall contains a remarkable quantity and variety of goods, it is only a tiny part of the national economy.

Who decided that the particular goods and services available at the mall and in the broader economy should be produced? How did the producers determine which technology and types of resources to use in producing these particular goods? Who will obtain these products? What accounts for the new and improved products among these goods? This chapter will answer these questions.

Economic Systems

Every society needs to develop an **economic system**—a particular set of institutional arrangements and a coordinating mechanism—to respond to the economic problem. The economic system has to determine what goods are produced, how they are produced, who gets them, and how to promote technological progress.

Economic systems differ as to (1) who owns the factors of production and (2) the method used to motivate, coordinate, and direct economic activity. There are two general types of economic systems: the command system and the market system.

economic system
A particular set of institutional arrangements and a coordinating mechanism for producing goods and services.

The Command System

The **command system** is also known as *socialism* or *communism*. In that system, government owns most property resources and economic decision making occurs through a central economic plan. A central planning board appointed by the government makes nearly all the major decisions concerning the use of resources, the composition and distribution of output, and the organization of production. The government owns most of the business firms, which produce according to government directives. The central planning board determines production goals for each enterprise and specifies the amount of resources to be allocated to each enterprise so that it can reach its production goals. The division of output between capital and consumer goods is centrally decided, and capital goods are allocated among industries on the basis of the central planning board's long-term priorities.

A pure command economy would rely exclusively on a central plan to allocate the government-owned property resources. But, in reality, even the preeminent command economy—the Soviet Union—tolerated some private ownership and incorporated some markets before its collapse in 1992. Recent reforms in Russia and most of the eastern European nations have to one degree or another transformed their command economies to capitalistic, market-oriented systems. China's reforms have not gone as far, but they have greatly reduced the reliance on central planning. Although there is still extensive government ownership of resources and capital in China, the nation has increasingly relied on free markets to organize and coordinate its economy. North Korea and Cuba are the last remaining examples of largely centrally planned economies. Global Snapshot 2.1 reveals how North Korea's centrally planned economy compares to the market economy of its neighbor, South Korea. Later in this chapter, we will explore the main reasons for the general demise of the command systems.

command system
An economic system in which most property resources are owned by the government and economic decisions are made by a central government body.

The Market System

The polar alternative to the command system is the **market system,** or *capitalism.* The system is characterized by the private ownership of resources and the use of markets and prices to coordinate and direct economic activity. Participants act in their own self-interest. Individuals and businesses seek to achieve their economic goals through their own decisions regarding work, consumption, or production. The system allows for the private ownership of capital, communicates through prices, and coordinates economic activity through *markets*—places where buyers and sellers come together. Goods and services are produced and resources are supplied by whoever is willing and able to do so. The result is competition among independently acting buyers and sellers of each product and resource. Thus, economic decision making is widely dispersed. Also, the high potential monetary rewards create powerful incentives for existing firms to innovate and entrepreneurs to pioneer new products and processes.

In *pure* capitalism—or *laissez-faire* capitalism—government's role would be limited to protecting private property and establishing an environment appropriate to the

market system
An economic system in which property resources are privately owned and markets and prices are used to direct and coordinate economic activities.

GLOBAL SNAPSHOT 2.1

The Two Koreas

North Korea is one of the few command economies still standing. After the Second World War, Korea was divided into North Korea and South Korea. North Korea, under the influence of the Soviet Union, established a command economy that emphasized government ownership and central government planning. South Korea, protected by the United States, established a market economy based upon private ownership and the profit motive. Today, the differences in the economic outcomes of the two systems are striking:

	North Korea	South Korea
GDP	$40 billion*	$1.2 trillion*
GDP per capita	$1,800*	$24,500*
Exports	$1.3 billion	$326 billion
Imports	$2.7 billion	$309.3 billion
Agriculture as % of GDP	30 percent	3 percent

*Based on purchasing power equivalencies to the U.S. dollar.
Source: CIA World Fact Book, **www.cia.gov.**

operation of the market system. The term "laissez-faire" means "let it be," that is, keep government from interfering with the economy. The idea is that such interference will disturb the efficient working of the market system.

But in the capitalism practiced in the United States and most other countries, government plays a substantial role in the economy. It not only provides the rules for economic activity but also promotes economic stability and growth, provides certain goods and services that would otherwise be underproduced or not produced at all, and modifies the distribution of income. The government, however, is not the dominant economic force in deciding what to produce, how to produce it, and who will get it. That force is the market.

Characteristics of the Market System

It will be very instructive to examine some of the key features of the market system in more detail.

Private Property

private property
The right of persons and firms to obtain, own, control, employ, dispose of, and bequeath land, capital, and other property.

In a market system, private individuals and firms, not the government, own most of the property resources (land and capital). It is this extensive private ownership of capital that gives capitalism its name. This right of **private property,** coupled with the freedom to negotiate binding legal contracts, enables individuals and businesses to obtain, use, and dispose of property resources as they see fit. The right of property owners to designate who will receive their property when they die sustains the institution of private property.

Property rights encourage investment, innovation, exchange, maintenance of property, and economic growth. Why would anyone stock a store, build a factory, or clear land for farming if someone else, or the government itself, could take that property for his or her own benefit?

Property rights also extend to intellectual property through patents, copyrights, and trademarks. Such long-term protection encourages people to write books, music, and computer programs and to invent new products and production processes without fear that others will steal them and the rewards they may bring.

Moreover, property rights facilitate exchange. The title to an automobile or the deed to a cattle ranch assures the buyer that the seller is the legitimate owner. Also, property rights encourage owners to maintain or improve their property so as to preserve or increase its value. Finally, property rights enable people to use their time and resources to produce more goods and services, rather than using them to protect and retain the property they have already produced or acquired.

Freedom of Enterprise and Choice

Closely related to private ownership of property is freedom of enterprise and choice. The market system requires that various economic units make certain choices, which are expressed and implemented in the economy's markets:

- **Freedom of enterprise** ensures that entrepreneurs and private businesses are free to obtain and use economic resources to produce their choice of goods and services and to sell them in their chosen markets.
- **Freedom of choice** enables owners to employ or dispose of their property and money as they see fit. It also allows workers to enter any line of work for which they are qualified. Finally, it ensures that consumers are free to buy the goods and services that best satisfy their wants.

These choices are free only within broad legal limitations, of course. Illegal choices such as selling human organs or buying illicit drugs are punished through fines and imprisonment. (Global Snapshot 2.2 reveals that the degree of economic freedom varies greatly from nation to nation.)

Self-Interest

In the market system, **self-interest** is the motivating force of the various economic units as they express their free choices. Self-interest simply means that each economic unit tries to achieve its own particular goal, which usually requires delivering something of value to others. Entrepreneurs try to maximize profit or minimize loss. Property owners try to get the highest price for the sale or rent of their resources. Workers try to maximize their utility (satisfaction) by finding jobs that offer the best combination of wages, hours, fringe benefits, and working conditions. Consumers try to obtain the products they want at the lowest possible price and apportion their expenditures to maximize their utility. The motive of self-interest gives direction and consistency to what might otherwise be a chaotic economy.

Competition

The market system depends on **competition** among economic units. The basis of this competition is freedom of choice exercised in pursuit of a monetary return. Very broadly defined, competition requires:

- Independently acting sellers and buyers operating in a particular product or resource market.
- Freedom of sellers and buyers to enter or leave markets, on the basis of their economic self-interest.

freedom of enterprise
The freedom of firms to obtain economic resources, to use those resources to produce products of the firms' own choosing, and to sell their products in markets of their choice.

freedom of choice
The freedom of owners of resources to employ or dispose of them as they see fit, and the freedom of consumers to spend their incomes in a manner they think is appropriate.

self-interest
The most-advantageous outcome as viewed by each firm, property owner, worker, or consumer.

competition
The presence in a market of independent buyers and sellers vying with one another, and the freedom of buyers and sellers to enter and leave the market.

GLOBAL SNAPSHOT 2.2

Index of Economic Freedom, Selected Economies

The Index of Economic Freedom measures economic freedom using 10 broad categories such as trade policy, property rights, and government intervention, with each category containing more than 50 specific criteria. The index then ranks 157 economies according to their degree of economic freedom. A few selected rankings for 2008 are listed below.

FREE
- 1 Hong Kong
- 4 Australia
- 5 United States

MOSTLY FREE
- 11 Denmark
- 23 Germany
- 48 France

MOSTLY UNFREE
- 96 Mozambique
- 126 China
- 134 Russia

REPRESSED
- 151 Iran
- 156 Cuba
- 157 North Korea

Source: Heritage Foundation (**www.heritage.org**) and *The Wall Street Journal.*

ORIGIN OF THE IDEA

O 2.1

Self-interest

Competition diffuses economic power within the businesses and households that make up the economy. When there are independently acting sellers and buyers in a market, no one buyer or seller is able to dictate the price of the product or resource because others can undercut that price.

Competition also implies that producers can enter or leave an industry; there are no insurmountable barriers to an industry's expanding or contracting. This freedom of an industry to expand or contract provides the economy with the flexibility needed to remain efficient over time. Freedom of entry and exit enables the economy to adjust to changes in consumer tastes, technology, and resource availability.

The diffusion of economic power inherent in competition limits the potential abuse of that power. A producer that charges more than the competitive market price will lose sales to other producers. An employer who pays less than the competitive market wage rate will lose workers to other employers. A firm that fails to exploit new technology will lose profits to firms that do. Competition is the basic regulatory force in the market system.

Markets and Prices

Markets and prices are key components of the market system. They give the system its ability to coordinate millions of daily economic decisions. A **market** is an institution or mechanism that brings buyers ("demanders") and sellers ("suppliers") into contact. A market system conveys the decisions made by buyers and sellers of products and resources. The decisions made on each side of the market determine a set of product and resource prices that guide resource owners, entrepreneurs, and consumers as they make and revise their choices and pursue their self-interest.

Just as competition is the regulatory mechanism of the market system, the market system itself is the organizing mechanism. It is an elaborate communication network through which innumerable individual free choices are recorded, summarized, and balanced. Those who respond to market signals and heed market dictates are rewarded with greater profit and income; those who do not respond to those signals and choose to ignore market dictates are penalized. Through this mechanism society decides what the economy should produce, how production can be organized efficiently, and how the fruits of production are to be distributed among the various units that make up the economy.

market
An institution or mechanism that brings buyers and sellers together.

Technology and Capital Goods

In the market system, competition, freedom of choice, self-interest, and personal reward provide the opportunity and motivation for technological advance. The monetary rewards for new products or production techniques accrue directly to the innovator. The market system therefore encourages extensive use and rapid development of complex capital goods: tools, machinery, large-scale factories, and facilities for storage, communication, transportation, and marketing.

Advanced technology and capital goods are important because the most direct methods of production are often the least efficient. The only way to avoid that inefficiency is to rely on capital goods. It would be ridiculous for a farmer to go at production with bare hands. There are huge benefits to be derived from creating and using such capital equipment as plows, tractors, storage bins, and so on. The more efficient production means much more abundant outputs.

Specialization

The extent to which market economies rely on **specialization** is extraordinary. Specialization is the use of resources of an individual, region, or nation to produce one or a few goods or services rather than the entire range of goods and services. Those goods and services are then exchanged for a full range of desired products. The majority of consumers produce virtually none of the goods and services they consume, and they consume little or nothing of the items they produce. The person working nine to five installing windows in commercial aircraft may rarely fly. Many farmers sell their milk to the local dairy and then buy margarine at the local grocery store. Society learned long ago that self-sufficiency breeds inefficiency. The jack-of-all-trades may be a very colorful individual but is certainly not an efficient producer.

specialization
The use of resources of an individual, region, or nation to produce one or a few goods and services rather than the entire range of goods and services.

Division of Labor Human specialization—called the **division of labor**—contributes to a society's output in several ways:

- *Specialization makes use of differences in ability* Specialization enables individuals to take advantage of existing differences in their abilities and skills. If Peyton is strong, athletic, and good at throwing a football and Beyonce is beautiful, agile, and can sing, their distribution of talents can be most efficiently used if Peyton plays professional football and Beyonce records songs and gives concerts.

division of labor
The separation of the work required to produce a product into a number of different tasks that are performed by different workers.

© Brent Smith/Reuters/Corbis   © PRNewsFoto/Diamond information Center

Photo Op Peyton Manning and Beyoncé Knowles

It makes economic sense for Peyton Manning and Beyoncé Knowles to specialize in what they do best.

ORIGIN OF THE IDEA

O 2.2

Specialization/division of labor

- *Specialization fosters learning by doing* Even if the abilities of two people are identical, specialization may still be advantageous. By devoting time to a single task rather than working at a number of different tasks, a person is more likely to develop the skills required and to improve techniques. You learn to be a good lawyer by studying and practicing law.
- *Specialization saves time* By devoting time to a single task, a person avoids the loss of time incurred in shifting from one job to another.

For all these reasons, specialization increases the total output society derives from limited resources.

Geographic Specialization Specialization also works on a regional and international basis. It is conceivable that oranges could be grown in Nebraska, but because of the unsuitability of the land, rainfall, and temperature, the costs would be very high. And it is conceivable that wheat could be grown in Florida, but such production would be costly for similar geographical reasons. So Nebraskans produce products—wheat in particular—for which their resources are best suited, and Floridians do the same, producing oranges and other citrus fruits. By specializing, both economies produce more than is needed locally. Then, very sensibly, Nebraskans and Floridians swap some of their surpluses—wheat for oranges, oranges for wheat.

Similarly, on an international scale, the United States specializes in producing such items as commercial aircraft and computers, which it sells abroad in exchange for video recorders from Japan, bananas from Honduras, and woven baskets from Thailand. Both human specialization and geographic specialization are needed to achieve efficiency in the use of limited resources.

Use of Money

A rather obvious characteristic of any economic system is the extensive use of money. Money performs several functions, but first and foremost it is a **medium of exchange**. It makes trade easier.

Specialization requires exchange. Exchange can, and sometimes does, occur through **barter**—swapping goods for goods, say, wheat for oranges. But barter poses serious problems because it requires a *coincidence of wants* between the buyer and the seller. In our example, we assumed that Nebraskans had excess wheat to trade and wanted oranges. And we assumed that Floridians had excess oranges to trade and wanted wheat. So an exchange occurred. But if such a coincidence of wants is missing, trade is stymied.

Suppose that Nebraska has no interest in Florida's oranges but wants potatoes from Idaho. And suppose that Idaho wants Florida's oranges but not Nebraska's wheat. And, to complicate matters, suppose that Florida wants some of Nebraska's wheat but none of Idaho's potatoes. We summarize the situation in Figure 2.1.

In none of the cases shown in the figure is there a coincidence of wants. Trade by barter clearly would be difficult. Instead, people in each state use **money,** which is simply a convenient social invention to facilitate exchanges of goods and services. Historically, people have used cattle, cigarettes, shells, stones, pieces of metal, and many other commodities, with varying degrees of success, as a medium of exchange. But to serve as money, an item needs to pass only one test: It must be generally acceptable to sellers in exchange for their goods and services. Money is socially defined; whatever society accepts as a medium of exchange *is* money.

Today, most economies use pieces of paper as money. The use of paper dollars (currency) as a medium of exchange is what enables Nebraska, Florida, and Idaho to overcome their trade stalemate, as demonstrated in Figure 2.1.

medium of exchange
Any item sellers generally accept and buyers generally use to pay for goods and services.

barter
The exchange of one good or service for another good or service.

money
Any item that is generally acceptable to sellers in exchange for goods and services.

FIGURE 2.1 **Money facilitates trade when wants do not coincide.** The use of money as a medium of exchange permits trade to be accomplished despite a noncoincidence of wants. (1) Nebraska trades the wheat that Florida wants for money from Floridians; (2) Nebraska trades the money it receives from Florida for the potatoes it wants from Idaho; (3) Idaho trades the money it receives from Nebraska for the oranges it wants from Florida.

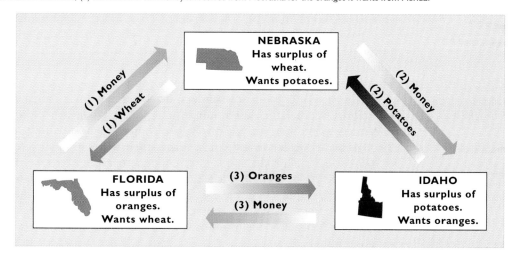

On a global basis different nations have different currencies, and that complicates specialization and exchange. But markets in which currencies are bought and sold make it possible for U.S. residents, Japanese, Germans, Britons, and Mexicans, through the swapping of dollars, yen, euros, pounds, and pesos, one for another, to exchange goods and services without resorting to barter.

Active, but Limited, Government

An active, but limited, government is the final characteristic of market systems in real-life advanced industrial economies. Although a market system promotes a high degree of efficiency in the use of its resources, it has certain inherent shortcomings. We will discover in Chapter 4 that government can increase the overall effectiveness of the economic system in several ways.

Four Fundamental Questions

The key features of the market system help explain how market economies respond to four fundamental questions:

- What goods and services will be produced?
- How will the goods and services be produced?
- Who will get the goods and services?
- How will the system promote progress?

These four questions highlight the economic choices underlying the production possibilities curve discussed in Chapter 1. They reflect the reality of scarce resources in a world of unlimited wants. All economies, whether market or command, must address these four questions.

What Will Be Produced?

How will a market system decide on the specific types and quantities of goods to be produced? The simple answer is this: The goods and services produced at a continuing profit will be produced, and those produced at a continuing loss will not. Profits and losses are the difference between the total revenue (TR) a firm receives from the sale of its products and the total cost (TC) of producing those products. (For economists, economic costs include not only wage and salary payments to labor, and interest and rental payments for capital and land, but also payments to the entrepreneur for organizing and combining the other resources to produce a commodity.)

Continuing economic profit (TR > TC) in an industry results in expanded production and the movement of resources toward that industry. The industry expands. Continuing losses (TC > TR) in an industry leads to reduced production and the exit of resources from that industry. The industry contracts.

In the market system, consumers are sovereign (in command). **Consumer sovereignty** is crucial in determining the types and quantities of goods produced. Consumers spend their income on the goods they are most willing and able to buy. Through these **"dollar votes"** they register their wants in the market. If the dollar votes for a certain product are great enough to create a profit, businesses will produce that product and offer it for sale. In contrast, if the dollar votes do not create sufficient revenues to cover costs, businesses will not produce the product. So the consumers are sovereign. They collectively direct resources to industries that are meeting consumer wants and away from industries that are not meeting consumer wants.

consumer sovereignty
Determination by consumers of the types and quantities of goods and services that will be produced with the economy's scarce resources.

dollar votes
The "votes" that consumers and entrepreneurs cast for the production of consumer and capital goods when they purchase them in product and resource markets.

McHits and McMisses

McDonald's has introduced several new menu items over the decades. Some have been profitable "hits," while others have been "misses." Ultimately, consumers decide whether a menu item is profitable and therefore whether it stays on the McDonald's menu.

- Hulaburger (1962)—McMiss
- Filet-O-Fish (1963)—McHit
- Strawberry shortcake (1966)—McMiss
- Big Mac (1968)—McHit
- Hot apple pie (1968)—McHit
- Egg McMuffin (1975)—McHit
- Drive-thru (1975)—McHit
- Chicken McNuggets (1983)—McHit
- Extra Value Meal (1991)—McHit
- McLean Deluxe (1991)—McMiss
- Arch Deluxe (1996)—McMiss
- 55-cent special (1997)—McMiss
- Big Xtra (1999)—McHit

Question:
Do you think McDonald's premium salads will be a lasting McHit, or do you think they eventually will become a McMiss?

Source: "Polishing the Golden Arches," *Forbes*, June 15, 1998, pp. 42–43, updated.

The dollar votes of consumers determine not only which industries will continue to exist but also which products will survive or fail. Only profitable industries, firms, and products survive.

How Will the Goods and Services Be Produced?

What combinations of resources and technologies will be used to produce goods and services? How will the production be organized? The answer: In combinations and ways that minimize the cost per unit of output. Because competition eliminates high-cost producers, profitability requires that firms produce their output at minimum cost per unit. Achieving this least-cost production necessitates, for example, that firms use the right mix of labor and capital, given the prices and productivity of those resources. It also means locating production facilities optimally to hold down production and transportation expenses. Finally, it means using the most appropriate technology in producing and distributing output. In a competitive market economy, high-cost producers lose business to low-cost producers of equal-quality products.

Who Will Get the Output?

The market system enters the picture in two ways when determining the distribution of total output. Generally, any product will be distributed to consumers on the basis of their ability and willingness to pay its existing market price. If the price of some product, say, a small sailboat, is $3000, then buyers who are willing and able to pay that price will "sail, sail away." Consumers who are unwilling or unable to pay the price will "sit on the dock of the bay."

The ability to pay the prices for sailboats and other products depends on the amount of income that consumers have, along with the prices of, and preferences for, various goods. If consumers have sufficient income and want to spend their money on a particular good, they can have it. And the amount of income they have depends on (1) the quantities of the property and human resources they supply and (2) the prices those resources command in the resource market. Resource prices (wages, interest, rent, profit) are key in determining the size of each household's income and therefore each household's ability to buy part of the economy's output.

How Will the System Promote Progress?

Society desires economic growth (greater output) and higher standards of living (greater income per person). How does the market system promote technological improvements and capital accumulation, both of which contribute to a higher standard of living for society?

Technological Advance The market system provides a strong incentive for technological advance and enables better products and processes to supplant inferior ones. An entrepreneur or firm that introduces a popular new product will gain revenue and economic profit at the expense of rivals. Firms that are highly profitable one year may find they are in financial trouble just a few years later.

Technological advance also includes new and improved methods that reduce production or distribution costs. By passing part of its cost reduction on to the consumer through a lower product price, the firm can increase sales and obtain economic profit at the expense of rival firms.

Moreover, the market system promotes the *rapid spread* of technological advance throughout an industry. Rival firms must follow the lead of the most innovative firm or else suffer immediate losses and eventual failure. In some cases, the result is **creative destruction:** The creation of new products and production methods completely destroys the market positions of firms that are wedded to existing products and older ways of doing business. Example: The advent of compact discs largely demolished long-play vinyl records, and iPods and other digital technologies are now supplanting CDs.

creative destruction
The idea that the creation of new products and production methods may simultaneously destroy the market power of existing firms.

Capital Accumulation Most technological advances require additional capital goods. The market system provides the resources necessary to produce those goods through increased dollar votes for capital goods. That is, the market system acknowledges dollar voting for capital goods as well as for consumer goods.

But who will register votes for capital goods? Answer: Entrepreneurs and owners of businesses. As receivers of profit income, they often use part of that income to purchase capital goods. Doing so yields even greater profit income in the future if the technological innovation is successful. Also, by paying interest or selling ownership shares, the entrepreneur and firm can attract some of the income of households to cast dollar votes for the production of more capital goods.

The "Invisible Hand"

In his 1776 book *The Wealth of Nations*, Adam Smith first noted that the operation of a market system creates a curious unity between private interests and social interests. Firms and resource suppliers, seeking to further their own self-interest and operating within the framework of a highly competitive market system, will simultaneously, as though guided by an **"invisible hand,"** promote the public or social interest. For example, we have seen that in a competitive environment, businesses seek to build new and improved products to increase profits. Those enhanced products increase society's well-being. Businesses also use the least costly combination of resources to produce a specific output because it is in their self-interest to do so. To act otherwise would be to forgo profit or even to risk business failure. But, at the same time, to use scarce resources in the least costly way is clearly in the social interest as well. It "frees up" resources to produce something else that society desires.

Self-interest, awakened and guided by the competitive market system, is what induces responses appropriate to the changes in society's wants. Businesses seeking to make higher profits and to avoid losses, and resource suppliers pursuing greater monetary rewards, negotiate changes in the allocation of resources and end up with the output that society wants. Competition controls or guides self-interest such that self-interest automatically and quite unintentionally furthers the best interest of society. The invisible hand ensures that when firms maximize their profits and resource suppliers maximize their incomes, these groups also help maximize society's output and income.

"invisible hand" The tendency of firms and resource suppliers that are seeking to further their own self-interest in competitive markets to also promote the interest of society as a whole.

Question:
Are "doing good for others" and "doing well for oneself" conflicting ideas, according to Adam Smith?

The Demise of the Command Systems

Now that you know how the market system answers the four fundamental questions, you can easily understand why command systems of the Soviet Union, eastern Europe, and prereform China failed. Those systems encountered two insurmountable problems.

The first difficulty was the *coordination problem*. The central planners had to coordinate the millions of individual decisions by consumers, resource suppliers, and businesses. Consider the setting up of a factory to produce tractors. The central planners had to establish a realistic annual production target, for example, 1000 tractors. They then had to make available all the necessary inputs—labor, machinery, electric power, steel, tires, glass, paint, transportation—for the production and delivery of those 1000 tractors.

Because the outputs of many industries serve as inputs to other industries, the failure of any single industry to achieve its output target caused a chain reaction of repercussions. For example, if iron mines, for want of machinery or labor or transportation, did not supply the steel industry with the required inputs of iron ore, the steel mills were unable to fulfill the input needs of the many industries that depended on steel. Those steel-using industries (such as tractor, automobile, and transportation) were unable to fulfill their planned production goals. Eventually the chain reaction spread to all firms that used steel as an input and from there to other input buyers or final consumers.

The coordination problem became more difficult as the economies expanded. Products and production processes grew more sophisticated, and the number of industries requiring planning increased. Planning techniques that worked for the simpler economy proved highly inadequate and inefficient for the larger economy. Bottlenecks and production stoppages became the norm, not the exception.

A lack of a reliable success indicator added to the coordination problem in the Soviet Union and prereform China. We have seen that market economies rely on profit as a success indicator. Profit depends on consumer demand, production efficiency, and product quality. In contrast, the major success indicator for the command economies usually was a quantitative production target that the central planners assigned. Production costs, product quality, and product mix were secondary considerations. Managers and workers often sacrificed product quality because they were being awarded bonuses for meeting quantitative, not qualitative, targets. If meeting production goals meant sloppy assembly work, so be it.

It was difficult at best for planners to assign quantitative production targets without unintentionally producing distortions in output. If the production target for an enterprise manufacturing nails was specified in terms of *weight* (tons of nails), the producer made only large nails. But if its target was specified as a *quantity* (thousands of nails), the producer made all small nails, and lots of them!

The command economies also faced an *incentive problem*. Central planners determined the output mix. When they misjudged how many automobiles, shoes, shirts, and chickens were wanted at the government-determined prices, persistent shortages and surpluses of those products arose. But as long as the managers who oversaw the production of those goods were rewarded for meeting their assigned production goals, they had no incentive to adjust production in response to the shortages and surpluses. And there were no fluctuations in prices and profitability to signal that more or less of certain products was desired. Thus, many products were unavailable or in short supply, while other products were overproduced and sat for months or years in warehouses.

The command systems of the Soviet Union and prereform China also lacked entrepreneurship. Central planning did not trigger the profit motive, nor did it reward innovation and enterprise. The route for getting ahead was through participation in the political hierarchy of the Communist Party. Moving up the hierarchy meant better housing, better access to health care, and the right to shop in special stores. Meeting production targets and maneuvering through the minefields of party politics were measures of success in "business." But a definition of business success based solely on political savvy is not conducive to technological advance, which is often disruptive to existing products, production methods, and organizational structures.

Question:
In market economies, firms rarely worry about the availability of inputs to produce their products, whereas in command economies input availability was a constant concern. Why the difference?

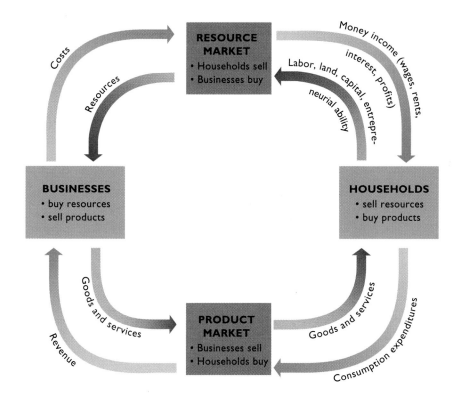

FIGURE 2.2 **The circular flow diagram.** Products flow from businesses to households through the product market, and resources flow from households to businesses through the resource market. Opposite those real flows are monetary flows. Households receive income from businesses (their costs) through the resource market, and businesses receive revenue from households (their expenditures) through the product market.

The Circular Flow Model

The dynamic market economy creates continuous, repetitive flows of goods and services, resources, and money. The **circular flow diagram,** shown in Figure 2.2, illustrates those flows. Observe that in the diagram we group private decision makers into *businesses* and *households* and group markets into the *resource market* and the *product market*.

Resource Market

The upper part of the circular flow diagram represents the **resource market:** the place where resources or the services of resource suppliers are bought and sold. In the resource market, households sell resources and businesses buy them. Households (that is, people) own all economic resources either directly as workers or entrepreneurs or indirectly through their ownership of business corporations. They sell their resources to businesses, which buy them because they are necessary for producing goods and services. The funds that businesses pay for resources are costs to businesses but are flows of wage, rent, interest, and profit income to the households. Productive resources therefore flow from households to businesses, and money flows from businesses to households.

circular flow diagram
The flow of resources from households to firms and of products from firms to households.

resource market
A market in which households sell and firms buy economic resources.

Product Market

Next consider the lower part of the diagram, which represents the **product market:** the place where goods and services produced by businesses are bought and sold. In the product market, businesses combine resources to produce and sell goods and services. Households use the (limited) income they have received from the sale of resources to buy goods and services. The monetary flow of consumer spending on goods and services yields sales revenues for businesses. Businesses compare those revenues to their costs in determining profitability and whether or not a particular good or service should continue to be produced.

product market
A market in which goods and services (products) are sold by firms and bought by households.

© T. O'Keefe/PhotoLink/Getty Images

© Royalty Free/CORBIS

Photo Op Resource Markets and Product Markets

The sale of a grove of orange trees would be a transaction in the resource market; the sale of oranges to final consumers would be a transaction in the product market.

The circular flow model depicts a complex, interrelated web of decision making and economic activity involving businesses and households. For the economy, it is the circle of life. Businesses and households are both buyers and sellers. Businesses buy resources and sell products. Households buy products and sell resources. As shown in Figure 2.2, there is a counterclockwise *real flow* of economic resources and finished goods and services and a clockwise *money flow* of income and consumption expenditures.

APPLYING THE ANALYSIS

Some Facts about U.S. Businesses

Businesses constitute one part of the private sector. The business population is extremely diverse, ranging from giant corporations such as ExxonMobil, with 2007 sales of $347 billion and thousands of employees, to neighborhood specialty shops with one or two employees and sales of only $200 to $300 per day. There are three major legal forms of businesses: sole proprietorships, partnerships, and corporations.

A *sole proprietorship* is a business owned and operated by one person. Usually, the proprietor (the owner) personally supervises its operation. In a *partnership*, two or more individuals (the partners) agree to own and operate a business together.

A *corporation* is a legal creation that can acquire resources, own assets, produce and sell products, incur debts, extend credit, sue and be sued, and perform the functions of any other type of enterprise. A corporation sells stocks (ownership shares) to raise funds but is legally distinct and separate from the individual stockholders.

FIGURE 2.3 **The business population and shares of total revenue.** (a) Sole proprietorships dominate the business population numerically, but (b) corporations dominate total sales revenue (total output). *Source:* U.S. Census Bureau, **www.census.gov.**

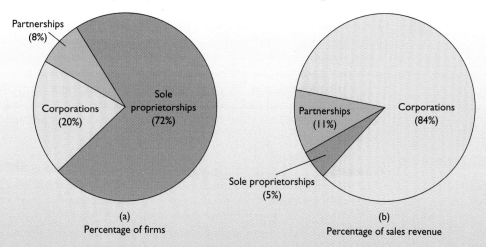

(a)
Percentage of firms

(b)
Percentage of sales revenue

The stockholders' legal and financial liability is limited to the loss of the value of their shares. Hired executives and managers operate corporations on a day-to-day basis.

Figure 2.3a shows how the business population is distributed among the three major legal forms. About 72% of firms are sole proprietorships, whereas only 20% are corporations. But as in Figure 2.3b indicates, corporations account for 84% of total sales revenue (and therefore total output) in the United States. Virtually all the nation's largest business enterprises are corporations. Global Snapshot 2.3 lists the world's largest corporations.

Question:
Why do you think sole proprietorships and partnerships typically incorporate (become corporations) when they experience rapid and sizable increases in their production, sales, and profits?

GLOBAL SNAPSHOT 2.3

The World's 10 Largest Corporations

Five of the world's ten largest corporations, based on dollar revenue in 2007, were headquartered in the United States.

Wal-Mart (USA) $351 billion

ExxonMobil (USA) $347 billion

Shell (Britain/Netherlands) $319 billion

BP (Britain) $274 billion

General Motors (USA) $207 billion

Toyota (Japan) $205 billion

Chevron (USA) $201 billion

DaimlerChrysler (Germany) $190 billion

ConocoPhillips (USA) $172 billion

Total (France) $168 billion

Source: Fortune Global 500, 2007, **www.fortune.com.**

Some Facts about U.S. Households

Households constitute the second part of the private sector. The U.S. economy currently has about 114 million households. These households consist of one or more persons occupying a housing unit and are both the ultimate suppliers of all economic resources *and* the major spenders in the economy.

The nation's earned income is apportioned among wages, rents, interest, and profits. *Wages* are paid to labor; *rents* and *interest* are paid to owners of property resources; and *profits* are paid to the owners of corporations and unincorporated businesses.

Figure 2.4a shows the categories of U.S. income earned in 2007. The largest source of income for households is the wages and salaries paid to workers. Notice that the bulk of total U.S. income goes to labor, not to capital. Proprietors' income—the income of doctors, lawyers, small-business owners, farmers, and owners of other unincorporated enterprises—also has a "wage" element. Some of this income is payment for one's own labor, and some of it is profit from one's own business.

FIGURE 2.4 **Sources of U.S. income and the composition of spending.** (a) Seventy-one percent of U.S. income is received as wages and salaries. Income to property owners—corporate profit, interest, and rents—accounts for about 20% of total income. (b) Consumers divide their spending among durable goods, nondurable goods, and services. Nearly 60% of consumer spending is for services; the rest is for goods.

Source: Bureau of Economic Analysis, **www.bea.gov.**

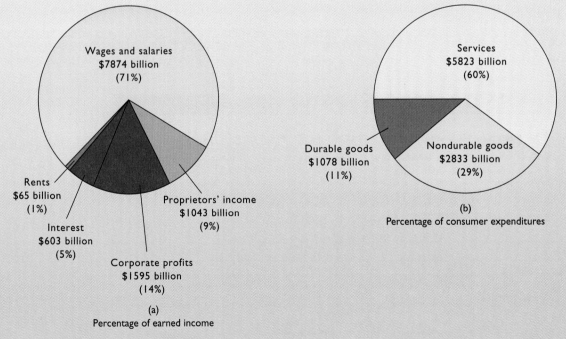

The other three types of income are self-evident: Some households own corporate stock and receive dividend incomes as their share of corporate profits. Many households also own bonds and savings accounts that yield interest income. And some households receive rental income by providing buildings and natural resources (including land) to businesses and other individuals.

U.S. households use their income to buy (spend), save, and pay taxes. Figure 2.4b shows how households divide their spending among three broad categories of goods and services: *consumer durables* (goods such as cars, refrigerators, and personal computers that have expected lives of 3 years or longer), *nondurables* (goods such as food, clothing, and gasoline that have lives of less than 3 years), and *services* (the work done by people such as lawyers, physicians, and recreational workers). Observe that nearly 60% of consumer spending is on services. For this reason, the United States is known as a *service-oriented economy*.

Question:
Over the past several decades, the service share of spending in the United States has increased relative to the goods share. Why do you think that trend has occurred?

Courtesy of Maytag Corporation.

© Ed Carey/Cole Group/Getty Images

© Royalty-Free/CORBIS

Photo Op Durable Goods, Nondurable Goods, and Services

Consumers collectively spend their income on durable goods (such as the washer-dryer combo), nondurable goods (such as the pizza), and services (such as hair care).

Summary

1. The market system and the command system are the two broad types of economic systems used to address the economic problem. In the market system (or capitalism), private individuals own most resources, and markets coordinate most economic activity. In the command system (or socialism or communism), government owns most resources, and central planners coordinate most economic activity.

2. The market system is characterized by the private ownership of resources, including capital, and the freedom of individuals to engage in economic activities of their choice to advance their material well-being. Self-interest is the driving force of such an economy, and competition functions as a regulatory or control mechanism.

3. In the market system, markets, prices, and profits organize and make effective the many millions of individual economic decisions that occur daily.

4. Specialization, use of advanced technology, and the extensive use of capital goods are common features of market systems. Functioning as a medium of exchange, money eliminates the problems of bartering and permits easy trade and greater specialization, both domestically and internationally.

5. Every economy faces four fundamental questions: (a) What goods and services will be produced? (b) How will the goods and services be produced? (c) Who will get the goods and services? (d) How will the system promote progress?

6. The market system produces products whose production and sale yield total revenue sufficient to cover total cost. It does not produce products for which total revenue continuously falls short of total cost. Competition forces firms to use the lowest-cost production techniques.

7. Economic profit (total revenue minus total cost) indicates that an industry is prosperous and promotes its expansion. Losses signify that an industry is not prosperous and hasten its contraction.

8. Consumer sovereignty means that both businesses and resource suppliers are subject to the wants of consumers. Through their dollar votes, consumers decide on the composition of output.

9. The prices that a household receives for the resources it supplies to the economy determine that household's income. This income determines the household's claim on the economy's output. Those who have income to spend get the products produced in the market system.

10. The market system encourages technological advance and capital accumulation, both of which raise a nation's standard of living.

11. Competition, the primary mechanism of control in the market economy, promotes a unity of self-interest and social interests. As directed by an invisible hand, competition harnesses the self-interested motives of businesses and resource suppliers to further the social interest.

12. The circular flow model illustrates the flows of resources and products from households to businesses and from businesses to households, along with the corresponding monetary flows. Businesses are on the buying side of the resource market and the selling side of the product market. Households are on the selling side of the resource market and the buying side of the product market.

Terms and Concepts

economic system	competition	consumer sovereignty
command system	market	dollar votes
market system	specialization	creative destruction
private property	division of labor	"invisible hand"
freedom of enterprise	medium of exchange	circular flow diagram
freedom of choice	barter	resource market
self-interest	money	product market

Study Questions ■ connect economics

1. Contrast how a market system and a command economy try to cope with economic scarcity. **LO1**

2. How does self-interest help achieve society's economic goals? Why is there such a wide variety of desired goods and services in a market system? In what way are entrepreneurs and businesses at the helm of the economy but commanded by consumers? **LO2**

3. Why is private property, and the protection of property rights, so critical to the success of the market system? **LO2**

4. What are the advantages of using capital in the production process? What is meant by the term "division of labor"? What are the advantages of specialization in the use of human and material resources? Explain why exchange is the necessary consequence of specialization. **LO2**

5. What problem does barter entail? Indicate the economic significance of money as a medium of exchange. What is meant by the statement "We want money only to part with it"? **LO2**

6. Evaluate and explain the following statements: **LO2**
   a. The market system is a profit-and-loss system.
   b. Competition is the disciplinarian of the market economy.

7. In the 1990s thousands of "dot-com" companies emerged with great fanfare to take advantage of the Internet and new information technologies. A few, like Yahoo, eBay, and Amazon, have generally thrived and prospered, but many others struggled and eventually failed. Explain these varied outcomes in terms of how the market system answers the question "What goods and services will be produced?" **LO3**

8. With current technology, suppose a firm is producing 400 loaves of banana bread daily. Also, assume that the least-cost combination of resources in producing those loaves is 5 units of labor, 7 units of land, 2 units of capital, and 1 unit of entrepreneurial ability, selling at prices of $40, $60, $60, and $20, respectively. If the firm can sell these 400 loaves at $2 per unit, will it continue to produce banana bread? If this firm's situation is typical for the other makers of banana bread, will resources flow to or away from this bakery good? **LO3**

9. Some large hardware stores such as Home Depot boast of carrying as many as 20,000 different products in each store.

What motivated the producers of those individual products to make them and offer them for sale? How did the producers decide on the best combinations of resources to use? Who made those resources available, and why? Who decides whether these particular hardware products should continue to be produced and offered for sale? **LO3**

10. What is meant by the term "creative destruction"? How does the emergence of iPod technology relate to this idea? **LO3**

11. In a sentence, describe the meaning of the phrase "invisible hand." **LO4**

12. Distinguish between the resource market and the product market in the circular flow model. In what way are businesses and households both sellers and buyers in this model? What are the flows in the circular flow model? **LO5**

13. What are the major forms of household income? Contrast the wage and salary share to the profit share in terms of relative size. Distinguish between a durable consumer good and a nondurable consumer good. How does the combined spending on both types of consumer goods compare to the spending on services? **LO5**

14. What are the three major legal forms of business enterprises? Which form is the most prevalent in terms of numbers? Which form is dominant in terms of total sales revenues? **LO5**

FURTHER TEST YOUR KNOWLEDGE AT
www.mcconnellbriefmacro1e.com

Web-Based Questions

At the text's Online Learning Center, **www.mcconnellbriefmacro 1e.com,** you will find a multiple-choice quiz on this chapter's content. We encourage you to take the quiz to see how you do.

Also, you will find one or more Web-based questions that require information from the Internet to answer.

IN THIS CHAPTER YOU WILL LEARN:

1 What demand is and what affects it.

2 What supply is and what affects it.

3 How supply and demand together determine market equilibrium.

4 How changes in supply and demand affect equilibrium prices and quantities.

5 What government-set prices are and how they can cause product surpluses and shortages.

3

Demand, Supply, and Market Equilibrium

According to an old joke, if you teach a parrot to say "demand and supply," you have an economist. There is an element of truth to this quip. The tools of demand and supply can take us far in understanding individual markets.

Markets bring together buyers ("demanders") and sellers ("suppliers") and exist in many forms. The corner gas station, an e-commerce site, the local music store, a farmer's roadside stand—all are familiar markets. The New York Stock Exchange and the Chicago Board of Trade are markets where buyers and sellers of stocks and bonds and farm commodities from all over the world communicate with one another to buy and sell. Auctioneers bring together potential buyers and sellers of art, livestock, used farm equipment, and, sometimes, real estate.

ORIGIN OF THE IDEA

O 3.1

Demand and supply

Some markets are local, while others are national or international. Some are highly personal, involving face-to-face contact between demander and supplier; others are faceless, with buyer and seller never seeing or knowing each other. But all competitive markets involve demand and supply.

Demand

demand
A schedule or curve that shows the various amounts of a product that consumers will buy at each of a series of possible prices during a specific period.

Demand is a schedule or a curve that shows the various amounts of a product that consumers will purchase at each of several possible prices during a specified period of time.[1] The table in Figure 3.1 is a hypothetical demand schedule for a *single consumer* purchasing a particular product, in this case, lattes. (For simplicity, we will categorize all espresso drinks as "lattes" and assume a highly competitive market.)

The table reveals that, if the price of lattes were $5 each, Joe Java would buy 10 lattes per month; if it were $4, he would buy 20 lattes per month; and so forth.

The table does not tell us which of the five possible prices will actually exist in the market. That depends on the interaction between demand and supply. Demand is simply a statement of a buyer's plans, or intentions, with respect to the purchase of a product.

To be meaningful, the quantities demanded at each price must relate to a specific period—a day, a week, a month. Here that period is 1 month.

Law of Demand

ORIGIN OF THE IDEA

O 3.2

Law of demand

A fundamental characteristic of demand is this: Other things equal, as price falls, the quantity demanded rises, and as price rises, the quantity demanded falls. In short, there

---

[1] This definition obviously is worded to apply to product markets. To adjust it to apply to resource markets, substitute the word "resource" for "product" and the word "businesses" for "consumers."

FIGURE 3.1 Joe Java's demand for lattes. Because price and quantity demanded are inversely related, an individual's demand schedule graphs as a downsloping curve such as *D*. Other things equal, consumers will buy more of a product as its price declines and less of the product as its price rises. (Here and in later figures, *P* stands for price and *Q* stands for quantity demanded or supplied.)

Joe Java's Demand for Lattes	
Price per Latte	Quantity Demanded per Month
$5	10
4	20
3	35
2	55
1	80

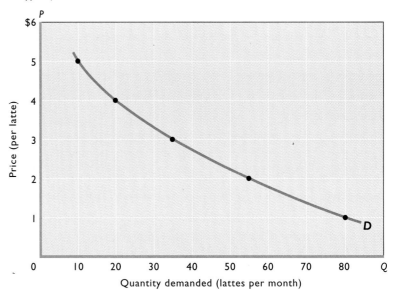

is an *inverse* relationship between price and quantity demanded. Economists call this inverse relationship the **law of demand.**

The other-things-equal assumption is critical here. Many factors other than the price of the product being considered affect the amount purchased. The quantity of lattes purchased will depend not only on the price of lattes but also on the prices of such substitutes as tea, soda, fruit juice, and bottled water. The law of demand in this case says that fewer lattes will be purchased if the price of lattes rises while the prices of tea, soda, fruit juice, and bottled water all remain constant.

The law of demand is consistent with both common sense and observation. People ordinarily *do* buy more of a product at a low price than at a high price. Price is an obstacle that deters consumers from buying. The higher that obstacle, the less of a product they will buy; the lower the obstacle, the more they will buy. The fact that businesses reduce prices to clear unsold goods is evidence of their belief in the law of demand.

The Demand Curve

The inverse relationship between price and quantity demanded for any product can be represented on a simple graph, in which, by convention, we measure *quantity demanded* on the horizontal axis and *price* on the vertical axis. In Figure 3.1 we have plotted the five price-quantity data points listed in the table and connected the points with a smooth curve, labeled *D*. This is a **demand curve.** Its downward slope reflects the law of demand: People buy more of a product, service, or resource as its price falls. They buy less as its price rises. There is an inverse relationship between price and quantity demanded.

The table and graph in Figure 3.1 contain exactly the same data and reflect the same inverse relationship between price and quantity demanded.

Market Demand

So far, we have concentrated on just one consumer, Joe Java. But competition requires that more than one buyer be present in each market. By adding the quantities demanded by all consumers at each of the various possible prices, we can get from *individual* demand to *market* demand. If there are just three buyers in the market (Joe Java, Sarah Coffee, and Mike Cappuccino), as represented by the table and graph in Figure 3.2, it is relatively easy to determine the total quantity demanded at each price. We simply sum the individual quantities demanded to obtain the total quantity demanded at each price. The particular price and the total quantity demanded are then plotted as one point on the market demand curve in Figure 3.2.

Competition, of course, ordinarily entails many more than three buyers of a product. To avoid hundreds or thousands of additions, let's simply suppose that the table and curve D_1 in Figure 3.3 show the amounts all the buyers in this market will purchase at each of the five prices.

In constructing a demand curve such as D_1 in Figure 3.3, economists assume that price is the most important influence on the amount of any product purchased. But economists know that other factors can and do affect purchases. These factors, called **determinants of demand,** are held constant when a demand curve like D_1 is drawn. They are the "other things equal" in the relationship between price and quantity demanded. When any of these determinants changes, the demand curve will shift to the right or left. For this reason, determinants of demand are sometimes referred to as *demand shifters.*

The basic determinants of demand are (1) consumers' tastes (preferences), (2) the number of consumers in the market, (3) consumers' incomes, (4) the prices of related goods, and (5) expected prices.

law of demand
The principle that, other things equal, as price falls, the quantity demanded rises, and as price rises, the quantity demanded falls.

demand curve
A curve illustrating the inverse relationship between the price of a product and the quantity of it demanded, other things equal.

determinants of demand
Factors other than price that locate the position of a demand curve.

FIGURE 3.2 **Market demand for lattes, three buyers.** We establish the market demand curve *D* by adding horizontally the individual demand curves (D_1, D_2, and D_3) of all the consumers in the market. At the price of $3, for example, the three individual curves yield a total quantity demanded of 100 lattes.

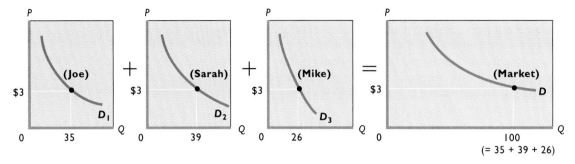

	Market Demand for Lattes, Three Buyers						
Price per Latte	Joe Java		Sarah Coffee		Mike Cappuccino		Total Quantity Demanded per Month
$5	10	+	12	+	8	=	30
4	20	+	23	+	17	=	60
3	35	+	39	+	26	=	100
2	55	+	60	+	39	=	154
1	80	+	87	+	54	=	221

FIGURE 3.3 **Changes in the demand for lattes.** A change in one or more of the determinants of demand causes a change in demand. An increase in demand is shown as a shift of the demand curve to the right, as from D_1 to D_2. A decrease in demand is shown as a shift of the demand curve to the left, as from D_1 to D_3. These changes in demand are to be distinguished from a change in *quantity demanded*, which is caused by a change in the price of the product, as shown by a movement from, say, point *a* to point *b* on fixed demand curve D_1.

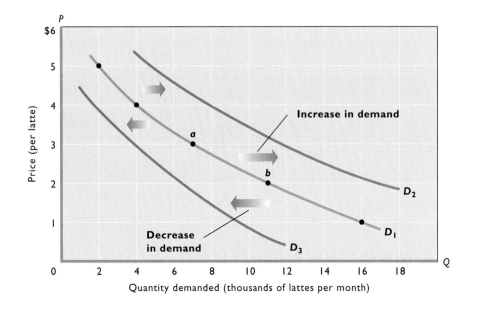

Market Demand for Lattes (D_1)	
(1)	(2)
Price per Latte	Total Quantity Demanded per Month
$5	2,000
4	4,000
3	7,000
2	11,000
1	16,000

Changes in Demand

A change in one or more of the determinants of demand will change the underlying demand data (the demand schedule in the table) and therefore the location of the demand curve in Figure 3.3. A change in the demand schedule or, graphically, a shift in the demand curve is called a *change in demand.*

If consumers desire to buy more lattes at each possible price, that *increase in demand* is shown as a shift of the demand curve to the right, say, from D_1 to D_2. Conversely, a *decrease in demand* occurs when consumers buy fewer lattes at each possible price. The leftward shift of the demand curve from D_1 to D_3 in Figure 3.3 shows that situation.

Now let's see how changes in each determinant affect demand.

Tastes   A favorable change in consumer tastes (preferences) for a product means more of it will be demanded at each price. Demand will increase; the demand curve will shift rightward. For example, greater concern about the environment has increased the demand for hybrid cars and other "green" technologies. An unfavorable change in consumer preferences will decrease demand, shifting the demand curve to the left. For example, the recent popularity of low-carbohydrate diets has reduced the demand for bread and pasta.

Number of Buyers   An increase in the number of buyers in a market increases product demand. For example, the rising number of older persons in the United States in recent years has increased the demand for motor homes and retirement communities. In contrast, the migration of people away from many small rural communities has reduced the demand for housing, home appliances, and auto repair in those towns.

Income   The effect of changes in income on demand is more complex. For most products, a rise in income increases demand. Consumers collectively buy more airplane tickets, projection TVs, and gas grills as their incomes rise. Products whose demand increases or decreases *directly* with changes in income are called *superior goods,* or **normal goods.**

Although most products are normal goods, there are a few exceptions. As incomes increase beyond some point, the demand for used clothing, retread tires, and soy-enhanced hamburger may decline. Higher incomes enable consumers to buy new clothing, new tires, and higher-quality meats. Goods whose demand increases or decreases *inversely* with money income are called **inferior goods.** (This is an economic term; we are not making personal judgments on specific products.)

Prices of Related Goods   A change in the price of a related good may either increase or decrease the demand for a product, depending on whether the related good is a substitute or a complement:

- A **substitute good** is one that can be used in place of another good.
- A **complementary good** is one that is used together with another good.

Beef and chicken are substitute goods or, simply, *substitutes.* When two products are substitutes, an increase in the price of one will increase the demand for the other. For example, when the price of beef rises, consumers will buy less beef and increase their demand for chicken. So it is with other product pairs such as Nikes and Reeboks, Budweiser and Miller beer, or Colgate and Crest toothpaste. They are *substitutes in consumption.*

normal good
A good (or service) whose consumption rises when income increases and falls when income decreases.

inferior good
A good (or service) whose consumption declines when income rises and rises when income decreases.

substitute good
A good (or service) that can be used in place of some other good (or service).

complementary good
A good (or service) that is used in conjunction with some other good (or service).

© Bambu Producoes/Getty Images   © Doug Menuez/Getty Images

Photo Op Normal versus Inferior Goods

New television sets are normal goods. People buy more of them as their incomes rise. Hand-pushed lawn mowers are inferior goods. As incomes rise, people purchase gas-powered mowers instead.

Complementary goods (or, simply, *complements*) are products that are used together and thus are typically demanded jointly. Examples include computers and software, cell phones and cellular service, and snowboards and lift tickets. If the price of a complement (for example, lettuce) goes up, the demand for the related good (salad dressing) will decline. Conversely, if the price of a complement (for example, tuition) falls, the demand for a related good (textbooks) will increase.

The vast majority of goods that are unrelated to one another are called *independent goods*. There is virtually no demand relationship between bacon and golf balls or pickles and ice cream. A change in the price of one will have virtually no effect on the demand for the other.

Expected Prices Changes in expected prices may shift demand. A newly formed expectation of a higher price in the future may cause consumers to buy now in order to "beat" the anticipated price rise, thus increasing current demand. For example, when freezing weather destroys much of Brazil's coffee crop, buyers may conclude that the price of coffee beans will rise. They may purchase large quantities now to stock up on beans. In contrast, a newly formed expectation of falling prices may decrease current demand for products.

© Michael Newman/PhotoEdit

© John A. Rizzo/Getty Images

Photo Op Substitutes versus Complements

Different brands of soft drinks are substitute goods; goods consumed jointly such as hot dogs and mustard are complementary goods.

Changes in Quantity Demanded

Be sure not to confuse a *change in demand* with a *change in quantity demanded*. A **change in demand** is a shift of the demand curve to the right (an increase in demand) or to the left (a decrease in demand). It occurs because the consumer's state of mind about purchasing the product has been altered in response to a change in one or more of the determinants of demand. Recall that "demand" is a schedule or a curve; therefore, a "change in demand" means a change in the schedule and a shift of the curve.

In contrast, a **change in quantity demanded** is a movement from one point to another point—from one price-quantity combination to another—on a fixed demand schedule or demand curve. The cause of such a change is an increase or decrease in the price of the product under consideration. In the table in Figure 3.3, for example, a decline in the price of lattes from $5 to $4 will increase the quantity of lattes demanded from 2000 to 4000.

In the graph in Figure 3.3, the shift of the demand curve D_1 to either D_2 or D_3 is a change in demand. But the movement from point *a* to point *b* on curve D_1 represents a change in quantity demanded: Demand has not changed; it is the entire curve, and it remains fixed in place.

Supply

Supply is a schedule or curve showing the amounts of a product that producers will make available for sale at each of a series of possible prices during a specific period.[2] The table in Figure 3.4 is a hypothetical supply schedule for Star Buck, a single supplier of lattes. Curve *S* incorporates the data in the table and is called a *supply curve*. The

change in demand
A change in the quantity demanded of a product at every price; a shift of the demand curve to the left or right.

change in quantity demanded
A movement from one point to another on a fixed demand curve.

supply
A schedule or curve that shows the amounts of a product that producers are willing to make available for sale at each of a series of possible prices during a specific period.

---

[2]This definition is worded to apply to product markets. To adjust it to apply to resource markets, substitute "resource" for "product" and "owners" for "producers."

FIGURE 3.4 **Star Buck's supply of lattes.** Because price and quantity supplied are directly related, the supply curve for an individual producer graphs as an upsloping curve. Other things equal, producers will offer more of a product for sale as its price rises and less of the product for sale as its price falls.

Star Buck's Supply of Lattes	
Price per Latte	Quantity Supplied per Month
$5	60
4	50
3	35
2	20
1	5

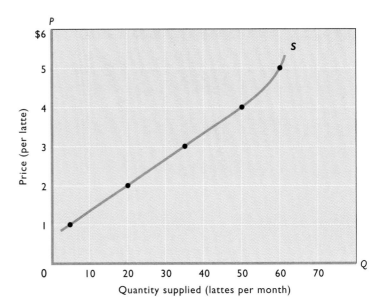

schedule and curve show the quantities of lattes that will be supplied at various prices, other things equal.

Law of Supply

Figure 3.4 shows a positive or direct relationship that prevails between price and quantity supplied. As price rises, the quantity supplied rises; as price falls, the quantity supplied falls. This relationship is called the **law of supply.** A supply schedule or curve reveals that, other things equal, firms will offer for sale more of their product at a high price than at a low price. This, again, is basically common sense.

Price is an obstacle from the standpoint of the consumer (for example, Joe Java), who is on the paying end. The higher the price, the less the consumer will buy. But the supplier (for example, Star Buck) is on the receiving end of the product's price. To a supplier, price represents *revenue*, which is needed to cover costs and earn a profit. Higher prices therefore create a profit incentive to produce and sell more of a product. The higher the price, the greater this incentive and the greater the quantity supplied.

Market Supply

Market supply is derived from individual supply in exactly the same way that market demand is derived from individual demand (Figure 3.2). We sum (not shown) the quantities supplied by each producer at each price. That is, we obtain the market **supply curve** by "horizontally adding" (also not shown) the supply curves of the individual producers. The price and quantity-supplied data in the table in Figure 3.5 are for an assumed 200 indentical producers in the market, each willing to supply lattes according to the supply schedule shown in Figure 3.4. Curve S_1 is a graph of the market supply data. Note that the axes in Figure 3.5 are the same as those used in our graph of market demand (Figure 3.3). The only difference is

law of supply
The principle that, other things equal, as price rises, the quantity supplied rises, and as price falls, the quantity supplied falls.

supply curve
A curve illustrating the direct relationship between the price of a product and the quantity of it supplied, other things equal.

that we change the label on the horizontal axis from "quantity demanded" to "quantity supplied."

Determinants of Supply

In constructing a supply curve, we assume that price is the most significant influence on the quantity supplied of any product. But other factors (the "other things equal") can and do affect supply. The supply curve is drawn on the assumption that these other things are fixed and do not change. If one of them does change, a *change in supply* will occur, meaning that the entire supply curve will shift.

The basic **determinants of supply** are (1) resource prices, (2) technology, (3) taxes and subsidies, (4) prices of other goods, (5) expected price, and (6) the number of sellers in the market. A change in any one or more of these determinants of supply, or *supply shifters*, will move the supply curve for a product either right or left. A shift to the *right*, as from S_1 to S_2 in Figure 3.5, signifies an *increase* in supply: Producers supply larger quantities of the product at each possible price. A shift to the *left*, as from S_1 to S_3, indicates a *decrease* in supply: Producers offer less output at each price.

> **determinants of supply**
> Factors other than price that locate the position of the supply curve.

Changes in Supply

Let's consider how changes in each of the determinants affect supply. The key idea is that costs are a major factor underlying supply curves; anything that affects costs (other than changes in output itself) usually shifts the supply curve.

Resource Prices The prices of the resources used in the production process help determine the costs of production incurred by firms. Higher *resource* prices raise production costs and, assuming a particular *product* price, squeeze profits. That

FIGURE 3.5 Changes in the supply of lattes. A change in one or more of the determinants of supply causes a change in supply. An increase in supply is shown as a rightward shift of the supply curve, as from S_1 to S_2. A decrease in supply is depicted as a leftward shift of the curve, as from S_1 to S_3. In contrast, a change in the *quantity supplied* is caused by a change in the product's price and is shown by a movement from one point to another, as from *a* to *b* on fixed supply curve S_1.

Market Supply of Lattes (S_1)	
(1) Price per Latte	(2) Total Quantity Supplied per Month
$5	12,000
4	10,000
3	7,000
2	4,000
1	1,000

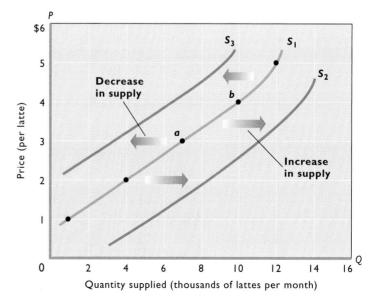

reduction in profits reduces the incentive for firms to supply output at each product price. For example, an increase in the prices of coffee beans and milk will increase the cost of making lattes and therefore reduce their supply.

In contrast, lower *resource* prices reduce production costs and increase profits. So when resource prices fall, firms supply greater output at each product price. For example, a decrease in the prices of sand, gravel, and limestone will increase the supply of concrete.

Technology Improvements in technology (techniques of production) enable firms to produce units of output with fewer resources. Because resources are costly, using fewer of them lowers production costs and increases supply. Example: Technological advances in producing flat-panel computer monitors have greatly reduced their cost. Thus, manufacturers will now offer more such monitors than previously at the various prices; the supply of flat-panel monitors has increased.

Taxes and Subsidies Businesses treat sales and property taxes as costs. Increases in those taxes will increase production costs and reduce supply. In contrast, subsidies are "taxes in reverse." If the government subsidizes the production of a good, it in effect lowers the producers' costs and increases supply.

Prices of Other Goods Firms that produce a particular product, say, soccer balls, can usually use their plant and equipment to produce alternative goods, say, basketballs and volleyballs. The higher prices of these "other goods" may entice soccer ball producers to switch production to those other goods in order to increase profits. This *substitution in production* results in a decline in the supply of soccer balls. Alternatively, when basketballs and volleyballs decline in price relative to the price of soccer balls, firms will produce fewer of those products and more soccer balls, increasing the supply of soccer balls.

Expected Prices Changes in expectations about the future price of a product may affect the producer's current willingness to supply that product. It is difficult, however, to generalize about how a new expectation of higher prices affects the present supply of a product. Farmers anticipating a higher wheat price in the future might withhold some of their current wheat harvest from the market, thereby causing a decrease in the current supply of wheat. In contrast, in many types of manufacturing industries, newly formed expectations that price will increase may induce firms to add another shift of workers or to expand their production facilities, causing current supply to increase.

Number of Sellers Other things equal, the larger the number of suppliers, the greater the market supply. As more firms enter an industry, the supply curve shifts to the right. Conversely, the smaller the number of firms in the industry, the less the market supply. This means that as firms leave an industry, the supply curve shifts to the left. Example: The United States and Canada have imposed restrictions on haddock fishing to replenish dwindling stocks. As part of that policy, the Federal government has bought the boats of some of the haddock fishers as a way of putting them out of business and decreasing the catch. The result has been a decline in the market supply of haddock.

Changes in Quantity Supplied

The distinction between a *change in supply* and a *change in quantity supplied* parallels the distinction between a change in demand and a change in quantity demanded. Because supply is a schedule or curve, a **change in supply** means a change in the schedule and a shift of the curve. An increase in supply shifts the curve to the right; a decrease in supply shifts it to the left. The cause of a change in supply is a change in one or more of the determinants of supply.

In contrast, a **change in quantity supplied** is a movement from one point to another on a fixed supply curve. The cause of such a movement is a change in the price of the specific product being considered. In Figure 3.5, a decline in the price of lattes from $4 to $3 decreases the quantity of lattes supplied per month from 10,000 to 7000. This movement from point *b* to point *a* along S_1 is a change in quantity supplied, not a change in supply. Supply is the full schedule of prices and quantities shown, and this schedule does not change when the price of lattes changes.

change in supply
A change in the quantity supplied of a product at every price; a shift of the supply curve to the left or right.

change in quantity supplied
A movement from one point to another on a fixed supply curve.

Market Equilibrium

With our understanding of demand and supply, we can now show how the decisions of Joe Java and other buyers of lattes interact with the decisions of Star Buck and other sellers to determine the price and quantity of lattes. In the table in Figure 3.6, columns 1 and 2 repeat the market supply of lattes (from Figure 3.5), and columns 2 and 3 repeat the market demand for lattes (from Figure 3.3). We assume this is a competitive market, so neither buyers nor sellers can set the price.

Equilibrium Price and Quantity

We are looking for the equilibrium price and equilibrium quantity. The **equilibrium price** (or *market-clearing price*) is the price at which the intentions of buyers and sellers match. It is the price at which quantity demanded equals quantity supplied. The table in Figure 3.6 reveals that at $3, *and only at that price*, the number of lattes that sellers wish to sell (7000) is identical to the number that consumers want to buy (also 7000). At $3 and 7000 lattes, there is neither a shortage nor a surplus of lattes. So 7000 lattes is the **equilibrium quantity:** the quantity demanded and quantity supplied that occur at the equilibrium price in a competitive market.

Graphically, the equilibrium price is indicated by the intersection of the supply curve and the demand curve in Figure 3.6. (The horizontal axis now measures both quantity demanded and quantity supplied.) With neither a shortage nor a surplus at $3, the market is in equilibrium, meaning "in balance" or "at rest."

To better understand the uniqueness of the equilibrium price, let's consider other prices. At any above-equilibrium price, quantity supplied exceeds quantity demanded. For example, at the $4 price, sellers will offer 10,000 lattes, but buyers will purchase only 4000. The $4 price encourages sellers to offer lots of lattes but discourages many consumers from buying them. The result is a **surplus** or *excess supply* of 6000 lattes. If latte sellers made them all, they would find themselves with 6000 unsold lattes.

Surpluses drive prices down. Even if the $4 price existed temporarily, it could not persist. The large surplus would prompt competing sellers to lower the price to encourage buyers to stop in and take the surplus off their hands. As the price fell, the incentive to produce lattes would decline and the incentive for consumers to buy lattes would increase. As shown in Figure 3.6, the market would move to its equilibrium at $3.

Any price below the $3 equilibrium price would create a shortage; quantity demanded would exceed quantity supplied. Consider a $2 price, for example. We see in column 4 of the table in Figure 3.6 that quantity demanded exceeds quantity

equilibrium price
The price in a competitive market at which the quantity demanded and quantity supplied of a product are equal.

equilibrium quantity
The quantity demanded and quantity supplied that occur at the equilibrium price in a competitive market.

surplus
The amount by which the quantity supplied of a product exceeds the quantity demanded at a specific (above-equilibrium) price.

FIGURE 3.6 Equilibrium price and quantity. The intersection of the downsloping demand curve *D* and the upsloping supply curve *S* indicates the equilibrium price and quantity, here $3 and 7000 lattes. The shortages of lattes at below-equilibrium prices (for example, 7000 at $2) drive up price. The higher prices increase the quantity supplied and reduce the quantity demanded until equilibrium is achieved. The surpluses caused by above-equilibrium prices (for example, 6000 lattes at $4) push price down. As price drops, the quantity demanded rises and the quantity supplied falls until equilibrium is established. At the equilibrium price and quantity, there are neither shortages nor surpluses of lattes.

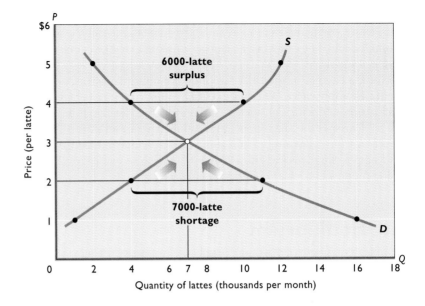

Market Supply of and Demand for Lattes			
(1) Total Quantity Supplied per Month	**(2)** Price per Latte	**(3)** Total Quantity Demanded per Month	**(4)** Surplus (+) or Shortage (−)*
12,000	$5	2,000	+10,000 ↓
10,000	4	4,000	+6,000 ↓
7,000	**3**	**7,000**	**0**
4,000	2	11,000	−7,000 ↑
1,000	1	16,000	−15,000 ↑

*Arrows indicate the effect on price.

shortage
The amount by which the quantity demanded of a product exceeds the quantity supplied at a specific (below-equilibrium) price.

supplied at that price. The result is a **shortage** or *excess demand* of 7000 lattes. The $2 price discourages sellers from devoting resources to lattes and encourages consumers to desire more lattes than are available. The $2 price cannot persist as the equilibrium price. Many consumers who want to buy lattes at this price will not obtain them. They will express a willingness to pay more than $2 to get them. Competition among these buyers will drive up the price, eventually to the $3 equilibrium level. Unless disrupted by supply or demand changes, this $3 price of lattes will continue.

Rationing Function of Prices
The ability of the competitive forces of supply and demand to establish a price at which selling and buying decisions are consistent is called the *rationing function of prices*. In our case, the equilibrium price of $3 clears the market, leaving no

burdensome surplus for sellers and no inconvenient shortage for potential buyers. And it is the combination of freely made individual decisions that sets this market-clearing price. In effect, the market outcome says that all buyers who are willing and able to pay $3 for a latte will obtain one; all buyers who cannot or will not pay $3 will go without one. Similarly, all producers who are willing and able to offer a latte for sale at $3 will sell it; all producers who cannot or will not sell for $3 will not sell their product.

> **INTERACTIVE GRAPHS**
>
> **G 3.1**
>
> Supply and demand

> **APPLYING THE ANALYSIS**

Ticket Scalping

Ticket prices for athletic events and musical concerts are usually set far in advance of the events. Sometimes the original ticket price is too low to be the equilibrium price. Lines form at the ticket window, and a severe shortage of tickets occurs at the printed price. What happens next? Buyers who are willing to pay more than the original price bid up the equilibrium price in resale ticket markets. The price rockets upward.

Tickets sometimes get resold for much greater amounts than the original price—market transactions known as "scalping." For example, an original buyer may resell a $75 ticket to a concert for $200, $250, or more. The media sometimes denounce scalpers for "ripping off" buyers by charging "exorbitant" prices.

But is scalping really a rip-off? We must first recognize that such ticket resales are voluntary transactions. If both buyer and seller did not expect to gain from the exchange, it would not occur! The seller must value the $200 more than seeing the event, and the buyer must value seeing the event at $200 or more. So there are no losers or victims here: Both buyer and seller benefit from the transaction. The "scalping" market simply redistributes assets (game or concert tickets) from those who would rather have the money (other things) to those who would rather have the tickets.

Does scalping impose losses or injury on the sponsors of the event? If the sponsors are injured, it is because they initially priced tickets below the equilibrium level. Perhaps they did this to create a long waiting line and the attendant media publicity. Alternatively, they may have had a genuine desire to keep tickets affordable for lower-income, ardent fans. In either case, the event sponsors suffer an opportunity cost in the form of less ticket revenue than they might have otherwise received. But such losses are self-inflicted and quite separate and distinct from the fact that some tickets are later resold at a higher price.

So is ticket scalping undesirable? Not on economic grounds! It is an entirely voluntary activity that benefits both sellers and buyers.

Question:
Why do you suppose some professional sports teams are setting up legal "ticket exchanges" (at buyer-and-seller-determined prices) at their Internet sites? (*Hint:* For the service, the teams charge a percentage of the transaction price of each resold ticket.)

Changes in Demand, Supply, and Equilibrium

We know that prices can and do change in markets. For example, demand might change because of fluctuations in consumer tastes or incomes, changes in expected price, or variations in the prices of related goods. Supply might change in response to changes in resource prices, technology, or taxes. How will such changes in demand and supply affect equilibrium price and quantity?

Changes in Demand

Suppose that the supply of some good (for example, health care) is constant and the demand for the good increases, as shown in Figure 3.7a. As a result, the new intersection of the supply and demand curves is at higher values on both the price and the quantity axes. Clearly, an increase in demand raises both equilibrium price and equilibrium quantity. Conversely, a decrease in demand, such as that shown in Figure 3.7b, reduces both equilibrium price and equilibrium quantity.

Changes in Supply

What happens if the demand for some good (for example, cell phones) is constant but the supply increases, as in Figure 3.7c? The new intersection of supply and demand is located at a lower equilibrium price but at a higher equilibrium quantity. An increase in supply reduces equilibrium price but increases equilibrium quantity. In contrast, if supply decreases, as in Figure 3.7d, the equilibrium price rises while the equilibrium quantity declines.

Complex Cases

When both supply and demand change, the effect is a combination of the individual effects.

Supply Increase; Demand Decrease
What effect will a supply increase for some good (for example, apples) and a demand decrease have on equilibrium price? Both changes decrease price, so the net result is a price drop greater than that resulting from either change alone.

What about equilibrium quantity? Here the effects of the changes in supply and demand are opposed: The increase in supply increases equilibrium quantity, but the decrease in demand reduces it. The direction of the change in quantity depends on the relative sizes of the changes in supply and demand. If the increase in supply is larger than the decrease in demand, the equilibrium quantity will increase. But if the decrease in demand is greater than the increase in supply, the equilibrium quantity will decrease.

Supply Decrease; Demand Increase
A decrease in supply and an increase in demand for some good (for example, gasoline) both increase price. Their combined effect is an increase in equilibrium price greater than that caused by either change separately. But their effect on equilibrium quantity is again indeterminate, depending on the relative sizes of the changes in supply and demand. If the decrease in supply is larger than the increase in demand, the equilibrium quantity will decrease. In contrast, if the increase in demand is greater than the decrease in supply, the equilibrium quantity will increase.

FIGURE 3.7 **Changes in demand and supply and the effects on price and quantity.** The increase in demand from D_1 to D_2 in (a) increases both equilibrium price and equilibrium quantity. The decrease in demand from D_3 to D_4 in (b) decreases both equilibrium price and equilibrium quantity. The increase in supply from S_1 to S_2 in (c) decreases equilibrium price and increases equilibrium quantity. The decrease in supply from S_3 to S_4 in (d) increases equilibrium price and decreases equilibrium quantity. The boxes in the top right summarize the respective changes and outcomes. The upward arrows in the boxes signify increases in equilibrium price (P) and equilibrium quantity (Q); the downward arrows signify decreases in these items.

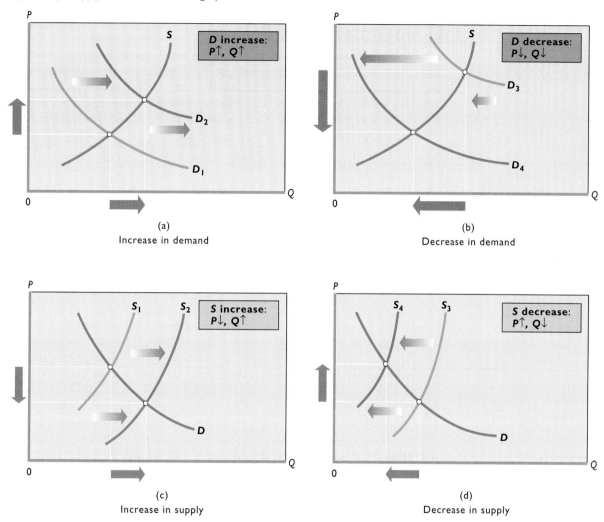

(a)
Increase in demand

(b)
Decrease in demand

(c)
Increase in supply

(d)
Decrease in supply

Supply Increase; Demand Increase

What if supply and demand both increase for some good (for example, sushi)? A supply increase drops equilibrium price, while a demand increase boosts it. If the increase in supply is greater than the increase in demand, the equilibrium price will fall. If the opposite holds, the equilibrium price will rise. If the two changes are equal and cancel out, price will not change.

The effect on equilibrium quantity is certain: The increases in supply and in demand each raise equilibrium quantity. Therefore, the equilibrium quantity will increase by an amount greater than that caused by either change alone.

Supply Decrease; Demand Decrease

What about decreases in both supply and demand for some good (for example, new homes)? If the decrease in supply is greater than the decrease in demand, equilibrium price will rise. If the reverse is true, equilibrium price will fall. If the two changes are of the same size and cancel out, price will not change. Because decreases in supply and in demand each reduce equilibrium quantity, we can be sure that equilibrium quantity will fall.

Government-Set Prices

In most markets, prices are free to rise or fall with changes in supply or demand, no matter how high or low those prices might be. However, government occasionally concludes that changes in supply and demand have created prices that are unfairly high to buyers or unfairly low to sellers. Government may then place legal limits on how high or low a price or prices may go. Our previous analysis of shortages and surpluses helps us evaluate the wisdom of government-set prices.

**APPLYING
THE
ANALYSIS**

Price Ceilings on Gasoline

price ceiling
A legally established maximum (below-equilibrium) price for a product.

A **price ceiling** sets the maximum legal price a seller may charge for a product or service. A price at or below the ceiling is legal; a price above it is not. The rationale for establishing price ceilings (or ceiling prices) on specific products is that they purportedly enable consumers to obtain some "essential" good or service that they could not afford at the equilibrium price.

Figure 3.8 shows the effects of price ceilings graphically. Let's look at a hypothetical situation. Suppose that rapidly rising world income boosts the purchase of automobiles and increases the demand for gasoline so that the equilibrium or market price reaches $3.50 per gallon. The rapidly rising price of gasoline greatly burdens low- and moderate-income households, which pressure government to "do something." To keep gasoline affordable for these households, the government imposes a ceiling price of $3 per gallon. To impact the market, a price ceiling must be below the equilibrium price. A ceiling price of $4, for example, would have had no immediate effect on the gasoline market.

What are the effects of this $3 ceiling price? The rationing ability of the free market is rendered ineffective. Because the $3 ceiling price is below the $3.50 market-clearing price, there is a lasting shortage of gasoline. The quantity of gasoline demanded at $3 is Q_d, and the quantity supplied is only Q_s; a persistent excess demand or shortage of amount $Q_d - Q_s$ occurs.

The $3 price ceiling prevents the usual market adjustment in which competition among buyers bids up price, inducing more production and rationing some buyers out of the market. That process would continue until the shortage disappeared at the equilibrium price and quantity, $3.50 and Q_0.

How will sellers apportion the available supply Q_s among buyers, who want the greater amount Q_d? Should they distribute gasoline on a first-come, first-served basis, that is, to those willing and able to get in line the soonest and stay in line? Or should gas stations distribute it on the basis of favoritism? Since an unregulated shortage does not lead to an equitable distribution of gasoline, the government must establish some formal system for rationing it to consumers. One option is to issue ration coupons, which authorize bearers to purchase a

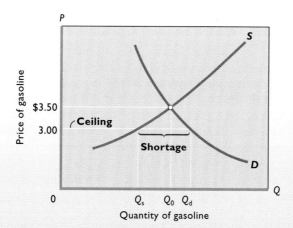

FIGURE 3.8 **A**
price ceiling. A price
ceiling is a maximum legal
price, such as $3, that is
below the equilibrium
price. It results in a
persistent product
shortage, here shown by
the distance between Q_d
and Q_s.

fixed amount of gasoline per month. The rationing system might entail first the printing of coupons for Q_s gallons of gasoline and then the equal distribution of the coupons among consumers so that the wealthy family of four and the poor family of four both receive the same number of coupons.

But ration coupons would not prevent a second problem from arising. The demand curve in Figure 3.8 reveals that many buyers are willing to pay more than the $3 ceiling price. And, of course, it is more profitable for gasoline stations to sell at prices above the ceiling. Thus, despite a sizable enforcement bureaucracy that would have to accompany the price controls, *black markets* in which gasoline is illegally bought and sold at prices above the legal limits will flourish. Counterfeiting of ration coupons will also be a problem. And since the price of gasoline is now "set by government," there might be political pressure on government to set the price even lower.

Question:
Why is it typically difficult to end price ceilings once they have been in place for a long time?

APPLYING
THE
ANALYSIS

Rent Controls

About 200 cities in the United States, including New York City, Boston, and San Francisco, have at one time or another enacted price ceilings in the form of rent controls—maximum rents established by law—or, more recently, have set maximum rent increases for existing tenants: Such laws are well intended. Their goals are to protect low-income families from escalating rents caused by demand increases that outstrip supply increases. Rent controls are designed to alleviate perceived housing shortages and make housing more affordable.

What have been the actual economic effects? On the demand side, it is true that as long as rents are below equilibrium, more families are willing to consume rental housing; the quantity of rental housing demanded increases at the lower price. But a large problem occurs on the supply side. Price controls make it less attractive for landlords to offer housing on the rental market. In the short run, owners may sell their rental units or convert them to condominiums. In the long run, low rents make it unprofitable for owners to repair or renovate their rental units. (Rent controls are one cause of the many abandoned apartment buildings found in some larger cities.) Also, insurance companies, pension funds, and other potential new investors in housing will find it more profitable to invest in office buildings, shopping malls, or motels, where rents are not controlled.

In brief, rent controls distort market signals, and thus resources are misallocated: Too few resources are allocated to rental housing, and too many to alternative uses. Ironically, although rent controls are often legislated to lessen the effects of perceived shortages, controls in fact are a primary cause of such shortages. For that reason, most American cities either have abandoned rent controls or are gradually phasing them out.

Question:
Why does maintenance tend to diminish in rent-controlled apartment buildings relative to maintenance in buildings where owners can charge market-determined rents?

APPLYING
THE
ANALYSIS

Price Floors on Wheat

price floor
A legally established minimum (above-equilibrium) price for a product.

A **price floor** is a minimum price fixed by the government. A price at or above the price floor is legal; a price below it is not. Price floors above equilibrium prices are usually invoked when society feels that the free functioning of the market system has not provided a sufficient income for certain groups of resource suppliers or producers. Supported prices for agricultural products and current minimum wages are two examples of price (or wage) floors. Let's look at the former.

Suppose the demand for wheat declines relative to supply, pushing down the equilibrium price of wheat to $2 per bushel. Because of that low price, many farmers have extremely low incomes. The government decides to help out by establishing a legal price floor (or "price support") of $3 per bushel.

What will be the effects? At any price above the equilibrium price, quantity supplied will exceed quantity demanded—that is, there will be a persistent surplus of the product. Farmers will be willing to produce and offer for sale more wheat than private buyers are willing to buy at the $3 price floor. As we saw with a price ceiling, an imposed legal price disrupts the rationing ability of the free market.

Figure 3.9 illustrates the effect of a price floor graphically. Suppose that S and D are the supply and demand curves for wheat. Equilibrium price and quantity are $2 and Q_0, respectively. If the government imposes a price floor of $3, farmers will produce Q_s but private buyers will purchase only Q_d. The surplus is the excess of Q_s over Q_d.

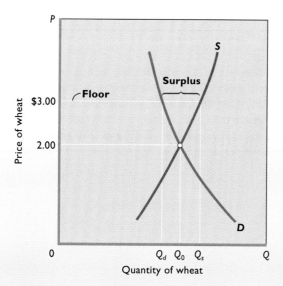

FIGURE 3.9 A
price floor. A price
floor is a minimum legal
price, such as $3, that
results in a persistent
product surplus, here
shown by the distance
between Q_s and Q_d.

The government may cope with the surplus resulting from a price floor in two ways:

- It can restrict supply (for example, by instituting acreage allotments by which farmers agree to take a certain amount of land out of production) or increase demand (for example, by researching new uses for the product involved). These actions may reduce the difference between the equilibrium price and the price floor and that way reduce the size of the resulting surplus.
- If these efforts are not wholly successful, then the government must purchase the surplus output at the $3 price (thereby subsidizing farmers) and store or otherwise dispose of it.

Price floors such as $3 in Figure 3.9 not only disrupt the rationing ability of prices but also distort resource allocation. Without the price floor, the $2 equilibrium price of wheat would cause financial losses and force high-cost wheat producers to plant other crops or abandon farming altogether. But the $3 price floor allows them to continue to grow wheat and remain farmers. So society devotes too many scarce resources to wheat production and too few to producing other, more valuable, goods and services. It fails to achieve an optimal allocation of resources.

That's not all. Consumers of wheat-based products pay higher prices because of the price floor. Taxpayers pay higher taxes to finance the government's purchase of the surplus. Also, the price floor causes potential environmental damage by encouraging wheat farmers to bring hilly, erosion-prone "marginal land" into production. The higher price also prompts imports of wheat. But, since such imports would increase the quantity of wheat supplied and thus undermine the price floor, the government needs to erect tariffs (taxes on imports) to keep the foreign wheat out. Such tariffs usually prompt other countries to retaliate with their own tariffs against U.S. agricultural or manufacturing exports.

Question:
To maintain price floors on milk, the U.S. government has at times bought out and destroyed entire dairy herds from dairy farmers. What's the economic logic of these actions?

INTERACTIVE GRAPHS

G 3.2

Price floors and ceilings

It is easy to see why economists "sound the alarm" when politicians advocate imposing price ceilings or price floors such as price controls, rent controls, interest-rate lids, or agricultural price supports. In all these cases, good intentions lead to bad economic outcomes. Government-controlled prices lead to shortages or surpluses, distort resource allocations, and cause negative side effects.

For additional examples of demand and supply, view the Chapter 3 Web appendix at www.mcconnellbriefmacro1e.com. There, you will find examples relating to such diverse products as lettuce, corn, salmon, gasoline, sushi, and Olympic tickets. Several of the examples depict simultaneous shifts in demand and supply curves—circumstances that often show up in exam questions!

Summary

1. Demand is a schedule or curve representing the willingness of buyers in a specific period to purchase a particular product at each of various prices. The law of demand implies that consumers will buy more of a product at a low price than at a high price. So, other things equal, the relationship between price and quantity demanded is inverse and is graphed as a downsloping curve.

2. Market demand curves are found by adding horizontally the demand curves of the many individual consumers in the market.

3. Changes in one or more of the determinants of demand (consumer tastes, the number of buyers in the market, the money incomes of consumers, the prices of related goods, and expected prices) shift the market demand curve. A shift to the right is an increase in demand; a shift to the left is a decrease in demand. A change in demand is different from a change in the quantity demanded, the latter being a movement from one point to another point on a fixed demand curve because of a change in the product's price.

4. Supply is a schedule or curve showing the amounts of a product that producers are willing to offer in the market at each possible price during a specific period. The law of supply states that, other things equal, producers will offer more of a product at a high price than at a low price. Thus, the relationship between price and quantity supplied is positive or direct, and supply is graphed as an upsloping curve.

5. The market supply curve is the horizontal summation of the supply curves of the individual producers of the product.

6. Changes in one or more of the determinants of supply (resource prices, production techniques, taxes or subsidies, the prices of other goods, expected prices, or the number of suppliers in the market) shift the supply curve of a product.

A shift to the right is an increase in supply; a shift to the left is a decrease in supply. In contrast, a change in the price of the product being considered causes a change in the quantity supplied, which is shown as a movement from one point to another point on a fixed supply curve.

7. The equilibrium price and quantity are established at the intersection of the supply and demand curves. The interaction of market demand and market supply adjusts the price to the point at which the quantities demanded and supplied are equal. This is the equilibrium price. The corresponding quantity is the equilibrium quantity.

8. A change in either demand or supply changes the equilibrium price and quantity. Increases in demand raise both equilibrium price and equilibrium quantity; decreases in demand lower both equilibrium price and equilibrium quantity. Increases in supply lower equilibrium price and raise equilibrium quantity; decreases in supply raise equilibrium price and lower equilibrium quantity.

9. Simultaneous changes in demand and supply affect equilibrium price and quantity in various ways, depending on their direction and relative magnitudes.

10. A price ceiling is a maximum price set by government and is designed to help consumers. Effective price ceilings produce persistent product shortages, and if an equitable distribution of the product is sought, government must ration the product to consumers.

11. A price floor is a minimum price set by government and is designed to aid producers. Price floors lead to persistent product surpluses; the government must either purchase the product or eliminate the surplus by imposing restrictions on production or increasing private demand.

12. Legally fixed prices stifle the rationing function of prices and distort the allocation of resources.

Terms and Concepts

demand

law of demand

demand curve

determinants of demand

normal good

inferior good

substitute good

complementary good

change in demand

change in quantity demanded

supply

law of supply

supply curve

determinants of supply

change in supply

change in quantity supplied

equilibrium price

equilibrium quantity

surplus

shortage

price ceiling

price floor

Study Questions connect economics

1. Explain the law of demand. Why does a demand curve slope downward? How is a market demand curve derived from individual demand curves? **LO1**

2. What are the determinants of demand? What happens to the demand curve when any of these determinants changes? Distinguish between a change in demand and a change in the quantity demanded, noting the cause(s) of each. **LO1**

3. What effect will each of the following have on the demand for small automobiles such as the Mini Cooper and Smart car? **LO1**

   a. Small automobiles become more fashionable.

   b. The price of large automobiles rises (with the price of small autos remaining the same).

   c. Income declines and small autos are an inferior good.

   d. Consumers anticipate that the price of small autos will greatly come down in the near future.

   e. The price of gasoline substantially drops.

4. Explain the law of supply. Why does the supply curve slope upward? How is the market supply curve derived from the supply curves of individual producers? **LO2**

5. What are the determinants of supply? What happens to the supply curve when any of these determinants changes? Distinguish between a change in supply and a change in the quantity supplied, noting the cause(s) of each. **LO2**

6. What effect will each of the following have on the supply of auto tires? **LO2**

   a. A technological advance in the methods of producing tires.

   b. A decline in the number of firms in the tire industry.

   c. An increase in the price of rubber used in the production of tires.

   d. The expectation that the equilibrium price of auto tires will be lower in the future than currently.

   e. A decline in the price of the large tires used for semitrucks and earth-hauling rigs (with no change in the price of auto tires).

   f. The levying of a per-unit tax on each auto tire sold.

   g. The granting of a 50-cent-per-unit subsidy for each auto tire produced.

7. "In the latte market, demand often exceeds supply and supply sometimes exceeds demand." "The price of a latte rises and falls in response to changes in supply and demand." In which of these two statements are the concepts of supply and demand used correctly? Explain. **LO4**

8. Suppose the total demand for wheat and the total supply of wheat per month in the Kansas City grain market are as shown below: **LO3**

Thousands of Bushels Demanded	Price per Bushel	Thousands of Bushels Supplied	Surplus (+) or Shortage (−)
85	$3.40	72	_____
80	3.70	73	_____
75	4.00	75	_____
70	4.30	77	_____
65	4.60	79	_____
60	4.90	81	_____

   a. What is the equilibrium price? What is the equilibrium quantity? Fill in the surplus-shortage column, and use it to explain why your answers are correct.

   b. Graph the demand for wheat and the supply of wheat. Be sure to label the axes of your graph correctly. Label equilibrium price P and equilibrium quantity Q.

   c. Why will $3.40 not be the equilibrium price in this market? Why not $4.90? "Surpluses drive prices up; shortages drive them down." Do you agree?

   d. Suppose government establishes a price ceiling of $3.70 for wheat. What might prompt it to establish this price ceiling? Explain carefully the main effects. Demonstrate your answer graphically.

e. Suppose government establishes a price floor of $4.60 for wheat. What will be the main effects of this price floor? Demonstrate your answer graphically.

9. How will each of the following changes in demand and/or supply affect equilibrium price and equilibrium quantity in a competitive market; that is, do price and quantity rise, fall, or remain unchanged, or are the answers indeterminate because they depend on the magnitudes of the shifts? Use supply and demand diagrams to verify your answers. **LO4**

   a. Supply decreases and demand is constant.

   b. Demand decreases and supply is constant.

   c. Supply increases and demand is constant.

   d. Demand increases and supply increases.

   e. Demand increases and supply is constant.

   f. Supply increases and demand decreases.

   g. Demand increases and supply decreases.

   h. Demand decreases and supply decreases.

10. For each stock in the stock market, the number of shares sold daily equals the number of shares purchased. That is, the quantity of each firm's shares demanded equals the quantity of its shares supplied. So, if this equality always occurs, why do the prices of stock shares ever change? **LO4**

11. Critically evaluate: "In comparing the two equilibrium positions in Figure 3.7a, I see that a larger amount is actually purchased at a higher price. This refutes the law of demand." **LO4**

FURTHER TEST YOUR KNOWLEDGE AT
www.mcconnellbriefmacro1e.com

Web-Based Questions

At the text's Online Learning Center, **www.mcconnellbriefmacro 1e.com,** you will find a multiple-choice quiz on this chapter's content. We encourage you to take the quiz to see how you do.

Also, you will find one or more Web-based questions that require information from the Internet to answer.

4

Public Goods and Externalities

Competitive markets usually do a remarkable job of allocating society's scarce resources to their highest-valued uses. But markets have certain limitations. In some circumstances, economically desirable goods are not produced at all. In other situations, they are either overproduced or underproduced. This chapter examines **market failure,** which occurs when the competitive market system (1) does not allocate any resources whatsoever to the production of certain goods or (2) either underallocates or overallocates resources to the production of certain goods.

Where private markets fail, an economic role for government may arise. In this chapter, we will examine that role as it relates to public goods and so-called externalities. Then we want to see how the government uses taxation to reallocate resources away from the private sector to the public sector. We conclude the chapter by noting potential government inefficiencies that can hinder government's economic efforts.

Private Goods

market failure
The inability of a market to produce a desirable product or produce it in the "right" amount.

Certain goods called **private goods** are produced through the competitive market system. Private goods encompass the full range of goods offered for sale in stores and shops. Examples include automobiles, clothing, personal computers, household appliances, and sporting goods. Private goods have two characteristics: rivalry and excludability.

private goods
Goods that people individually buy and consume and that private firms can profitably provide because they keep people who do not pay from receiving the benefits.

- *Rivalry* (in consumption) means that when one person buys and consumes a product, it is not available for another person to buy and consume. When Adams purchases and drinks a bottle of mineral water, it is not available for Benson to purchase and consume.
- *Excludability* means that sellers can keep people who do not pay for a product from obtaining its benefits. Only people who are willing and able to pay the market price for bottles of water can obtain these drinks and the benefits they confer.

Profitable Provision

Consumers fully express their personal demands for private goods in the market. If Adams likes bottled mineral water, that fact will be known by her desire to purchase the product. Other things equal, the higher the price of bottled water, the fewer bottles she will buy. So Adams' demand for bottled water will reflect an inverse relationship between the price of bottled water and the quantity of it demanded. This is simply *individual* demand, as described in Chapter 3.

The *market* demand for a private good is the horizontal summation of the individual demand schedules (review Figure 3.2). Suppose there are just two consumers in the market for bottled water and the price is $1 per bottle. If Adams will purchase 3 bottles and Benson will buy 2, the market demand will reflect that consumers demand 5 bottles at the $1 price. Similar summations of quantities demanded at other prices will generate the market demand schedule and curve.

Suppose the equilibrium price of bottled water is $1. Adams and Benson will buy a total of 5 bottles, and the sellers will obtain total revenue of $5 (= $1 × 5). If the sellers' cost per bottle is $.80, their total cost will be $4 (= $.80 × 5). So sellers charging $1 per bottle will obtain $5 of total revenue, incur $4 of total cost, and earn $1 of profits for the 5 bottles sold.

Because firms can profitably "tap market demand" for private goods, they will produce and offer them for sale. Consumers demand private goods, and profit-seeking suppliers produce goods that satisfy the demand. Consumers willing to pay the market price obtain the goods; nonpayers go without.

Efficient Allocation

productive efficiency
The production of a good in the least costly way.

A competitive market not only makes private goods available to consumers but also allocates society's resources efficiently to the particular product. Competition among producers forces them to use the best technology and right mix of productive resources. Otherwise, lower-cost producers will drive them out of business. The result is **productive efficiency:** the production of any particular good in the least costly way. When society produces, say, bottled water, at the lowest achievable per-unit cost, it is expending the smallest amount of resources to produce that product and therefore is making available the largest amount of resources to produce other desired goods. Suppose society has only $100 worth of resources available. If it can produce a bottle of water using only $1 of those resources, then it will have available $99 of resources to produce other goods. This is clearly better than producing the bottle of water for $5 and having only $95 of resources available for alternative uses.

Competitive markets also produce **allocative efficiency:** the *particular mix* of goods and services most highly valued by society (minimum-cost production assumed). For example, society wants high-quality mineral water to be used for bottled water, not for gigantic blocks of refrigeration ice. It wants MP3 players (such as iPods), not phonographs and 45-rpm records. Moreover, society does not want to devote all its resources to bottled water and MP3 players. It wants to assign some resources to automobiles and personal computers. Competitive markets make those proper assignments.

The equilibrium price and quantity in competitive markets usually produce an assignment of resources that is "right" from an economic perspective. Demand reflects the marginal benefit (MB) of the good, and supply reflects its marginal cost (MC). The market ensures that firms produce all units of goods for which MB exceeds MC and no units for which MC exceeds MB. At the intersection of the demand and supply curves, MB equals MC and allocative efficiency results. There is neither underproduction nor overproduction of the product.

allocative efficiency
The production of the "right" mix of goods and services (minimum-cost production assumed).

Public Goods

Certain other goods and services called **public goods** have the opposite characteristics of private goods. Public goods are distinguished by nonrivalry and nonexcludability.

- *Nonrivalry* (in consumption) means that one person's consumption of a good does not preclude consumption of the good by others. Everyone can simultaneously obtain the benefit from a public good such as a global positioning system, national defense, street lighting, and environmental protection.
- *Nonexcludability* means there is no effective way of excluding individuals from the benefit of the good once it comes into existence.

public goods
Goods that everyone can simultaneously consume and from which no one can be excluded, even if they do not pay.

These two characteristics create a **free-rider problem.** Once a producer has provided a public good, everyone including nonpayers can obtain the benefit. Most people do not voluntarily pay for something they can obtain for free!

With only free riders, the demand for a public good does not get expressed in the market. With no market demand, there is no potential for firms to "tap the demand" for revenues and profits. The free-rider problem makes it impossible for firms to gather together resources and profitably provide the good. If society wants a public good, society will have to direct government to provide it. We will soon see that government can finance the provision of such goods through taxation.

A significant example of a public good is homeland defense. The vast majority of Americans think this public good is economically justified because they perceive the benefits as exceeding the costs. Once homeland defense efforts are undertaken, however, the benefits accrue to all Americans (nonrivalry). And there is no practical way to exclude any American from receiving those benefits (nonexcludability).

No private firm will undertake overall homeland defense because the free-rider problem means that benefits cannot be profitably sold. So here we have a service that yields substantial net benefits but to which the market system will not allocate sufficient resources. Like national defense in general, homeland defense is a public good. Society signals its desire for such goods by voting for particular political candidates who support their provision. Because of the free-rider problem, government provides these goods and finances them through compulsory charges in the form of taxes.

free-rider problem
The inability of a firm to profitably provide a good because everyone, including nonpayers, can obtain the benefit.

© Steven P. Lynch/The McGraw-Hill Companies, Inc.   © S. Solum/PhotoLink/Getty Images

Photo Op Private versus Public Goods

Apples, distinguished by rivalry (in consumption) and excludability, are examples of private goods. In contrast, streetlights, distinguished by nonrivalry (in consumption) and nonexcludability, are examples of public goods.

ILLUSTRATING THE IDEA

Art for Art's Sake

Suppose an enterprising sculptor creates a piece of art costing $600 and, with permission, places it in the town square. Also suppose that Jack gets $300 of enjoyment from the art and Diane gets $400. Sensing this enjoyment and hoping to make a profit, the sculptor approaches Jack for a donation equal to his satisfaction. Jack falsely says that, unfortunately, he does not particularly like the piece. The sculptor then tries Diane, hoping to get $400 or so. Same deal: Diane professes not to like the piece either. Jack and Diane have become free riders. Although feeling a bit guilty, both reason that it makes no sense to pay for something when anyone can receive the benefits without paying for them. The artist is a quick learner; he vows never to try anything like that again.

Question:
What is the rationale for government funding for art placed in town squares and other public spaces?

Optimal Quantity of a Public Good

If consumers need not reveal their true demand for a public good in the marketplace, how can society determine the optimal amount of that good? The answer is that the government has to try to estimate the demand for a public good through surveys or public votes. It can then compare the marginal benefit of an added unit of the good against the government's marginal cost of providing it. Adhering to the MB = MC rule, it can provide the "right" amount of the public good.

Measuring Demand

Suppose that Adams and Benson are the only two people in the society and that their willingness to pay for a public good, this time the war on terrorism, is as shown in columns 1 and 2 and columns 1 and 3 in Table 4.1. Economists might have discovered these schedules through a survey asking hypothetical questions about how much each citizen was willing to pay for various types and amounts of public goods rather than go without them.

Notice that the schedules in the first four columns of Table 4.1 are price-quantity schedules, meaning they are demand schedules. Rather than depicting demand in the usual way—the quantity of a product someone is willing to buy at each possible price—these schedules show the price someone is willing to pay for the extra unit of each possible quantity. That is, Adams is willing to pay $4 for the first unit of the public good, $3 for the second, $2 for the third, and so on.

Suppose the government produces 1 unit of this public good. Because of nonrivalry, Adams' consumption of the good does not preclude Benson from also consuming it, and vice versa. So both people consume the good, and neither volunteers to pay for it. But from Table 4.1 we can find the amount these two people would be willing to pay, together, rather than do without this 1 unit of the good. Columns 1 and 2 show that Adams would be willing to pay $4 for the first unit of the public good, whereas columns 1 and 3 reveal that Benson would be willing to pay $5 for it. Adams and Benson therefore are jointly willing to pay $9 (= $4 + $5) for this first unit.

For the second unit of the public good, the collective price they are willing to pay is $7 (= $3 from Adams + $4 from Benson); for the third unit they will pay $5 (= $2 + $3); and so on. By finding the collective willingness to pay for each additional unit (column 4), we can construct a collective demand schedule (a willingness-to-pay schedule) for the public good. Here we are *not* adding the quantities demanded at each possible price, as with the market demand for a private good. Instead, we are adding the prices that people are willing to pay for the last unit of the public good at each possible quantity demanded.

What does it mean in columns 1 and 4 of Table 4.1 that, for example, Adams and Benson are collectively willing to pay $7 for the second unit of the public good? It means

(1) Quantity of Public Good	(2) Adams' Willingness to Pay (Price)		(3) Benson's Willingness to Pay (Price)		(4) Collective Willingness to Pay (Price)	(5) Marginal Cost
1	$4	+	$5	=	$9	$3
2	3	+	4	=	7	4
3	2	+	3	=	5	5
4	1	+	2	=	3	6
5	0	+	1	=	1	7

TABLE 4.1
Optimal Quantity of a Public Good, Two Individuals

that they jointly expect to receive $7 of extra benefit or utility from that unit. Column 4, in effect, reveals the collective marginal benefit of each unit of the public good.

Comparing Marginal Benefit and Marginal Cost

Now let's suppose the marginal cost of providing the public good is as shown in column 5 of Table 4.1. As explained in Chapter 1, marginal cost tends to rise as more of a good is produced. In view of the marginal-cost data shown, how much of the good should government provide? The optimal amount occurs at the quantity where marginal benefit equals marginal cost. In Table 4.1 that quantity is 3 units, where the collective willingness to pay for the third unit—the $5 marginal benefit—just matches that unit's $5 marginal cost. As we saw in Chapter 1, equating marginal benefit and marginal cost efficiently allocates society's scarce resources.

Cost-Benefit Analysis

The above example suggests a practical means, called **cost-benefit analysis,** for deciding whether to provide a particular public good and how much of it to provide. Like our example, cost-benefit analysis (or marginal-benefit–marginal-cost analysis) involves a comparison of marginal costs and marginal benefits.

Suppose the Federal government is contemplating a highway construction plan. Because the economy's resources are limited, any decision to use more resources in the public sector will mean fewer resources for the private sector. There will be both a cost and a benefit. The cost is the loss of satisfaction resulting from the accompanying decline in the production of private goods; the benefit is the extra satisfaction resulting from the output of more public goods. Should the needed resources be shifted from the private to the public sector? The answer is yes if the benefit from the extra public goods exceeds the cost that results from having fewer private goods. The answer is no if the cost of the forgone private goods is greater than the benefit associated with the extra public goods.

Cost-benefit analysis, however, can indicate more than whether a public program is worth doing. It can also help the government decide on the extent to which a project should be pursued. Real economic questions cannot usually be answered simply by "yes" or "no" but, rather, involve questions such as "how much" or "how little."

Although private toll roads exist, highways clearly have public goods characteristics because the benefits are widely diffused and highway use is relatively difficult to price. Should the Federal government expand the Federal highway system? If so, what is the proper size or scope for the overall project?

Table 4.2 lists a series of increasingly ambitious and increasingly costly highway projects: widening existing two-lane highways; building new two-lane highways; building new four-lane highways; building new six-lane highways. The extent to which government should undertake highway construction depends on the costs and benefits. The costs are largely the costs of constructing and maintaining the highways; the benefits are improved flows of people and goods throughout the nation.

TABLE 4.2 Cost-Benefit Analysis for a National Highway Construction Project (in Billions)

(1) Plan	(2) Total Cost of Project	(3) Marginal Cost	(4) Total Benefit	(5) Marginal Benefit	(6) Net Benefit (4) − (2)
No new construction	$ 0		$ 0		$ 0
		$ 4		$ 5	
A: Widen existing highways	4		5		1
		6		8	
B: New 2-lane highways	10		13		3
		8		10	
C: New 4-lane highways	18		23		5
		10		3	
D: New 6-lane highways	28		26		−2

The table shows that total annual benefit (column 4) exceeds total annual cost (column 2) for plans A, B, and C, indicating that some highway construction is economically justifiable. We see this directly in column 6, where total costs (column 2) are subtracted from total annual benefits (column 4). Net benefits are positive for plans A, B, and C. Plan D is not economically justifiable because net benefits are negative.

But the question of optimal size or scope for this project remains. Comparing the marginal cost (the change in total cost) and the marginal benefit (the change in total benefit) relating to each plan determines the answer. The guideline is well known to you from previous discussions: Increase an activity, project, or output as long as the marginal benefit (column 5) exceeds the marginal cost (column 3). Stop the activity at, or as close as possible to, the point at which the marginal benefit equals the marginal cost. Do not undertake a project for which marginal cost exceeds marginal benefit.

In this case plan C (building new four-lane highways) is the best plan. Plans A and B are too modest; the marginal benefits exceed the marginal costs. Plan D's marginal cost ($10 billion) exceeds the marginal benefit ($3 billion) and therefore cannot be justified; it overallocates resources to the project. Plan C is closest to the theoretical optimum because its marginal benefit ($10 billion) still exceeds marginal cost ($8 billion) but approaches the MB = MC (or MC = MB) ideal.

This marginal-cost–marginal-benefit rule tells government which plan provides the maximum excess of total benefits over total costs or, in other words, the plan that provides society with the maximum net benefit. You can confirm directly in column 6 that the maximum net benefit ($5 billion) is associated with plan C.

Question:
Do you think it is generally easier to measure the costs of public goods or their benefits? Explain your reasoning.

Externalities

When we say that competitive markets automatically bring about allocative efficiency, we assume that all the benefits and costs for each product are fully reflected in the market demand and supply curves. That is not always the case. In some markets certain benefits or costs may escape the buyer or seller.

An *externality* occurs when some of the costs or the benefits of a good are passed on, or "spill over," to someone other than the immediate buyer or seller. Externalities are benefits or costs that accrue to some third party that is external to the market transaction.

Negative Externalities

Production or consumption costs inflicted on a third party without compensation are called **negative externalities** or *spillover costs*. Environmental pollution is an example. When a chemical manufacturer or a meatpacking plant dumps its wastes into a lake or river, water users such as swimmers, fishers, and boaters suffer negative externalities. When a petroleum refinery pollutes the air with smoke or a paper mill creates obnoxious odors, the community experiences negative externalities for which it is not compensated.

Figure 4.1a illustrates how negative externalities affect the allocation of resources. When producers shift some of their costs onto the community as spillover costs, producers' marginal costs are lower than otherwise. So their supply curves do not include or "capture" all the costs legitimately associated with the production of their goods. A supply curve such as S in Figure 4.1a therefore understates the total cost of production for a polluting firm. Its supply curve lies to the right of (or below) the full-cost supply curve S_t, which would include the negative externality. Through polluting and thus transferring cost to society, the firm enjoys lower production costs and has the supply curve S.

The resource allocation outcome is shown in Figure 4.1a, where equilibrium output Q_e is larger than the optimal output Q_o. This is a market failure because resources are *overallocated* to the production of this commodity; too many units of it are produced.

Positive Externalities

Sometimes spillovers appear as external benefits. The production or consumption of certain goods and services may confer spillover or external benefits on third parties or on the community at large without compensating payment. Immunization against measles and polio results in direct benefits to the immediate consumer of

negative externalities
Spillover production or consumption costs imposed on third parties without compensation to them.

INTERACTIVE GRAPHS

G 4.1

Externalities

FIGURE 4.1 **Negative externalities and positive externalities.** (a) With negative externalities (spillover costs) borne by society, the producers' supply curve S is to the right of (below) the full-cost curve S_t. Consequently, the equilibrium output Q_e is greater than the optimal output Q_o. (b) When positive externalities (spillover benefits) accrue to society, the market demand curve D is to the left of (below) the full-benefit demand curve D_t. As a result, the equilibrium output Q_e is less than the optimal output Q_o.

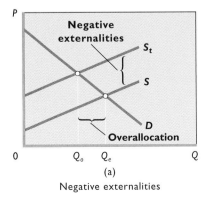

(a)
Negative externalities

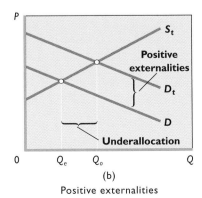

(b)
Positive externalities

those vaccines. But it also results in widespread substantial positive externalities to the entire community.

Education is another example of **positive externalities.** Education benefits individual consumers: Better-educated people generally achieve higher incomes than less-well-educated people. But education also benefits society through a more versatile and more productive labor force, on the one hand, and smaller outlays for crime prevention, law enforcement, and welfare programs, on the other.

Figure 4.1b shows the impact of positive externalities on resource allocation. When positive externalities occur, the market demand curve D lies to the left of (or below) the full-benefits demand curve. That is, D does not include the positive externalities of the product, whereas D_t does. Consider inoculations against a communicable disease. Alvarez and Anderson benefit when they get vaccinated, but so do their associates Bronson and Berkshire, who are less likely to contract the disease from them. The market demand curve reflects only the direct, private benefits to Alvarez and Anderson. It does not reflect the positive externalities—the spillover benefits—to Bronson and Berkshire, which are included in D_t.

The outcome, as shown in Figure 4.1b, is that the equilibrium output Q_e is less than the optimal output Q_o. The market fails to produce enough vaccinations, and resources are *underallocated* to this product.

Economists have explored several approaches to the problems of negative and positive externalities. Let's first look at situations where government intervention is not needed and then at some possible government solutions.

positive externalities
Spillover production or consumption benefits conferred on third parties without compensation from them.

ORIGIN OF THE IDEA

O 4.1

Externalities

© Paul Taylor/Photolibrary

© Charles Smith/Corbis

Photo Op Positive and Negative Consumption Externalities

Homeowners create positive externalities when they put up nice holiday lighting displays. Not only does the homeowner benefit from consuming the sight, but so do people who pass by the house. In contrast, when people consume roads (drive) during rush hour, it creates a negative externality. This takes the form of traffic congestion, imposing time and fuel costs on other drivers.

Individual Bargaining: Coase Theorem

Coase theorem
The idea that externality problems can be resolved through private negotiations by the affected parties when property rights are clearly established.

In the **Coase theorem**, conceived decades ago by economist Ronald Coase at the University of Chicago, government is not needed to remedy negative or positive externalities where (1) property ownership is clearly defined, (2) the number of people involved is small, and (3) bargaining costs are negligible. Under these circumstances, the government should confine its role to encouraging bargaining between affected individuals or groups. Property rights place a price tag on an externality, creating opportunity costs for all parties. Because the economic self-interests of the parties are at stake, bargaining will enable them to find a mutually acceptable solution to the externality problem.

ILLUSTRATING THE IDEA

A Forest Tale

Suppose the owner of a large parcel of forestland is considering a plan to clear-cut (totally level) thousands of acres of mature fir trees. The complication is that the forest surrounds a lake with a popular resort on its shore. The resort is on land owned by the resort. The unspoiled beauty of the general area attracts vacationers from all over the nation to the resort, and the resort owner is against the clear-cutting. Should state or local government intervene to allow or prevent the tree cutting?

According to the Coase theorem, the forest owner and the resort owner can resolve this situation without government intervention. As long as one of the parties to the dispute has property rights to what is at issue, an incentive will exist for both parties to negotiate a solution acceptable to each. In our example, the owner of the timberland holds the property rights to the land to be logged and thus has the right to clear-cut it. The owner of the resort therefore has an economic incentive to negotiate with the forest owner to reduce the logging impact. Excessive logging of the forest surrounding the resort will reduce tourism and revenues to the resort owner.

But less clear is the reason why the forest owner has an incentive to negotiate with the resort owner. The rationale draws directly on the idea of opportunity cost. One cost to the forest owner incurred in logging the forest is the forgone payment that he or she could obtain from the resort owner for agreeing not to clear-cut the fir trees. The resort owner might be willing to make a lump-sum or annual payment to the owner of the forest to avoid or minimize the negative externality. Or perhaps the resort owner might be willing to buy the forested land to prevent the logging. As viewed by the forest owner, a payment for not clear-cutting or a purchase price above the prior market value of the land is an opportunity cost of logging the land.

Both parties would probably regard a negotiated agreement as better than clear-cutting the firs.

Question:
Suppose the resort, not the timber company, owned the surrounding forest. Why would there still be an incentive for both to negotiate about the type and degree of logging in the forest?

Unfortunately, many externalities involve huge numbers of affected parties, high bargaining costs, and community property such as air and water. In such situations private bargaining cannot be used as a remedy. As an example, the climate change problem affects millions of people in many nations. The vast number of affected parties could not individually negotiate an agreement to reduce the greenhouse gases that contribute to climate change. Instead, they must rely on their governments to represent the millions of affected parties and find an acceptable solution.

Liability Rules and Lawsuits

Although private negotiation may not be a realistic solution to many externality problems, clearly established property rights may help in another way. The government has erected a framework of laws that define private property and protect it from damage done by other parties. Those laws, and the damage recovery system to which they give rise, permit parties suffering negative externalities to sue for compensation.

Suppose the Ajax Degreaser Company regularly dumps leaky barrels containing solvents into a nearby canyon owned by Bar Q Ranch. Bar Q eventually discovers this dump site and, after tracing the drums to Ajax, immediately contacts its lawyer. Soon after, Bar Q sues Ajax. If Ajax loses the case, it will have to pay for the cleanup and may also have to pay Bar Q additional damages for ruining its property.

Clearly defined property rights and government liability laws thus help remedy some externality problems. They do so directly by forcing the perpetrator of the harmful externality to pay damages to those injured. They do so indirectly by discouraging firms and individuals from generating negative externalities for fear of being sued. It is not surprising, then, that many spillovers do not involve private property but rather property held in common by society. It is the public bodies of water, the public lands, and the public air, where ownership is less clear, that often bear the brunt of spillovers.

Caveat: Like private negotiations, private lawsuits to resolve externalities have their own limitations. Large legal fees and major time delays in the court system are commonplace. Also, the uncertainty associated with the court outcome reduces the effectiveness of this approach. Will the court accept your claim that your emphysema has resulted from the smoke emitted by the factory next door, or will it conclude that your ailment is unrelated to the plant's pollution? Can you prove that a specific firm in the area is the source of the contamination of your well? What happens to Bar Q's suit if Ajax Degreaser goes out of business during the litigation?

Government Intervention

Government intervention may be needed to achieve economic efficiency when externalities affect large numbers of people or when community interests are at stake. Government can use direct controls and taxes to counter negative externalities (spillover costs); it may provide subsidies or public goods to deal with positive externalities (spillover benefits).

Direct Controls
The direct way to reduce negative externalities from a certain activity is to pass legislation limiting that activity. Such direct controls force the offending firms to incur the actual costs of the offending activity. To date, this approach has dominated public policy in the United States. Clean-air legislation has created uniform emission standards—limits on allowable pollution—and has forced factories and businesses to install "maximum achievable control technology"

FIGURE 4.2 **Correcting for negative externalities.** (a) Negative externalities (spillover costs) result in an overallocation of resources. (b) Government can correct this overallocation in two ways: (1) using direct controls, which would shift the supply curve from S to S_t and reduce output from Q_e to Q_o, or (2) imposing a specific tax T, which would also shift the supply curve from S to S_t, eliminating the overallocation of resources.

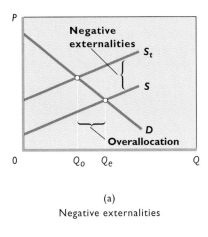

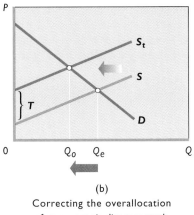

(a)
Negative externalities

(b)
Correcting the overallocation
of resources via direct controls
or via a tax

to reduce emissions of toxic chemicals. It has also mandated reductions in (1) tail-pipe emissions from automobiles, (2) use of chlorofluorocarbons (CFCs) that deplete the ozone layer, and (3) emissions of sulfur dioxide by coal-burning utilities to prevent the acid-rain destruction of lakes and forests. Also, clean-water legislation has limited the amounts of heavy metals and detergents that firms can discharge into rivers and bays. Toxic-waste laws dictate special procedures and dump sites for disposing of contaminated soil and solvents. Violating these laws means fines and, in some cases, imprisonment.

Direct controls raise the marginal cost of production because the firms must operate and maintain pollution-control equipment. The supply curve S in Figure 4.2b, which does not reflect the negative externalities, shifts leftward (upward) to the full-cost supply curve, S_t. Product price increases, equilibrium output falls from Q_e to Q_o, and the initial overallocation of resources shown in Figure 4.2a is corrected.

Specific Taxes   A second policy approach to negative externalities is for government to levy taxes or charges specifically on the related good. For example, the government has placed a manufacturing excise tax on CFCs, which deplete the stratospheric ozone layer protecting the earth from excessive solar ultraviolet radiation. Facing such an excise tax, manufacturers must decide whether to pay the tax or expend additional funds to purchase or develop substitute products. In either case, the tax raises the marginal cost of producing CFCs, shifting the private supply curve for this product leftward (or upward).

In Figure 4.2b, a tax equal to T per unit increases the firm's marginal cost, shifting the supply curve from S to S_t. The equilibrium price rises, and the equilibrium output declines from Q_e to the economically efficient level Q_o. The tax thus eliminates the initial overallocation of resources associated with the negative externality.

FIGURE 4.3 **Correcting for positive externalities.** (a) Positive externalities (spillover benefits) result in an underallocation of resources. (b) Government can correct this underallocation through a subsidy to consumers, which shifts market demand from D to D_t and increases output from Q_e to Q_o. (c) Alternatively, government can eliminate the underallocation by giving producers a subsidy of U, which shifts their supply curve from S_t to S'_t, increasing output from Q_e to Q_o.

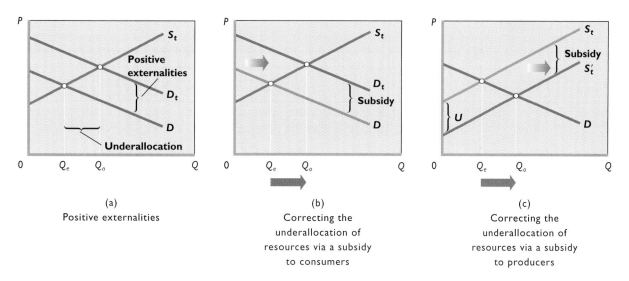

(a)
Positive externalities

(b)
Correcting the
underallocation of
resources via a subsidy
to consumers

(c)
Correcting the
underallocation of
resources via a subsidy
to producers

Subsidies and Government Provision
What policies might be useful in dealing with *positive* externalities? Where positive externalities are large and diffuse, as in our earlier example of inoculations, government has three options for correcting the underallocation of resources:

- *Subsidies to buyers* Figure 4.3a again shows the supply-demand situation for positive externalities. Government could correct the underallocation of resources, for example, to inoculations, by subsidizing consumers of the product. It could give each new mother in the United States a discount coupon to be used to obtain a series of inoculations for her child. The coupon would reduce the "price" to the mother by, say, 50 percent. As shown in Figure 4.3b, this program would shift the demand curve for inoculations from too low D to the appropriate D_t. The number of inoculations would rise from Q_e to the economically optimal Q_o, eliminating the underallocation of resources shown in Figure 4.3a.

- *Subsidies to producers* A subsidy to producers is a specific tax in reverse. Taxes impose an extra cost on producers, while subsidies reduce producers' costs. As shown in Figure 4.3c, a subsidy of U per inoculation to physicians and medical clinics would reduce their marginal costs and shift their supply curve rightward from S_t to S'_t. The output of inoculations would increase from Q_e to the optimal level Q_o, correcting the underallocation of resources shown in Figure 4.3a.

- *Government provision* Finally, where positive externalities are extremely large, the government may decide to provide the product for free or for a minimal charge. Government provides many goods that could be produced and delivered in such a way that exclusion would be possible. Such goods, called **quasi-public goods,** include education, streets and highways, police and fire protection, libraries and museums, preventive medicine, and sewage disposal. They could all be priced and provided by private firms through the market system because the free-rider problem would be minimal. But, because spillover benefits extend well beyond the individual buyer, the market system may underproduce them. Therefore, government often provides quasi-public goods.

quasi-public goods
Goods for which exclusion could occur but which government provides because of perceived widespread and diffuse benefits.

Lojack: A Case of Positive Externalities

Economists Ayres and Levitt point out that some forms of private crime prevention simply redistribute crime rather than reduce it. For example, car alarm systems that have red blinking warning lights may simply divert professional auto thieves to vehicles that do not have such lights and alarms. The owner of a car with such an alarm system benefits through reduced likelihood of theft but imposes a cost on other car owners who do not have such alarms. Their cars are more likely to be targeted for theft by thieves because other cars have visible security systems.

In contrast, some private crime prevention measures actually reduce crime, rather than simply redistribute it. One such measure is installation of a Lojack (or some similar) car retrieval system. Lojack is a tiny radio transmitter that is hidden in one of many possible places within the car. When an owner reports a stolen car, the police can remotely activate the transmitter. Police then can determine the car's precise location and track its subsequent movements.

The owner of the car benefits because the 95 percent retrieval rate on cars with the Lojack system is higher than the 60 percent retrieval rate for cars without the system. But, according to a study by Ayres and Levitt, the benefit to the car owner is only 10 percent of the total benefit. Ninety percent of the total benefit is external; it is a spillover benefit to other car owners in the community.

There are two sources of this positive externality. First, the presence of the Lojack device sometimes enables police to intercept the car while the thief is still driving it. For example, in California the arrest rate for cars with Lojack was three times greater than that for cars without it. The arrest puts the car thief out of commission for a time and thus reduces subsequent car thefts in the community. Second, and far more important, the device enables police to trace cars to "chop shops," where crooks disassemble cars for resale of the parts. When police raid the chop shop, they put the entire theft ring out of business. In Los Angeles alone, Lojack has eliminated 45 chop shops in just a few years. The purging of the chop shop and theft ring reduces auto theft in the community. So auto owners who do not have Lojack devices in their cars benefit from car owners who do. Ayres and Levitt estimate the *marginal social benefit* of Lojack—the marginal benefit to the Lojack car owner *plus* the spillover benefit to other car owners—is 15 times greater than the marginal cost of the device.

We saw in Figure 4.3a that the existence of positive externalities causes an insufficient quantity of a product and thus an underallocation of scarce resources to its production. The two general ways to correct the outcome are to subsidize the consumer, as shown in Figure 4.3b, or to subsidize the producer, as shown in Figure 4.3c. Currently, there is only one form of government intervention in place: state-mandated insurance discounts for people who install auto retrieval systems such as Lojack. In effect, those discounts on insurance premiums subsidize the consumer by lowering the "price" of the system to consumers. The lower price raises the number of systems installed. But, on the basis of their research, Ayres and Levitt contend that the current levels of insurance discounts are far too small to correct the underallocation that results from the positive externalities created by Lojack.

Question:
Other than mandating lower insurance premiums for Lojack users, what might government do to increase the use of Lojack devices in automobiles?

Source: Based on Ian Ayres and Steven D. Levitt, "Measuring Positive Externalities from Unobservable Victim Precaution: An Empirical Analysis of Lojack," *Quarterly Journal of Economics*, February 1998, pp. 43–77. The authors point out that Lojack did not fund their work; nor do they have any financial stake in Lojack.

A Market-Based Approach

One novel approach to negative externalities involves only limited government action. The idea is to create a market for externality rights.

Operation of the Market

In this market-based approach—commonly called a cap-and-trade program—an appropriate pollution-control agency determines the amount of pollutants that firms can discharge into the water or air of a specific region annually while maintaining the water or air quality at some acceptable level. Suppose the agency ascertains that 500 tons of pollutants can be discharged into Metropolitan Lake and "recycled" by nature each year. Then 500 pollution rights, each entitling the owner to dump 1 ton of pollutants into the lake in 1 year, are made available for sale to producers each year. The supply of these pollution rights is fixed and therefore perfectly inelastic, as shown in Figure 4.4.

The demand for pollution rights, represented by D_{2008} in the figure, takes the same downsloping form as the demand for any other input. At higher prices there is less pollution, as polluters either stop polluting or pollute less by acquiring pollution-abatement equipment. An equilibrium market price for pollution rights, here $100, will be determined at which the environment-preserving quantity of pollution rights is rationed to polluters. Figure 4.4 shows that if the use of the lake as a dump site for pollutants were instead free, 750 tons of pollutants would be discharged into the lake; it would be "overconsumed," or polluted, in the amount of 250 tons.

Over time, as human and business populations expand, demand will increase, as from D_{2008} to D_{2018}. Without a market for pollution rights, pollution in 2018 would be 1000 tons, 500 tons beyond what can be assimilated by nature. With the market for pollution rights, the price would rise from $100 to $200, and the amount of pollutants would remain at 500 tons—the amount that the lake can recycle.

Advantages

This scheme has several advantages over direct controls. Most important, it reduces society's costs by allowing pollution rights to be bought and sold.

FIGURE 4.4 **A market for pollution rights.** The supply of pollution rights S is set by the government, which determines that a specific body of water can safely recycle 500 tons of waste. In 2008, the demand for pollution rights is D_{2008} and the 1-ton price is $100. The quantity of pollution is 500 tons, not the 750 tons it would have been without the pollution rights. Over time, the demand for pollution rights increases to D_{2018} and the 1-ton price rises to $200. But the amount of pollution stays at 500 tons, rather than rising to 1000 tons.

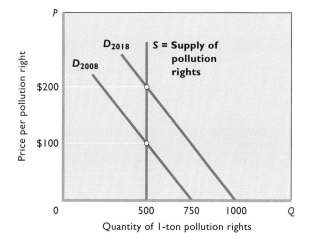

This trading of pollution rights is the "trade" portion of the "cap-and-trade" terminology given to this type of scheme. Let's see how this cost reduction works. Assume that the present equilibrium price of pollution rights is $100, as shown by the intersection of the supply curve and demand curve (2008) in Figure 4.4. Next, suppose that the pollution in question is some specific noxious discharge into Metropolitan Lake. Suppose that it costs Acme Pulp Mill $20 a year to reduce this pollution by 1 ton while it costs Zemo Chemicals $800 a year to accomplish the same 1-ton reduction. Also assume that Zemo wants to expand production but doing so will increase its pollution discharge by 1 ton.

Without a market for pollution rights, Zemo would have to use $800 of society's scarce resources to keep the 1-ton pollution discharge from occurring. But with a market for pollution rights, Zemo has a better option: It buys 1 ton of pollution rights for the $100 price shown in Figure 4.4. Acme is willing to sell Zemo 1 ton of pollution rights for $100 because that amount is more than Acme's $20 cost of reducing its pollution by 1 ton. Zemo increases its discharge by 1 ton; Acme reduces its discharge by 1 ton. Zemo benefits by paying $100 for something that would otherwise cost $800. Acme benefits by selling something for $100 that costs only $20 to "produce." Society saves $780. Rather than using $800 of its scarce resources to hold the discharge at the specified level, society uses only $20 of those resources.

Market-based plans have other advantages. Potential polluters have a monetary incentive not to pollute because they must pay for the right to discharge effluent. Conservation groups can fight pollution by buying up and withholding pollution rights, thereby reducing pollution below governmentally determined standards. As the demand for pollution rights increases over time, the growing revenue from the sale of a fixed quantity of pollution rights could be devoted to environmental improvement. At the same time, the rising price of pollution rights should stimulate the search for improved pollution-control techniques.

APPLYING THE ANALYSIS

Reducing Greenhouse Gases

Climate change, to the extent it is caused by human-generated greenhouse gases, is a negative externality problem. Suggested policies to reduce carbon emissions, a major greenhouse gas, include carbon taxes and a cap-and-trade program.

A tax imposed on each ton of carbon emitted would increase the marginal cost of production to all firms that release carbon into the air through their production processes. Because of the added marginal cost, the supply curves within affected markets would shift to the left (as illustrated by the move from S to S_t in Figure 4.1). The reduced market supply would increase equilibrium price and reduce equilibrium quantity. With the lower output, carbon, emissions in these industries would fall.

A carbon tax would require minimum government interference in the economy once the tax was in place. The Federal government could direct the revenues from the tax to research on cleaner production technologies or simply use the new revenues to reduce other taxes. But there would be no free lunch here: According to a 2007 study, a proposed $15 tax per ton of carbon emitted would add an estimated 14 cents to a gallon of gasoline, $1.63 to a kilowatt hour of electricity, $28.50 to a ton of coal, and $6.48 to a barrel of crude oil.

An alternative approach is a cap-and-trade program, based on the concepts embodied within Figure 4.4. As it currently does with sulfur dioxide emissions, the Federal government could place a cap or lid on total carbon emissions and then either hand out emission rights or auction them off. In ways previously discussed, the cap-and-trade program would reduce society's overall cost of lowering carbon emissions. In that regard, it would be more efficient than direct controls requiring each producer of greenhouse gas to reduce emissions by a fixed percentage amount. Existing cap-and-trade programs—including current European markets for carbon certificates—prove that this program can work. But such programs require considerable government oversight and enforcement of the rules.

Question:
Why would rising prices of emission rights increase the incentive for firms to use cleaner production methods?

Financing the Public Sector: Taxation

How are resources reallocated from the production of private goods to the production of public goods (and quasi-public goods)? How are government programs to deal with externalities funded? If the resources of the economy are fully employed, government must free up resources from the production of private goods and make them available for producing public and quasi-public goods. It does so by reducing the demand for private goods. And it does that by levying taxes on households and businesses, taking some of their income out of the circular flow. With lower incomes and therefore reduced purchasing power, households and businesses must curtail their spending.

As a result, the private demand for goods and services declines, as does the private demand for resources. So by diverting purchasing power from private spenders to government, taxes remove resources from private use.

Government then spends the tax proceeds to provide public and quasi-public goods and services. Taxation releases resources from the production of private consumer goods (food, clothing, television sets) and private investment goods (printing presses, boxcars, warehouses). Government shifts those resources to the production of public and quasi-public goods (post offices, submarines, parks), changing the composition of the economy's total output.

Apportioning the Tax Burden

Once government has decided on the total tax revenue it needs to finance its activities, including the provision of public and quasi-public goods, it must determine how to apportion the tax burden among the citizens. (By "tax burden" we mean the total cost of taxes imposed on society.) This apportionment question affects each of us. The overall level of taxes is important, but the average citizen is much more concerned with his or her share of taxes.

Benefits Received versus Ability to Pay

Two basic philosophies coexist on how the economy's tax burden should be assigned.

Benefits-Received

The **benefits-received principle** of taxation states that households and businesses should purchase the goods and services of government in the same way they buy other commodities. Those who benefit most from government-supplied goods or services should pay the taxes necessary to finance them. A few public goods are now financed on this basis. For example, money collected as gasoline taxes is typically used to finance highway construction and repairs. Thus people who benefit from good roads pay the cost of those roads. Difficulties immediately arise, however, when we consider widespread application of the benefits-received principle:

- How will the government determine the benefits that individual households and businesses receive from national defense, education, the court system, and police and fire protection? Recall that public goods are characterized by nonrivalry and nonexcludability. So benefits from public goods are especially widespread and diffuse. Even in the seemingly straightforward case of highway financing it is difficult to measure benefits. Good roads benefit the owners of cars in different degrees. But others also benefit. For example, businesses benefit because good roads bring them workers and customers.

- Government cannot logically apply the benefits-received principle to some government programs such as "safety net" programs. It would be absurd to ask poor families to pay the taxes needed to finance their welfare payments. It would be ridiculous to think of taxing only unemployed workers to finance the unemployment compensation payments they receive.

Ability to Pay

The **ability-to-pay principle** of taxation states that government should apportion the tax burden according to taxpayers' income. In the United States this means that individuals and businesses with larger incomes should pay more taxes in both absolute and relative terms than those with smaller incomes.

The rationale of ability-to-pay taxation is the proposition that each additional dollar of income received by a household yields a smaller amount of satisfaction or marginal utility when it is spent. Because consumers act rationally, the first dollars of income received in any time period will be spent on high-urgency goods that yield the greatest marginal utility. Successive dollars of income will go for less urgently needed goods and finally for trivial goods and services. This means that a dollar taken through taxes from a poor person who has few dollars represents a greater utility sacrifice than a dollar taken through taxes from a rich person who has many dollars. To balance the sacrifices that taxes impose on income receivers, taxes should be apportioned according to the amount of income a taxpayer receives.

This argument is appealing, but application problems arise here too. Although we might agree that the household earning $100,000 per year has a greater ability to pay taxes than a household receiving $10,000, we don't know exactly how much more ability to pay the first family has. Should the wealthier family pay the same percentage of its larger income, and hence a larger absolute amount, as taxes? Or should it be made to pay a larger fraction of its income as taxes? And how much larger should that fraction be? Who is to decide?

There is no scientific way of making utility comparisons among individuals and thus of measuring someone's relative ability to pay taxes. That is the main problem. In practice, the solution hinges on guesswork, expediency, the tax views of the political party in power, and how urgently the government needs revenue.

Progressive, Proportional, and Regressive Taxes

Any discussion of taxation leads ultimately to the question of tax rates. The **marginal tax rate** is the rate paid on each additional dollar of income (or purchases). The **average tax rate** is the total tax paid as a percentage of income.

Taxes are classified as progressive, regressive, or proportional taxes, depending on the relationship between average tax rates and taxpayer incomes. We focus on incomes because all taxes, whether on income or on a product or a building or a parcel of land, are ultimately paid out of someone's income.

- A tax is **progressive** if its average rate increases as income increases. Such a tax claims not only a larger absolute (dollar) amount but also a larger percentage of income as income increases.
- A tax is **regressive** if its average rate declines as income increases. Such a tax takes a smaller proportion of income as income increases. A regressive tax may or may not take a larger absolute amount of income as income increases. (You may want to derive an example to substantiate this conclusion.)
- A tax is **proportional** if its average rate remains the same regardless of the size of income.

We can illustrate these ideas with the personal income tax. Suppose tax rates are such that a household pays 10 percent of its income in taxes regardless of the size of its income. This is a proportional income tax. Now suppose the rate structure is such that a household with an annual taxable income of less than $10,000 pays 5 percent in income taxes; a household with an income of $10,000 to $19,999 pays 10 percent; one with a $20,000 to $29,999 income pays 15 percent; and so forth. This is a progressive income tax. Finally, suppose the rate declines as taxable income rises: You pay 15 percent if you earn less than $10,000; 10 percent if you earn $10,000 to $19,999; 5 percent if you earn $20,000 to $29,999; and so forth. This is a regressive income tax.

In general, progressive taxes are those that fall relatively more heavily on people with high incomes; regressive taxes are those that fall relatively more heavily on the poor.

Tax Progressivity in the United States

The progressivity or regressivity of taxes varies by type of tax in the United States. As shown in Table 4.3, the Federal *personal income tax* is progressive. Marginal tax rates (column 2)—those assessed on additional income—ranged from 10 to 35 percent in 2008. Rules that allow individuals to deduct from income interest on home mortgages

marginal tax rate
The tax rate paid on each additional dollar of income.

average tax rate
The total tax paid divided by total taxable income, as a percentage.

progressive tax
A tax whose average tax rate increases as the taxpayer's income increases.

regressive tax
A tax whose average tax rate decreases as the taxpayer's income increases.

proportional tax
A tax whose average tax rate remains constant as the taxpayer's income increases.

(1) Total Taxable Income	(2) Marginal Tax Rate, %	(3) Total Tax on Highest Income in Bracket	(4) Average Tax Rate on Highest Income in Bracket, % (3) ÷ (1)
$1–$16,050	10.0	$ 1610	10
$16,051–$65,100	15.0	8963	14
$65,101–$131,450	25.0	25,550	19
$131,451–$200,300	28.0	44,828	22
$200,301–$375,700	33.0	96,770	27
Over $375,700	35.0		

TABLE 4.3
Federal Personal Income Tax Rates, 2008*

* For a married couple filing a joint return.

and property taxes and that exempt interest on state and local bonds from taxation tend to make the tax less progressive than these marginal rates suggest. Nevertheless, average tax rates (column 4) rise with income.

At first thought, a *general sales tax* with, for example, a 5 percent rate would seem to be proportional. But in fact it is regressive with respect to income (rather than purchases). A larger portion of a low-income person's income is exposed to the tax than is the case for a high-income person; the rich pay no tax on the part of income that is saved, whereas the poor are unable to save. Example: "Low-income" Smith has an income of $15,000 and spends it all. "High-income" Jones has an income of $300,000 but spends only $200,000 and saves the rest. Assuming a 5 percent sales tax applies to all expenditures of each individual, we find that Smith pays $750 (= 5 percent of $15,000) in sales taxes and Jones pays $10,000 (= 5 percent of $200,000). But Smith pays $750/$15,000, or 5 percent of income, as sales taxes, while Jones pays $10,000/$300,000, or 3.3 percent of income. The general sales tax therefore is regressive.

The Federal *corporate income tax* is essentially a proportional tax with a flat 35 percent tax rate. In the short run, the corporate owners (shareholders) bear the tax through lower dividends and share values. In the long run, workers may bear some of the tax since it reduces the return on investment and therefore slows capital accumulation. It also causes corporations to relocate to other countries that have lower tax rates. With less capital per worker, U.S. labor productivity may decline and wages may fall. To the extent this happens, the corporate income tax may be somewhat regressive.

Payroll taxes (Social Security and Medicare) are regressive because the Social Security tax applies to only a fixed amount of income. For example, in 2008 the Social Security tax rate was 6.2 percent, but only of the first $102,000 of a person's wage income. The Medicare tax was 1.45 percent of all wage income. Someone earning exactly $102,000 would pay $7803, or 7.65 percent (6.2 percent + 1.45 percent) of his or her income. Someone with twice that wage income, or $204,000, would pay $9282 (= $7803 on the first $102,000 + $1479 on the second $102,000), which is only 5 percent of his or her wage income. So the average payroll tax falls as income rises, confirming that the payroll tax is regressive.

Most economists conclude that *property taxes* on buildings are regressive for the same reasons as are sales taxes. First, property owners add the tax to the rents they charge tenants. Second, property taxes, as a percentage of income, are higher for low-income families than for high-income families because the poor must spend a larger proportion of their incomes for housing. This alleged regressivity of property taxes may be increased by differences in property-tax rates from locality to locality. In general, property-tax rates are higher in poorer areas, to make up for lower property values.

Is the overall U.S. tax structure—Federal, state, and local taxes combined—progressive, proportional, or regressive? This question is difficult to answer. Estimates of the distribution of the total tax burden depend on the extent to which the various taxes are shifted to others, and who bears the ultimate burden is subject to dispute. But the majority view of economists is as follows:

- The Federal tax system is progressive. In 2005 (the latest year for which data have been compiled), the 20 percent of households with the lowest income paid an average Federal tax rate (on Federal income, payroll, and excise taxes) of 4.3 percent. The 20 percent with the highest income paid a 25.5 percent average rate; the top 10 percent paid 27.4 percent; and the top 1 percent paid 31.2 percent.[1]

---

[1]*Historical Effective Federal Tax Rates, 1979–2005*, Congressional Budget Office, December 2007.

- The state and local tax structures are largely regressive. As a percentage of income, property taxes and sales taxes fall as income rises. Also, state income taxes are generally less progressive than the Federal income tax.
- The overall U.S. tax system is slightly progressive. Higher-income people carry a slightly larger tax burden, as a percentage of their income, than do lower-income people.

Government's Role: A Qualification

Along with providing public goods and correcting externalities, government's economic role includes setting the rules and regulations for the economy, redistributing income when desirable, and taking macroeconomic actions to stabilize the economy.

Government does not have an easy task in performing its economic functions. In a democracy, government undertakes its economic role in the context of politics. To serve the public, politicians need to get elected. To stay elected, officials (presidents, senators, representatives, mayors, council members, school board members) need to satisfy their particular constituencies. At best, the political realities complicate government's role in the economy; at worst, they sometimes produce undesirable economic outcomes.

In the political context, some public goods and quasi-public goods may get produced not because their benefits exceed their costs but because their benefits accrue to firms located in states served by powerful elected officials. Inefficiency can easily creep into government activities because of the lack of a profit incentive to hold down costs. Indeed, the failure of programs to achieve their goals may simply lead to calls for more funding for the failed programs. Policies to correct negative externalities can be politically blocked by the very parties that are producing the spillovers. Overregulation can occur in some cases; underregulation, in others. Income can be redistributed to such an extent that incentives to work, save, and invest suffer. In short, the economic role of government, although critical to a well-functioning economy, is not always perfectly carried out.

Summary

1. Private goods are distinguished by rivalry (in consumption) and excludability. One person's purchase and consumption of a private good precludes others from also buying and consuming it. Producers can exclude nonpayers (free riders) from receiving the benefits. Competitive markets usually ensure that private goods are (a) available, (b) produced at minimum average cost, and (c) produced and sold in the "right" amounts.

2. Public goods are distinguished by nonrivalry (in consumption) and nonexcludability. Public goods are not profitable to private firms because nonpayers (free riders) can obtain and consume those goods. Only government is willing to provide desirable public goods.

3. The collective demand schedule for a particular public good is found by summing the prices that each individual is willing to pay for an additional unit. The optimal quantity of a public good occurs where the society's willingness to pay for the last unit—the marginal benefit of the good—equals the marginal cost of the good.

4. Cost-benefit analysis can provide guidance as to the economic desirability and optimal scope of public goods output.

5. Externalities cause the equilibrium output of certain goods to vary from their optimal output. Negative externalities (spillover costs) result in an overallocation of resources, which society can correct through private bargaining, legislation, or specific taxes. Positive externalities (spillover benefits) are accompanied by an underallocation of resources, which society can correct through private bargaining, subsidies to consumers, subsidies to producers, or government provision.

6. The Coase theorem holds that private bargaining is capable of solving potential externality problems where (a) the property rights are clearly defined, (b) the number of people involved is small, and (c) bargaining costs are negligible.

7. Clearly established property rights and liability rules enable private lawsuits that can prevent or remedy some negative externalities. Lawsuits, however, can be costly, time-consuming, and of uncertain result.

8. Direct controls and specific taxes can improve resource allocation in situations where negative externalities affect many people and community resources. Both direct controls (for example, smokestack emission standards) and specific taxes (for example, taxes on firms producing toxic chemicals) increase production costs and raise product price. As product price rises, the externality declines because less of the output is produced and purchased.

9. Markets for pollution rights, where firms can buy and sell the right to discharge a fixed amount of pollution, put a price on pollution and encourage firms to reduce or eliminate it. Markets for such rights (or "tradable credits") currently exist under terms of U.S. antipollution laws.

10. Government reallocates resources from the private sector to the public sector through taxation, which decreases after-tax income and therefore reduces the demand for private goods. Government then uses the tax revenues to finance the provision of public goods and quasi-public goods.

11. The benefits-received principle of taxation states that those who receive the benefits of goods and services provided by government should pay the taxes required to finance them. The ability-to-pay principle states that those who have greater income should be taxed more, absolutely and relatively, than those who have less income.

12. The Federal income tax is progressive (average tax rate rises as income rises). The corporate income tax is roughly proportional (average tax rate remains constant as income rises). General sales, excise, payroll, and property taxes are regressive (average tax rate falls as income rises). Overall, the U.S. tax system is slightly progressive.

Terms and Concepts

market failure	cost-benefit analysis	ability-to-pay principle
private goods	negative externalities	marginal tax rate
productive efficiency	positive externalities	average tax rate
allocative efficiency	Coase theorem	progressive tax
public goods	quasi-public goods	regressive tax
free-rider problem	benefits-received principle	proportional tax

Study Questions ![Mc Graw Hill] connect | economics

1. Use the characteristics of private goods to explain why firms can profitably offer them for sale. Why do competitive firms tend to produce private goods at minimum average cost? What do economists mean when they say that private goods tend to be produced in the "right" amounts? **LO1**

2. Contrast the characteristics of public goods with those of private goods. Why won't private firms produce public goods? **LO1**

3. The accompanying table relating to a public good provides information on the prices Young and Zorn are willing to pay for various quantities of that public good. These two people are the only members of society. Determine the price that society is willing to pay for the public good at each quantity of output. If the government's marginal cost of providing this public good is constant at $7, how many units of the public good should government provide? Why not less? Why not more? **LO2**

Young		Zorn		Society	
P	**Q$_d$**	**P**	**Q$_d$**	**P**	**Q$_d$**
$8	0	$8	1	$ ___	1
7	0	7	2	___	2
6	0	6	3	___	3
5	1	5	4	___	4
4	2	4	5	___	5
3	3	3	6	___	6
2	4	2	7	___	7
1	5	1	8	___	8

4. The table below shows the total costs and total benefits in billions for four different antipollution programs of increasing scope. Use cost-benefit analysis to determine which program should be undertaken. Explain. **LO2**

Program	Total Cost	Total Benefit
A	$ 3	$ 7
B	7	12
C	12	16
D	18	19

5. Why are negative externalities and positive externalities also called spillover costs and spillover benefits? Show graphically how a tax can correct for a negative externality and how a subsidy to producers can correct for a positive externality. How does a subsidy to consumers differ from a subsidy to producers in correcting for a positive externality? **LO3**

6. An apple grower's orchard provides nectar to a neighbor's bees, while the beekeeper's bees help the apple grower by pollinating the apple blossoms. Use Figure 4.1b to explain why this situation of dual positive externalities might lead to an underallocation of resources to apple growing and to beekeeping. How might this underallocation get resolved via the means suggested by the Coase theorem? **LO3**

7. Explain: "Without a market for pollution rights, dumping pollutants into the air or water is costless; in the presence of the right to buy and sell pollution rights, dumping pollutants creates an opportunity cost for the polluter." What is the significance of this opportunity cost to the search for better technology to reduce pollution? **LO3**

8. Explain the following statement, using cost-benefit analysis: "The optimal amount of pollution abatement for some substances, say, water from storm drains, is very low; the optimal amount of abatement for other substances, say, cyanide poison, is close to 100 percent." **LO3**

9. Explain how marketable emission credits add to overall economic efficiency, compared to across-the-board limitations on maximum discharges of air pollutants by firms. **LO3**

10. Contrast the benefits-received and ability-to-pay principles of taxation. Which of the following taxes mainly adhere to the benefits-received principle? Which mainly to the ability-to-pay principle? **LO4**

   a. An admission tax on tickets to sporting events at public stadiums.

   b. The Federal personal income tax.

   c. A sales tax applied only to certain luxury goods such as expensive automobiles, yachts, and private airplanes.

   d. A toll charge required for driving on a public highway.

   e. The Federal and state gasoline tax.

11. Suppose in Fiscalville there is no tax on the first $10,000 of income, but a 20 percent tax on earnings between $10,001 and $20,000 and a 30 percent tax on income between $20,001 and $30,000. Any income above $30,000 is taxed at 40 percent. If your income is $50,000, how much will you pay in taxes? Determine your marginal and average tax rates. Is this a progressive tax? Explain. **LO5**

Web-Based Questions

At the text's Online Learning Center, **www.mcconnellbriefmacro 1e.com,** you will find a multiple-choice quiz on this chapter's content. We encourage you to take the quiz to see how you do.

Also, you will find one or more Web-based questions that require information from the Internet to answer.

PART THREE

GDP, Growth, and Instability

5

GDP and Economic Growth

As you learned in Chapter 2, economists represent the economy as a circular flow of output (goods and services), income, and spending (Figure 2.2, p. 43). In our discussion of microeconomics, we examined how society can maximize output and income at any point in time by using the market system and government decisions to allocate society's limited resources to their highest valued uses.

We now want to turn to macroeconomics: the part of economics concerned with the economy as a whole. In this chapter we are interested in how economists measure the overall (aggregate) flow of goods and services in the circular flow diagram, both in total and on a per-person basis. Once that is established, we can examine the factors that expand the flow of goods and services over time and thus improve a society's standard of living. What are the main sources of such economic growth? Is economic growth desirable?

Gross Domestic Product

To examine the level of total output, total income, and total spending, we need to combine and measure the production, income, and spending of all the participants in the economy. The Bureau of Economic Analysis (BEA), an agency of the Commerce Department, does just that when it compiles the **national income and product accounts (NIPA)** for the U.S. economy. The BEA derives the NIPA data from Census Bureau surveys and information available from government agencies.

The primary measure of the economy's performance is its annual total output of goods and services. This output is called **gross domestic product (GDP):** the total market value of all final goods and services produced within the borders of a given country during a given period of time, typically a year. GDP includes all goods and services produced by either citizen-supplied or foreign-supplied resources employed within the country. If a final good or service is produced in the United States, it is part of U.S. GDP.

A Monetary Measure

If the economy produces three sofas and two computers in year 1 and two sofas and three computers in year 2, in which year is output greater? We can't answer that question until we attach a price tag to each of the two products to indicate how society evaluates their relative worth.

That's what GDP does. It is a *monetary measure*. Without such a measure we would have no way of comparing the relative values of the vast number of goods and services produced in different years. In Table 5.1 the price of sofas is $500 and the price of computers is $2000. GDP would gauge the output of year 2 ($7000) as greater than the output of year 1 ($5500) because society places a higher monetary value on the output of year 2. Society is willing to pay $1500 more for the combination of goods produced in year 2 than for the combination of goods produced in year 1.

Avoiding Multiple Counting

To measure aggregate output accurately, all goods and services produced in a particular year must be counted once and only once. Because most products go through a series of production stages before they reach the market, some of their components are bought and sold many times. To avoid counting those components each time, GDP includes only the market value of *final goods* and ignores *intermediate goods* altogether.

Intermediate goods are goods and services that are purchased for resale or for further processing or manufacturing. **Final goods** are consumption goods, capital goods, and services that are purchased by their final users, rather than for resale or for further processing or manufacturing.

Including the value of intermediate goods in calculating GDP would amount to *multiple counting*, and that would distort the value of GDP. For example, suppose that among other inputs an automobile manufacturer uses $4000 of steel, $2000 of glass, and $1000 of tires in producing a new automobile that sells for $20,000. The $20,000 final good already includes the $7000 of steel, glass, and tires. We would be greatly overstating GDP if we added the $7000 of components to the $20,000 price of the auto and obtained $27,000 of output.

national income and product accounts (NIPA)
The national accounts that measure the overall production and income of the economy for the nation as a whole.

gross domestic product (GDP)
The total market value of all final goods and services produced annually within the borders of the United States, whether by U.S. or foreign-supplied resources.

intermediate goods
Products that are purchased for resale or further processing or manufacturing.

final goods
Products, capital goods, and services that have been purchased for final use and not for resale or further processing or manufacturing.

TABLE 5.1 Comparing Heterogeneous Output by Using Money Prices

Year	Annual Output	Market Value
I	3 sofas and 2 computers	3 at $500 + 2 at $2000 = $5500
2	2 sofas and 3 computers	2 at $500 + 3 at $2000 = $7000

© Brand X Pictures/Punchstock

© Royalty-Free/CORBIS

Photo Op Intermediate versus Final Goods

Lumber is an intermediate good, and a new townhouse is a final good.

Excluding Secondhand Sales

Secondhand sales do not contribute to current production and therefore are excluded from GDP. If you sell your 1965 Ford Mustang to a friend, that transaction would be ignored in determining this year's GDP because it generates no current production. The same would be true if you sold a brand-new Mustang to a neighbor a week after you purchased it. It has already been counted in GDP.

© PhotoLink/Getty Images

Photo Op New Goods versus Secondhand Goods

The goods offered for sale at a shopping mall are new goods and therefore included in current GDP. In contrast, many of the goods sold through eBay are secondhand items and thus not part of current GDP.

Measuring GDP

The simplest way to measure GDP is to add up all that was spent to buy total output in a certain year. Economists use precise terms for the four categories of spending.

Personal Consumption Expenditures (C)

personal consumption expenditures (C)
Expenditures by households for durable goods, nondurable goods, and services.

The symbol C designates the **personal consumption expenditures** component of GDP. That term covers all expenditures by households on *durable consumer goods* (automobiles, refrigerators, cameras) that have lives of more than 3 years, *nondurable consumer goods* (bread, milk, toothpaste), and *consumer expenditures for services* (of lawyers, doctors, mechanics).

Gross Private Domestic Investment (I_g)

gross private domestic investment (I_g)
Expenditures for newly produced capital goods (such as plant and equipment) and for additions to inventories.

Under the heading **gross private domestic investment** are included (1) all final purchases of machinery, equipment, and tools by business enterprises; (2) all construction; and (3) changes in inventories.

Notice that this list, except for the first item, includes more than we have meant by "economic investment" so far. The second item includes residential construction as well as the construction of new factories, warehouses, and stores. Why is residential construction investment rather than consumption? Because apartment buildings and houses, like factories and stores, earn income when they are rented or leased. Owner-occupied houses are treated as investment goods because they *could be* rented to bring in an income return. So all residential construction is treated as investment. Finally, an increase in inventories (unsold goods) is investment because it is "unconsumed output." For economists, all new output either is consumed or is capital. An increase in inventories is an addition (although temporary) to the stock of capital goods, and such additions are precisely how we define investment.

Positive and Negative Changes in Inventories

We need to look at changes in inventories more closely. Inventories can either increase or decrease over some period. Suppose inventories rose by $10 billion between December 31, 2006, and December 31, 2007. That means the economy produced $10 billion more output than was purchased in 2007. We need to count all output produced in 2007 as part of that year's GDP, even though some of it remained unsold at the end of the year. This is accomplished by including the $10 billion increase in inventories as investment in 2007. That way the expenditures in 2007 will correctly measure the output produced that year.

Alternatively, suppose inventories fell by $10 billion in 2007. This "drawing down of inventories" means that the economy sold $10 billion more of output in 2007 than it produced that year. It did this by selling goods produced in prior years—goods already counted as GDP in those years. Unless corrected, expenditures in 2007 will overstate GDP for 2007. So in 2007 we consider the $10 billion decline in inventories as "negative investment" and subtract it from total investment that year. Thus, expenditures in 2007 will correctly measure the output produced in 2007.

Noninvestment Transactions

So much for what investment *is*. You also need to know what it *isn't*. Investment does *not* include the transfer of paper assets (stocks, bonds) or the resale of tangible assets (houses, factories). Such transactions merely transfer the ownership of existing assets. Investment has to do with the creation of *new* capital assets. The mere transfer (sale) of claims to existing capital goods does not create new capital.

Gross Investment As we have seen, the category "gross private domestic investment" includes (1) all final purchases of machinery, equipment, and tools; (2) all construction; and (3) changes in inventories. The words "private" and "domestic" mean that we are speaking of spending by private businesses, not by government (public) agencies, and that the investment is taking place inside the country, not abroad.

The word "gross" means that we are referring to *all* investment goods—both those that replace machinery, equipment, and buildings that were used up (worn out or made obsolete) in producing the current year's output and any net additions to the economy's stock of capital. Gross investment includes investment in replacement capital *and* in added capital. [As opposed to net investment, for which replacement capital (depreciation) is subtracted from gross investment.]

The symbol I represents private domestic investment spending, along with the subscript g to signify gross investment.

Government Purchases (G)

The third category of expenditures in the national income accounts is **government purchases,** officially labeled "government consumption expenditures and gross investment." These expenditures have two components: (1) expenditures for goods and services that government consumes in providing public services and (2) expenditures for *publicly owned capital* such as schools and highways, which have long lifetimes. Government purchases (Federal, state, and local) include all government expenditures on final goods and all direct purchases of resources, including labor. It does *not* include government transfer payments such as Social Security payments, unemployment compensation, and veterans' benefits, because they merely transfer government receipts to certain households and generate no *current* production. The symbol G signifies government purchases.

> government purchases (G)
> Government expenditures on final goods, services, and publicly owned capital.

Net Exports (X_n)

International trade transactions are a significant item in national income accounting. But when calculating U.S. GDP, we must keep in mind that we want to total up only those expenditures that are used to purchase goods and services produced *within the borders of the United States*. Thus, we must add in the value of exports, X, since exports are by definition goods and services produced within the borders of the United States. Don't be confused by the fact that the expenditures made to buy up our exports are made by foreigners. The definition of GDP does not care about *who* is making expenditures on U.S.-made goods and services—only that the goods and services that they buy are made within the borders of the United States. Thus, foreign spending on our exports must be included in GDP.

At this point, you might incorrectly think that GDP should be equal to the sum of $C + I_g + G + X$. But this sum overstates GDP. The problem is that, once again, we must consider only expenditures made on *domestically produced* goods and services. As it stands, C, I_g, and G count up expenditures on consumption, investment, and government purchases regardless of where those goods and services are made. Crucially, not all of the C, I_g, or G expenditures are for domestically produced goods and services. Some of the expenditures are for imports—goods and services produced outside of the United States. Thus, since we wish to count *only* the part of C, I_g, and G that goes to purchasing domestically produced goods and services, we must subtract off the spending that goes to imports, M. Doing so yields the correct formula for calculating gross domestic product:

$$GDP = C + I_g \times G + X - M.$$

net exports (X_n)
Exports minus imports.

Accountants simplify this formula for GDP by defining **net exports**, X_n, to be equal to exports minus imports:

$$\text{Net exports } (X_n) = \text{exports } (X) - \text{imports } (M).$$

Using this definition of net exports, the formula for gross domestic product simplifies to

$$\text{GDP} = C + I_g + G + X_n.$$

In 2007 Americans spent $708 billion more on imports than foreigners spent on U.S. exports. That is, net exports in 2007 were a minus $708 billion.

Adding It Up: GDP = $C + I_g + G + X_n$

Taken together, these four categories of expenditures provide a measure of the market value of a given year's total output—its GDP. For the United States in 2007,

$$\text{GDP} = \$9734 + 2125 + 2690 - 708 = \$13,841 \text{ billion (or }\$13.841 \text{ trillion)}$$

Global Snapshot 5.1 compares GDP in the United States to GDP in several other countries for 2007.

GLOBAL SNAPSHOT 5.1

Comparative GDPs in Trillions of U.S. Dollars, Selected Nations, 2007

The United States, Japan, and Germany have the world's highest GDPs. The GDP data charted below have been converted to dollars via international exchange rates.

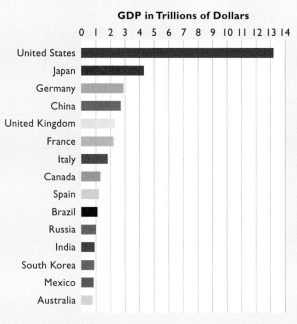

Source: World Bank, **www.worldbank.org**.

Nominal GDP versus Real GDP

Recall that GDP is a measure of the market or money value of all final goods and services produced by the economy in a given year. We use money or nominal values as a common denominator in order to sum that heterogeneous output into a meaningful total. But that creates a problem: How can we compare the market values of GDP from year to year if the value of money itself changes in response to inflation or deflation? After all, we determine the value of GDP by multiplying total output by market prices.

Whether there is a 5 percent increase in output with no change in prices or a 5 percent increase in prices with no change in output, the change in the monetary value of GDP will be the same. And yet it is the *quantity* of goods that get produced and distributed to households that affects our standard of living, not the price of the goods. The McDonald's hamburger that sold for 89 cents in 2007 yielded the same satisfaction as the nearly identical McDonald's hamburger that sold for 18 cents in 1967.

The way around this problem is to *deflate* GDP when prices rise and to *inflate* GDP when prices fall. These adjustments give us a measure of GDP for various years as if the value of the dollar had always been the same as it was in some reference year. A GDP based on the prices that prevailed when the output was produced is called *unadjusted GDP*, or **nominal GDP.** A GDP that has been deflated or inflated to reflect changes in the price level is called *adjusted GDP*, or **real GDP.**

Let's see how real GDP can be found. For simplicity, suppose the economy produces only one good, pizza, in the amounts indicated in Table 5.2 for years 1, 2, 3, 4, and 5. Also assume that we gather output and price data directly from the pizza business in various years. That is, we collect separate data on physical outputs (as in column 1) and their prices (as in column 2).

We can then determine the unadjusted, or nominal, GDP in each year by multiplying the number of units of output by the price per unit. Nominal GDP—here, the market value of pizza—is shown for each year in column 3.

We can also determine adjusted, or real, GDP from the data in Table 5.2. We want to know the market value of outputs in successive years *if the base-year price ($10) had prevailed.* In year 2, the 7 units of pizza would have a value of $70 (= 7 units × $10) at the year-1 price. As column 4 shows, that $70 worth of output is year 2's real GDP. Similarly, we can determine the real GDP for year 3 by multiplying the 8 units of output that year by the $10 price in the base year. You should check your understanding of nominal versus real GDP by completing columns 3 and 4, where we purposely left the last rows blank.

nominal GDP
Gross domestic product measured in terms of the price level at the time of measurement (i.e., GDP that is unadjusted for inflation).

real GDP
Gross domestic product measured in terms of the price level in a base period (i.e., GDP that is adjusted for inflation).

WORKED PROBLEMS

W 5.1

Real GDP and price indexes

TABLE 5.2 **Calculating Real GDP (Base Year = Year 1)**

Year	(1) Units of Output	(2) Price of Pizza per Unit	(3) Unadjusted, or Nominal, GDP, (1) × (2)	(4) Adjusted, or Real, GDP
1	5	$10	$ 50	$50
2	7	20	140	70
3	8	25	200	80
4	10	30	___	___
5	11	28	___	___

Let's return to the real economy. As previously determined, nominal GDP in the United States was $13,841 billion in 2007. What was real GDP that year? Because prices rose between the 2000 base year and 2007, real GDP in 2007 turned out to be $11,567 billion. Or, in the language of economics, "GDP in 2007 was $11,567 billion in 2000 (base-year) prices."

APPLYING THE ANALYSIS

The Underground Economy

Real GDP is a reasonably accurate and highly useful measure of how well or how poorly the economy is performing. But some production never shows up in GDP, which measures only the *market value* of output. Embedded in the U.S. economy is a flourishing, productive underground sector. Some of the people who conduct business there are gamblers, smugglers, prostitutes, "fences" of stolen goods, drug producers, and drug dealers. They have good reason to conceal their economic activities. When they do, their "contributions" to output do not show up in GDP.

Most participants in the underground economy, however, engage in perfectly legal activities but choose not to report their full incomes to the Internal Revenue Service (IRS). A bell captain at a hotel may report just a portion of the tips received from customers. Storekeepers may report only a portion of their sales receipts. Workers who want to hold on to their unemployment compensation benefits may take an "off-the-books" or "cash-only" job. A brick mason may agree to rebuild a neighbor's fireplace in exchange for the neighbor's repairing his boat engine. The value of none of these transactions shows up in GDP.

The value of underground transactions is estimated to be about 8 percent of the recorded GDP in the United States. That would mean that GDP in 2007 was understated by about $1107 billion. Global Snapshot 5.2 shows estimates of the relative sizes of underground economies in selected nations.

Question:
How would decriminalization of drugs instantly increase a nation's real GDP? What might be the downside of decriminalization of drugs for growth of real GDP over time?

Economic Growth

economic growth
The expansion of real GDP (or real GDP per capita) over time.

real GDP per capita
Real output divided by population.

The NIPA data enable economists to calculate and analyze economic growth rates. Economists define and measure **economic growth** as either an *increase in real* GDP occurring over time or an *increase in real GDP per capita* occurring over time. **Real GDP per capita** (or output per person) is found by dividing real GDP by the size of the population. With either definition, economic growth is calculated as a percentage rate of growth per quarter (3-month period) or per year.

GLOBAL SNAPSHOT 5.2

The Underground Economy as a Percentage of GDP, Selected Nations

Underground economies vary in size worldwide. Three factors that help explain the variation are (1) the extent and complexity of regulation, (2) the type and degree of taxation, and (3) the effectiveness of law enforcement.

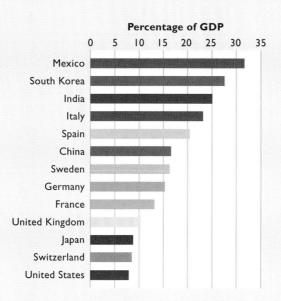

Source: Friedrich Schneider, "Shadow Economies and Corruption All over the World: New Estimates for 145 Countries," Economics: The Open Access—Open Assessment, E-Journal No. 2007–09, July 24, 2007.

For measuring expansion of military potential or political preeminence, the growth of real GDP is more useful. Unless specified otherwise, growth rates reported in the news and by international agencies use this definition of economic growth. For comparing living standards, however, the second definition is superior. While China's GDP in 2006 was $2644 billion compared with Denmark's $275 billion, Denmark's real GDP per capita was $52,110 compared with China's $2000.

Growth as a Goal

Economic growth is a widely held economic goal. The expansion of total output relative to population results in rising real wages and incomes and thus higher standards of living. An economy that is experiencing economic growth is better able to meet people's wants and resolve socioeconomic problems. Rising real wages and income provide richer opportunities to individuals and families—a vacation trip, a personal computer, a higher education—without sacrificing other opportunities and pleasures. A growing economy can undertake new programs to alleviate poverty and protect the environment without impairing existing levels of consumption, investment, and public goods production.

In short, *growth lessens the burden of scarcity.* A growing economy, unlike a static economy, can consume more today while increasing its capacity to produce more in the future. By easing the burden of scarcity—by relaxing society's constraints on production—economic growth enables a nation to attain its economic goals more readily and to undertake new endeavors that require the use of goods and services to be accomplished.

Arithmetic of Growth

WORKED PROBLEMS

W 5.2

GDP growth

The mathematical approximation called the *rule of 70* shows the effect of compounding of economic growth rates over time. It tells us that we can find the number of years it will take for some measure to double, given its annual percentage increase, by dividing that percentage increase into the number 70. So

$$\text{Approximate number of years required to double real GDP} = \frac{70}{\text{annual percentage rate of growth}}$$

Examples: A 3 percent annual rate of growth will double real GDP in about 23 (= 70/3) years. Growth of 8 percent per year will double it in about 9 (= 70/8) years.

ILLUSTRATING THE IDEA

Growth Rates Matter!

Small absolute differences in rates of economic growth add up to substantial differences in real GDP and standards of living. Consider three hypothetical countries—Slogo, Sumgo, and Speedo. Suppose that in 2008 these countries have identical levels of real GDP ($6 trillion), population (200 million), and real GDP per capita ($30,000). Also, assume that annual real GDP growth is 2 percent in Slogo, 3 percent in Sumgo, and 4 percent in Speedo.

How will these alternative growth rates affect real GDP and real GDP per capita over a long period, say, the 70-year average life span of an American? By 2078 the 2, 3, and 4 percent growth rates would boost real GDP from $6 trillion to $24 trillion in Slogo, $47 trillion in Sumgo, and $93 trillion in Speedo.

For illustration, let's assume that each country experienced an average annual population growth of 1 percent over the 70 years. Then, in 2078 real GDP per capita would be about $60,000 in Slogo, $118,000 in Sumgo, and $233,000 in Speedo.

No wonder economists pay so much attention to small changes in the rate of economic growth. For the United States, with a current real GDP of about $12 trillion, the difference between a 3 percent and a 4 percent rate of growth is about $120 billion of output each year. For a poor country, a difference of one-half of a percentage point in the rate of growth may mean the difference between starvation and mere hunger. Economic growth rates matter!

Question:
Why would gaps in GDP per capita for Slogo and Speedo be even more dramatic if population growth was faster in Slogo than in Speedo?

Growth in the United States

Table 5.3 gives an overview of economic growth in the United States over past periods. Column 2 reveals strong growth as measured by increases in real GDP. Note that real GDP increased more than sixfold between 1950 and 2007. But the U.S. population also increased over these years. Nevertheless, in column 4 we find that real GDP per capita rose more than threefold.

What has been the *rate* of U.S. growth? Real GDP grew at an annual rate of about 3.5 percent between 1950 and 2007. Real GDP per capita increased about 2.3 percent per year over that time.

Viewed from the perspective of the last half-century, economic growth in the United States lagged behind that in Japan, Germany, Italy, Canada, and France. Japan's annual growth rate, in fact, averaged twice that of the United States. But economic growth since 1997 is quite another matter. As shown in Global Snapshot 5.3, until 2007, the U.S. growth rate generally topped the rates of growth in Japan and other major industrial nations.

(1) Year	(2) Real GDP, Billions of 2000 $	(3) Population, Millions	(4) Real Per Capita GDP, 2000 $ (2) ÷ (3)
1950	$ 1777	152	$11,691
1960	2502	181	13,823
1970	3772	205	18,400
1980	5162	228	22,640
1990	7113	250	28,452
2000	9817	282	34,812
2005	11,135	297	37,491
2007	11,567	303	38,174

TABLE 5.3 **Real GDP and per Capita Real GDP, Selected Years, 1950–2007**

Source: Bureau of Economic Analysis, **www.bea.doc.gov,** and U.S. Census Bureau, **www.census.gov.**

GLOBAL SNAPSHOT 5.3

Average Annual Growth Rates, 1997–2007, Selected Nations

Between 1997 and 2006, economic growth in the United States exceeded that of several other major countries. U.S. economic growth greatly slowed in 2001 and 2002 before rising again in 2003 and 2004. U.S. growth slowed again in 2007.

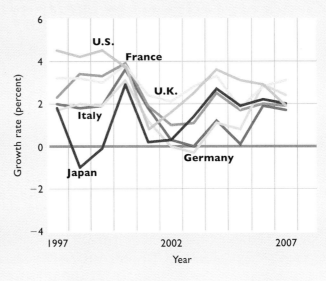

Source: *Economic Report of the President, 2006 and 2008.*

Ingredients of Growth

There are six main ingredients in economic growth. We can group them as supply, demand, and efficiency factors.

Supply Factors

Four of the ingredients of economic growth relate to the physical ability of the economy to expand. They are:

- Increases in the quantity and quality of natural resources.
- Increases in the quantity and quality of human resources.
- Increases in the supply (or stock) of capital goods.
- Improvements in technology.

These *supply factors*—changes in the physical and technical agents of production—enable an economy to expand its potential GDP.

Demand Factor

The fifth ingredient of economic growth is the *demand factor:*

- To achieve the higher production potential created by the supply factors, households, businesses, and government must *purchase* the economy's expanding output of goods and services.

When that occurs, there will be no unplanned increases in inventories and resources will remain fully employed. Economic growth requires increases in total spending to realize the output gains made available by increased production capacity.

Efficiency Factor
The sixth ingredient of economic growth is the *efficiency factor:*

- To reach its full production potential, an economy must achieve economic efficiency as well as full employment.

The economy must use its resources in the least costly way (productive efficiency) to produce the specific mix of goods and services that maximizes people's well-being (allocative efficiency). The ability to expand production, together with the full use of available resources, is not sufficient for achieving maximum possible growth. Also required is the efficient use of those resources.

The supply, demand, and efficiency factors in economic growth are related. Unemployment caused by insufficient total spending (the demand factor) may lower the rate of new capital accumulation (a supply factor) and delay expenditures on research (also a supply factor). Conversely, low spending on investment (a supply factor) may cause insufficient spending (the demand factor) and unemployment. Widespread inefficiency in the use of resources (the efficiency factor) may translate into higher costs of goods and services and thus lower profits, which in turn may slow innovation and reduce the accumulation of capital (supply factors). Economic growth is a dynamic process in which the supply, demand, and efficiency factors all interact.

ORIGIN OF THE IDEA

O 5.1

Growth theory

Production Possibilities Analysis
To put the six factors affecting the rate of economic growth into better perspective, let's use the production possibilities analysis introduced in Chapter 1.

Growth and Production Possibilities
Recall that a curve like *AB* in Figure 5.1 is a production possibilities curve. It indicates the various *maximum* combinations of products an economy can produce with its fixed quantity and quality of natural, human, and capital resources and its stock of technological knowledge. An improvement in any of the supply factors will push the production possibilities curve outward, as from *AB* to *CD*.

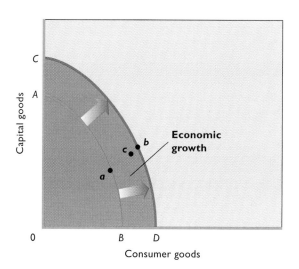

FIGURE 5.1 Economic growth and the production possibilities curve. Economic growth is made possible by the four supply factors that shift the production possibilities curve outward, as from *AB* to *CD*. Economic growth is realized when the demand factor and the efficiency factor move the economy from point *a* to *b*.

But the demand factor reminds us that an increase in total spending is needed to move the economy from a point like *a* on curve *AB* to any of the points on the higher curve *CD*. And the efficiency factor reminds us that we need least-cost production and an optimal location on *CD* for the resources to make their maximum possible dollar contribution to total output. You will recall from Chapter 1 that this "best allocation" is determined by expanding production of each good until its marginal cost equals its marginal benefit. Here, we assume that this optimal combination of capital and consumer goods occurs at point *b*.

Example: The net increase in the size of the labor force in the United States in recent years has been 1.5 million to 2 million workers per year. That increment raises the economy's production capacity. But obtaining the extra output that these added workers could produce depends on their success in finding jobs. It also depends on whether or not the jobs are in firms and industries where the workers' talents are fully and optimally used. Society does not want new labor-force entrants to be unemployed. Nor does it want pediatricians working as plumbers or pediatricians producing services for which marginal costs exceed marginal benefits.

Normally, increases in total spending match increases in production capacity, and the economy moves from a point on the previous production possibilities curve to a point on the expanded curve. Moreover, the competitive market system tends to drive the economy toward productive and allocative efficiency. Occasionally, however, the curve may shift outward but leave the economy behind at some level of operation such as *c* in Figure 5.1. Because *c* is inside the new production possibilities curve *CD*, the economy has not realized its potential for economic growth.

Inputs and Productivity

Society can increase its output and income in two fundamental ways: (1) by increasing its inputs of resources and (2) by raising the productivity of those inputs. Figure 5.2 concentrates on the input of *labor* and provides a useful framework for discussing the role of supply factors in growth. A nation's real GDP in any year depends on the input of labor (measured in hours of work) multiplied by **labor productivity** (measured as real output per hour of work).

So, thought of this way, a nation's economic growth from one year to the next depends on its *increase* in labor inputs (if any) and its *increase* in labor productivity (if any).

Illustration: Assume that the cool economy of Rapland has 10 workers in year 1, each working 2000 hours per year (50 weeks at 40 hours per week). The total input of

labor productivity
Real output per hour of work.

FIGURE 5.2 **The supply determinants of real output.** Real GDP is usefully viewed as the product of the quantity of labor inputs (hours of work) multiplied by labor productivity.

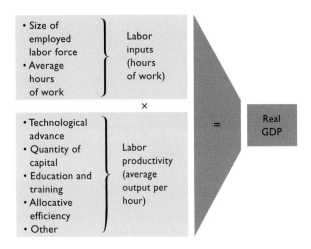

labor therefore is 20,000 hours. If productivity (average real output per hour of work) is $10, then real GDP in Rapland will be $200,000 (= 20,000 × $10). If work hours rise to 20,200 and labor productivity rises to $10.40, Rapland's real GDP will increase to $210,080 in year 2. Rapland's rate of economic growth will be about 5 percent [= ($210,080 − $200,000)/$200,000] for the year.

Hours of Work   What determines the number of hours worked each year? As shown in Figure 5.2, the hours of labor input depend on the size of the employed labor force and the length of the average workweek. Labor-force size depends on the size of the working-age population and the **labor-force participation rate**—the percentage of the working-age population actually in the labor force. The length of the average workweek is governed by legal and institutional considerations and by collective bargaining.

labor-force participation rate
The percentage of the working-age population actually in the labor force.

Labor Productivity   Figure 5.2 tells us that labor productivity is determined by technological progress, the quantity of capital goods available to workers, the quality of the labor itself, and the efficiency with which inputs are allocated, combined, and managed. Productivity rises when the health, training, education, and motivation of workers improve, when workers have more and better machinery and natural resources with which to work, when production is better organized and managed, and when labor is reallocated from less efficient industries to more efficient industries.

Accounting for Growth

The Council of Economic Advisers uses a system called **growth accounting** to assess the relative importance of the supply-side elements that contribute to changes in real GDP. This system groups these elements into the two main categories we have just discussed:

growth accounting
The bookkeeping of the supply-side elements that contribute to changes in real GDP.

- Increases in hours of work.
- Increases in labor productivity.

Labor Inputs versus Labor Productivity

Table 5.4 provides the relevant data for four periods. The symbol "Q" in the table stands for "quarter" of the year. The beginning points for three of the four periods are business-cycle peaks, and the last column includes future projections by the Council of Economic Advisers. It is clear from the table that both increases in the quantity of labor and rises in labor productivity are important sources of economic growth. Between 1953 and 2007, the labor force increased from 63 million to 154 million workers. Over that period the average length of the workweek remained relatively stable. Falling birthrates slowed the growth of the native population, but increased immigration partly

TABLE 5.4
Accounting for Growth of Real GDP, 1953–2013 (Average Annual Percentage Changes)*

Item	1953 Q2 to 1973 Q4	1973 Q4 to 1995 Q2	1995 Q2 to 2001 Q1	2001 Q1 to 2007 Q3	2007 Q3 to 2013 Q4*
Increase in real GDP	3.6	2.8	3.8	2.6	2.8
Increase in quantity of labor	1.1	1.3	1.4	−0.1	0.3
Increase in labor productivity	2.5	1.5	2.4	2.7	2.5

*Rates beyond 2007 are projected rates.

Source: Derived from *Economic Report of the President, 2008,* p. 45.

offset that slowdown. Of particular significance was a surge of women's participation in the labor force, from 34 percent in 1953 to 59 percent in 2007. Partly as a result, U.S. labor-force growth averaged 1.7 million workers per year over the past 54 years.

The growth of labor productivity has also been important to economic growth. In fact, productivity growth has usually been the more significant factor, with the exception of 1973–1995 when productivity growth greatly slowed. For example, between 2001 and 2007, productivity growth was responsible for all of the 2.6 percent average annual economic growth. Between 2007 and 2013, productivity growth is projected to account for 90 percent of the growth of real GDP.

Because increases in labor productivity are so important to economic growth, economists go to the trouble of investigating and assessing the relative importance of the factors that contribute to productivity growth. There are five factors that, together, appear to explain changes in productivity growth rates. They are technological advance, the amount of capital each worker has to work with, education and training, economies of scale, and resource allocation. We will examine each factor in turn, noting how much each factor contributes to productivity growth.

Technological Advance

The largest contributor to productivity growth is technological advance, which is thought to account for about 40 percent of productivity growth. As economist Paul Romer has stated, "Human history teaches us that economic growth springs from better recipes, not just from more cooking."

Technological advance includes not only innovative production techniques but new managerial methods and new forms of business organization that improve the process of production. Generally, technological advance is generated by the discovery of new knowledge, which allows resources to be combined in improved ways that increase output. Once discovered and implemented, new knowledge soon becomes available to entrepreneurs and firms at relatively low cost. Technological advance therefore eventually spreads through the entire economy, boosting productivity and economic growth.

Technological advance and capital formation (investment) are closely related because technological advance usually promotes investment in new machinery and equipment. In fact, technological advance is often *embodied* within new capital. For example, the purchase of new computers brings into industry speedier, more powerful computers that incorporate new technology.

Technological advance has been both rapid and profound. Gas and diesel engines, conveyor belts, and assembly lines are significant developments of the past. So, too, are fuel-efficient commercial aircraft, integrated microcircuits, personal computers, digital photography, and containerized shipping. More recently, technological advance has exploded, particularly in the areas of computers, wireless communications, and the Internet. Other fertile areas of recent innovation are medicine and biotechnology.

Quantity of Capital

A second major contributor to productivity growth is increased capital, which explains roughly 30 percent of productivity growth. More and better plant and equipment make workers more productive. And a nation acquires more capital by saving some of its income and using that saving to invest in plant and equipment.

Although some capital substitutes for labor, most capital is complementary to labor—it makes labor more productive. A key determinant of labor productivity is the amount of capital goods available *per worker*. If both the aggregate stock of capital goods and the size of the labor force increase over a given period, the individual worker is not necessarily better equipped and productivity will not necessarily rise. But the quantity of capital equipment available per U.S. worker has increased greatly over time. (In 2006 it was about $97,140 per worker.)

Public investment in the U.S. **infrastructure** (highways and bridges, public transit systems, water and sewage systems, airports, industrial parks, educational facilities, and so on) has also grown over the years. This publicly owned capital complements private capital. Investments in new highways promote private investment in new factories and retail stores along their routes. Industrial parks developed by local governments attract manufacturing and distribution firms.

Private investment in infrastructure also plays a large role in economic growth. One example is the tremendous growth of private capital relating to communications systems over the years.

Education and Training

Ben Franklin once said, "He that hath a trade hath an estate," meaning that education and training contribute to a worker's stock of **human capital**—the knowledge and skills that make a worker productive. Investment in human capital includes not only formal education but also on-the-job training. Like investment in physical capital, investment in human capital is an important means of increasing labor productivity and earnings. An estimated 15 percent of productivity growth derives from investments in people's education and skills.

infrastructure
Public and private capital goods that buttress an economy's production capacity (for example, highways, bridges, airports, public transit systems, waste-water treatment facilities, educational facilities, and telecommunications systems that complement private capital).

human capital
The knowledge and skills that make a worker productive.

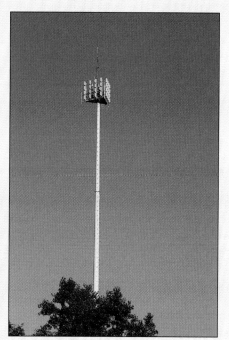

© Medioimages/Superstock   © Royalty-Free/CORBIS

PHOTO OP Public and Private Investment in Infrastructure

Both public infrastructure investments (such as highways and bridges) and private infrastructure investments (such as wireless communications systems) have increased the nation's stock of private and public capital and help expand real GDP.

FIGURE 5.3 Changes in the educational attainment of the U.S. adult population. The percentage of the U.S. adult population, age 25 or more, completing high school and college has been rising over recent decades. Source: U.S. Census Bureau, **www.census.gov**.

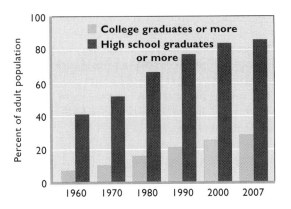

One measure of a nation's quality of labor is its level of educational attainment. Figure 5.3 shows large gains in educational attainment over the past several decades. In 1960 only 41 percent of the U.S. population age 25 or older had at least a high school education; and only 8 percent had a college education or more. By 2007, those numbers had increased to 86 and 29 percent, respectively. Clearly, more people are receiving an education than ever before.

But all is not upbeat with education in the United States. Many observers think that the quality of education in the United States has declined. For example, U.S. students in science and mathematics perform poorly on tests on those subjects relative to students in many other nations. The United States has been producing fewer native-born engineers and scientists, a problem that may trace back to inadequate training in math and science in elementary and high schools. For these reasons, much recent public policy discussion and legislation have been directed toward improving the quality of the U.S. education and training system.

Economies of Scale and Resource Allocation

Economies of scale and improved resource allocation are a fourth and fifth source of productivity growth, and together they explain about 15 percent of productivity growth.

Economies of Scale

economies of scale Reductions in per-unit production costs that result from increases in the size of markets and firms.

Reductions in per-unit production costs that result from increases in output levels are called **economies of scale.** Markets have increased in size over time, allowing firms to increase output levels and thereby achieve production advantages associated with greater size. As firms expand their size and output, they are able to use larger, more productive equipment and employ methods of manufacturing and delivery that increase productivity. They also are better able to recoup substantial investments in developing new products and production methods. Examples: A large manufacturer of autos can use elaborate assembly lines with computerization and robotics, while smaller producers must settle for less-advanced technologies using more labor inputs. Large pharmaceutical firms greatly reduce the average amount of labor (researchers, production workers) needed to produce each pill as they increase the number of pills produced. Accordingly, economies of scale result in greater real GDP and thus contribute to economic growth.

Improved Resource Allocation

Improved resource allocation means that workers over time have moved from low-productivity employment to high-productivity employment. Historically, many workers have shifted from agriculture, where labor productivity is low, to manufacturing, where it is quite high. More recently, labor has shifted away from some manufacturing industries to even higher-productivity industries such as computer software, business consulting, and pharmaceuticals. As a result of such shifts, the average productivity of U.S. workers has increased.

Also, we will discover in Chapter 12 that tariffs, import quotas, and other barriers to international trade tend to relegate resources to relatively unproductive pursuits. The long-run movement toward liberalized international trade through international agreements has improved the allocation of resources, increased labor productivity, and expanded real output, both here and abroad.

Finally, discrimination in education and the labor market has historically deterred some women and minorities from entering high-productivity jobs. With the decline of such discrimination over time, many members of those groups have shifted from low-productivity jobs to higher-productivity jobs. The result has been higher overall labor productivity and real GDP.

Institutional Structures That Promote Growth

Economic historians have identified several institutional structures that promote and sustain modern economic growth. Some structures increase the savings and investment that are needed to fund the construction and maintenance of the huge amounts of infrastructure required to run modern economies. Other institutional structures promote the development of new technologies. And still others act to ensure that resources flow efficiently to their most productive uses. These growth-promoting institutional structures include

- *Strong property rights*   These appear to be absolutely necessary for rapid and sustained economic growth. People will not invest if they believe that thieves, bandits, or a rapacious and tyrannical government will steal their investments or their expected returns.

- *Patents and copyrights*   These are necessary if a society wants a constant flow of innovative new technologies and sophisticated new ideas. Before patents and copyrights were first issued and enforced, inventors and authors usually saw their ideas stolen before they could profit from them. By giving inventors and authors the exclusive right to market and sell their creations, patents and copyrights give a strong financial incentive to invent and create.

- *Efficient financial institutions*   These are needed to channel the savings generated by households towards the businesses, entrepreneurs, and inventors that do most of society's investing and inventing. Banks as well as stock and bond markets appear to be institutions crucial to modern economic growth.

- *Free trade*   Free trade promotes economic growth by allowing countries to specialize so that different types of output can be produced in the countries where they can be made most efficiently. In addition, free trade promotes the rapid spread of new ideas so that innovations made in one country quickly spread to other countries.

- *A competitive market system*   Under a market system, prices and profits serve as the signals that tell firms what to make and how much of it to make. Rich leader countries vary substantially in terms of how much government regulation they impose on markets, but in all cases, firms have substantial autonomy to follow market signals not only in terms of current production but also in terms of the investments they will currently make to produce what they believe consumers will demand in the future.

Other Factors

Several other difficult-to-measure factors also influence a nation's capacity for economic growth. The overall social-cultural-political environment of the United States, for example, has encouraged economic growth. Beyond the market system that has prevailed in the United States, the nation also has had a stable political system characterized by democratic principles, internal order, the right of property ownership, the legal status of enterprise, and the enforcement of contracts. Economic freedom and political freedom have been "growth-friendly."

In addition, and unlike some nations, there are virtually no social or moral taboos on production and material progress in the United States. The nation's social philosophy has embraced wealth creation as an attainable and desirable goal and the inventor, the innovator, and the businessperson are accorded high degrees of prestige and respect in American society. Finally, Americans have a positive attitude toward work and risk taking, resulting in an ample supply of willing workers and innovative entrepreneurs. A flow of energetic immigrants has greatly augmented that supply.

The Recent Productivity Acceleration

Figure 5.4 shows the growth of labor productivity (as measured by changes in the index of labor productivity for the full business sector) in the United States from 1973 to 2007, along with separate trend lines for 1973–1995 and 1995–2007. Labor productivity grew by an average of only 1.4 percent yearly over the 1973–1995 period. But productivity growth averaged 2.7 percent between 1995 and 2007. Many economists believe that this higher productivity growth resulted from a significant new wave of technological advance, coupled with global competition. Some economists are hopeful that the higher trend rates of productivity growth may be permanent.

This increase in productivity growth is important because real output, real income, and real wages are linked to labor productivity. To see why, suppose you are alone on an uninhabited island. The number of fish you can catch or coconuts you can pick per hour—your productivity—is your real wage (or real income) per hour. By *increasing* your productivity, you can improve your standard of living because greater output per hour means there are more fish and coconuts (goods) available to consume.

FIGURE 5.4 Growth of labor productivity in the United States, 1973–2007. U.S. labor productivity (here, for the business sector) increased at an average annual rate of only 1.4 percent from 1973 to 1995. But between 1995 and 2007 it accelerated to an annual rate of 2.7 percent. Source: U.S. Bureau of Labor Statistics, **www.bls.gov**.

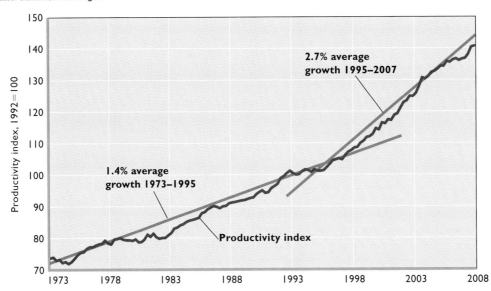

So it is for the economy as a whole: Over long periods, the economy's labor productivity determines its average real hourly wage. The economy's income per hour is equal to its output per hour. Productivity growth therefore is its main route for increasing its standard of living. It allows firms to pay higher wages without lowering their business profits. Even a seemingly small percentage change in productivity growth, if sustained over several years, can make a substantial difference as to how fast a nation's standard of living rises. We know from the *rule of 70* that if a nation's productivity grows by 2.7 percent annually rather than 1.4, its standard of living will double in 26 years rather than 50 years. That is a big deal!

Reasons for the Productivity Acceleration

Why has productivity growth increased relative to earlier periods?

The Microchip and Information Technology The core element of the productivity speedup is an explosion of entrepreneurship and innovation based on the microprocessor, or *microchip*, which bundles transistors on a piece of silicon. Some observers liken the invention of the microchip to that of electricity, the automobile, air travel, the telephone, and television in importance and scope.

The microchip has found its way into thousands of applications. It has helped create a wide array of new products and services and new ways of doing business. Its immediate results were the pocket calculator, the bar-code scanner, the personal computer, the laptop computer, and more powerful business computers. But the miniaturization of electronic circuits also advanced the development of many other products such as cell phones and pagers, computer-guided lasers, deciphered genetic codes, global positioning equipment, energy conservation systems, Doppler radar, and digital cameras.

Perhaps of greatest significance, the widespread availability of personal and laptop computers stimulated the desire to tie them together. That desire promoted rapid development of the Internet and all its many manifestations, such as business-to-household and business-to-business electronic commerce (*e-commerce*). The combination of the computer, fiber optic cable, wireless technology, and the Internet constitutes a spectacular advance in **information technology**, which has been used to connect all parts of the world.

> **information technology**
> New and more efficient methods of delivering and receiving information through use of computers, fax machines, wireless phones, and the Internet.

New Firms and Increasing Returns Hundreds of new **start-up firms** advanced various aspects of the new information technology. Many of these firms created more "hype" than goods and services and quickly fell by the wayside. But a number of firms flourished, eventually to take their places among the nation's largest firms. Examples of those firms include Intel (microchips); Apple and Dell (personal computers); Microsoft and Oracle (computer software); Cisco Systems (Internet switching systems); Yahoo and Google (Internet search engines); and Amazon.com (electronic commerce). There are scores more! Most of these firms were either "not on the radar" or "a relatively small blip on the radar" 30 years ago. Today each of them has large annual revenue and employs thousands of workers.

> **start-up firms**
> New firms focused on creating and introducing particular new products or employing specific new production or distribution methods.

Successful new firms often experience **increasing returns,** a situation in which a given percentage increase in the amount of inputs a firm uses leads to an even larger percentage increase in the amount of output the firm produces. For example, suppose that a company called Techco decides to double the size of its operations to meet the growing demand for its services. After doubling its plant and equipment and doubling its workforce, say, from 100 workers to 200 workers, it finds that its total output has tripled from 8000 units to 24,000 units. Techco has experienced increasing returns; its output has increased by 200 percent, while its inputs have increased by only

> **increasing returns**
> A firm's output increases by a larger percentage than the increase in its inputs.

100 percent. That is, its labor productivity has gone up from 80 units per worker (= 8000 units/100 workers) to 120 units per worker (= 24,000 units/200 workers). Increasing returns boost labor productivity and lower per-unit production costs. Since these cost reductions result from increases in output levels, they are examples of *economices of scale.*

Both emerging firms as well as established firms can exploit several different sources of increasing returns and economies of scale:

- *More specialized inputs*   Firms can use more specialized and thus more productive capital and workers as they expand their operations. A growing new e-commerce business, for example, can purchase highly specialized inventory management systems and hire specialized personnel such as accountants, marketing managers, and system maintenance experts.
- *Spreading of development costs*   Firms can spread high product development costs over greater output. For example, suppose that a new software product costs $100,000 to develop and only $2 per unit to manufacture and sell. If the firm sells 1000 units of the software, its cost per unit will be $102 [= ($100,000 + $2000)/1000], but if it sells 500,000 units, that cost will drop to only $2.20 [= ($100,000 + $1 million)/500,000].
- *Simultaneous consumption*   Many recently developed products and services can satisfy large numbers of customers at the same time. Unlike a gallon of gas that needs to be produced for each buyer, a software program needs to be produced only once. It then becomes available at very low expense to thousands or even millions of buyers. The same is true of entertainment delivered on CDs, movies distributed on DVDs, and information disseminated through the Internet.
- *Network effects*   Software and Internet service become more beneficial to a buyer the greater the number of households and businesses that also buy them. When others have Internet service, you can send e-mail messages to them. And when they also have software that allows display of documents and photos, you can attach those items to your e-mail messages. These system advantages are called **network effects,** which are increases in the value of the product to each user, including existing users, as the total number of users rises. The domestic and global expansion of the Internet in particular has produced network effects, as have cell phones, pagers, palm computers, and other aspects of wireless communication. Network effects magnify the value of output well beyond the costs of inputs.
- *Learning by doing*   Finally, firms that produce new products or pioneer new ways of doing business experience increasing returns through **learning by doing.** Tasks that initially may have taken firms hours may take them only minutes once the methods are perfected.

network effects
Increases in the value of a product to each user, including existing users, as the total number of users rises.

learning by doing
Achieving greater productivity and lower average total costs through gains in knowledge and skill that accompany repetition of a task.

Whatever the particular source of increasing returns, the result is higher productivity, which tends to reduce the per-unit cost of producing and delivering products.

Global Competition

The recent economy is characterized not only by information technology and increasing returns but also by heightened global competition. The collapse of the socialist economies in the late 1980s and early 1990s, together with the success of market systems, has led to a reawakening of capitalism throughout the world. The new information technologies have "shrunk the globe" and made it imperative for all firms to lower their costs and prices and to innovate in order to remain competitive. Free-trade zones such as those created by the North American Free Trade Agreement (NAFTA) and the European Union (EU) also have heightened competition internationally by removing trade protection from domestic firms. So, too, has trade liberalization through the World Trade Organization (WTO). The larger geographic markets and lower tariffs, in turn, have enabled emerging and old-line firms to expand beyond their national borders.

Implication: More Rapid Economic Growth

Other things equal, stronger productivity growth and heightened global competition allow the economy to achieve a higher rate of economic growth. A glance back at Figure 5.1 will help make this point. Suppose that the shift of the production possibilities curve from *AB* to *CD* reflects annual changes in potential output levels before the recent increase in growth rates. Then the higher growth rates of the more recent period of accelerated productivity growth would be depicted by a *larger* outward shift of the economy's production possibilities from *AB* to a curve beyond *CD*. When coupled with economic efficiency and increased total spending, the economy's real GDP would rise by more than that shown.

A caution: Economists who believe that the higher productivity growth rates experienced in recent years are likely to continue do not believe that the business cycle is dead. Their contention is limited to the belief that the *trend lines* of productivity growth and economic growth have become steeper. Real output may periodically deviate below and above the steeper trend; in 2001 the economy slowed in the first two months and receded over the following eight months of that year. The economy slowed again during the fourth quarter of 2007 and receded in 2008.

© Royalty-Free/CORBIS

Courtesy of Google Inc.

© age fotostock/SuperStock

Photo Op Key Elements of the U.S. Productivity Acceleration

A combination of information technology, emerging new firms, and globalization helps explain the speedup in U.S. productivity growth since 1995.

Skepticism about Permanence

Although most macroeconomists have revised their forecasts for long-term productivity growth upward, at least slightly, others are still skeptical and urge a "wait-and-see" approach. These macroeconomists acknowledge that the economy has experienced a rapid advance of new technology, some new firms have experienced increasing returns, and global competition has increased. But they wonder if these factors are sufficiently profound to produce a 15- to 20-year period of substantially higher rates of productivity growth and real GDP growth.

They also point out that productivity surged between 1975 and 1978 and between 1983 and 1986 but in each case soon reverted to its lower long-run trend. The higher trend line of productivity inferred from the short-run spurt of productivity could prove to be an illusion. Only by looking backward over long periods can economists distinguish the start of a new long-run trend from a shorter-term boost in productivity related to the business cycle and temporary factors.

What Can We Conclude?

Given the different views on the recent productivity acceleration, what should we conclude? Perhaps the safest conclusions are these:

- The prospects for a lasting increase in productivity growth are good (see Global Snapshot 5.4). Studies indicate that productivity increases related to information technology have spread to a wide range of industries, including services. Even in the recession year 2001 and in 2002, when the economy was sluggish, productivity growth remained strong. Specifically, it averaged about 3.3 percent in the business sector over those two years. Productivity rose by 4.1 percent in 2003, 3.5 percent in 2004, and 2.7 percent in 2005 as the economy vigorously expanded.

- Time will tell. Productivity growth was just 1.0 percent in 2006 and 1.9 percent in 2007. Whether this is a temporary decline or not is uncertain. It will be several more years before economists can declare the post-1995 productivity acceleration to be a sustained, long-term trend.

GLOBAL SNAPSHOT 5.4

Global Competitiveness Index

The World Economic Forum annually compiles a global competitiveness index, which uses various factors (such as innovativeness, effective transfer of technology among sectors, efficiency of the financial system, rates of investment, and degree of integration with the rest of the world) to measure the ability of a country to achieve economic growth over time. Here is its top 10 list for 2007.

Country	Global Competitiveness Ranking, 2007
United States	1
Switzerland	2
Denmark	3
Sweden	4
Germany	5
Finland	6
Singapore	7
Japan	8
United Kingdom	9
Netherlands	10

Source: World Economic Forum, **www.weforum.org**.

Is Growth Desirable and Sustainable?

Economists typically see economic growth as desirable and sustainable. But not all social observers agree.

The Antigrowth View

Critics of growth say industrialization and growth result in pollution, global warming, ozone depletion, and other environmental problems. These adverse spillover costs occur because inputs in the production process reenter the environment as some form of waste. The more rapid our growth and the higher our standard of living, the more waste the environment must absorb—or attempt to absorb. In an already wealthy society, further growth usually means satisfying increasingly trivial wants at the cost of mounting threats to the ecological system.

Critics of growth also argue that there is little compelling evidence that economic growth has solved sociological problems such as poverty, homelessness, and discrimination. Consider poverty: In the antigrowth view, American poverty (and, for that matter, world poverty) is a problem of distribution, not production. The requisite for solving the problem is commitment and political courage to redistribute wealth and income, not further increases in output.

Antigrowth sentiment also says that while growth may permit us to "make a better living," it does not give us "the good life." We may be producing more and enjoying it less. Growth means frantic paces on jobs, worker burnout, and alienated employees who have little or no control over decisions affecting their lives. The changing technology at the core of growth poses new anxieties and new sources of insecurity for workers. Both high-level and low-level workers face the prospect of having their hard-earned skills and experience rendered obsolete by an onrushing technology. High-growth economies are high-stress economies, which may impair our physical and mental health.

Finally, critics of high rates of growth doubt that they are sustainable. The planet Earth has finite amounts of natural resources available, and they are being consumed at alarming rates. Higher rates of economic growth simply speed up the degradation and exhaustion of the earth's resources. In this view, slower economic growth that is sustainable is preferable to faster growth.

In Defense of Economic Growth

The primary defense of growth is that it is the path to the greater material abundance and higher living standards desired by the vast majority of people. Rising output and incomes allow people to buy

> more education, recreation, and travel, more medical care, closer communications, more skilled personal and professional services, and better-designed as well as more numerous products. It also means more art, music, and poetry, theater, and drama. It can even mean more time and resources devoted to spiritual growth and human development.[1]

Growth also enables society to improve the nation's infrastructure, enhance the care of the sick and elderly, provide greater access for the disabled, and provide more police and fire protection. Economic growth may be the only realistic way to reduce poverty, since there is little political support for greater redistribution of income. The way to improve the economic position of the poor is to increase household incomes through higher productivity and economic growth. Also, a no-growth policy among industrial nations might severely limit growth in poor nations. Foreign investment and development assistance in those nations would fall, keeping the world's poor in poverty longer.

Economic growth has not made labor more unpleasant or hazardous, as critics suggest. New machinery is usually less taxing and less dangerous than the machinery it replaces. Air-conditioned workplaces are more pleasant than steamy workshops. Furthermore, why would an end to economic growth reduce materialism or alienation? The loudest protests against materialism are heard in those nations and groups that

---

[1] Alice M. Rivlin, *Reviving the American Dream* (Washington, D.C.: Brookings Institution, 1992), p. 36.

now enjoy the highest levels of material abundance! The high standard of living that growth provides has increased our leisure and given us more time for reflection and self-fulfillment.

Does growth threaten the environment? The connection between growth and environment is tenuous, say growth proponents. Increases in economic growth need not mean increases in pollution. Pollution is not so much a by-product of growth as it is a "problem of the commons." Much of the environment—streams, lakes, oceans, and the air—is treated as "common property," with insufficient or no restrictions on its use. The commons have become our dumping grounds; we have overused and debased them. Environmental pollution is a case of spillover or external costs, and correcting this problem involves regulatory legislation, specific taxes ("effluent charges"), or market-based incentives to remedy misuse of the environment.

Those who support growth admit there are serious environmental problems but say that limiting growth is the wrong solution. Growth has allowed economies to reduce pollution, be more sensitive to environmental considerations, set aside wilderness, create national parks and monuments, and clean up hazardous waste, while still enabling rising household incomes.

Is growth sustainable? Yes, say the proponents of growth. If we were depleting natural resources faster than their discovery, we would see the prices of those resources rise. That has not been the case for most natural resources; in fact, the prices of most of them have declined. And if one natural resource becomes too expensive, another resource will be substituted for it. Moreover, say economists, economic growth has to do with the expansion and application of human knowledge and information, not of extractable natural resources. In this view, economic growth—and solving any problems it may create—is limited only by human imagination.

Summary

1. Gross domestic product (GDP) is the market value of all final goods and services produced within the borders of a nation in a year. Intermediate goods and secondhand sales are purposely excluded in calculating GDP.

2. GDP can be calculated by adding consumer purchases of goods and services, gross investment spending by businesses, government purchases, and net exports: $GDP = C + I_g + G + X_n$.

3. Nominal (current-dollar) GDP measures each year's output valued in terms of the prices prevailing in that year. Real (constant-dollar) GDP measures each year's output in terms of the prices that prevailed in a selected base year. Because real GDP is adjusted for price-level changes, differences in real GDP are due only to differences in output.

4. Economic growth is either (a) an increase of real GDP over time or (b) an increase in real GDP per capita over time. Growth lessens the burden of scarcity and provides increases in real GDP that can be used to resolve socioeconomic problems.

5. The supply factors in economic growth are (a) the quantity and quality of a nation's natural resources, (b) the quantity and quality of its human resources, (c) its stock of capital facilities, and (d) its technology. Two other factors—a

sufficient level of aggregate demand and economic efficiency—are necessary for the economy to realize its growth potential.

6. The growth of production capacity is shown graphically as an outward shift of a nation's production possibilities curve. Growth is realized when total spending rises sufficiently to match the growth of production capacity.

7. U.S. real GDP has grown partly because of increased inputs of labor and primarily because of increases in the productivity of labor. The increases in productivity have resulted mainly from technological progress, increases in the quantity of capital per worker, improvements in the quality of labor, economies of scale, and an improved allocation of labor.

8. Over long time periods, the growth of labor productivity underlies an economy's growth of real wages and its standard of living.

9. Productivity rose by 2.7 percent annually between 1995 and 2007, compared to 1.4 percent annually between 1973 and 1995. Some economists think this productivity acceleration will be long-lasting and allow the economy to experience greater noninflationary economic growth.

10. The productivity speedup is based on (a) rapid technological change in the form of the microchip and information technology, (b) increasing returns and lower per-unit costs, and (c) heightened global competition that holds down prices.

11. The main sources of increasing returns in recent years are (a) the use of more specialized inputs as firms grow, (b) the spreading of development costs, (c) simultaneous consumption by consumers, (d) network effects, and (e) learning by doing. Increasing returns mean higher productivity and lower per-unit production costs.

12. Some economists wonder if the recent productivity speedup is permanent, and therefore they urge a wait-and-see approach.

They point out that surges in productivity and real GDP growth have previously occurred during vigorous economic expansions but do not necessarily represent long-lived trends.

13. Critics of rapid growth say that it adds to environmental degradation, increases human stress, and exhausts the earth's finite supply of natural resources. Defenders of rapid growth say that it is the primary path to the rising living standards nearly universally desired by people, that it need not debase the environment, and that there are no indications that we are running out of resources. Growth is based on the expansion and application of human knowledge, which is limited only by human imagination.

Terms and Concepts

national income and product accounts (NIPA)

gross domestic product (GDP)

intermediate goods

final goods

personal consumption expenditures (*C*)

gross private domestic investment (*I_g*)

government purchases (*G*)

net exports (*X_n*)

nominal GDP

real GDP

economic growth

real GDP per capita

labor productivity

labor-force participation rate

growth accounting

infrastructure

human capital

economies of scale

information technology

start-up firms

increasing returns

network effects

learning by doing

Study Questions

1. Why do national income accountants compare the market value of the total outputs in various years rather than actual physical volumes of production? What problem is posed by any comparison over time of the market values of various total outputs? How is this problem resolved? **LO1**

2. Why are only final goods counted in measuring GDP for a particular year? Why is the value of used furniture that's bought and sold not counted? **LO1**

3. What are the three main types of consumption expenditures? Why are purchases of new houses considered to be investment expenditures rather than consumption expenditures? **LO1**

4. Why are changes in inventories included as part of investment spending? Suppose inventories declined by $1 billion during 2008. How would this affect the size of gross private domestic investment and gross domestic product in 2008? Explain. **LO1**

5. Suppose foreigners spend $7 billion on U.S. exports in a specific year and Americans spend $5 billion on imports

from abroad in the same year. What is the amount of the United States' net exports? Explain how net exports might be a negative amount. **LO1**

6. Which of the following are included in this year's GDP? Explain your answer in each case. **LO1**

    a. The services of a commercial painter in painting the family home.

    b. An auto dealer's sale of a new car to a nonbusiness customer.

    c. The money received by Smith when she sells her biology textbook to a used-book buyer.

    d. The publication and sale of a new economics textbook.

    e. A $2 billion increase in business inventories.

    f. Government purchases of newly produced aircraft.

7. Using the following NIPA data, compute GDP. All figures are in billions. **LO1**

Personal consumption expenditures	$245
Wages and salaries	223
Imports	18
Corporate profits	42
Depreciation	28
Gross private domestic investment	86
Government purchases	82
Exports	9

8. Suppose that in 1984 the total output in a single-good economy was 7000 buckets of chicken. Also suppose that in 1984 each bucket of chicken was priced at $10. Finally, assume that in 2004 the price per bucket of chicken was $16 and that 22,000 buckets were produced. Determine real GDP for 1984 and 2004, in 1984 prices. **LO2**

9. Suppose an economy's real GDP is $30,000 in year 1 and $31,200 in year 2. What is the growth rate of its real GDP? Assume that population is 100 in year 1 and 102 in year 2. What is the growth rate of GDP per capita? **LO2**

10. What are the four supply factors of economic growth? What is the demand factor? What is the efficiency factor? Illustrate these factors in terms of the production possibilities curve. **LO4**

11. Suppose that work hours in New Zombie are 200 in year 1 and productivity is $8. What is New Zombie's real GDP? If work hours increase to 210 in year 2 and productivity rises to $10, what is New Zombie's rate of economic growth? **LO4**

12. To what extent have increases in U.S. real GDP resulted from more labor inputs? From higher labor productivity? Rearrange the following contributors to the growth of real GDP in order of their quantitative importance: economies of scale, quantity of capital, improved resource allocation, education and training, technological advance. **LO5**

13. True or false? If false, explain why. **LO5**
    a. Technological advance, which to date has played a relatively small role in U.S. economic growth, is destined to play a more important role in the future.
    b. Many public capital goods are complementary to private capital goods.
    c. Immigration has slowed economic growth in the United States.

14. Explain why there is such a close relationship between changes in a nation's rate of productivity growth and changes in its average real hourly wage. **LO4**

15. Relate each of the following to the recent productivity speedup: **LO6**
    a. Information technology
    b. Increasing returns
    c. Network effects
    d. Global competition

16. Provide three examples of products or services that can be simultaneously consumed by many people. Explain why labor productivity greatly rises as the firm sells more units of the product or service. Explain why the higher level of sales greatly reduces the per-unit cost of the product. **LO6**

FURTHER TEST YOUR KNOWLEDGE AT
www.mcconnellbriefmacro1e.com

Web-Based Questions

At the text's Online Learning Center, **www.mcconnellbriefmacro 1e.com,** you will find a multiple-choice quiz on this chapter's content. We encourage you to take the quiz to see how you do.

Also, you will find one or more Web-based questions that require information from the Internet to answer.

6

Business Cycles, Unemployment, and Inflation

Between 1996 and 2000, real GDP in the United States expanded briskly and the price level rose only slowly. The economy experienced neither significant unemployment nor inflation. Some observers felt that the United States had entered a "new era" in which the business cycle was dead. But that wishful thinking came to an end in March 2001, when the economy entered its ninth recession since 1950. In December 2007, the tenth recession since 1950 began. At first mild, the recession gained traction from extreme instability in the financial industry, and toward the end of 2008 became severe. Since 1970, real GDP has declined in the United States in six periods: 1973–1975, 1980, 1981–1982, 1990–1991, 2001, and 2007–?

Although the U.S. economy has experienced remarkable economic growth over time, high unemployment or inflation has sometimes been a problem. For example, between December 2007 and

December 2008, unemployment rose by 3.6 million workers. The U.S. rate of inflation was 13.5 percent in 1980 and 5.4 percent in 1990. Further, other nations have suffered high unemployment rates or inflation rates in recent years. For example, the unemployment rate in Germany reached 10.7 percent in 2005. The inflation rate was 26,000 percent in Zimbabwe in 2007.

In this chapter, we provide an introductory look at macroeconomic instability. Our specific topics are the business cycle, unemployment, and inflation.

ORIGIN OF THE IDEA

O 6.1

Business cycles

business cycles
Recurring increases and decreases in the level of economic activity over periods of time.

recession
A period of declining real GDP, accompanied by lower income and higher unemployment.

expansion
A generalized increase in output, income, and business activity.

Business Cycles

The long-run growth trend of the U.S. economy is one of expansion. But growth has been interrupted by periods of economic instability usually associated with *business cycles*. **Business cycles** are alternating rises and declines in the level of economic activity, sometimes over several years. Individual cycles (one "up" followed by one "down") vary substantially in duration and intensity.

As shown in Figure 6.1, the two primary phases of business cycles are recessions and expansions ("peaks" and "troughs" are merely turning points). A **recession** is a period of decline in total output, income, and employment. This downturn, which lasts 6 months or more, is marked by the widespread contraction of business activity in many sectors of the economy. Along with declines in real GDP, significant increases in unemployment occur. Table 6.1 documents the 10 recessions in the United States since 1950.

A recession is usually followed by a recovery and **expansion,** a period in which real GDP, income, and employment rise. At some point, full employment is again achieved. If spending then expands more rapidly than does production capacity, prices of nearly all goods and services will rise. In other words, inflation will occur.

Causes of Business Cycles

The long-run trend of the U.S. economy is expansion and growth. That is why the business cycles in Figure 6.1 are drawn against a trend of economic growth. A key issue in macroeconomics is why the economy sees business cycle fluctuations rather than slow, smooth growth. In terms of Figure 6.1, why does output go up and down rather than just staying on the smooth growth trend line?

FIGURE 6.1 **The business cycle.** Economists distinguish two primary phases of the business cycle (recession and expansion); the duration and strength of each phase may vary.

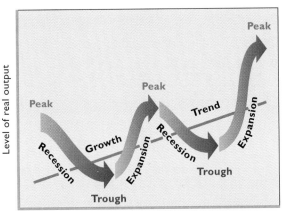

TABLE 6.1
**U.S. Recessions since
1950**

Period	Duration, Months	Depth (Decline in Real Output)
1953–54	10	−3.7%
1957–58	8	−3.9
1960–61	10	−1.6
1969–70	11	−1.0
1973–75	16	−4.9
1980	6	−2.3
1981–82	16	−3.3
1990–91	8	−1.8
2001	8	−0.5
2007–?	?	−?

Source: *Economic Report of the President, 1993*, p. 58. We have extended the 1993 table by appending 2001 data from the Council of Economic Advisers.

Economists have come up with several theories to explain business cycles. These theories are founded on the idea that fluctuations are driven by **shocks**—situations in which individuals and firms were expecting one thing to happen but then something else happened. For instance, consider a situation in which a firm decides to build a high-speed railroad that will shuttle passengers between Washington, D.C., and New York. They do so expecting it to be very popular and make a handsome profit. But if it unexpectedly turns out to be unpopular and loses money, the railroad must figure out how to respond. Should the railroad go out of business, change the service it provides, or spend millions on a massive advertising campaign? These sorts of decisions are necessitated by the shock and surprise of having to deal with an unexpected situation.

Economies are exposed to both demand shocks and supply shocks. **Demand shocks** are unexpected changes in the demand for goods and services. **Supply shocks** are unexpected changes in the supply of goods and services. Please note that the word *shock* only tells us that something unexpected has happened. It does not tell us whether what has happened is unexpectedly good or unexpectedly bad. To make things more clear, economists use more specific terms. For instance, a *positive demand shock* refers to a situation in which demand turns out to be higher than expected, while a *negative demand shock* refers to a situation in which demand turns out to be lower than expected.

Shocks to the economy, particularly those with significant negative impacts, often lead to calls for government action. But why are shocks a big enough problem to justify calling in the government for help? Why can't firms deal with shocks on their own? Why don't product and resource markets respond quickly to correct imbalances?

The answer to these questions is that the prices of many goods and services are inflexible (slow to change, also known as **sticky prices**) in the short run. This implies that price changes do not quickly equalize the quantities demanded of such goods and services with their respective quantities supplied. Instead, because prices are inflexible, the economy is forced to respond in the short run to demand shocks primarily through changes in output and employment rather than through changes in prices. If negative effects on output and employment effects are severe and/or long-lasting, government is generally called upon to take corrective action. We will address government policy options in upcoming chapters; for now we resume our focus on business cycles.

shocks
Situations in which events don't meet expectations.

demand shocks
Unexpected changes in the demand for goods and services.

supply shocks
Unexpected changes in the supply of goods and services.

sticky prices
A situation where prices of goods and services are slow to respond to changes in supply and demand.

Economists fall into several different camps when it comes to the types of shocks that they believe to be responsible for business cycles. One group, for instance, stresses supply shocks caused by momentous innovations such as the railroad, the automobile, microchips, and the Internet. They believe that major inventions like these have a large impact on investment spending and consumption spending—and therefore on output, employment, and the price level. Because such major inventions occur irregularly and unexpectedly, they contribute to the variability of economic activity.

Another school of thought sees shocks to productivity as the major cause of business cycles. When productivity unexpectedly increases, the economy booms; when productivity unexpectedly falls, the economy goes into a recession. Others view the business cycle as a purely monetary phenomenon. They say that when a country's central bank shocks the economy by creating more money than people were expecting, an inflationary boom occurs. By contrast, printing less money than people were expecting triggers a decline in output and employment and, eventually, in the price level. Still others say that business cycles result from unexpected financial bubbles and bursts, which spill over through optimism or pessimism to affect the production of goods and services. And, finally, unexpected political events like wars or the 9/11 terrorist attacks also constitute major economic shocks to which the economy must adjust.

But whatever they see as the underlying forces driving economic shocks, most economists agree that the *immediate* cause of the large majority of cyclical changes in the levels of real output and employment is unexpected changes in the level of total spending. If total spending unexpectedly sinks and firms cannot lower prices, firms will find themselves selling fewer units of output (since, with prices fixed, a decreased amount of spending implies fewer items purchased). Slower sales will cause firms to cut back on production. As they do, GDP will fall. And since fewer workers will be needed to produce less output, employment also will fall. The economy will contract and enter a recession.

By contrast, if the level of spending unexpectedly rises, output, employment, and incomes will rise. This is true because with prices sticky, the increased spending will mean that consumers will be buying a larger volume of goods and services (since, with prices fixed, more spending means more items purchased). Firms will respond by increasing output. This will increase GDP. And because they will need to hire more workers to produce the larger volume of output, employment also will increase. The economy will boom and enjoy an expansion. Eventually, as time passes and prices become more flexible, prices are also likely to rise as a result of the increased spending.

Cyclical Impact: Durables and Nondurables

Although the business cycle is felt everywhere in the economy, it affects different segments in different ways and to different degrees.

Firms and industries producing *capital goods* (for example, housing, commercial buildings, heavy equipment, and farm implements) and *consumer durables* (for example, automobiles, personal computers, refrigerators) are affected most by the business cycle. Within limits, firms can postpone the purchase of capital goods. For instance, when the economy goes into recession, producers frequently delay the purchase of new equipment and the construction of new plants. The business outlook simply does not warrant increases in the stock of capital goods. In good times, capital goods are usually replaced before they depreciate completely. But when recession strikes, firms patch up their old equipment and make do. As a result, investment in capital goods declines sharply. Firms that have excess plant capacity may not even bother to replace all the capital that is depreciating. For them, net investment may be negative. The pattern is much the same for consumer durables such as automobiles and major appliances. When recession occurs and households must trim their budgets, purchases of these goods are often deferred. Families repair their old cars and appliances rather than buy new ones, and the firms producing these products suffer. (Of course, producers of capital goods and consumer durables also benefit most from expansions.)

In contrast, *service* industries and industries that produce *nondurable consumer goods* are somewhat insulated from the most severe effects of recession. People find it difficult to cut back on needed medical and legal services, for example. And a recession actually helps some service firms, such as pawnbrokers and law firms that specialize in bankruptcies. Nor are the purchases of many nondurable goods such as food and clothing easy to postpone. The quantity and quality of purchases of nondurables will decline, but not so much as will purchases of capital goods and consumer durables.

Stock Prices and Macroeconomic Instability

APPLYING THE ANALYSIS

Every day, the individual stocks (ownership shares) of thousands of corporations are bought and sold in the stock market. The owners of the individual stocks receive dividends—a portion of the firm's profit. Supply and demand in the stock market determine the price of each firm's stock, with individual stock prices generally rising and falling in concert with the collective expectations for each firm's profits. Greater profits normally result in higher dividends to the stock owners, and, in anticipation of higher dividends, people are willing to pay a higher price for the stock.

The media closely monitor and report stock market averages such as the Dow Jones Industrial Average (DJIA)—the weighted-average price of the stocks of 30 major U.S. industrial firms. It is common for these price averages to change over time or even to rise or fall sharply during a single day. On "Black Monday," October 19, 1987, the DJIA fell by 20 percent. In contrast, the stock market averages rose spectacularly in 1998 and 1999, with the DJIA rising 16 and 25 percent in those two years. In 2002, the DJIA fell 17 percent. In 2003, it rose by 25 percent. In the last three months of 2008, the DJIA plummeted by over 19 percent, and was down by nearly 34 percent for the full year.

The volatility of the stock market raises this question: Do changes in stock price averages and thus stock market wealth cause macroeconomic instability? Linkages between the stock market and the economy might lead us to answer "yes." Consider a sharp increase in stock prices. Feeling wealthier, stock owners respond by increasing their spending (the *wealth effect*). Firms react by increasing their purchases of new capital goods because they can finance such purchases through issuing new shares of high-valued stock (the *investment effect*). Of course, sharp declines in stock prices would produce the opposite results.

Studies find that changes in stock prices do affect consumption and investment but that these consumption and investment impacts are relatively weak. For example, a 10 percent sustained increase in stock market values in 1 year is associated with a 4 percent increase in consumption spending over the next 3 years. The investment response is even weaker. So typical day-to-day and year-to-year changes in stock market values have little impact on the macroeconomy.

In contrast, *stock market bubbles* can be detrimental to an economy. Such bubbles are huge run-ups of overall stock prices, caused by excessive optimism and frenzied buying. The rising stock values are unsupported by realistic prospects of the future strength of the economy and the firms operating in it. Rather than slowly decompress, such bubbles may burst and cause harm to the economy. The free fall of stock values, if long-lasting, causes reverse wealth effects. The stock market crash also may create an overall pessimism about the economy that undermines consumption and investment spending even further. Indeed, although not the precipitating cause of the Great Depression of the 1930s, the stock market crash of 1929 contributed to it by creating a tremendous amount of anxiety and pessimism about the future.

Question:
Suppose that your college savings fund of $100,000, all invested in stocks, was reduced in value to $25,000 because of a stock market crash. Explain how that would affect your spending for college (including your choice of school) and spending for other goods and services.

Unemployment

Two problems that arise over the course of the business cycle are unemployment and inflation. Let's look at unemployment first.

Measurement of Unemployment

The U.S. Bureau of Labor Statistics (BLS) conducts a nationwide random survey of some 60,000 households each month to determine who is employed and who is not employed. In a series of questions it asks which members of the household are working, unemployed and looking for work, not looking for work, and so on. From the answers it determines an unemployment rate for the entire nation.

Figure 6.2 helps explain the mathematics. It divides the total U.S. population into three groups. One group is made up of people less than 16 years of age and people who are institutionalized, for example, in mental hospitals or correctional institutions. Such people are not considered potential members of the labor force. A second group, labeled "Not in labor force," is composed of adults who are potential workers but are not employed and are not seeking work. For example, they are homemakers, full-time students, or retirees. The third group is the **labor force** which constituted about 50 percent of the total population in 2007. The labor force consists of people who are able and willing to work. Both those who are employed full-time and part-time and those who are unemployed but actively seeking work are counted as being in the labor force. The **unemployment rate** is the percentage of the labor force unemployed:

labor force
Persons 16 years and older who are not in institutions and who are either employed or unemployed and seeking work.

unemployment rate
The percentage of the labor force unemployed.

$$\text{Unemployment rate} = \frac{\text{unemployed}}{\text{labor force}} \times 100$$

The statistics included in Figure 6.2 show that in 2007 the unemployment rate averaged

$$\frac{7{,}078{,}000}{153{,}124{,}000} \times 100 = 4.6\%$$

WORKED PROBLEMS

W 6.1

Unemployment rate

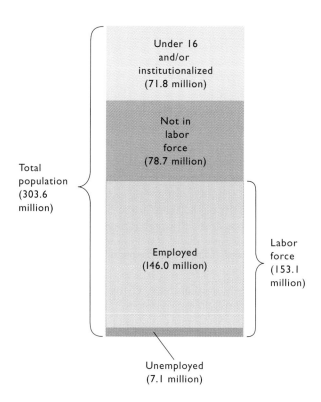

FIGURE 6.2 **The labor force, employment, and unemployment, 2007.** The labor force consists of persons 16 years of age or older who are not in institutions and who are (1) employed or (2) unemployed but seeking employment. Source: Bureau of Labor Statistics, **www.bls.gov** (civilian labor force data, which excludes military employment).

Types of Unemployment

There are three *types* of unemployment: frictional, structural, and cyclical.

Frictional Unemployment

At any moment some workers are "between jobs." Some of them will be moving voluntarily from one job to another. Others will have been fired and will be seeking reemployment. Still others will have been laid off temporarily because of seasonal demand. In addition to those between jobs, many young workers will be searching for their first jobs.

As these unemployed people find jobs or are called back from temporary layoffs, other job seekers and laid-off workers will replace them in the "unemployment pool." It is important to keep in mind that while the pool itself persists because there are always newly unemployed workers flowing into it, most workers do *not* stay in the unemployment pool for very long. Indeed, when the economy is strong, the majority of unemployed workers find new jobs within a couple of months. One should be careful not to make the mistake of confusing the permanence of the pool itself with the false ideal that the pool's membership is permanent, too. On the other hand, there *are* workers who do remain unemployed and in the pool for very long periods of time— sometimes for many years. As we discuss the different types of unemployment below, notice that certain types tend to be transitory while others are associated with much longer spells of unemployment.

Economists use the term **frictional unemployment**—consisting of *search unemployment* and *wait unemployment*—for workers who are either searching for jobs or waiting to take jobs in the near future. The word "frictional" implies that the labor market does not operate perfectly and instantaneously (without friction) in matching workers and jobs.

Frictional unemployment is inevitable and, at least in part, desirable. Many people who are frictionally unemployed are moving into the labor force or from low-paying,

frictional unemployment
Unemployment that is associated with people searching for jobs or waiting to take jobs in the near future.

low-productivity jobs to higher-paying, higher-productivity positions. That means greater income for the workers, a better allocation of labor resources, and a larger real GDP for the economy.

Structural Unemployment

structural unemployment
Unemployment that is associated with a mismatch between available jobs and the skills or locations of those unemployed.

Structural Unemployment Frictional unemployment blurs into a category called **structural unemployment.** Here, economists use "structural" in the sense of "compositional." Changes over time in consumer demand and in technology alter the "structure" of the total demand for labor, both occupationally and geographically.

Occupationally, the demand for certain skills (for example, sewing clothes or working on farms) may decline or even vanish. The demand for other skills (for example, designing software or maintaining computer systems) will intensify. Unemployment results because the composition of the labor force does not respond immediately or completely to the new structure of job opportunities. Workers who find that their skills and experience have become obsolete or unneeded thus find that they have no marketable talents. They are structurally unemployed until they adapt or develop skills that employers want.

Geographically, the demand for labor also changes over time. An example: migration of industry and thus of employment opportunities from the Snow Belt to the Sun Belt over the past few decades. Another example is the movement of jobs from inner-city factories to suburban industrial parks. As job opportunities shift from one place to another, some workers become structurally unemployed.

cyclical unemployment
Unemployment that is associated with the recessionary phase of a business cycle.

Cyclical Unemployment Unemployment caused by a decline in total spending is called **cyclical unemployment** and typically begins in the recession phase of the business cycle. As the demand for goods and services decreases, employment falls and unemployment rises. The 25 percent unemployment rate in 1933 reflected mainly cyclical unemployment, as did significant parts of the 9.7 percent unemployment rate in 1982 and the 7.5 percent rate in 1992. Cyclical unemployment is also the main contributor to the rising unemployment rate in the current recession (2007–?).

Cyclical unemployment is a very serious problem when it occurs. To understand its costs, we need to define "full employment."

Definition of Full Employment

Because frictional and structural unemployment are largely unavoidable in a dynamic economy, *full employment* is something less than 100 percent employment of the labor force. Economists say that the economy is "fully employed" when it is experiencing only frictional and structural unemployment. That is, full employment occurs when there is no cyclical unemployment. Today, most economists believe that the economy is fully employed when the unemployment rate is less than 5 percent. The level of real GDP that would occur precisely at "full employment" is called **potential output** (or *potential GDP*).

potential output
The level of real GDP that would occur if there was full employment.

Economic Cost of Unemployment

GDP gap
The negative or positive difference between actual GDP and potential GDP.

The basic economic cost of unemployment is forgone output. When the economy fails to create enough jobs for all who have the necessary skills and are willing to work, potential production of goods and services is irretrievably lost. In terms of Chapter 1's analysis, cyclical unemployment means that society is operating at some point inside its production possibilities curve. Economists call this sacrifice of output a **GDP gap**—the difference between actual and potential GDP. That is:

$$\text{GDP gap} = \text{actual GDP} - \text{potential GDP}$$

The GDP gap can be either a negative number (actual GDP is less than potential GDP) or a positive number (actual GDP exceeds potential GDP). There is a close correlation between the actual unemployment rate and the GDP gap. The higher the unemployment rate, the greater is the negative GDP gap.

Society's cost of unemployment—its forgone output—translates to forgone income for individuals. This loss of income is borne unequally. Some groups have higher unemployment rates than others and bear the brunt of rising rates during recessions. For instance, workers in lower-skilled occupations (for example, laborers) have higher unemployment rates than workers in higher-skilled occupations (for example, professionals). Lower-skilled workers have more and longer spells of structural unemployment than higher-skilled workers. They also are less likely to be self-employed than are higher-skilled workers. Moreover, lower-skilled workers usually bear the brunt of recessions. Businesses generally retain most of their higher-skilled workers, in whom they have invested the expense of training.

Also, teenagers have much higher unemployment rates than adults. Teenagers have lower skill levels, quit their jobs more frequently, are more frequently "fired," and have less geographic mobility than adults. Many unemployed teenagers are new in the labor market, searching for their first jobs. Male African-American teenagers, in particular, have very high unemployment rates.

Finally, the overall unemployment rate for African Americans and Hispanics is higher than that for whites and Asians. The causes of the higher rates include lower rates of educational attainment, greater concentration in lower-skilled occupations, and discrimination in the labor market. In general, the unemployment rate for African Americans is twice that of whites.

International Comparisons

Unemployment rates differ greatly among nations at any given time. One reason is that nations have different unemployment rates when their economies are fully employed. Another is that nations may be in recessions or expansions. Global Snapshot 6.1 shows unemployment rates for six industrialized nations in recent years. Between 1997 and 2007, the U.S. unemployment rate was considerably lower than the rates in Germany, France, and Italy.

Inflation

We now turn to inflation, another aspect of macroeconomic instability. The problems inflation poses are subtler than those posed by unemployment.

Meaning of Inflation

Inflation is a rise in the *general level of prices*. When inflation occurs, each dollar of income will buy fewer goods and services than before. Inflation reduces the "purchasing power" of money. But inflation does not mean that *all* prices are rising. Even during periods of rapid inflation, some prices may be relatively constant and others may even fall. For example, although the United States experienced high rates of inflation in the 1970s and early 1980s, the prices of video recorders, digital watches, and personal computers declined.

Measurement of Inflation

The main measure of inflation in the United States is the **Consumer Price Index (CPI),** compiled by the Bureau of Labor Statistics (BLS). The government uses this

inflation
A rise in the general level of prices in an economy.

Consumer Price Index (CPI)
An index that compares the price of a market basket of consumer goods and services in one period with the price of the same (or highly similar) market basket in a base period.

GLOBAL SNAPSHOT 6.1

Unemployment Rates in Six Industrial Nations, 1997–2007

Compared with Germany, France, and Italy, the United States has had a relatively low unemployment rate in recent years.

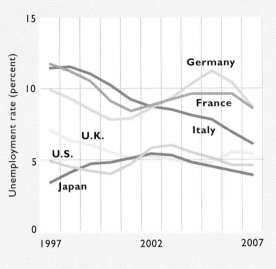

Source: Bureau of Labor Statistics, **www.bls.gov.**

index to report inflation rates each month and each year. It also uses the CPI to adjust Social Security benefits and income tax brackets for inflation. The CPI reports the price of a "market basket" of some 300 consumer goods and services that are purchased by a typical urban consumer.

The composition of the market basket for the CPI is based on spending patterns of urban consumers in a specific period, presently 2005–2006. The BLS updates the composition of the market basket every 2 years so that it reflects the most recent patterns of consumer purchases and captures the inflation that consumers are currently experiencing. The BLS arbitrarily sets the CPI equal to 100 for 1982–1984. So the CPI for any particular year is found as follows:

$$\text{CPI} = \frac{\text{price of the most recent market basket in the particular year}}{\text{price of the same market basket in } 1982{-}1984}$$

The rate of inflation for a certain year is found by comparing, in percentage terms, that year's index with the index in the previous year. For example, the CPI rose from 201.6 in 2006 to 207.3 in 2007. So the rate of inflation for 2007 was 2.8 percent.

$$\text{Rate of inflation} = \frac{207.3 - 201.6}{201.6} \times 100 = 2.8\%$$

In Chapter 5 we discussed the mathematical approximation called the *rule of 70*, which tells us that we can find the number of years it will take for some measure to double, given its annual percentage increase, by dividing that percentage increase into the number 70. For example, annual rates of inflation of 3 percent will double the price level in about 23 (= 70/3) years.

FIGURE 6.3 **Annual inflation rates in the United States, 1960–2007.** The major periods of inflation in the United States in the past 47 years were in the 1970s and 1980s.
Source: Bureau of Labor Statistics, **www.bls.gov** (December-to-December data).

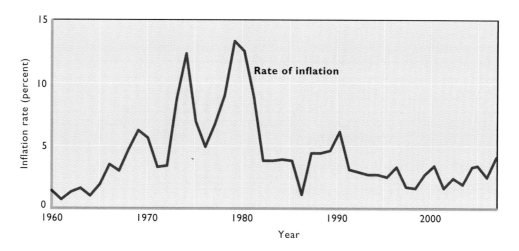

Facts of Inflation

Figure 6.3 shows the annual rates of inflation in the United States between 1960 and 2007. Observe that inflation reached double-digit rates in the 1970s and early 1980s but has since declined and has been relatively mild recently.

In recent years U.S. inflation has been neither unusually high nor unusually low relative to inflation in several other industrial countries (see Global Snapshot 6.2).

GLOBAL SNAPSHOT 6.2

Inflation Rates in Six Industrial Nations, 1997–2007

Inflation rates in the United States in recent years were neither extraordinarily high nor extraordinarily low relative to rates in other industrial nations.

Source: Bureau of Labor Statistics, **www.bls.gov.**

Some nations (not shown) have had double-digit or even higher annual rates of inflation in recent years. In 2007, for example, the annual inflation rate in Venezuela was 21 percent; in Afghanistan, 16 percent; in Burma, 39 percent; and in Zimbabwe, according to official data, 26,470 percent.

Types of Inflation

Nearly all prices in the economy are set by supply and demand. Consequently, if the economy is experiencing inflation and the overall level of prices is rising, we need to look for an explanation in terms of supply and demand. Reflecting this, economists distinguish between two types of inflation: *demand-pull inflation* and *cost-push inflation*.

Demand-Pull Inflation

Usually, increases in the price level are caused by an excess of total spending beyond the economy's capacity to produce. Where inflation is rapid and sustained, the cause invariably is an overissuance of money by the central bank (the Federal Reserve in the United States). When resources are already fully employed, the business sector cannot respond to excess demand by expanding output. So the excess demand bids up the prices of the limited output, producing **demand-pull inflation.** The essence of this type of inflation is "too much spending chasing too few goods."

demand-pull inflation
Inreases in the price level (inflation) caused by excessive spending.

ILLUSTRATING
THE
IDEA

Clipping Coins

Some interesting early episodes of demand-pull inflation occurred in Europe during the ninth to the fifteenth centuries under feudalism. In that economic system, *lords* (or *princes*) ruled individual fiefdoms, and their *vassals* (or *peasants*) worked the fields. The peasants initially paid parts of their harvest as taxes to the princes. Later, when the princes began issuing "coins of the realm," peasants began paying their taxes with gold coins.

Some princes soon discovered a way to transfer purchasing power from their vassals to themselves without explicitly increasing taxes. As coins came into the treasury, princes clipped off parts of the gold coins, making them slightly smaller. From the clippings they minted new coins and used them to buy more goods for themselves.

This practice of clipping coins was a subtle form of taxation. The quantity of goods being produced in the fiefdom remained the same, but the number of gold coins increased. With "too much money chasing too few goods," inflation occurred. Each gold coin earned by the peasants therefore had less purchasing power than previously because prices were higher. The increase of the money supply shifted purchasing power away from the peasants and toward the princes just as surely as if the princes had increased taxation of the peasants.

In more recent eras, some dictators have simply printed money to buy more goods for themselves, their relatives, and their key loyalists. These dictators, too, have levied hidden taxes on their population by creating inflation.

The moral of the story is quite simple: A society that values price-level stability should not entrust the control of its money supply to people who benefit from inflation.

Question:
Why might a government with a huge foreign debt be tempted to increase its domestic money supply and cause inflation?

Cost-Push Inflation Inflation may also arise on the supply, or cost, side of the economy. During some periods in U.S. economic history, including the mid-1970s, the price level increased even though total spending was not excessive. These were periods when output and employment were both *declining* (evidence that total spending was not excessive) while the general price level was *rising*.

The theory of **cost-push inflation** explains rising prices in terms of factors that raise the average cost of a particular level of output. Rising average production costs squeeze profits and reduce the economy's supply of goods and services. In this scenario, costs are *pushing* the price level upward, whereas in demand-pull inflation demand is *pulling* it upward.

The major source of cost-push inflation has been so-called *supply shocks*. Specifically, abrupt increases in the costs of raw materials or energy inputs have on occasion driven up per-unit production costs and thus product prices. The rocketing prices of imported oil in 1973–1974 and again in 1979–1980 are good illustrations. As energy prices surged upward during these periods, the costs of producing and transporting virtually every product in the economy rose. Cost-push inflation ensued.

> **cost-push inflation**
> Increases in the price level (inflation) caused by sharp rises in the cost of key resources.

Redistribution Effects of Inflation

Inflation redistributes real income. This redistribution helps some people and hurts others, while leaving many people largely unaffected. Who gets hurt? Who benefits? Before we can answer, we need some terminology. There is a difference between money (or nominal) income and real income. **Nominal income** is the number of dollars received as wages, rent, interest, or profits. **Real income** is a measure of the amount of goods and services nominal income can buy; it is the purchasing power of nominal income, or income adjusted for inflation. That is,

$$\text{Real income} = \frac{\text{nominal income}}{\text{price index (in hundredths)}}$$

Inflation need not alter an economy's overall real income—its total purchasing power. It is evident from the above equation that real income will remain the same when nominal income and the price index rise at the same percentage rate.

But when inflation occurs, not everyone's nominal income rises at the same pace as the price level. Therein lies the potential for redistribution of real income from

> **nominal income**
> The number of dollars received as wages, rent, interest, and profit.
>
> **real income**
> The purchasing power of nominal income; the amount of goods and services that nominal income can buy.

> **WORKED PROBLEMS**
>
> **W 6.2**
>
> Nominal and real income

some to others. If the change in the price level differs from the change in a person's nominal income, his or her real income will be affected. The following approximation (shown by the ≅ sign) tells us roughly how much real income will change:

$$
\begin{array}{ccc}
\text{Percentage} & \text{percentage} & \text{percentage} \\
\text{change in} \quad \cong & \text{change in} \quad - & \text{change in} \\
\text{real income} & \text{nominal income} & \text{price level}
\end{array}
$$

For example, suppose that the price level rises by 6 percent in some period. If Bob's nominal income rises by 6 percent, his real income will *remain unchanged*. But if his nominal income instead rises by 10 percent, his real income will *increase* by about 4 percent. And if Bob's nominal income rises by only 2 percent, his real income will *decline* by about 4 percent.

The redistribution effects of inflation depend on whether or not it is expected. With fully expected or *anticipated inflation*, an income receiver may be able to avoid or lessen the adverse effects of inflation on real income. The generalizations that follow assume *unanticipated inflation*—inflation whose full extent was not expected.

Who Is Hurt by Inflation?

Unanticipated inflation hurts fixed-income recipients, savers, and creditors. It redistributes real income away from them and toward others.

Fixed-Income Receivers People whose incomes are fixed see their real incomes fall when inflation occurs. The classic case is the elderly couple living on a private pension or annuity that provides a fixed amount of nominal income each month. They may have retired on what appeared to be an adequate pension. However, years later they discover that inflation has severely cut the purchasing power of that pension—their real income.

Similarly, landlords who receive lease payments of fixed dollar amounts will be hurt by inflation as they receive dollars of declining value over time. Likewise, public sector workers whose incomes are dictated by fixed pay schedules may suffer from inflation. The fixed "steps" (the upward yearly increases) in their pay schedules may not keep up with inflation. Minimum-wage workers and families living on fixed welfare incomes also will be hurt by inflation.

Savers Unanticipated inflation hurts savers. As prices rise, the real value, or purchasing power, of an accumulation of savings deteriorates. Paper assets such as savings accounts, insurance policies, and annuities, which once were adequate to meet rainy-day contingencies or provide for a comfortable retirement, decline in real value during periods of inflation.

Creditors Unanticipated inflation harms creditors (lenders). Suppose Chase Bank lends Bob $1000, to be repaid in 2 years. If in that time the price level doubles, the $1000 that Bob repays will have only half the purchasing power of the $1000 he borrowed. True, if we ignore interest charges, the same number of dollars will be repaid as was borrowed. But because of inflation, each of those dollars will buy only half as much as it did when the loan was negotiated. As prices go up, the value of the dollar goes down. So the borrower pays back less-valuable dollars than those received from the lender. The owners of Chase Bank suffer a loss of real income.

Who Is Unaffected or Helped by Inflation?

Some people are unaffected by inflation, and others are actually helped by it. For the second group, inflation redistributes real income toward them and away from others.

Flexible-Income Receivers People who have flexible incomes may escape inflation's harm or even benefit from it. For example, individuals who derive their incomes solely from Social Security are largely unaffected by inflation because Social Security payments are *indexed* to the CPI. Benefits automatically increase when the CPI increases, preventing erosion of benefits from inflation. Some union workers also get automatic *cost-of-living adjustments (COLAs)* in their pay when the CPI rises, although such increases rarely equal the full percentage rise in inflation.

Some flexible-income receivers are helped by unanticipated inflation. The strong product demand and labor shortages implied by rapid demand-pull inflation may cause some nominal incomes to spurt ahead of the price level, thereby enhancing real incomes. As an example, property owners faced with an inflation-induced real estate boom may be able to boost rents more rapidly than the rate of inflation. Also, some business owners may benefit from inflation. If their product prices rise faster than their resource prices, business revenues will increase more rapidly than costs. In those cases, the growth rate of profit incomes will outpace the rate of inflation.

Debtors Unanticipated inflation benefits debtors (borrowers). In our earlier example, Chase Bank's loss of real income from inflation is Bob's gain of real income. Debtor Bob borrows "dear" dollars but, because of inflation, pays back the principal and interest with "cheap" dollars whose purchasing power has been eroded by inflation. Real income is redistributed away from the owners of Chase Bank toward borrowers such as Bob.

Anticipated Inflation

The redistribution effects of inflation are less severe or are eliminated altogether if people anticipate inflation and can adjust their nominal incomes to reflect the expected price-level rises. The prolonged inflation that began in the late 1960s prompted many workers in the 1970s to insist on high wage and salary increases that would protect them from expected inflation.

Similarly, if inflation is anticipated, the redistribution of income from lender to borrower may be altered. Suppose a lender (perhaps a bank) and a borrower (a household) both agree that 5 percent is a fair rate of interest on a 1-year loan provided the price level is stable. But assume that inflation has been occurring and is expected to be 6 percent over the next year. The lender will neutralize inflation by charging an *inflation premium* of 6 percent, the amount of the anticipated inflation.

Our example reveals the difference between the real rate of interest and the nominal rate of interest. The **real interest rate** is the percentage increase in *purchasing power* that the borrower pays the lender. In our example the real interest rate is 5 percent. The **nominal interest rate** is the percentage increase in *money* that the borrower pays the lender, including that resulting from the built-in expectation of inflation, if any. In equation form:

$$\text{Nominal interest rate} = \text{real interest rate} + \text{inflation premium}$$
$$\text{(the expected rate of inflation)}$$

real interest rate
The percentage increase in purchasing power that a borrower pays a lender; the nominal interest rate less the expected rate of inflation.

nominal interest rate
The percentage increase in money that a borrower pays a lender.

FIGURE 6.4 **The inflation premium and nominal and real interest rates.** The inflation premium—the expected rate of inflation—gets built into the nominal interest rate. Here, the nominal interest rate of 11 percent comprises the real interest rate of 5 percent plus the inflation premium of 6 percent.

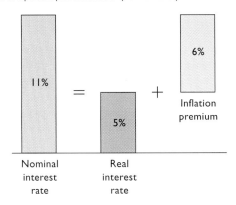

As illustrated in Figure 6.4, the nominal interest rate in our example is 11 percent.

Does Inflation Affect Output?

Thus far, our discussion has focused on how inflation redistributes a given level of total real income. But inflation also may affect an economy's level of real output (and thus its level of real income). The direction and significance of this effect on output depends on the type of inflation and its severity.

Cost-Push Inflation and Real Output

Recall that abrupt and unexpected rises in key resource prices such as oil can sufficiently drive up overall production costs to cause cost-push inflation. As prices rise, the quantity of goods and services demanded falls. So firms respond by producing less output, and unemployment goes up. In short, cost-push inflation reduces real output. It redistributes a decreased level of real income.

Demand-Pull Inflation and Real Output

Economists do not fully agree on the effects of mild inflation (less than 3 percent) on real output. One perspective is that even low levels of inflation reduce real output because inflation diverts time and effort toward activities designed to hedge against inflation. For example, businesses must incur the cost of changing thousands of prices on their shelves and in their computers simply to reflect inflation. Also, households and businesses must spend considerable time and effort obtaining the information they need to distinguish between real and nominal values such as prices, wages, and interest rates. Further, to limit the loss of purchasing power from inflation, people try to limit the amount of money they hold in their billfolds and checking accounts at any one time and instead put more money into interest-bearing accounts and stock and bond funds. But cash and checking deposits are needed in even greater amounts to buy the higher-priced goods and services. Therefore, people must make more frequent trips, phone calls, or Internet visits to financial institutions to transfer funds to checking accounts and billfolds, when needed. Bottom line: From this perspective even mild inflation reduces total output.

In contrast, other economists point out that full employment and economic growth depend on strong levels of total spending. Such spending creates high profits, strong demand for labor, and a powerful incentive for firms to expand their plants and equipment. In this view, the mild inflation that is a by-product of strong spending is a small price to pay for full employment and continued economic growth. Defenders of mild inflation say that it is much better for an economy to err on the side of strong spending, full employment, economic growth, and mild inflation than on the side of weak spending, unemployment, recession, and **deflation**—a decline in the general level of prices in the economy.

deflation
A decline in the general level of prices in the economy.

APPLYING THE ANALYSIS

Hyperinflation

All economists agree that *hyperinflation*, which is extraordinarily rapid inflation, can have a devastating impact on real output and employment.

As prices shoot up sharply and unevenly during hyperinflation, normal economic relationships are disrupted. Business owners do not know what to charge for their products. Consumers do not know what to pay. Resource suppliers want to be paid with actual output, rather than with rapidly depreciating money. Money eventually becomes almost worthless and ceases to do its job as a medium of exchange. The economy may be thrown into a state of barter, and production and exchange drop dramatically. The net result is economic, social, and possibly political chaos.

Examples of hyperinflation are Germany after the First World War and Japan after the Second World War. In Germany, "prices increased so rapidly that waiters changed the prices on the menu several times during the course of a lunch. Sometimes customers had to pay double the price listed on the menu when they ordered."[*] In postwar Japan, in 1947 "fishermen and farmers…used scales to weigh currency and change, rather than bothering to count it."[†]

There are also more recent examples: Between June 1986 and March 1991 the cumulative inflation in Nicaragua was 11,895,866,143 percent. From November 1993 to December 1994 the cumulative inflation rate in the Democratic Republic of Congo was 69,502 percent. From February 1993 to January 1994 the cumulative inflation rate in Serbia was 156,312,790 percent.[‡]

Such dramatic hyperinflations are always the consequence of highly imprudent expansions of the money supply by government. The rocketing money supply produces frenzied total spending and severe demand-pull inflation.

Question:
How would you alter your present spending plans if you were quite certain that the prices of everything were going to double in the coming week?

[*] Theodore Morgan, *Income and Employment*, 2d ed. (Englewood Cliffs, N.J.: Prentice-Hall, 1952), p. 361.
[†] Raburn M. Williams, *Inflation! Money, Jobs, and Politicians* (Arlington Heights, Ill.: AHM Publishing, 1980), p. 2.
[‡] Stanley Fischer, Ratna Sahay, and Carlos Végh, "Modern Hyper- and High Inflations," *Journal of Economic Literature*, September 2002, p. 840.

Summary

1. Business cycles are recurring ups and downs in economic activity. Their two primary phases are expansions and recessions.

2. Economists distinguish between frictional, structural, and cyclical unemployment. The rate of unemployment at full employment consists of frictional and structural unemployment and currently is about 5 percent.

3. The economic cost of unemployment, as measured by the negative GDP gap, consists of the goods and services forgone by society when its resources are involuntarily idle.

4. Inflation is a rise in the general price level and is measured in the United States by the Consumer Price Index (CPI). When inflation occurs, each dollar of income will buy fewer goods and services than before. That is, inflation reduces the purchasing power of money.

5. Economists discern both demand-pull and cost-push (supply-side) inflation. Demand-pull inflation results from an excess of total spending relative to the economy's capacity to produce. The main source of cost-push inflation is abrupt and rapid increases in the prices of key resources. These supply shocks push up per-unit production costs and ultimately the prices of consumer goods.

6. Unanticipated inflation arbitrarily redistributes real income at the expense of fixed-income receivers, creditors, and savers. If inflation is anticipated, individuals and businesses may be able to take steps to lessen or eliminate adverse redistribution effects.

7. Cost-push inflation reduces real output and employment. Proponents of zero inflation argue that even mild demand-pull inflation (1 to 3 percent) reduces the economy's real output. Other economists say that mild inflation may be a necessary by-product of the high and growing spending that produces high levels of output, full employment, and economic growth.

8. Hyperinflation, caused by highly imprudent expansions of the money supply, may undermine the monetary system and cause severe declines in real output.

Terms and Concepts

business cycles	unemployment rate	demand-pull inflation
recession	frictional unemployment	cost-push inflation
expansion	structural unemployment	nominal income
shocks	cyclical unemployment	real income
demand shocks	potential output	real interest rate
supply shocks	GDP gap	nominal interest rate
sticky prices	inflation	deflation
labor force	Consumer Price Index (CPI)	

Study Questions

1. What are the two primary phases of the business cycle? What tends to happen to real GDP, unemployment, and inflation during these phases? **LO1**

2. How many recessions has the U.S. experienced since 1950? Which ones were the longest in duration? Which ones were the most severe in terms of declines in real output? **LO1**

3. Use the following data to calculate (a) the size of the labor force and (b) the official unemployment rate: total population, 500; population under 16 years of age or institutionalized, 120; not in labor force, 150; unemployed, 23; part-time workers looking for full-time jobs, 10. **LO2**

4. Since the United States has an unemployment compensation program that provides income for those out of work, why should we worry about unemployment? **LO3**

5. What are the three types of unemployment? Unemployment is seen by some as undesirable. Are all three types of unemployment undesirable? Explain. **LO3**

6. What is the Consumer Price Index (CPI), and how is it determined each month? What effect does inflation have on the purchasing power of a dollar? How does it explain differences between nominal and real interest rates? How does deflation differ from inflation? **LO2**

7. If the CPI was 110 last year and is 121 this year, what is this year's rate of inflation? What is the "rule of 70"? How long would it take for the price level to double if inflation persisted at (a) 2 percent, (b) 5 percent, and (c) 10 percent per year? **LO2**

8. Briefly distinguish between demand-pull inflation and cost-push inflation. **LO3**

9. How does unanticipated inflation hurt creditors and help borrowers? How can anticipating the inflation make these effects less severe? **LO3**

10. Explain how hyperinflation might lead to a severe decline in total output. **LO3**

FURTHER TEST YOUR KNOWLEDGE AT
www.mcconnellbriefmacro1e.com

Web-Based Questions

At the text's Online Learning Center, **www.mcconnellbriefmacro 1e.com,** you will find a multiple-choice quiz on this chapter's content. We encourage you to take the quiz to see how you do.

Also, you will find one or more Web-based questions that require information from the Internet to answer.

7

Aggregate Demand and Aggregate Supply

In early 2000, Alan Greenspan, chair of the Federal Reserve, made the following statement:

> Through the so-called wealth effect, the [recent stock market gains] have tended to foster increases in aggregate demand beyond the increases in supply. It is this imbalance . . . that contains the potential seeds of rising inflationary . . . pressures that could undermine the current expansion. Our goal [at the Federal Reserve] is to extend the expansion by containing its imbalances and avoiding the very recession that would complete the business cycle.[1]

Although the Federal Reserve held inflation in check, it did not accomplish its goal of extending the decade-long economic expansion. In March 2001 the U.S. economy experienced a recession and the

---

[1] Alan Greenspan, speech to the New York Economics Club, Jan. 13, 2000.

expansionary phase of the business cycle ended. Recovery and expansion resumed in 2002 and picked up considerable strength over the next two years, so that the the economy was again operating at full employment by late 2004. In December, 2007, however, the expansion came to an end. Largely because of a mortgage debt crisis, a new recession began.

We will say more about the expansion and recession soon, but our immediate focus is the terminology in the Greenspan quotation. This is precisely the language of the **aggregate demand–aggregate supply model (AD-AS model).** The AD-AS model—the subject of this chapter—enables us to analyze changes in real GDP and the price level simultaneously. The AD-AS model therefore provides keen insights on inflation, recession, unemployment, and economic growth. In later chapters, we will also see how the model nicely depicts macroeconomic stabilization policies, such as those used in 2008 to try to counter the recession that was occuring.

Aggregate Demand

Aggregate demand is a schedule or curve that shows the quantities of real domestic output (real GDP) that buyers collectively want to purchase at each possible price level. The relationship between the price level (as measured by the GDP price index) and the amount of real output demanded is inverse or negative: When the price level rises, the quantity of real GDP demanded falls; when the price level falls, the quantity of real GDP demanded rises.

Figure 7.1 shows the inverse relationship between the price level and real GDP. The downward slope of the AD curve reflects the fact that higher U.S. price levels discourage domestic buyers (households and businesses) and foreign buyers from purchasing U.S. real GDP. Lower price levels encourage them to buy more U.S. real output.

Changes in Aggregate Demand

Other things equal, a change in the price level will change the amount of total spending and therefore change the amount of real GDP demanded by the economy. Movements along a fixed aggregate demand curve represent these changes in real GDP. However, if one or more of those "other things" change, the entire aggregate demand curve will

aggregate demand–aggregate supply (AD-AS) model
The macroeconomic model that uses aggregate demand and aggregate supply to determine and explain the price level and level of real domestic output.

aggregate demand
A schedule or curve that shows the total quantity of goods and services demanded (purchased) at different price levels.

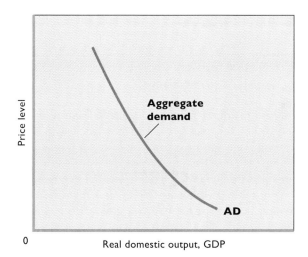

FIGURE 7.1 **The aggregate demand curve.** The downsloping aggregate demand curve AD indicates an inverse (or negative) relationship between the price level and the amount of real output purchased.

FIGURE 7.2 Changes in aggregate demand. A change in one or more of the listed determinants of aggregate demand will shift the aggregate demand curve. The rightward shift from AD_1 to AD_2 represents an increase in aggregate demand; the leftward shift from AD_1 to AD_3 shows a decrease in aggregate demand.

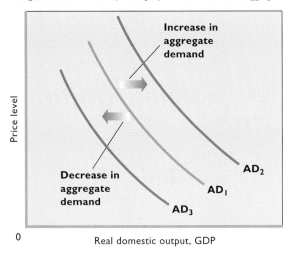

Determinants of Aggregate Demand: Factors That Shift the Aggregate Demand Curve

1. Change in consumer spending
   a. Consumer wealth
   b. Household borrowing
   c. Consumer expectations
   d. Personal taxes
2. Change in investment spending
   a. Interest rates
   b. Expected returns
      • Expected future business conditions
      • Technology
      • Degree of excess capacity
      • Business taxes
3. Change in government spending
4. Change in net export spending
   a. National income abroad
   b. Exchange rates

determinants of aggregate demand Factors that shift the aggregate demand curve when they change.

shift. We call these other things **determinants of aggregate demand.** When they change, they shift the AD curve. These AD shifters are listed in the table in Figure 7.2. In that figure, the rightward shift of the curve from AD_1 to AD_2 shows an increase in aggregate demand. The leftward shift from AD_1 to AD_3 shows a decrease in aggregate demand. Notice that the categories of spending are the same as those in the national income and product accounts (Chapter 5). To provide a clear understanding of these AD shifters, we need to elaborate on them.

Consumer Spending

If consumers decide to buy more output at each price level, the aggregate demand curve will shift to the right, as from AD_1 to AD_2 in Figure 7.2. If they decide to buy less output, the aggregate demand curve will shift to the left, as from AD_1 to AD_3.

Several factors can change consumer spending and therefore shift the aggregate demand curve. As the table in Figure 7.2 shows, those factors are real consumer wealth, household borrowing, consumer expectations, and personal taxes.

Consumer Wealth
Consumer wealth is the total dollar value of all assets owned by consumers in the economy less the dollar value of their liabilities (debts). Assets include stocks, bonds, and real estate. Liabilities include mortgages, car loans, and credit card balances.

Consumer wealth sometimes changes suddenly and unexpectedly due to surprising changes in asset values. An unforeseen increase in the stock market is a good example. The increase in wealth prompts pleasantly surprised consumers to save less and buy more out of their current incomes than they had previously been planning. The resulting increase in consumer spending—the so-called *wealth effect*—shifts the aggregate demand curve to the right. In contrast, an unexpected decline in asset values will cause an unanticipated reduction in consumer wealth at each price level. As consumers tighten their belts in response to the bad news, a "reverse wealth effect" sets in. Unpleasantly surprised consumers increase savings and reduce consumption, thereby shifting the aggregate demand curve to the left.

Household Borrowing Consumers can increase their consumption spending by borrowing. Doing so shifts the aggregate demand curve to the right. By contrast, a decrease in borrowing for consumption purposes shifts the aggregate demand curve to the left. The aggregate demand curve also will shift to the left if consumers increase their savings rates in order to pay off their debts. With more money flowing to debt repayment, consumption expenditures decline and the AD curve shifts left.

Consumer Expectations Changes in expectations about the future may alter consumer spending. When people expect their future real incomes to rise, they tend to spend more of their current incomes. Thus, current consumption spending increases (current saving falls), and the aggregate demand curve shifts to the right. Similarly, a widely held expectation of surging inflation in the near future may increase aggregate demand today because consumers will want to buy products before their prices escalate. Conversely, expectations of lower future income or lower future prices may reduce current consumption and shift the aggregate demand curve to the left.

Personal Taxes A reduction in personal income tax rates raises take-home income and increases consumer purchases at each possible price level. Tax cuts shift the aggregate demand curve to the right. Tax increases reduce consumption spending and shift the curve to the left.

APPLYING THE ANALYSIS

What Wealth Effect?

The consumption component of aggregate demand is usually relatively stable even during rather extraordinary times. Between March 2000 and July 2002, the U.S. stock market lost a staggering $3.7 trillion of value (yes, trillion). Yet consumption spending was greater at the end of that period than at the beginning. How can that be? Why didn't a negative wealth effect reduce consumption?

There are a number of reasons. Of greatest importance, the amount of consumption spending in the economy depends mainly on the *flow* of income, not the *stock* of wealth. Disposable income (after-tax income) in the United States is nearly $9 trillion annually, and consumers spend a large portion of it. Even though there was a mild recession in 2001, disposable income and consumption spending were both greater in July 2002 than in March 2000. Second, the Federal government cut personal income tax rates during this period, and that bolstered consumption spending. Third, household wealth did not fall by the full amount of the $3.7 trillion stock market loss because the value of houses increased dramatically over this period. Finally, lower interest rates during this period enabled many households to refinance their mortgages, reduce monthly loan payments, and increase their current consumption.

For all these offsetting reasons, the consumption component of aggregate demand held up in the face of the extraordinary loss of stock market value.

Question:
Which do you think will decrease consumption more: a 10 percent decrease in after-tax income or a 10 percent decrease in stock market values? Explain.

Investment Spending

Investment spending (the purchase of capital goods) is a second major determinant of aggregate demand. Increases in investment spending at each price level boost aggregate demand, and decreases in investment spending reduce it.

The investment decision is a marginal-benefit–marginal-cost decision. The marginal benefit of the investment is a stream of higher profits that is expected to result from the investment. In percentage terms, economists call these higher profits (net of new operation expenses) the *expected return on the investment, r*. For example, suppose the owner of a small cabinetmaking shop is considering whether to invest in a new sanding machine that costs $1000, expands output, and has a useful life of only 1 year. (Extending the life of the machine beyond 1 year complicates the economic calculation but does not change the fundamental analysis.) Suppose the net expected revenue from the machine (that is, after such operating costs as power, lumber, labor, and certain taxes have been subtracted) is $1100. Then the expected net revenue is sufficient to cover the initial $1000 cost of the machine and leave a profit of $100. Comparing this $100 to the $1000 initial cost of the machine, we find that the expected rate of return, r, on the investment is 10 percent (= $100/$1000).

It is important to note that the return just discussed is an *expected* rate of return, not a *guaranteed* rate of return. Investment involves risk, so the investment may or may not pay off as anticipated. Moreover, investment faces diminishing returns. As more of it occurs, the best investment projects are completed and the subsequent projects produce lower expected rates of return. So, the expected return, r, tends to fall as firms undertake more and more investment.

The marginal cost of the investment to a firm is reflected in either the explicit costs of borrowing money from others or the implicit cost of using its own retained earnings to make the investment. In percentage terms, and adjusted for expected inflation, this cost is the real interest rate, i.

The business firm compares the real interest rate (marginal cost) with the expected return on investment (marginal benefit). If the expected rate of return (for example, 6 percent) exceeds the interest rate (say, 5 percent), the investment is undertaken. The firm expects the investment to be profitable. But if the interest rate (for example, 7 percent) exceeds the expected rate of return (6 percent), the investment will not be undertaken. The firm expects the investment to be unprofitable. The profit-maximizing firm will undertake all investment that it thinks will be profitable. That means it will invest up to the point where $r = i$ in order to exhaust all investment possibilities for which r exceeds i.

So real interest rates and expected returns are the two main determinants of investment spending.

Real Interest Rates We will discover that a nation's central bank—the Federal Reserve in the United States—can take monetary actions to increase and decrease interest rates. When it takes those actions, it shifts the nation's aggregate demand curve. Other things equal, increases in real interest rates will lower investment spending and reduce aggregate demand. Declines in interest rates will have the opposite effects.

Expected Returns Higher expected returns on investment projects will increase the demand for capital goods and shift the aggregate demand curve to the right. Alternatively, declines in expected returns will decrease investment and shift the curve to the left. Expected returns are influenced by several factors:

- *Future business conditions* If firms are generally optimistic about future business conditions, they are more likely to forecast high rates of return on current investment and therefore may invest more today. In contrast, if they think the economy will deteriorate in the future, they will forecast low rates of return and perhaps will invest less today.

- *Technology* New and improved technologies enhance expected returns on investment and thus increase aggregate demand. For example, recent advances in microbiology have motivated pharmaceutical companies to establish new labs and production facilities.

- *Degree of excess capacity* A rise in excess capacity—unused capital—will reduce the expected return on new investment and hence decrease aggregate demand. Other things equal, firms operating factories at well below capacity have little incentive to build new factories. But when firms realize that their excess capacity is dwindling or has completely disappeared, their expected returns on new investment in factories and capital equipment rise. Thus, they increase their investment spending, and the aggregate demand curve shifts to the right.

- *Business taxes* An increase in business taxes will reduce after-tax profits from capital investment and lower expected returns. So investment and aggregate demand will decline. A decrease in business taxes will have the opposite effects.

The variability of interest rates and investment expectations makes investment quite volatile. In contrast to consumption, investment spending rises and falls quite often, independent of changes in total income. Investment, in fact, is the least stable component of aggregate demand.

Global Snapshot 7.1 compares investment spending relative to GDP for several nations in 2006.

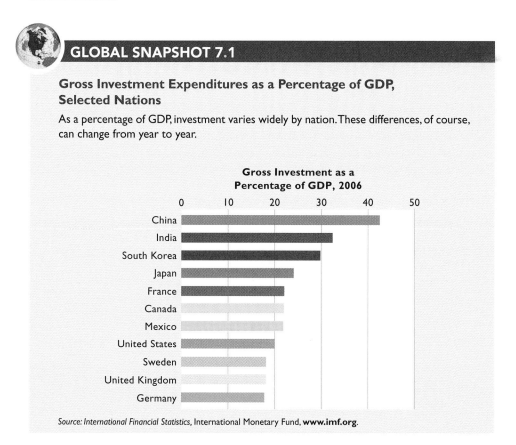

GLOBAL SNAPSHOT 7.1

Gross Investment Expenditures as a Percentage of GDP, Selected Nations

As a percentage of GDP, investment varies widely by nation. These differences, of course, can change from year to year.

Gross Investment as a Percentage of GDP, 2006

Source: *International Financial Statistics,* International Monetary Fund, **www.imf.org**.

Government Spending

Government purchases are the third determinant of aggregate demand. An increase in government purchases (for example, more military equipment) will shift the aggregate demand curve to the right, as long as tax collections and interest rates do not change as a result. In contrast, a reduction in government spending (for example, fewer transportation projects) will shift the curve to the left.

Net Export Spending

The final determinant of aggregate demand is net export spending. Other things equal, higher U.S. *exports* mean an increased foreign demand for U.S. goods. So a rise in net exports (higher exports relative to imports) shifts the aggregate demand curve to the right. In contrast, a decrease in U.S. net exports shifts the aggregate demand curve leftward.

What might cause net exports to change, other than the price level? Two possibilities are changes in national income abroad and changes in exchange rates.

National Income Abroad
Rising national income abroad encourages foreigners to buy more products, some of which are made in the United States. So U.S. net exports rise, and the U.S. aggregate demand curve shifts to the right. Declines in national income abroad do the opposite: They reduce U.S. net exports and shift the U.S. aggregate demand curve to the left.

Exchange Rates
Changes in **exchange rates**—the prices of foreign currencies in terms of one's own currency—may affect U.S. net exports and therefore aggregate demand. When the dollar *depreciates* (declines in value) against foreign currencies, it takes more dollars to buy foreign goods. So foreign goods become more expensive in dollar terms, and Americans reduce their imports. On the opposite side, the depreciation of the dollar means that other currencies *appreciate* (rise in value) relative to the dollar. U.S. exports rise because those foreign currencies can buy more American goods. Conclusion: Dollar depreciation increases net exports (imports go down; exports go up) and therefore increases aggregate demand.

Dollar appreciation has the opposite effects: Net exports fall (imports go up; exports go down) and aggregate demand declines.

As shown in Global Snapshot 7.2, net exports vary greatly among the major industrial nations.

exchange rates
The prices of foreign currencies in terms of one's own currency.

GLOBAL SNAPSHOT 7.2

Net Exports of Goods, Selected Nations, 2006

Some nations, such as Germany and Japan, have positive net exports; other countries, such as the United States and the United Kingdom, have negative net exports.

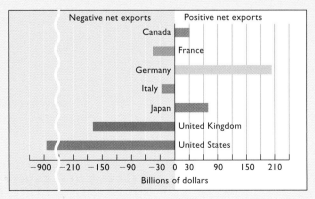

Source: World Trade Organization, **www.wto.org**.

Aggregate Supply

Aggregate supply is a schedule or curve showing the relationship between the price level and the amount of real domestic output that firms in the economy produce. This relationship varies depending on the time horizon and how quickly output prices and input prices can change. We will define three time horizons.

- In the *immediate short run*, both input prices as well as output prices are fixed.
- In the *short run*, input prices are fixed, but output prices can vary.
- In the *long run*, input prices as well as output prices can vary.

In Chapter 6, we introduced the concept of inflexible (or "sticky") prices. Here we consider different degrees of stickiness in order to discuss how total output varies with the price level in the immediate short run, the short run, and the long run. As you will see, the relationship between the price level and total output is different in each of the three time horizons because input prices are stickier than output prices. While both become more flexible as time passes, output prices usually adjust more rapidly.

Aggregate Supply in the Immediate Short Run

Depending on the type of firm, the immediate short run can last anywhere from a few days to a few months. It lasts as long as *both* input prices and output prices stay fixed. Input prices are fixed in both the immediate short run and the short run by contractual agreements. In particular, 75 percent of the average firm's costs are wages and salaries—and these are almost always fixed by labor contracts for months or years at a time. As a result, they are usually fixed for a much longer duration than output prices, which can begin to change within a few days or a few months depending upon the type of firm.

That being said, output prices are also typically fixed in the immediate short run. This is most often caused by firms setting fixed prices for their customers and then agreeing to supply whatever quantity demanded results at those fixed prices. For instance, once an appliance manufacturer sets its annual list prices for refrigerators, stoves, ovens, and microwaves, it is obligated to supply however many or few appliances customers want to buy at those prices. Similarly, a catalogue company is obliged to sell however much customers want to buy of its products at the prices listed in its current catalogue. And it is obligated to supply those quantities demanded until it sends out its next catalogue.

With output prices fixed and firms selling however much customers want to purchase at those fixed prices, the **immediate-short-run aggregate supply curve** AS_{ISR} is a horizontal line, as shown in Figure 7.3. The AS_{ISR} curve is horizontal at the overall price level P_1, which is calculated from all of the individual prices set by the various firms in the economy. Its horizontal shape implies that the total amount of output supplied in the economy depends directly on the volume of spending that results at price level P_1. If total spending is low at price level P_1, firms will supply a small amount to match the low level of spending. If total spending is high at price level P_1, they will supply a high level of output to match the high level of spending. The amount of output that results may be higher than or lower than the economy's full-employment output level Q_f.

Notice, however, that firms will respond in this manner to changes in total spending only as long as output prices remain fixed. As soon as firms are able to change their product prices, they can respond to changes in aggregate spending not only by increasing or decreasing output but also by raising or lowering prices. This is the situation that leads to the upward-sloping short-run aggregate supply curve that we discuss next.

aggregate supply
A schedule or curve that shows the total quantity of goods and services supplied (produced) at different price levels.

immediate-short-run aggregate supply curve
The aggregate supply curve associated with a period of time in which neither input nor output prices respond to changes in the level of spending or production.

FIGURE 7.3 **Aggregate supply in the immediate short run.** In the immediate short run, the aggregate supply curve AS_{ISR} is horizontal at the economy's current price level, P_1. With output prices fixed, firms collectively supply the level of output that is demanded at those prices.

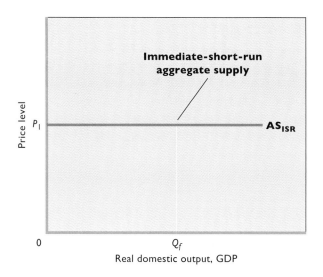

short-run aggregate supply curve
An aggregate supply curve relevant to a time period in which output prices are flexible, but input prices are sticky.

Aggregate Supply in the Short Run

The short run begins after the immediate short run ends. As it relates to macroeconomics, the short run is a period of time during which output prices are flexible but input prices are either totally fixed or highly inflexible.

These assumptions about output prices and input prices are general—they relate to the economy in the aggregate. Naturally, some input prices are more flexible than others. Since gasoline prices are quite flexible, a package delivery firm like UPS that uses gasoline as an input will have at least one very flexible input price. On the other hand, wages at UPS are set by five-year labor contracts negotiated with its drivers' union, the Teamsters. Because wages are the firm's largest and most important input cost, it is the case that, overall, UPS faces input prices that are inflexible for several years at a time. Thus, its "short run"—during which it can change the shipping prices that it charges its customers but during which it must deal with substantially fixed input prices—is actually quite long. Keep this in mind as we derive the short-run aggregate supply for the entire economy. Its applicability does not depend on some arbitrary definition of how long the "short run" should be. Instead, the short run for which the model is relevant is any period of time during which output prices are flexible but input prices are fixed or nearly fixed.

As illustrated in Figure 7.4, the **short-run aggregate supply curve** AS slopes upward because, with input prices fixed, changes in the price level will raise or lower real firm profits. To see how this works, consider an economy that has only a single multiproduct firm called Mega Buzzer and in which the firm's owners must receive a real profit of $20 in order to produce the full-employment output of 100 units. Assume the owner's only input (aside from entrepreneurial talent) is 10 units of hired labor at $8 per worker, for a total wage cost of $80. Also, assume that the 100 units of output sell for $1 per unit, so total revenue is $100. Mega Buzzer's nominal profit is $20 (= $100 − $80), and using the $1 price to designate the base-price index of 100, its real profit is also $20 (= $20/1.00). Well and good; the full-employment output is produced.

Next, consider what will happen if the price of Mega Buzzer's output doubles. The doubling of the price level will boost total revenue from $100 to $200, but

FIGURE 7.4 **The aggregate supply curve (short run).** The upsloping aggregate supply curve AS indicates a direct (or positive) relationship between the price level and the amount of real output that firms will offer for sale. The AS curve is relatively flat below the full-employment output because unemployed resources and unused capacity allow firms to respond to price-level rises with large increases in real output. It is relatively steep beyond the full-employment output because resource shortages and capacity limitations make it difficult to expand real output as the price level rises.

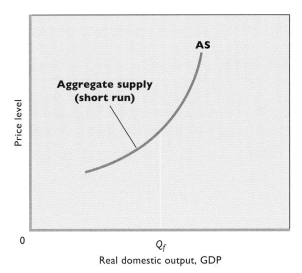

since we are discussing the short run during which input prices are fixed, the $8 nominal wage for each of the 10 workers will remain unchanged so that total costs stay at $80. Nominal profit will rise from $20 (= $100 − $80) to $120 (= $200 − $80). Dividing that $120 profit by the new price index of 200 (= 2.0 in hundredths), we find that Mega Buzzer's real profit is now $60. The rise in the real reward from $20 to $60 prompts the firm (economy) to produce more output. Conversely, price-level declines reduce real profits and cause the firm (economy) to reduce its output. So, in the short run, there is a direct, or positive, relationship between the price level and real output. When the price level rises, real output rises and when the price level falls, real output falls. The result is an upward-sloping short-run aggregate supply curve.

Notice, however, that the slope of the short-run aggregate supply curve is not constant. It is relatively flat at outputs below the full-employment output level Q_f and relatively steep at outputs above it. This has to do with the fact that per-unit production costs underlie the short-run aggregate supply curve. In equation form,

$$\text{Per-unit production cost} = \frac{\text{total input cost}}{\text{units of output}}.$$

The per-unit production cost of any specific level of output establishes that output's price level because the associated price level must cover all the costs of production, including profit "costs."

As the economy expands in the short run, per-unit production costs generally rise because of reduced efficiency. But the extent of that rise depends on where the economy is operating relative to its capacity. When the economy is operating below its full-employment output, it has large amounts of unused machinery and equipment and large numbers of unemployed workers. Firms can put these idle human and property resources back to work with little upward pressure on per-unit production costs. And as output expands, few if any shortages of inputs or production bottlenecks will arise to raise per-unit production costs. That is why the slope of the short-run aggregate supply curve increases only slowly at output levels below the full-employment output level Q_f.

On the other hand, when the economy is operating beyond Q_f, the vast majority of its available resources are already employed. Adding more workers to a relatively fixed number of highly used capital resources such as plant and equipment creates congestion in the workplace and reduces the efficiency (on average) of workers. Adding more capital, given the limited number of available workers, leaves equipment idle and reduces the efficiency of capital. Adding more land resources when capital and labor are highly constrained reduces the efficiency of land resources. Under these circumstances, total input costs rise more rapidly than total output. The result is rapidly rising per-unit production costs that give the short-run aggregate supply curve its rapidly increasing slope at output levels beyond Q_f.

Aggregate Supply in the Long Run

In macroeconomics, the long run is the time horizon over which both input prices as well as output prices are flexible. It begins after the short run ends. Depending on the type of firm and industry, this may be from a couple of weeks to several years in the future. But for the economy as a whole, it is the time horizon over which all output and input prices—including wage rates—are fully flexible.

The **long-run aggregate supply curve** AS_{LR} is vertical at the economy's full-employment output Q_f, as shown in Figure 7.5. The vertical curve means that in the long run the economy will produce the full employment output level no matter what the price level is. How can this be? Shouldn't higher prices cause firms to increase output? The explanation lies in the fact that in the long run, when both input prices as well as output prices are flexible, profit levels will always adjust so as to give firms exactly the right profit incentive to produce exactly the full-employment output level, Q_f.

long-run aggregate supply curve
The aggregate supply curve associated with a period of time in which both input and output prices are fully flexible.

FIGURE 7.5 **Aggregate supply in the long run.** The long-run aggregate supply curve AS_{LR} is vertical at the full-employment level of real GDP (Q_f) because in the long run wages and other input prices rise and fall to match changes in the price level. So price-level changes do not affect firms' profits, and thus they create no incentive for firms to alter their output.

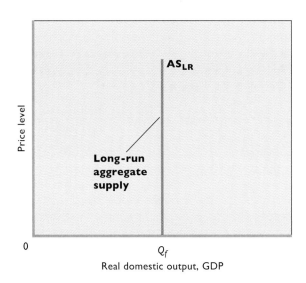

To see why this is true, look back at the short-run aggregate supply curve AS shown in Figure 7.4. Suppose that the economy starts out producing at the full-employment output level Q_f and that the price level at that moment has an index value of 100. Now suppose that output prices double, so that the price index goes to 200. We previously demonstrated for our single-firm economy that this doubling of the price level would cause profits to rise in the short run and that the higher profits would motivate the firm to increase output.

This outcome, however, is totally dependent upon the fact that input prices are fixed in the short run. Consider what will happen in the long run when they are free to change. Firms can only produce beyond the full-employment output level by running factories and businesses at extremely high rates. This creates a great deal of demand for the economy's limited supply of productive resources. In particular, labor is in great demand because the only way to produce beyond full employment is if workers are working overtime.

As time passes and input prices are free to change, the high demand will start to raise input prices. In particular, overworked employees will demand and receive raises as employers scramble to deal with the labor shortages that arise when the economy is producing at above its full-employment output level. As input prices increase, firm profits will begin to fall. And as they decline, so does the motive firms have to produce more than the full-employment output level. This process of rising input prices and falling profits continues until the rise in input prices exactly matches the initial change in output prices (in our example, they both double). When that happens, firm profits in real terms return to their original level so that firms are once again motivated to produce at exactly the full-employment output level. This adjustment process means that in the long run the economy will produce at full employment regardless of the price level (in our example, at either $P = 100$ or $P = 200$). That is why the long-run aggregate supply curve AS_{LR} is vertical above the full-employment output level. Every possible price level on the vertical axis is associated with the economy producing at the full-employment output level in the long run once input prices adjust to exactly match changes in output prices.

Focusing on the Short Run

The immediate-short-run aggregate supply curve, the short-run aggregate supply curve, and the long-run aggregate supply curve are all important. Each curve is appropriate to situations that match their respective assumptions about the flexibility of input and output prices. But our focus in the rest of this chapter and the chapters that immediately follow will be on short-run aggregate supply curves such as the AS curve shown in Figure 7.4. Indeed, unless explicitly stated otherwise, all references to "aggregate supply" will be to aggregate supply in the short run.

Our emphasis on the short-run aggregate supply curve stems from our interest in understanding the business cycle in the simplest possible way. It is a fact that real-world economies typically manifest simultaneous changes in both their price levels and their levels of real output. The upward-sloping short-run AS curve is the only version of aggregate supply that can handle simultaneous movements in both of these variables. By contrast, the price level is assumed fixed in the immediate-short-run version of aggregate supply illustrated in Figure 7.3 and the economy's output is always equal to the full-employment output level in the long-run version of aggregate supply shown in Figure 7.5. This renders these versions of the aggregate supply curve less useful as part of a core model for analyzing business cycles and demonstrating the short-run government policies designed to deal with them.

Changes in Aggregate Supply

An existing aggregate supply curve identifies the relationship between the price level and real output, other things equal. But when other things change, the curve itself shifts. The rightward shift of the curve from AS_1 to AS_2 in Figure 7.6 represents an increase in aggregate supply, indicating that firms are willing to produce and sell more real output at each price level. A decrease in aggregate supply is shown by the leftward shift of the curve from AS_1 to AS_3. At each price level, firms produce less output than before.

determinants of aggregate supply Factors that shift the aggregate supply curve when they change.

The table in Figure 7.6 lists the factors that collectively position the aggregate supply curve. They are called the **determinants of aggregate supply** and shift the curve when they change. Changes in these determinants raise or lower per-unit production costs *at each price level (or each level of output)*. These changes in per-unit production costs affect profits, thereby leading firms to alter the amount of output they are willing to produce *at each price level*. For example, firms may collectively offer $7 trillion of real output at a price level of 1.0 (= 100 in index-value terms), rather than $6.8 trillion. Or they may offer $6.5 trillion rather than $7 trillion. The point is that when one of the determinants listed in Figure 7.6 changes, the aggregate supply curve shifts to the right or left. Changes that reduce per-unit production costs shift the aggregate supply curve to the right, as from AS_1 to AS_2; changes that increase per-unit production costs shift it to the left, as from AS_1 to AS_3. *When per-unit production costs change for reasons other than changes in real output, the aggregate supply curve shifts.*

The aggregate supply determinants listed in Figure 7.6 are very important and therefore require more discussion.

Input Prices

Input or resource prices—to be distinguished from the output prices that make up the price level—are a major ingredient of per-unit production costs and therefore a key determinant of aggregate supply. These resources can be either domestic or imported.

FIGURE 7.6 Changes in aggregate supply. A change in one or more of the listed determinants of aggregate supply will shift the aggregate supply curve. The rightward shift of the aggregate supply curve from AS_1 to AS_2 represents an increase in aggregate supply; the leftward shift of the curve from AS_1 to AS_3 shows a decrease in aggregate supply.

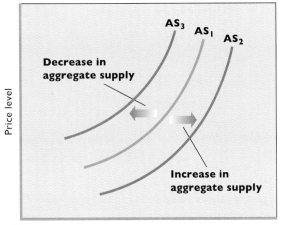

Determinants of Aggregate Supply: Factors That Shift the Aggregate Supply Curve

1. Change in input prices
   a. Domestic resource prices
   b. Prices of imported resources
2. Change in productivity
3. Change in legal-institutional environment
   a. Business taxes
   b. Government regulations

Domestic Resource Prices As stated earlier, wages and salaries make up about 75 percent of all business costs. Other things equal, decreases in wages reduce per-unit production costs. So the aggregate supply curve shifts to the right. Increases in wages shift the curve to the left. Examples:

- Labor supply increases because of substantial immigration. Wages and per-unit production costs fall, shifting the AS curve to the right.
- Labor supply decreases because a rapid increase in pension income causes many older workers to opt for early retirement. Wage rates and per-unit production costs rise, shifting the AS curve to the left.

Similarly, the aggregate supply curve shifts when the prices of land and capital inputs change. Examples:

- The price of machinery and equipment falls because of declines in the prices of steel and electronic components. Per-unit production costs decline, and the AS curve shifts to the right.
- The supply of available land resources expands through discoveries of mineral deposits, irrigation of land, or technical innovations that transform "nonresources" (say, vast desert lands) into valuable resources (productive lands). The price of land declines, per-unit production costs fall, and the AS curve shifts to the right.

Prices of Imported Resources Just as foreign demand for U.S. goods contributes to U.S. aggregate demand, resources imported from abroad (such as oil, tin, and copper) add to U.S. aggregate supply. Added supplies of resources—whether domestic or imported—typically reduce per-unit production costs. A decrease in the price of imported resources increases U.S. aggregate supply, while an increase in their price reduces U.S. aggregate supply.

A good example of the major effect that changing resource prices can have on aggregate supply is the oil price hikes of the 1970s. At that time, a group of oil-producing nations called the Organization of Petroleum Exporting Countries (OPEC) worked in concert to decrease oil production in order to raise the price of oil. The 10-fold increase in the price of oil that OPEC achieved during the 1970s drove up per-unit production costs and jolted the U.S. aggregate supply curve leftward. By contrast, a sharp decline in oil prices in the mid-1980s resulted in a rightward shift of the U.S. aggregate supply curve. In 1999 OPEC again reasserted itself, raising oil prices and therefore per-unit production costs for some U.S. producers including airlines and shipping companies like FedEx and UPS. Increases in the price of oil in 2008 were mostly due to increases in demand rather than changes in supply caused by OPEC. But keep in mind that no matter what their cause, increases in the price of oil and other resources raise production costs and decrease aggregate supply.

Exchange-rate fluctuations are one factor that may alter the price of imported resources. Suppose that the dollar appreciates, enabling U.S. firms to obtain more foreign currency with each dollar. This means that domestic producers face a lower *dollar* price of imported resources. U.S. firms will respond by increasing their imports of foreign resources, thereby lowering their per-unit production costs at each level of output. Falling per-unit production costs will shift the U.S. aggregate supply curve to the right.

A depreciation of the dollar will have the opposite set of effects and will shift the aggregate supply curve to the left.

productivity
A measure of real
output per unit of
input.

Productivity

The second major determinant of aggregate supply is **productivity,** which is a measure of the relationship between a nation's level of real output and the amount of resources used to produce that output. Thus productivity is a measure of average real output, or of real output per unit of input:

$$\text{Productivity} = \frac{\text{total output}}{\text{total inputs}}$$

WORKED PROBLEMS

W 7.1

Productivity and costs

With no change in resource prices, increases in productivity reduce the per-unit production cost of output. Recall that this cost is determined by dividing the total cost of production by the dollar amount of output. For example, if the total cost of production is $20 billion and total output is $40 billion, per-unit production cost is $.50. If productivity rises such that output increases from $40 billion to $60 billion, the per-unit production cost will fall from $.50 (= $20/$40) to $.33 (= $20/$60).

The generalization is this: By reducing per-unit production costs, increases in productivity shift the aggregate supply curve to the right. The main source of productivity advance is improved production technology, often embodied within new plant and equipment that replaces old plant and equipment. Other sources of productivity increases are a better-educated and better-trained workforce, improved forms of business enterprises, and the reallocation of labor resources from lower-productivity to higher-productivity uses.

Much rarer, decreases in productivity increase per-unit production costs and therefore reduce aggregate supply (shift the AS curve to the left).

Legal-Institutional Environment

Changes in the legal-institutional setting in which businesses operate are the final determinant of aggregate supply. Such changes may alter the per-unit costs of output and, if so, shift the aggregate supply curve. Two changes of this type are (1) changes in business taxes and (2) changes in the extent of regulation.

Business Taxes Higher business taxes, such as sales, excise, and payroll taxes, increase per-unit costs and reduce short-run aggregate supply in much the same way as a wage increase does. An increase in such taxes paid by businesses will increase per-unit production costs and shift aggregate supply to the left.

Government Regulation It is usually costly for businesses to comply with government regulations. More regulation therefore tends to increase per-unit production costs and shift the aggregate supply curve to the left. "Supply-side" proponents of deregulation of the economy have argued forcefully that, by increasing efficiency and reducing the paperwork associated with complex regulations, deregulation will reduce per-unit costs and shift the aggregate supply curve to the right. Other economists are less certain. Deregulation that results in accounting manipulations, monopolization, and business failures is likely to shift the AS curve to the left rather than to the right.

Equilibrium Price Level and Real GDP

Of all the possible combinations of price levels and levels of real GDP, which combination will the economy gravitate toward, at least in the short run? Figure 7.7 and its accompanying table provide the answer. Equilibrium occurs at the price level that equalizes the amounts of real output demanded and supplied. The intersection of the

FIGURE 7.7 **The equilibrium price level and equilibrium real GDP.** The intersection of the aggregate demand curve and the aggregate supply curve determines the economy's equilibrium price level. At the equilibrium price level of 100 (in index-value terms), the $510 billion of real output demanded matches the $510 billion of real output supplied. So equilibrium real GDP is $510 billion.

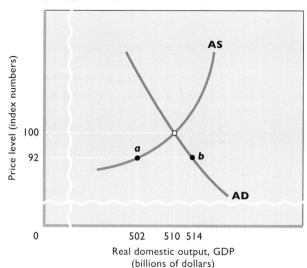

Real Output Demanded (Billions)	Price Level (Index Number)	Real Output Supplied (Billions)
$506	108	$513
508	104	512
510	*100*	*510*
512	96	507
514	92	502

aggregate demand curve AD and the aggregate supply curve AS establishes the economy's **equilibrium price level** and **equilibrium real output.** So aggregate demand and aggregate supply jointly establish the price level and level of real GDP.

In Figure 7.7 the equilibrium price level and level of real output are 100 and $510 billion, respectively. To illustrate why, suppose the price level is 92 rather than 100. We see from the table that the lower price level will encourage businesses to produce real output of $502 billion. This is shown by point *a* on the AS curve in the graph. But, as revealed by the table and point *b* on the aggregate demand curve, buyers will want to purchase $514 billion of real output at price level 92. Competition among buyers to purchase the lesser available real output of $502 billion will eliminate the $12 billion (= $514 billion − $502 billion) shortage and pull up the price level to 100.

As the table and graph show, the rise in the price level from 92 to 100 encourages producers to increase their real output from $502 billion to $510 billion and causes buyers to scale back their purchases from $514 billion to $510 billion. When equality occurs between the amounts of real output produced and purchased, as it does at price level 100, the economy has achieved equilibrium (here, at $510 billion of real GDP).

equilibrium price level
The price level at which the aggregate demand curve and the aggregate supply curve intersect.

equilibrium real output
The level of real GDP at which the aggregate demand curve and aggregate supply curve intersect.

INTERACTIVE GRAPHS

G 7.1
Aggregate demand–aggregate supply

Changes in the Price Level and Real GDP

Aggregate demand and aggregate supply typically change from one period to the next. If aggregate demand and aggregate supply increase proportionately over time, real GDP will expand and neither demand-pull inflation nor cyclical unemployment will occur. But we know from our discussion of the business cycle that macroeconomic stability is not always certain. A number of less-desirable situations can confront the economy. Let's apply the model to several such situations. For simplicity we will use *P* and *Q* symbols, rather than actual numbers. Remember that these symbols represent price index values and amounts of real GDP.

Demand-Pull Inflation

Suppose the economy is operating at its full-employment output and businesses and government increase their spending—actions that shift the aggregate demand curve to the right. Our list of determinants of aggregate demand (Figure 7.2) provides several reasons why this shift might occur. Perhaps firms boost their investment spending because they anticipate higher future profits from investments in new capital. Those profits are predicated on having new equipment and facilities that incorporate a number of new technologies. And perhaps government increases spending to expand national defense.

As shown by the rise in the price level from P_1 to P_2 in Figure 7.8, the increase in aggregate demand beyond the full-employment level of output moves the economy from a to b and causes inflation. This is *demand-pull inflation* because the price level is being pulled up by the increase in aggregate demand. Also, observe that the increase in demand expands real output from the full-employment level Q_f to Q_1. The distance between Q_1 and Q_f is a positive, or "inflationary" *GDP gap*: Actual GDP exceeds potential GDP.*

A classic American example of demand-pull inflation occurred in the late 1960s. The escalation of the war in Vietnam resulted in a 40 percent increase in defense spending between 1965 and 1967 and another 15 percent increase in 1968. The rise in government spending, imposed on an already growing economy, shifted the economy's aggregate demand curve to the right, producing the worst inflation in two decades. Actual GDP exceeded potential GDP, thereby creating an inflationary GDP gap. Inflation jumped from 1.6 percent in 1965 to 5.7 percent by 1970.

A more recent example of demand-pull inflation occurred in the late 1980s. As aggregate demand expanded beyond its full-employment level between 1986

---

* This positive GDP gap cannot last forever because eventually the price of labor and other inputs will increase and therefore shift the short-run AS curve leftward. The economy will eventually return to its full-employment output, Q_f, along its vertical long-run aggregate supply curve (not shown) that is located there.

FIGURE 7.8
Demand-pull inflation. The increase of aggregate demand from AD_1 to AD_2 moves the economy from a to b, causing demand-pull inflation of P_1 to P_2. It also causes a positive GDP gap of Q_1 minus Q_f.

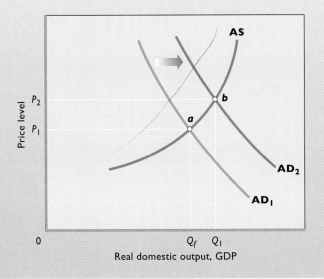

and 1990, the price level rose at an increasing rate. Specifically, the annual rate of inflation increased from 1.9 percent in 1986 to 3.6 percent in 1987 to 4.1 percent in 1988 to 4.8 percent in 1989. In terms of Figure 7.8, the aggregate demand curve moved rightward from year to year, raising the price level and the size of the positive GDP gap. The gap closed and the rate of inflation fell as the expansion gave way to the recession of 1990–1991.

Question:
How is the upward slope of the aggregate supply curve important in explaining demand-pull inflation?

Cost-Push Inflation

Inflation also can arise on the aggregate supply side of the economy. Suppose that warfare in the Middle East severely disrupts world oil supplies and drives up oil prices by some huge amount, say, 300 percent. Higher energy prices would spread through the economy, driving up production and distribution costs on a wide variety of goods. The U.S. aggregate supply curve would spring to the left, say, from AS_1 to AS_2 in Figure 7.9. The resulting increase in the price level would be *cost-push inflation*.

The effects of a leftward shift in aggregate supply are doubly bad. When aggregate supply shifts from AS_1 to AS_2, the economy moves from *a* to *b*. The price level rises from P_1 to P_2 and real output declines from Q_f to Q_1. Along with the cost-push inflation, a recession (and negative GDP gap) occurs. That is exactly

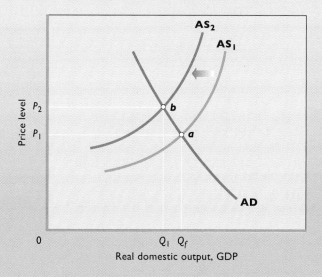

FIGURE 7.9
Cost-push inflation. A leftward shift of aggregate supply from AS_1 to AS_2 moves the economy from *a* to *b*, raises the price level from P_1 to P_2, and produces cost-push inflation. Real output declines and a negative GDP gap (of Q_1 minus Q_f) occurs.

what happened in the United States in the mid-1970s when the price of oil rocketed upward.

Today, the effect of oil prices on the U.S. economy has weakened relative to earlier periods. In the mid-1970s, oil expenditures were about 10 percent of U.S. GDP, compared to only 3 percent today. So the U.S. economy is now less vulnerable to cost-push inflation arising from oil-related "aggregate supply shocks."

Question:
Which is costlier to an economy in terms of lost real output, an equal degree of demand-pull inflation or cost-push inflation?

© Royalty-Free/CORBIS

© Royalty-Free/CORBIS

Photo Op Demand-Pull versus Cost-Push Inflation

A boom in investment spending, such as that for new construction, can cause demand-pull inflation. Soaring prices of key resources, such as oil, can cause cost-push inflation.

Downward Price-Level Inflexibility

We have just seen examples where, despite what we have learned about price "stickiness," the price level is readily flexible upward. But in the U.S. economy, deflation (a decline in the price level) rarely occurs even though the rate of inflation rises and falls. Why is the price level "sticky" or inflexible, particularly on the downside? Economists have offered several possible reasons for this:

- *Fear of price wars* Some oligopolists may be concerned that if they reduce their prices, rivals not only will match their price cuts but may retaliate by making even deeper cuts. An initial price cut may touch off an unwanted *price war:* successively deeper and deeper rounds of price cuts. In such a situation, all the firms end up with far less profit or higher losses than would be the case if they had simply maintained their prices. For this reason, each firm may resist making the initial price cut, choosing instead to reduce production and lay off workers.

- **Menu costs** Firms that think a recession will be relatively short-lived may be reluctant to cut their prices. One reason is what economists metaphorically call *menu costs*, named after their most obvious example: the cost of printing new menus when a restaurant decides to reduce its prices. But lowering prices also creates other costs. There are the costs of (1) estimating the magnitude and duration of the shift in demand to determine whether prices should be lowered, (2) repricing items held in inventory, (3) printing and mailing new catalogs, and (4) communicating new prices to customers, perhaps through advertising. When menu costs are present, firms may choose to avoid them by retaining current prices. That is, they may wait to see if the decline in aggregate demand is permanent.
- **Wage contracts** It usually is not profitable for firms to cut their product prices if they cannot also cut their wage rates. Wages are usually inflexible downward because large parts of the labor force work under contracts prohibiting wage cuts for the duration of the contract. (It is not uncommon for collective bargaining agreements in major industries to run for 3 years.) Similarly, the wages and salaries of nonunion workers are usually adjusted once a year, rather than quarterly or monthly.
- **Morale, effort, and productivity** Wage inflexibility downward is reinforced by the reluctance of many employers to reduce wage rates. If worker productivity (output per hour of work) remains constant, lower wages *do* reduce labor costs per unit of output. But lower wages might impair worker morale and work effort, thereby reducing productivity. Considered alone, lower productivity raises labor costs per unit of output because less output is produced. If the higher labor costs resulting from reduced productivity exceed the cost savings from the lower wage, then wage cuts will increase rather than reduce labor costs per unit of output. In such situations, firms will resist lowering wages when they are faced with a decline in aggregate demand.
- **Minimum wage** The minimum wage imposes a legal floor under the wages of the least skilled workers. Firms paying those wages cannot reduce that wage rate when aggregate demand declines.

Conclusion: In the United States, the price level readily rises but only reluctantly falls.

ILLUSTRATING
THE
IDEA

The Ratchet Effect

A *ratchet analogy* is a good way to think about the asymmetry of price-level changes. A ratchet is a tool or mechanism such as a winch, car jack, or socket wrench that cranks a wheel forward but does not allow it to go backward. Properly set, each allows the operator to move an object (boat, car, or nut) in one direction while preventing it from moving in the opposite direction.

The price level, wage rates, and per-unit production costs readily rise when aggregate demand increases along the aggregate supply curve. In the United States, the price level has increased in every year but one since 1950.

But the price level, wage rates, and per-unit production costs are inflexible downward when aggregate demand declines. The U.S. price level has fallen in only a single year (1955) since 1950, even though aggregate demand and real output have declined in a number of years.

In terms of our analogy, increases in aggregate demand ratchet the U.S. price level upward. Once in place, the higher price level remains until it is ratcheted up again. The higher price level tends to remain even with declines in aggregate demand. Inflation rates *do* rise and fall in the United States, but the price level mainly rises.

Question:
Does the ratchet analogy also apply to changes in real GDP? Why or why not?

APPLYING THE ANALYSIS

Recession and Cyclical Unemployment

Decreases in aggregate demand, combined with downward price-level inflexibility, can create recessions. For example, suppose that for some reason investment spending sharply declines. In Figure 7.10 we show the resulting decline in aggregate demand as a leftward shift from AD_1 to AD_2.

With the price level inflexible downward at P_1, the decline in aggregate demand moves the economy from *a* to *b* and reduces real output from Q_f to Q_1. The distance between Q_1 and Q_f measures the negative GDP gap—the amount by which actual output falls short of potential output. Because fewer workers are needed to produce the lower output, *cyclical unemployment* arises.

All recent demand-caused recessions in the United States have mimicked the "GDP gap but no deflation" scenario shown in Figure 7.10. Consider the recession that began in December 2007. In 2008, home foreclosures skyrocketed, several major financial institutions failed, and credit became very tight. New

FIGURE 7.10
A recession. If the price level is downwardly inflexible, a decline of aggregate demand from AD_1 to AD_2 will move the economy from *a* to *b* and reduce real GDP from Q_f to Q_1. Idle production capacity, cyclical unemployment, and a negative GDP gap (of Q_1 minus Q_f) will result.

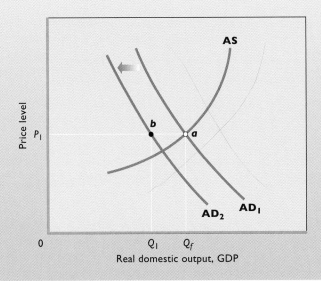

construction and other investment spending plummeted. Because of the resulting decline of aggregate demand, GDP fell short of potential output. In 2008, the unemployment rate rose from 4.9 to 7.2 percent. Although the rate of inflation declined (an outcome called *disinflation*), the price level was no lower at the end of 2008 than at the beginning.

Question:
How can a decline in expected investment returns on the construction of new houses, condominiums, and office buildings contribute to a recession?

The Multiplier Effect

Before leaving the topic of aggregate demand and aggregate supply, we need to supply two additional insights. First, shifts in the aggregate demand curves such as those in Figures 7.8 and 7.10 embody an "initial change" in spending, say, an increase in investment, followed by successive rounds of additional spending by businesses and households that are on the receiving end of the prior spending. Our shifts from one AD curve to another AD curve simply show the final results.

Assuming an economy has room to expand, an initial change in investment spending changes aggregate demand and GDP (and thus income) by more than the initial spending change. That surprising result is called the *multiplier effect*. The **multiplier** measures how much larger the final change in GDP will be; it is the ratio of a change in GDP to the initial change in spending (in this case, investment). Stated generally,

multiplier
The ratio of a change in GDP to an initial change in spending.

Multiplier = change in real GDP / initial change in spending

By rearranging this equation, we can also say that

Change in real GDP = multiplier × initial change in spending

So if investment in an economy rises by $30 billion and aggregate demand and real GDP increase by $90 billion as a result, we then know from our first equation that the multiplier is 3 (= $90/30).

Note these two points about the multiplier:

- The initial change in spending is often associated with investment spending because of investment's volatility. But changes in consumption spending (unrelated to change in income), government purchases, and net exports also lead to the multiplier effect.
- The multiplier works in both directions. An increase in initial spending may create a multiple increase in GDP, and a decrease in spending may be multiplied into a larger decrease in GDP.

The multiplier effect follows from the fact that the economy supports repetitive, continuous flows of expenditures and income, as we saw in the circular flow model in Chapter 2. Through this process, dollars spent by Smith are received as income by Chin, who then spends a portion that is received as income by Gonzales, and so on. Because a portion of new income is saved (not spent), the amount of new spending in each successive round declines, eventually bringing the multiplier process to an end.

Self-Correction?

The second insight is a caution: There is some evidence that the price level and average level of wages are becoming more flexible downward in the United States. Intense international competition and the declining power of unions in the United States seem to be undermining the ability of firms and workers to resist price and wage cuts when faced with falling aggregate demand. This increased flexibility of some prices and wages may be one reason the recession of 2001 was relatively mild. The U.S. auto manufacturers, for example, maintained output in the face of falling demand by offering zero-interest loans on auto purchases. This, in effect, was a disguised price cut.

In theory, fully flexible downward prices and wages would automatically "self-correct" a recession. Reduced aggregate demand, with its accompanying negative GDP gap and greater unemployment, would reduce the price level and level of (nominal) wages. In Figure 7.10, the lower wages would reduce per-unit production costs and shift the AS curve rightward. Eventually the economy would return to its full-employment output, but at a considerably lower price level than before. That is, the economy would move back to its long-run aggregate supply curve, like the one shown in Figure 7.5. (We will demonstrate this adjustment mechanism graphically in Chapter 11, "Long-Run Aggregate Supply and Aggregate Demand.")

In reality, the government and monetary authorities have been reluctant to wait for these slow and uncertain "corrections." Instead, they focus on trying to move the aggregate demand curve to its prerecession location. For example, throughout 2001 the Federal Reserve lowered interest rates to try to halt the recession and promote recovery. Those Fed actions, along with large Federal tax cuts, increased military spending, and strong demand for new housing, helped increase aggregate demand and spur recovery. The economy haltingly resumed its economic growth in 2002 and 2003, and then expanded rapidly in 2004 and 2005. Robust growth continued in 2006 and for the first three quarters of 2007.

Toward the end of 2007, however, crises in the housing and credit markets precipitated a new recession, prompting the Fed to begin a series of interest rate cuts to try to boost spending. In February 2008, the Federal government passed a tax rebate package, also in an effort to support aggregate demand and deal with the recession. We will examine stabilization policies such as these in the chapters that follow.

Summary

1. The aggregate demand–aggregate supply model (AD-AS model) enables analysis of simultaneous changes of real GDP and the price level.

2. The aggregate demand curve shows the level of real output that the economy will purchase at each price level. It slopes downward because higher price levels dissuade U.S. businesses and households, along with foreign buyers, from purchasing as much output as before.

3. The determinants of aggregate demand consist of spending by domestic consumers, businesses, and government and by foreign buyers. Changes in the factors listed in Figure 7.2 alter the spending by these groups and shift the aggregate demand curve.

4. The aggregate supply curve shows the levels of real output that businesses will produce at various possible price levels. The slope of the aggregate supply curve depends upon the flexibility of input and output prices. Since these vary over time, aggregate supply curves are categorized into three time horizons, each having different underlying assumptions about the flexibility of input and output prices.

5. The *immediate-short-run aggregate supply curve* assumes that both input prices and output prices are fixed. With output prices fixed, the aggregate supply curve is a horizontal line at the current price level. The *short-run aggregate supply curve* assumes nominal wages and other input prices remain fixed while output prices vary. The aggregate supply curve is generally upsloping because per-unit production costs, and hence the prices that firms must receive, rise as real output expands. The aggregate supply curve is relatively steep to

the right of the full-employment output level and relatively flat to the left of it. The *long-run aggregate supply curve* assumes that nominal wages and other input prices fully match any change in the price level. The curve is vertical at the full-employment output level.

6. Because the short-run aggregate supply curve is the only version of aggregate supply that can handle simultaneous changes in the price level and real output, it serves well as the core aggregate supply curve for analyzing the business cycle and economic policy. Unless stated otherwise, all references to "aggregate supply" refer to the short-run aggregate supply curve.

7. Figure 7.6 lists the determinants of aggregate supply: input prices, productivity, and the legal-institutional environment. A change in any one of these factors will change per-unit production costs at each level of output and therefore will shift the aggregate supply curve.

8. The intersection of the aggregate demand and aggregate supply curves determines an economy's equilibrium price level and real GDP. At the intersection, the quantity of real GDP demanded equals the quantity of real GDP supplied.

9. Increases in aggregate demand beyond the full-employment output cause inflation and positive GDP gaps (actual GDP exceeds potential GDP). Such gaps eventually evaporate as wages and other input prices rise to match the increase in the price level.

10. Leftward shifts of the aggregate supply curve reflect increases in per-unit production costs at each level of output and cause cost-push inflation, with accompanying negative GDP gaps.

11. Shifts of the aggregate demand curve to the left of the full-employment output cause recession, negative GDP gaps, and cyclical unemployment. The price level typically does not fall during U.S. recessions because of downwardly inflexible prices and wages. This inflexibility results from fear of price wars, menu costs, wage contracts, morale concerns, and minimum wages.

12. In theory, price and wage flexibility would allow the economy automatically to self-correct from a recession. In reality, downward price and wage flexibility make the process slow and uncertain. Recessions usually prompt the Federal government and the Federal Reserve to take actions to try to increase aggregate demand.

13. Changes in spending (consumption, investment, government purchases, and net exports) will lead to larger changes in GDP through the multiplier effect.

Terms and Concepts

aggregate demand–aggregate supply (AD-AS) model

aggregate demand

determinants of aggregate demand

exchange rates

aggregate supply

immediate-short-run aggregate supply curve

short-run aggregate supply curve

long-run aggregate supply curve

determinants of aggregate supply

productivity

equilibrium price level

equilibrium real output

multiplier

Study Questions

1. What is the general relationship between a country's price level and the quantity of its domestic output (real GDP) demanded? Who are the buyers of U.S. real GDP? **LO1**

2. What assumptions cause the immediate-short-run aggregate supply curve to be horizontal? Why is the long-run aggregate supply curve vertical? Explain the shape of the short-run aggregate supply curve. Why is the short-run curve relatively flat to the left of the full-employment output and relatively steep to the right? **LO2**

3. Suppose that the aggregate demand and supply schedules for an economy are as shown to the right: **LO3**

Amount of Real GDP Demanded, Billions	Price Level (Price Index)	Amount of Real GDP Supplied, Billions
$100	300	$450
200	250	400
300	200	300
400	150	200
500	100	100

a. Use these sets of data to graph the aggregate demand and aggregate supply curves. What are the equilibrium price level and the equilibrium level of real output in this hypothetical economy? Is the equilibrium real output also necessarily the full-employment real output? Explain.

b. Why will a price level of 150 not be an equilibrium price level in this economy? Why not 250?

c. Suppose that buyers desire to purchase $200 billion of extra real output at each price level. Sketch in the new aggregate demand curve as AD_1. What factors might cause this change in aggregate demand? What are the new equilibrium price level and level of real output?

4. Suppose that a hypothetical economy has the following relationship between its real output and the input quantities necessary for producing that output: **LO2**

Input Quantity	Real GDP
150.0	$400
112.5	300
75.0	200

a. What is productivity in this economy?

b. What is the per-unit cost of production if the price of each input unit is $2?

c. Assume that the input price increases from $2 to $3 with no accompanying change in productivity. What is the new per-unit cost of production? In what direction would the $1 increase in input price push the economy's aggregate supply curve? What effect would this shift of aggregate supply have on the price level and the level of real output?

d. Suppose that the increase in input price does not occur but, instead, that productivity increases by 100 percent. What would be the new per-unit cost of production? What effect would this change in per-unit production cost have on the economy's aggregate supply curve? What effect would this shift of aggregate supply have on the price level and the level of real output?

5. Other things equal, what effects would each of the following have on aggregate demand or aggregate supply? In each case use a diagram to show the expected effects on the equilibrium price level and the level of real output. **LO1, LO2**

a. A reduction in the economy's real interest rate.

b. A major increase in Federal spending for health care (with no increase in taxes).

c. The complete disintegration of OPEC, causing oil prices to fall by one-half.

d. A 10 percent reduction in personal income tax rates (with no change in government spending).

e. A sizable increase in labor productivity (with no change in nominal wages).

f. A 12 percent increase in nominal wages (with no change in productivity).

g. A sizable depreciation in the international value of the dollar.

6. Other things equal, what effect will each of the following have on the equilibrium price level and level of real output? **LO3**

a. An increase in aggregate demand in the steep portion of the aggregate supply curve.

b. An increase in aggregate supply, with no change in aggregate demand (assume that prices and wages are flexible upward and downward).

c. Equal increases in aggregate demand and aggregate supply.

d. A reduction in aggregate demand in the relatively flat portion of the aggregate supply curve.

e. An increase in aggregate demand and a decrease in aggregate supply.

7. Why does a reduction in aggregate demand tend to reduce real output, rather than the price level? **LO4**

8. Explain: "Unemployment can be caused by a decrease of aggregate demand or a decrease of aggregate supply." In each case, specify the price-level outcomes. **LO4**

9. In early 2001 investment spending sharply declined in the United States. In the 2 months following the September 11, 2001, attacks on the United States, consumption also declined. Use AD-AS analysis to show the two impacts on real GDP. **LO4**

10. Using the concept of the multiplier, explain why mass layoffs by large companies such as Boeing or General Motors are a concern to the citizens and leaders where those firms are located. **LO4**

FURTHER TEST YOUR KNOWLEDGE AT
www.mcconnellbriefmacro1e.com

Web-Based Questions

At the text's Online Learning Center, **www.mcconnellbriefmacro1e.com**, you will find a multiple-choice quiz on this chapter's content. We encourage you to take the quiz to see how you do. Also, you will find one or more Web-based questions that require information from the Internet to answer.

8

Fiscal Policy, Deficits, and Debt

In the previous chapter we saw that an excessive increase in aggregate demand can cause demand-pull inflation and that a significant decline in aggregate demand can cause recession and cyclical unemployment. For those reasons, central governments sometimes use budgetary actions to try to "stimulate the economy" or "rein in inflation." Such countercyclical **fiscal policy** consists of deliberate changes in government spending and tax collections designed to achieve full employment, control inflation, and encourage economic growth. (The adjective "fiscal" simply means "financial.")

ORIGIN OF THE IDEA

O 8.1

Fiscal policy

We begin this chapter by examining the logic behind fiscal policy, its current status, and its limitations. Then we examine two related topics: the U.S. public debt and the Social Security funding problem.

fiscal policy
Changes in government spending or taxation to promote full employment, price-level stability, and economic growth

Council of Economic Advisers (CEA)
A group of three economists appointed by the U.S. president to provide advice and assistance on economic matters.

expansionary fiscal policy
An increase in government spending, a decrease in taxes, or some combination of the two for the purpose of increasing aggregate demand and real output.

budget deficit
The amount by which expenditures of the Federal government exceed its revenues in any year.

Fiscal Policy and the AD-AS Model

The fiscal policy that we have been describing is *discretionary* (or "active"). It is often initiated on the advice of the president's **Council of Economic Advisers (CEA),** a group of three economists appointed by the president to provide expertise and assistance on economic matters. Such changes in government spending and taxes are *at the option* of the Federal government. They do not occur automatically, independent of congressional action. The latter changes are *nondiscretionary* (or "passive" or "automatic"), and we will examine them later in this chapter.

Expansionary Fiscal Policy

When recession occurs, an **expansionary fiscal policy** may be in order. Consider Figure 8.1, where we suppose that a sharp decline in investment spending has shifted the economy's aggregate demand curve to the left from AD₁ to AD₂. (Disregard the arrow for now.) The cause of the recession may be that profit expectations on investment projects have dimmed, curtailing investment spending and reducing aggregate demand.

Suppose the economy's potential or full-employment output is $510 billion in Figure 8.1. If the price level is inflexible downward at P_1, the aggregate demand curve slides leftward at that price level and reduces real GDP to $490 billion. A negative GDP gap of $20 billion (= $490 billion − $510 billion) arises. An increase in unemployment accompanies this negative GDP gap because fewer workers are needed to produce the reduced output. In short, the economy depicted is suffering both recession and cyclical unemployment.

What fiscal policy should the Federal government adopt to try to remedy the situation? It has three main options: (1) government-spending increases, (2) tax reductions, or (3) some combination of the two. If the Federal budget is balanced at the outset, expansionary fiscal policy will create a government **budget deficit** (government spending in excess of tax revenues).

FIGURE 8.1 Expansionary fiscal policy. Expansionary fiscal policy uses increases in government spending, tax cuts, or a combination of both to increase aggregate demand and push the economy out of recession. Here, this policy increases aggregate demand from AD₂ to AD₁, increases real GDP from $490 billion to $510 billion, and restores full employment.

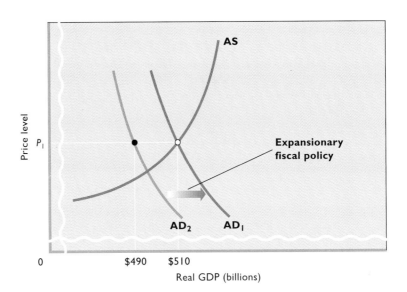

Government Spending Increases To increase aggregate demand, the Federal government can increase its spending. For example, it might boost spending on highways, education, and health care. Other things equal, a sufficient increase in government spending will shift an economy's aggregate demand curve to the right, as from AD_2 to AD_1 in Figure 8.1. Observe that real output rises to $510 billion, up $20 billion from its recessionary level of $490 billion. Firms increase their employment to the full-employment level, output increases, and the negative GDP gap disappears.

Tax Reductions Alternatively, the government could reduce taxes to shift the aggregate demand curve rightward, as from AD_2 to AD_1. Suppose the government cuts personal income taxes, which increases disposable income. Households will spend a large part of that income and save the rest. The part spent—the new consumption spending—will increase aggregate demand. In Figure 8.1, this increase in aggregate demand from AD_2 to AD_1 expands real GDP by $20 billion, eliminating the negative GDP gap. Employment increases accordingly, and the unemployment rate falls.

A tax cut must be larger than an increase in government spending to achieve the same rightward shift of the aggregate demand curve. This is because households save part of the higher after-tax income provided by the tax cut. Only the part of the tax cut that increases consumption spending shifts the aggregate demand curve to the right.

Combined Government Spending Increases and Tax Reductions
The government may combine spending increases and tax cuts to produce the desired initial increase in spending and the eventual increase in aggregate demand and real GDP. In the economy depicted in Figure 8.1, there is some combination of greater government spending and lower taxes (increased consumption spending) that will shift the aggregate demand curve from AD_2 to AD_1 and remove the negative GDP gap.

Contractionary Fiscal Policy

When demand-pull inflation occurs, a restrictive or **contractionary fiscal policy** may help control it. Take a look at Figure 8.2, where the full-employment level of real GDP is $510 billion. Suppose a sharp increase in investment and net export spending shifts the aggregate demand curve from AD_3 to AD_4. The outcomes are demand-pull inflation, as shown by the rise of the price level from P_1 to P_2, and a positive GDP gap of $12 billion (=$522 billion − $510 billion).

If the government decides on fiscal policy to control this inflation, its options are the opposite of those used to combat recession. It can (1) decrease government spending, (2) raise taxes, or (3) use some combination of those two policies. When the economy faces demand-pull inflation, fiscal policy should move toward a government **budget surplus** (tax revenues in excess of government spending).

Government Spending Decreases Reduced government spending shifts the aggregate demand curve leftward to control demand-pull inflation. In Figure 8.2, this spending cut shifts the aggregate demand curve leftward from AD_4 to AD_3. If the price level were downwardly flexible, the price level would return to P_1, where it was before demand-pull inflation occurred. That is, deflation would occur.

contractionary fiscal policy
A decrease in government spending, an increase in taxes, or some combination of the two for the purpose of decreasing aggregate demand and halting inflation.

budget surplus
The amount by which revenues of the Federal government exceed its expenditures in any year.

FIGURE 8.2 **Contractionary fiscal policy.** Contractionary fiscal policy uses decreases in government spending, increases in taxes, or a combination of both to reduce aggregate demand and slow or eliminate demand-pull inflation. Here, this policy shifts the aggregate demand curve from AD_4 to AD_3, removes the upward pressure on the price level, and halts the demand-pull inflation. Note, however, that even though the inflation is stopped, the presence of inflexible ("sticky") prices may prevent the price level from falling to P_1.

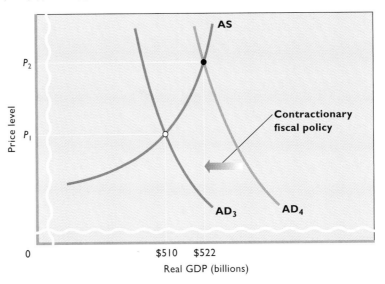

Unfortunately, the actual economy is not as simple and tidy as Figure 8.2 suggests. Increases in aggregate demand tend to ratchet the price level upward, but declines in aggregate demand do not seem to push the price level downward. So stopping inflation is a matter of halting the rise of the price level, not trying to lower it to the previous level. Demand-pull inflation usually is experienced as a continual rightward shifting of the aggregate demand curve. Contractionary fiscal policy is designed to stop a further shift, not to restore a lower price level. Successful fiscal policy eliminates a continuing positive (and thus inflationary) GDP gap and prevents the price level from continuing its inflationary rise. Nevertheless, Figure 8.2 displays the basic principle: Reductions in government expenditures can be used as a fiscal policy action to tame demand-pull inflation.

Tax Increases Just as government can use tax cuts to increase consumption spending, it can use tax increases to reduce consumption spending. In the economy in Figure 8.2, the government must raise taxes sufficiently to reduce consumption such that the aggregate demand curve will shift leftward from AD_4 to AD_3. That way, the demand-pull inflation will have been controlled.

Because part of any tax increase reduces saving rather than consumption, a tax increase must exceed a decrease in government spending to cause the same leftward shift of the aggregate demand curve. Only the part of the tax increase that lowers consumption spending reduces aggregate demand.

Combined Government Spending Decreases and Tax Increases
The government may choose to combine spending decreases and tax increases in order to reduce aggregate demand and check inflation. Some combination of lower government spending and higher taxes will shift the aggregate demand curve from AD_4 to AD_3.

Built-In Stability

To some degree, government tax revenues change automatically over the course of the business cycle and in ways that stabilize the economy. This automatic response, or built-in stability, constitutes nondiscretionary (or "passive" or "automatic") budgetary policy and results from the makeup of most tax systems. We did not include this built-in stability in our discussion of fiscal policy because we implicitly assumed that the same amount of tax revenue was being collected at each level of GDP. But the actual U.S. tax system is such that *net tax revenues* vary directly with GDP. (*Net taxes* are tax revenues less transfers and subsidies. From here on, we will use the simpler "taxes" to mean "net taxes.")

Virtually any tax will yield more tax revenue as GDP (and therefore total income) rises. In particular, personal income taxes have progressive rates and thus generate more-than-proportionate increases in tax revenues as GDP expands. Furthermore, as GDP rises and more goods and services are purchased, revenues from corporate income taxes and from sales taxes and excise taxes also increase. And, similarly, revenues from payroll taxes rise as economic expansion creates more jobs and income. Conversely, when GDP declines, tax receipts from all these sources also decline.

Transfer payments (or "negative taxes") behave in the opposite way from tax revenues. For example, welfare and unemployment compensation payments decline during an economic expansion and increase during an economic contraction.

Automatic or Built-In Stabilizers

A **built-in stabilizer** is anything that increases the government's budget deficit (or reduces its budget surplus) during a recession and increases its budget surplus (or reduces its budget deficit) during inflation without requiring explicit action by policymakers. As Figure 8.3 reveals, this is precisely what the U.S. tax system does. Government expenditures *G* are fixed and assumed to be independent of the level of GDP. Congress decides on a particular level of spending, but it does not determine the magnitude of tax revenues. Instead, it establishes tax rates, and the tax revenues then vary directly with the level of GDP that the economy achieves. Line *T* represents that direct relationship between tax revenues and GDP.

built-in stabilizer
Anything that increases the government's budget deficit (or reduces its budget surplus) during a recession and increases its budget surplus (or reduces its budget deficit) during expansion without requiring explicit action by policymakers.

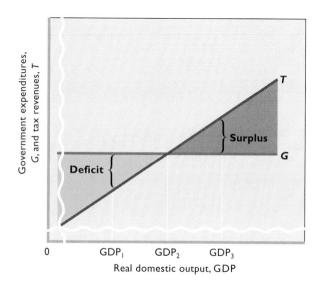

FIGURE 8.3 Built-in stability. Tax revenues *T* vary directly with GDP, and government spending *G* is assumed to be independent of GDP. As GDP falls in a recession, deficits occur automatically and help alleviate the recession. As GDP rises during expansion, surpluses occur automatically and help offset possible inflation.

Economic Importance

The economic importance of the direct relationship between tax receipts and GDP becomes apparent when we consider that:

- Taxes reduce spending and aggregate demand.
- Reductions in spending are desirable when the economy is moving toward inflation, whereas increases in spending are desirable when the economy is slumping.

As shown in Figure 8.3, tax revenues automatically increase as GDP rises during prosperity, and since taxes reduce household and business spending, they restrain the economic expansion. That is, as the economy moves toward a higher GDP, tax revenues automatically rise and move the budget from deficit toward surplus. In Figure 8.3, observe that the high and perhaps inflationary income level GDP_3 automatically generates a contractionary budget surplus.

Conversely, as output and income fall during recession, tax revenues automatically decline, increasing spending and cushioning the economic contraction. With a falling GDP, tax receipts decline and move the government's budget from surplus toward deficit. In Figure 8.3, the low level of income GDP_1 will automatically yield an expansionary budget deficit.

Built-in stability has reduced the severity of U.S. business fluctuations, perhaps by as much as 8 to 10 percent of the change in GDP that otherwise would have occurred.[1] For example, as the economy expanded vigorously in the late 1990s, the Federal budget swung from deficit to surplus. That swing helped dampen private spending and forestall demand-pull inflation. When the recession of 2001 hit, tax revenues automatically dropped off, slowing the decline in aggregate demand. But built-in stabilizers can only diminish, not eliminate, swings in real GDP. Discretionary fiscal policy (changes in tax rates and expenditures) or monetary policy (central bank-caused changes in interest rates) may be needed to correct recession or inflation of any appreciable magnitude. For example, both expansionary monetary policy and expansionary fiscal policy were used in the recessionary year 2008 to try to boost the economy.

Evaluating Fiscal Policy

How can we determine whether a government's discretionary fiscal policy is expansionary, neutral, or contractionary? We cannot simply examine the actual budget deficits or surpluses that take place under the current policy because they will necessarily include the automatic changes in tax revenues that accompany every change in GDP. In addition, the expansionary or contractionary strength of any change in discretionary fiscal policy depends not on its absolute size but on how large it is relative to the size of the economy. So, in evaluating the status of fiscal policy, we must adjust deficits and surpluses to eliminate automatic changes in tax revenues and also compare the sizes of the adjusted budget deficits and surpluses to the level of potential GDP.

standardized budget
A measure of what the Federal budget deficit or surplus would be with existing tax rates and government spending programs if the economy had achieved its full-employment GDP in the year.

Economists use the **standardized budget** (or *full-employment budget*) to adjust actual Federal budget deficits and surpluses to account for the changes in tax revenues that happen automatically whenever GDP changes. The standardized budget measures what the Federal budget deficit or surplus would have been under existing tax rates and government spending programs if the economy had achieved its full-employment level of GDP (its potential output). The idea is to compare *actual* government

---

[1] Alan J. Auerbach and Daniel Feenberg, "The Significance of Federal Taxes as Automatic Stabilizers," *Journal of Economic Perspectives*, Summer 2000, p. 54.

expenditures with the tax revenues *that would have occurred* if the economy had achieved full-employment GDP. That procedure removes budget deficits or surpluses that arise simply because of changes in GDP and thus tell us nothing about whether the government's current discretionary fiscal policy is fundamentally expansionary, contractionary, or neutral.

Consider Figure 8.4, where line G represents government expenditures and line T represents tax revenues. In full-employment year 1, government expenditures of $500 billion equal tax revenues of $500 billion, as indicated by the intersection of lines G and T at point a. The actual budget deficit and the standardized budget deficit in year 1 are zero—government expenditures equal tax revenues, and government spending equals the tax revenues forthcoming at the full-employment output GDP_1. Obviously, the standardized budget deficit *as a percentage of potential GDP* is also zero. The government's fiscal policy is neutral.

Now suppose that a recession occurs and GDP falls from GDP_1 to GDP_2, as shown in Figure 8.4. Let's also assume that the government takes no discretionary action, so lines G and T remain as shown in the figure. Tax revenues automatically fall to $450 billion (point c) at GDP_2, while government spending (we assume) remains unaltered at $500 billion (point b). A $50 billion actual budget deficit (represented by distance bc) arises. But this **cyclical deficit** is simply a by-product of the economy's slide into recession, not the result of discretionary fiscal actions by the government. We would be wrong to conclude from this deficit that the government is engaging in an expansionary fiscal policy. The government's fiscal policy has not changed; it is still neutral.

That fact is highlighted when we consider the standardized budget deficit for year 2 in Figure 8.4. The $500 billion of government expenditures in year 2 is shown by b on line G. And, as shown by a on line T, $500 billion of tax revenues would have occurred if the economy had achieved its full-employment GDP.

cyclical deficit
A Federal budget deficit that is caused by a recession and the consequent decline in tax revenues.

FIGURE 8.4 Standardized budget deficits. The standardized budget deficit is zero at the full-employment output GDP_1. But it is also zero at the recessionary output GDP_2, because the $500 billion of government expenditures at GDP_2 equals the $500 billion of tax revenues that would be forthcoming at the full-employment GDP_1. Here, fiscal policy did not change as the economy slid into recession. The deficit that arose is simply a cyclical deficit.

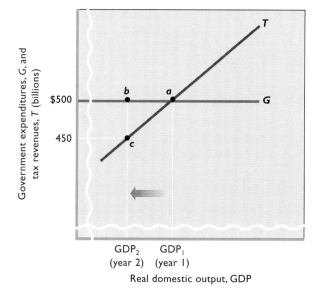

Real domestic output, GDP

Because both *b* and *a* represent $500 billion, the standardized budget deficit in year 2 is zero, as is this deficit as a percentage of potential GDP. Since the full-employment deficits are zero in both years, we know that government did not change its discretionary fiscal policy, even though a recession occurred and an actual deficit of $50 billion resulted.

In contrast, if we observed a standardized deficit of zero in a specific year, followed by a standardized budget deficit in the next, we could conclude that fiscal policy is expansionary. Because the standardized budget adjusts for automatic changes in tax revenues, the increase in the standardized budget deficit reveals that government either increased its spending (*G*) or decreased tax rates such that tax revenues (*T*) decreased. In Figure 8.4, the government either shifted the line *G* upward or the line *T* downward. These changes in *G* and *T* are precisely the discretionary actions that we have identified as elements of an *expansionary* fiscal policy. Similarly, if we observed a standardized deficit of zero in one year, followed by a standardized budget surplus in the next, we could conclude that fiscal policy is contractionary. Government either decreased its spending (*G*) or increased tax rates such that tax revenues (*T*) increased. We know that these changes in *G* and *T* are elements of a *contractionary* fiscal policy.

Global Snapshot 8.1 shows the extent of the standardized budget deficits or surpluses of a number of countries in a recent year.

GLOBAL SNAPSHOT 8.1

Standardized Budget Deficits or Surpluses as a Percentage of Potential GDP, Selected Nations

In 2007 some nations had standardized budget surpluses, while others had standardized budget deficits. These surpluses and deficits varied as a percentage of each nation's potential GDP. Generally, the surpluses represented contractionary fiscal policy and the deficits expansionary fiscal policy.

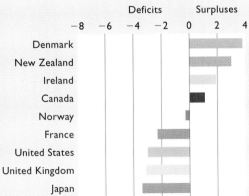

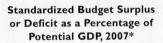

*The standardized deficit shown for the United States is larger than the standardized budget deficit listed for 2007 in the United States in Table 8.1 because the data here include all levels of government, not just the Federal government.

Source: OECD Economic Outlook, Organization for Economic Cooperation and Development, **www.oecd.org**.

Recent U.S. Fiscal Policy

Table 8.1 lists the actual U.S. budget deficits and surpluses (column 2) and the standardized deficits and surpluses (column 3), as percentages of actual and potential GDP, respectively, for recent years. Observe that the standardized deficits are generally smaller than the actual deficits. This is because the actual deficits include cyclical deficits, whereas the standardized deficits do not. The latter deficits provide the information needed to assess discretionary fiscal policy.

Column 3 shows that fiscal policy was expansionary in the early to mid-1990s. Consider 1992, for example. From the table we see that the actual budget deficit was 4.5 percent of GDP and the standardized budget deficit was 2.9 percent of potential GDP. The economy was recovering from the 1990–1991 recession, so tax revenues were relatively low. But even if the economy were at full employment in 1992, with the greater tax revenues that would imply, the Federal budget would have been in deficit by 2.9 percent. And that percentage was greater than the deficits in the prior 2 years. So the standardized budget deficit in 1992 clearly reflected expansionary fiscal policy.

But the large standardized budget deficits were projected to continue even when the economy fully recovered from the 1990–1991 recession. The concern was that the large actual and full-employment deficits would cause high interest rates, low levels of investment, and slow economic growth. In 1993 the Clinton administration and Congress increased personal income and corporate income tax

(1) Year	(2) Actual Deficit or Surplus	(3) Standardized Deficit or Surplus*
1992	−4.5	−2.9
1993	−3.8	−2.9
1994	−2.9	−2.1
1995	−2.2	−2.0
1996	−1.4	−1.2
1997	−0.3	−1.0
1998	+0.8	−0.4
1999	+1.4	+0.1
2000	+2.5	+1.1
2001	+1.3	+1.0
2002	−1.5	−1.2
2003	−3.4	−2.5
2004	−3.5	−2.4
2005	−2.6	−1.9
2006	−1.9	−1.8
2007	−1.2	−1.4

TABLE 8.1

Federal Deficits (−) and Surpluses (+) as Percentages of GDP, 1992–2007

* As a percentage of potential GDP.

Source: Congressional Budget Office. www.cbo.gov.

rates to prevent these potential outcomes. Observe from column 3 of Table 8.1 that the standardized budget deficits shrunk each year and eventually gave way to surpluses in 1999, 2000, and 2001.

U.S. stock markets crashed in 2000 and the economy began to slow later that year, with the economy slipping into recession by March 2001. The Congress and the Bush administration responded by passing tax cuts of $44 billion in 2001 and $52 billion in 2002. This fiscal policy action helped to stimulate the economy and offset the recession as well as the second economic blow that arrived with the September 11, 2001, terrorist attacks. Further tax cuts totaling $122 billion over two years, as well as an extension of unemployment benefits, were passed in March 2002.

As seen in Table 8.1, the standardized budget moved from a *surplus* of 1.1 percent of potential GDP in 2000 to a *deficit* of 1.2 percent in 2002. Clearly, fiscal policy had turned expansionary. Nevertheless, the economy remained very sluggish through 2002 and into 2003. In June of that year, Congress again cut taxes, this time by an enormous $350 billion over several years. Specifically, the tax legislation accelerated the reduction of marginal tax rates already scheduled for future years and slashed tax rates on income from dividends and capital gains. It also increased tax breaks for families and small businesses. This tax package, along with expanded government spending, increased the standardized budget deficit greatly. As a percentage of potential GDP, it rose to −2.5 percent in 2003 and to −2.4 percent in 2004.

The economy strengthened and real output grew between 2003 and 2007; full employment was restored. But starting in the summer of 2007, a crisis in the market for mortgage loans occurred and spread quickly to other financial markets. Households in particular retrenched on their spending and in the last quarter of 2007 the economy slowed. In December 2007, a recession began. Congress acted quickly to enact expansionary fiscal policy in the form of the Economic Stimulus Act of 2008. This law provided a total of $152 billion in stimulus. Some of it came in the form of tax breaks for businesses, but most of it arrived in the form of checks of up to $600 each that were mailed to taxpayers, veterans, and Social Security recipients in May of 2008. The government hoped that those receiving checks would spend the money, thereby boosting consumption and aggregate demand. But further shocks to the fragile financial system overrode the fiscal stimulus. Real GDP declined sharply in the last half of 2008. The in-coming Obama administration proposed a massive new round of expansionary fiscal policy for 2009.

Figure 8.5 shows the actual and projected budget deficits and surpluses (both nonstandardized) from 1994–2014. Clearly, the United States has been experiencing large budget deficits recently and these are expected to continue for several years. But projected deficits and surpluses change periodically as government alters fiscal policy and the growth of GDP rises or slows. To see the most up-to-date figures, visit the Congressional Budget Office Web site, **www.cbo.gov,** and selecting "Current Budget Projections" and then "CBO's Baseline Budget Projections." The relevant numbers are in the row "Surplus or Deficit (−)."

Question:
Use Figure 8.5 to demonstrate how each of the following contributed to increased actual budget deficits in recent years: (a) the recession of 2001; (b) the war on terrorism in the United States and abroad; and (c) the Bush administration tax cuts.

FIGURE 8.5 Federal budget deficits and surpluses, actual and projected, fiscal years 1994–2014 (in billions of nominal dollars). The annual budget deficits of 1992 through 1997 gave way to budget surpluses from 1998 through 2001. Deficits reappeared in 2002 and are projected to continue through 2014.
Source: Congressional Budget Office, **www.cbo.gov**.

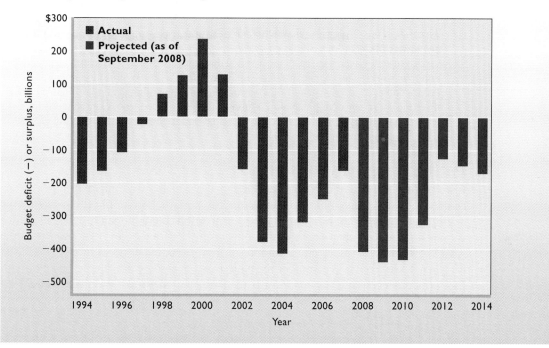

Problems, Criticisms, and Complications

Economists recognize that governments may encounter a number of significant problems in enacting and applying fiscal policy.

Problems of Timing

Several problems of timing may arise in connection with fiscal policy:

- *Recognition lag* The recognition lag is the time between the beginning of recession or inflation and the certain awareness that it is actually happening. This lag arises because the economy does not move smoothly through the business cycle. Even during good times, the economy has slow months interspersed with months of rapid growth and expansion. This makes recognizing a recession difficult since several slow months will have to happen in succession before people can conclude with any confidence that the good times are over and a recession has begun. The same is true with inflation. Several high-inflation months must come in sequence before people can confidently conclude that inflation has moved to a higher level. Efforts to get a jump on the recognition lag by attempting to predict the future course of the economy have also proven to be largely futile. As a result, the economy is often 4 to 6 months into a recession or inflation before the situation is clearly discernible in the relevant statistics. Due to this recognition lag, the economic downslide or the inflation may become more serious than it would have if the situation had been identified and acted on sooner.

- *Administrative lag*   The wheels of democratic government turn slowly. There will typically be a significant lag between the time the need for fiscal action is recognized and the time action is taken. Following the terrorist attacks of September 11, 2001, the U.S. Congress was stalemated for 5 months before passing a compromise economic stimulus law in March 2002. (In contrast, the Federal Reserve began lowering interest rates the week after the attacks.)
- *Operational lag*   A lag also occurs between the time fiscal action is taken and the time that action affects output, employment, or the price level. Although changes in tax rates can be put into effect relatively quickly once new laws are passed, government spending on public works—new dams, interstate highways, and so on—requires long planning periods and even longer periods of construction. Such spending is of questionable use in offsetting short (for example, 6- to 12-month) periods of recession. Consequently, discretionary fiscal policy has increasingly relied on tax changes rather than on changes in spending as its main tool.

Political Considerations

Fiscal policy is conducted in a political arena. That reality not only may slow the enactment of fiscal policy but also may create the potential for political considerations swamping economic considerations in its formulation. It is a human trait to rationalize actions and policies that are in one's self-interest. Politicians are very human—they want to get reelected. A strong economy at election time will certainly help them. So they may favor large tax cuts under the guise of expansionary fiscal policy even though that policy is economically inappropriate. Similarly, they may rationalize increased government spending on popular items such as farm subsidies, health care, education, and homeland security.

At the extreme, elected officials and political parties might collectively "hijack" fiscal policy for political purposes, cause inappropriate changes in aggregate demand, and thereby cause (rather than avert) economic fluctuations. For instance, before an election they may try to stimulate the economy to improve their reelection hopes. And then after the election they may try to use contractionary fiscal policy to dampen the excessive aggregate demand that they caused with their pre-election stimulus. Such **political business cycles** are difficult to document and prove, but there is little doubt that political considerations weigh heavily in the formulation of fiscal policy. The question is how often, if ever, those political considerations run counter to "sound economics."

An example of the interaction of political and economic considerations—and a notable exception to the administrative lag mentioned previously—was the Economic Stimulus Act of 2008. The proposal was unveiled by President Bush on January 28, 2008, passed through both houses of Congress less than two weeks later, and signed into law on February 14, 2008. While there seemed to be strong consensus among lawmakers that the U.S. economy needed a boost, some have also suggested that the looming 2008 elections provided additional motivation to act quickly.

Future Policy Reversals

Fiscal policy may fail to achieve its intended objectives if households expect future reversals of policy. Consider a tax cut, for example. If taxpayers believe the tax reduction is temporary, they may save a large portion of their tax cut, reasoning that rates will return to their previous level in the future. They save more now so that they will be able to draw on this extra savings to maintain their future consumption levels if taxes do indeed rise again in the future. So a tax reduction thought to be temporary may not increase present consumption spending and aggregate demand by as much as our simple model (Figure 8.1) suggests.

political business cycle
The alleged tendency of presidential administrations and Congress to create macroeconomic instability by reducing taxes and increasing government spending before elections, and by raising taxes and reducing expenditures after elections.

The opposite may be true for a tax increase. If taxpayers think it is temporary, they may reduce their saving to pay the tax while maintaining their present consumption. They may reason that they can restore their saving when the tax rate again falls. So the tax increase may not reduce current consumption and aggregate demand by as much as policymakers intended.

To the extent that this so-called *consumption smoothing* occurs over time, fiscal policy will lose some of its strength. The lesson is that tax-rate changes that households view as permanent are more likely to alter consumption and aggregate demand than tax changes they view as temporary.

Offsetting State and Local Finance

The fiscal policies of state and local governments are frequently *pro-cyclical*, meaning that they worsen rather than correct recession or inflation. Unlike the Federal government, most state and local governments face constitutional or other legal requirements to balance their budgets. Like households and private businesses, state and local governments increase their expenditures during prosperity and cut them during recession. During the Great Depression of the 1930s, most of the increase in Federal spending was offset by decreases in state and local spending. During and immediately following the recession of 2001, many state and local governments had to offset lower tax revenues resulting from the reduced personal income and spending of their citizens. They offset the decline in revenues by raising tax rates, imposing new taxes, and reducing spending.

Crowding-Out Effect

Another potential flaw of fiscal policy is the so-called **crowding-out effect:** An expansionary fiscal policy (deficit spending) may increase the interest rate and reduce investment spending, thereby weakening or canceling the stimulus of the expansionary policy. The rising interest rate might also potentially crowd out interest sensitive consumption spending (such as purchasing automobiles on credit). But since investment is the most volatile component of GDP, the crowding out effect focuses its attention on investment and whether the stimulus provided by deficit spending may be partly or even fully neutralized by an offsetting reduction in investment spending.

To see the potential problem, realize that whenever the government borrows money (as it must if it is deficit spending), it increases the overall demand for money. If the monetary authorities are holding the money supply constant, this increase in demand will raise the price paid for borrowing money: the interest rate. Because investment spending varies inversely with the interest rate, some investment will be choked off or "crowded out."

Economists vary in their opinions about the strength of the crowding-out effect. An important thing to keep in mind is that crowding out is likely to be less of a problem when the economy is in recession. This is true because investment demand tends to be low during recessions. Why? Because sales are slow during recessions, so that most businesses end up with substantial amounts of excess capacity. As a result, they do not have much incentive to add new machinery or build new factories. After all, why should they add capacity when some of the capacity they already have is lying idle?

With investment demand low during a recession, the crowding out effect is likely to be very small. Simply put, with investment demand at such a low level due to the recession, there isn't much investment for the government to crowd out. Even if deficit spending does increase the interest rate, investment spending cannot fall by that much for the simple reason that it is only a small number to begin with.

By contrast, when the economy is operating at or near full capacity, investment demand is likely to be quite high so that crowding out is likely to be a much more

crowding-out effect
A decrease in private investment caused by higher interest rates that result from the Federal government's increased borrowing to finance deficits (or debt).

INTERACTIVE GRAPHS

G 8.1
Crowding out

ORIGIN OF THE IDEA

O 8.2
Crowding out

serious problem. When the economy is booming, factories will be running at or near full capacity and firms will have investment demand for two reasons. First, equipment running at full capacity wears out fast, so that firms will be doing a lot of investment just to replace machinery and equipment that wears out and depreciates. Second, the economy is likely to be growing overall so that firms will be investing not just to replace worn out equipment in order to keep their productive capacity from deteriorating, but also so that they can make *additions* to their productive capacity.

Current Thinking on Fiscal Policy

Where do these complications leave us as to the advisability and effectiveness of discretionary fiscal policy? In view of the complications and uncertain outcomes of fiscal policy, some economists argue that it is better not to engage in it at all. Those holding that view point to the superiority of monetary policy (changes in interest rates engineered by the Federal Reserve) as a stabilizing device or believe that most economic fluctuations tend to be mild and self-correcting.

But most economists believe that fiscal policy remains an important, useful policy lever in the government's macroeconomic toolkit. The current popular view is that fiscal policy can help "push the economy" in a particular direction but cannot "fine-tune it" to a precise macroeconomic outcome. Mainstream economists generally agree that monetary policy is the best month-to-month stabilization tool for the U.S. economy. If monetary policy is doing its job, the government should maintain a relatively neutral fiscal policy, with a standardized budget deficit or surplus of no more than 2 percent of potential GDP. It should hold major discretionary fiscal policy in reserve to help counter situations where recession threatens to be deep and long-lasting (as in 2008 and early 2009) or where a substantial reduction in aggregate demand might help to eliminate a large inflationary gap and aid the Federal Reserve in its efforts to quell the inflation caused by that inflationary gap.

Finally, there is general agreement that proposed fiscal policy should be evaluated for its potential positive and negative impacts on long-run productivity growth. The short-run policy tools used for conducting active fiscal policy often have long-run impacts. Countercyclical fiscal policy should be shaped to strengthen, or at least not impede, the growth of long-run aggregate supply (shown as a rightward shift of the long-run aggregate supply curve in Figure 7.5). For example, a tax cut might be structured to enhance work effort, strengthen investment, and encourage innovation. Or an increase in government spending might center on preplanned projects for "public capital" (highways, mass transit, ports, airports) that are complementary to private investment and thus conducive to long-term economic growth.

The Public Debt

public debt
The total amount of money owed by the Federal government to the owners of government securities; equal to the sum of past government budget deficits less government budget surpluses.

The national or **public debt** is essentially the total accumulation of the deficits (minus the surpluses) the Federal government has incurred through time. These deficits have emerged mainly because of war financing, recessions, and fiscal policy. In 2007 the total public debt was $9.01 trillion–$4.27 trillion held by the public and $4.73 held by agencies of the Federal government.

Ownership

U.S. securities
Treasury bills, Treasury notes, Treasury bonds, and U.S. savings bonds issued by the Federal government to finance expenditures that exceed tax revenues.

The total public debt represents the total amount of money owed by the Federal government to the holders of **U.S. securities:** Treasury bills, Treasury notes, Treasury

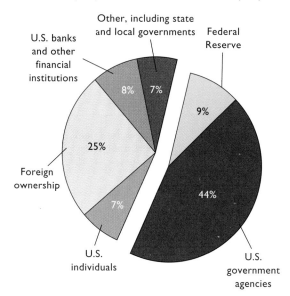

Debt held outside the Federal government and Federal Reserve (47%)

Debt held by the Federal government and Federal Reserve (53%)

Other, including state and local governments

U.S. banks and other financial institutions

Federal Reserve

8% 7%

25%

9%

Foreign ownership

44%

7%

U.S. individuals

U.S. government agencies

Total debt: $9.01 trillion

FIGURE 8.6 Ownership of the total public debt, 2007. The total public debt can be divided into the proportion held by the public (47 percent) and the proportion held by Federal agencies and the Federal Reserve System (53 percent). Of the total debt, 25 percent is foreign-owned.   Source: U.S. Treasury, **www.fms.treas.gov**/.

bonds, and U.S. savings bonds. Figure 8.6 shows that the public held 47 percent of the public debt in 2007 and that Federal government agencies and the Federal Reserve (the U.S. central bank) held the other 53 percent. In this case the "public" consists of individuals here and abroad, state and local governments, and U.S. financial institutions. People and institutions abroad held about 25 percent of the total debt. So most of the debt is internally held, not externally held. Americans owe roughly three-fourths of the debt to Americans.

Debt and GDP

A simple statement of the absolute size of the debt ignores the fact that the wealth and productive ability of the U.S. economy is also vast. A wealthy, highly productive nation can incur and carry a large public debt more easily than a poor nation can. It is more meaningful to measure the public debt in relation to an economy's GDP. Figure 8.7 shows the relative size of the Federal debt held by the public (as opposed to the Federal Reserve and Federal agencies) over time. Notice this percentage has increased since 2001, but remains below the percentages in the 1990s.

International Comparisons

It is not uncommon for countries to have public debts. Global Snapshot 8.2 lists publicly held government debts as percentages of GDP for several countries.

Interest Charges

Many economists conclude that the primary burden of the debt is the annual interest charge accruing on the bonds sold to finance the debt. In 2007 interest on the total public debt was $237 billion and is now the fourth-largest item in the Federal budget (behind income security, national defense, and health).

FIGURE 8.7 Federal debt held by the public as a percentage of GDP, 1970–2007. As a percentage of GDP, the Federal debt held by the public (held outside the Federal Reserve and government agencies) increased sharply over the 1980–1995 period and declined significantly between 1995 and 2001. Since 2001, the percentage has gone up again, but remains lower than it was in the 1990s.
Source: Economic Report of the President, **www.gpoaccess.gov/eop/index.html**.

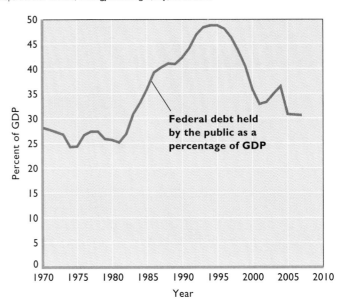

GLOBAL SNAPSHOT 8.2

Publicly Held Debt: International Comparisons

Although the United States has the world's largest public debt, a number of other nations have larger publicly held debts as a percentage of their GDPs.

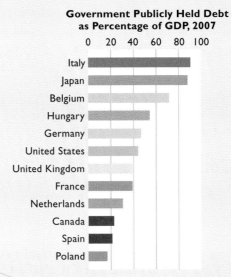

Source: Economic Outlook, Organization of Economic Cooperation and Development, **www.oecd.org**. These debt calculations included federal, state, and local debt (not just federal debt as in Figure 8.7)

Interest payments were 1.7 percent of GDP in 2007. That percentage reflects the level of taxation (the average tax rate) required to pay the interest on the public debt. That is, in 2007 the Federal government had to collect taxes equal to 1.7 percent of GDP to service the total public debt.

False Concerns

You may wonder if the large public debt might bankrupt the United States or at least place a tremendous burden on your children and grandchildren. Fortunately, these are false concerns.

Bankruptcy

The large U.S. public debt does not threaten to bankrupt the Federal government, leaving it unable to meet its financial obligations. There are two main reasons: refinancing and taxation.

Refinancing The public debt is easily refinanced. As portions of the debt come due on maturing Treasury bills, notes, and bonds each month, the government does not cut expenditures or raise taxes to provide the funds required. Rather, it refinances the debt by selling new bonds and using the proceeds to pay off holders of the maturing bonds. The new bonds are in strong demand, because lenders can obtain a relatively good interest return with no risk of default by the Federal government.

Taxation The Federal government has the constitutional authority to levy and collect taxes. A tax increase is a government option for gaining sufficient revenue to pay interest and principal on the public debt. Financially distressed private households and corporations cannot extract themselves from their financial difficulties by taxing the public. If their incomes or sales revenues fall short of their expenses, they can indeed go bankrupt. But the Federal government does have the option to impose new taxes or increase existing tax rates if necessary to finance its debt.

Burdening Future Generations

In 2007 public debt per capita was $29,987. Was each child born in 2007 handed a bill for $29,987 from the Federal government? Not really. The public debt does not impose as much of a burden on future generations as commonly thought.

The United States owes a substantial portion of the public debt to itself. U.S. citizens and institutions (banks, businesses, insurance companies, governmental agencies, and trust funds) own about 75 percent of the U.S. government securities. While that part of the public debt is a liability to Americans (as taxpayers), it is simultaneously an asset to Americans (as holders of Treasury bills, Treasury notes, Treasury bonds, and U.S. savings bonds).

To eliminate the American-owned part of the public debt would require a gigantic transfer payment from Americans to Americans. Taxpayers would pay higher taxes, and holders of the debt would receive an equal amount for their U.S. securities. Purchasing power in the United States would not change. Only the repayment of the 25 percent of the public debt owned by foreigners would negatively impact U.S. purchasing power.

The public debt increased sharply during the Second World War. But the decision to finance military purchases through the sale of government bonds did not shift the economic burden of the war to future generations. The economic cost of the Second World War consisted of the civilian goods society had to forgo in shifting scarce resources to war goods production (recall production possibilities analysis). Regardless of whether society financed this reallocation through higher taxes or through borrowing, the real economic burden of the war would have been the same. That burden was borne almost entirely by those who lived during the war. They were the ones who did without a multitude of consumer goods to enable the United States to arm itself and its allies. The next generation inherited the debt from the war but also an equal amount of government bonds. It also inherited the enormous benefits from the victory—namely, preserved political and economic systems at home and the "export" of those systems to Germany, Italy, and Japan. Those outcomes enhanced postwar U.S. economic growth and helped raise the standard of living of future generations of Americans.

Substantive Issues

Although the above issues are of false concern, there are a number of substantive issues relating to the public debt. Economists, however, attach varying degrees of importance to them.

Income Distribution

The distribution of ownership of government securities is highly uneven. Some people own much more than the $29,987-per-person portion of government securities; other people own less or none at all. In general, the ownership of the public debt is concentrated among wealthier groups who own a large percentage of all stocks and bonds. Because the overall Federal tax system is only mildly progressive, payment of interest on the public debt probably increases income inequality. Income is transferred from people who, on average, have lower incomes to the higher-income bondholders. If greater income equality is one of society's goals, then this redistribution is undesirable.

Incentives

The current public debt necessitates annual interest payments of $237 billion. With no increase in the size of the debt, that interest charge must be paid out of tax revenues. Higher taxes may dampen incentives to bear risk, to innovate, to invest, and to work. So, in this indirect way, a large public debt may impair economic growth.

Foreign-Owned Public Debt

external public debt
The part of the public debt owed to foreign citizens, firms, and institutions.

The 25 percent of the U.S. debt held by citizens and institutions of foreign countries *is* an economic burden to Americans. Because we do not owe that portion of the debt "to ourselves," the payment of interest and principal on this **external public debt** enables foreigners to buy some of our output. In return for the benefits derived from the borrowed funds, the United States transfers goods and services to foreign lenders. Of course, Americans also own debt issued by foreign governments, so payment of principal and interest by those governments transfers some of their goods and services to Americans.

Crowding Out Revisited

There is a potentially more serious problem. The financing (and continual refinancing) of the large public debt can transfer a real economic burden to future generations by passing a smaller stock of capital goods on to them. This possibility involves the previously discussed crowding-out effect: the idea that public borrowing drives up real interest rates, which reduces private investment spending. As we mentioned earlier, if public borrowing only happened during recessions, crowding out would not likely be much of

FIGURE 8.8 **The investment demand curve and the crowding-out effect.** If the investment demand curve (ID_1) is fixed, the increase in the interest rate from 6 to 10 percent caused by financing a large public debt will move the economy from *a* to *b* and crowd out $10 billion of private investment and decrease the size of the capital stock inherited by future generations. However, if the public goods enabled by the debt improve the investment prospects of businesses, the private investment demand curve will shift rightward, as from ID_1 to ID_2. That shift may offset the crowding-out effect wholly or in part. In this case, it moves the economy from *a* to *c*.

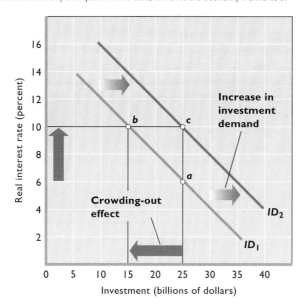

a problem. Because private investment demand tends to be low during recessions, any increase in interest rates caused by public borrowing will at most cause a small reduction in investment spending. By contrast, a large public debt may cause crowding out problems because the need to continuously refinance the debt will entail large amounts of borrowing not just during recessions but also during times when the economy is at full employment and investment demand tends to be very high. In such situations, any increase in interest rates caused by the borrowing necessary to refinance the debt may result in a substantial decline in investment spending. If the amount of current investment crowded out is extensive, future generations will inherit an economy with a smaller production capacity and, other things equal, a lower standard of living.

A Graphical Look at Crowding Out
We know from Chapter 7 there is an inverse relationship between the real interest rate and the amount of investment spending. When graphed, that relationship is shown as a downward-sloping **investment demand curve,** such as either ID_1 or ID_2 in Figure 8.8. Let's first consider curve ID_1. (Ignore curve ID_2 for now.) Suppose that government borrowing increases the real interest rate from 6 to 10 percent. Then, investment spending will fall from $25 billion to $15 billion, as shown by the economy's move from *a* to *b*. That is, the financing of the debt will compete with the financing of private investment projects and crowd out $10 billion of private investment. So the stock of private capital handed down to future generations will be $10 billion less than it would have been without the need to finance the public debt.

Public Investments and Public-Private Complementarities
But even with crowding out, there are two factors that could partly or fully offset the net economic burden shifted to future generations. First, just as private expenditures may involve either consumption or investment, so it is with public goods. Part of the government spending enabled by the public debt is for public investment outlays (for

investment demand curve
A curve that shows the amount of investment forthcoming in an economy at each real interest rate in a series of such rates.

example, highways, mass-transit systems, and electric power facilities) and "human capital" (for example, investments in education, job training, and health). Like private expenditures on machinery and equipment, those **public investments** increase the economy's future production capacity. Because of the financing through debt, the stock of public capital passed on to future generations may be higher than otherwise. That greater stock of public capital may offset the diminished stock of private capital resulting from the crowding-out effect, leaving overall production capacity unimpaired.

So-called public-private complementarities are a second factor that could reduce the crowding-out effect. Some public and private investments are complementary. Thus, the public investment financed through the debt could spur some private sector investment by increasing its expected rate of return. For example, a Federal building in a city may encourage private investment in the form of nearby office buildings, shops, and restaurants. Through its complementary effect, the spending on public capital may shift the private investment demand curve to the right, as from ID_1 to ID_2 in Figure 8.8. Even though the government borrowing boosts the interest rate from 6 to 10 percent, total private investment need not fall. In the case shown as the move from a to c in Figure 8.8, it remains at $25 billion. Of course, the increase in investment demand might be smaller than that shown. If it were smaller, the crowding-out effect would not be fully offset. But the point is that an increase in private investment demand may counter the decline in investment that would otherwise result from the higher interest rate.

The Long-Run Fiscal Imbalance: Social Security

The most significant fiscal issue in the United States is not the budget deficit or the public debt but, rather, the long-term funding imbalance in the Social Security and Medicare programs. In 2007, the total projected funding shortfall for Social Security and Medicare (including its prescription drug benefit) was $24 trillion through 2080. We will focus our attention on Social Security.

The Future Funding Shortfall

The Social Security program (excluding Medicare) has grown from less than one-half of 1 percent of U.S. GDP in 1950 to 4.2 percent of GDP today. That percentage is projected to grow to 6.2 percent of GDP in 2030 and even higher thereafter. There is a severe long-run shortfall in Social Security funding because of growing payments to retiring baby boomers.

The $461 billion Social Security program is largely a "pay-as-you-go" plan, meaning that most of the current revenues from the 12.4 percent Social Security tax (the rate when the 2.9 percent Medicare tax is excluded) are paid out to current Social Security retirees. In anticipation of the large benefits owed to the baby boomers when they retire, however, the Social Security Administration has been placing an excess of current revenues over current payouts into the **Social Security trust fund,** consisting of U.S. Treasury securities. But the accumulation of money in the trust fund will be greatly inadequate for paying the retirement benefits promised to all future retirees.

In 2017 Social Security retirement revenues will fall below Social Security retirement benefits, and the system will begin dipping into the trust fund to make up the difference. The trust fund will be exhausted in 2041, after which the annual tax revenues will cover only 75 percent of the promised benefits. The Federal government faces a several-trillion-dollar shortfall of long-run revenues for funding Social Security.

As shown in Figure 8.9, the problem is one of demographics. The percentage of the American population age 62 or older will rise substantially over the next several

public investments
Government expenditures on public capital (such as highways, bridges, mass-transit systems, and electric power facilities) and on human capital (such as education, training, and health).

Social Security trust fund
A Federal fund that saves excessive Social Security tax revenues received in one year to meet Social Security benefit obligations that exceed Social Security tax revenues in some subsequent year.

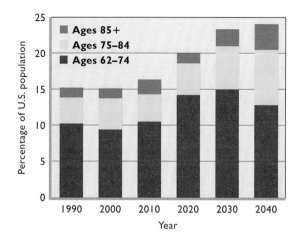

FIGURE 8.9 **The aging U.S.
population.** The percentage of the
U.S. population that is age 62 or older is
rapidly rising. Depending on policy
responses, this could result in a severe
funding shortfall for Social Security in the
decades ahead.

decades, with the greatest increases for people who are age 75 and older. High fertility rates during the "baby boom" (1946–1964), declining birthrates thereafter, and rising life expectancies have combined to produce an aging population. In the future, more people will be receiving Social Security benefits for longer periods, and fewer workers will pay for each person's benefits. The number of workers per Social Security beneficiary was 5:1 in 1960. Today it is 3:1, and by 2040 it will be only 2:1.

There is no easy way to restore long-run balance to Social Security funding. Either benefits must be reduced or revenues must be increased. The Social Security Administration concludes that bringing projected Social Security revenues and payments into balance over the next 75 years would require a 13 percent permanent reduction in Social Security benefits, a 16 percent permanent increase in tax revenues, or some combination of the two.[2]

© Purestock/PunchStock

© Royalty-Free/CORBIS

Photo Op Will Social Security Be There for You?

Social Security is largely a "pay-as-you-go" plan, in which current retirement benefits are paid out of current payroll taxes. But the number of retirees in the United States is growing faster than the number of workers, foretelling a future funding shortfall.

---

[2]Social Security Board of Trustees, "Status of the Social Security and Medicare Programs: A Summary of the 2007 Annual Reports," **www.ssa.gov**.

Policy Options

Several suggestions have been offered to help make Social Security financially sound. These ideas include increasing the retirement age, subjecting a larger portion of total earnings to the Social Security tax, and reducing benefits for wealthy retirees.

Other ideas are more novel. For example, one suggestion is to boost the trust fund by investing all or part of it in corporate stocks and bonds. The Federal government would own the stock investments, and an appointed panel would oversee the direction of those investments. The presumed higher returns on the investments relative to the lower returns on U.S. securities would stretch out the life of the trust fund. Nevertheless, a substantial increase in the payroll tax would still be needed to cover the shortfalls after the trust fund is exhausted.

Another option is to increase the payroll tax immediately—perhaps by as much as 1.5 percentage points—and allocate the new revenues to individual accounts. Government would own the accumulations in the accounts, but individuals could direct their investments to a restricted list of broad stock or bond funds. When they retire, recipients could convert these individual account balances to annuities—securities paying monthly payments for life. That annuity income would supplement reduced monthly benefits from the pay-as-you-go system when the trust fund is exhausted.

A different route is to place half the payroll tax into accounts that individuals, not the government, would own, maintain, and bequeath. Individuals could invest these funds in bank certificates of deposit or in approved stock and bond funds and draw upon the accounts when they reach retirement age. A flat monthly benefit would supplement the accumulations in the private accounts. The personal security accounts would be phased in over time, so people now receiving or about to receive Social Security benefits would continue to receive benefits.

These general ideas do not exhaust the possible reforms, since the variations on each plan are nearly endless. Reaching consensus on Social Security reform will be difficult because every citizen has a direct economic stake in the outcome and little agreement is present among them on the proper magnitude of the benefits, how the program should be structured, and how we should pay for the projected funding shortfall. Nevertheless, Americans will eventually need to confront the problem of trillions of dollars of unfunded Social Security liabilities.

Summary

1. Fiscal policy consists of deliberate changes in government spending, taxes, or some combination of both to promote full employment, price-level stability, and economic growth. Fiscal policy requires increases in government spending, decreases in taxes, or both—a budget deficit—to increase aggregate demand and push an economy from a recession. Decreases in government spending, increases in taxes, or both—a budget surplus—are appropriate fiscal policy for dealing with demand-pull inflation.

2. Built-in stability arises from net tax revenues, which vary directly with the level of GDP. During recession, the Federal budget automatically moves toward a stabilizing deficit; during expansion, the budget automatically moves toward an anti-inflationary surplus. Built-in stability lessens, but does not fully correct, undesired changes in real GDP.

3. The standardized budget measures the Federal budget deficit or surplus that would occur if the economy operated at full employment throughout the year. Cyclical deficits or surpluses are those that result from changes in GDP. Changes in the standardized deficit or surplus provide meaningful information as to whether the government's fiscal policy is expansionary, neutral, or contractionary. Changes in the actual budget deficit or surplus do not, since such deficits or surpluses can include cyclical deficits or surpluses.

4. Certain problems complicate the enactment and implementation of fiscal policy. They include (a) timing problems

associated with recognition, administrative, and operational lags; (b) the potential for misuse of fiscal policy for political rather than economic purposes; (c) the fact that state and local finances tend to be pro-cyclical; (d) potential ineffectiveness if households expect future policy reversals; and (e) the possibility of fiscal policy crowding out private investment.

5. Most economists believe that fiscal policy can help move the economy in a desired direction but cannot reliably be used to fine-tune the economy to a position of price stability and full employment. Nevertheless, fiscal policy is a valuable backup tool for aiding monetary policy in fighting significant recession or inflation.

6. The large Federal budget deficits of the 1980s and early 1990s prompted Congress in 1993 to increase tax rates and limit government spending. As a result of these policies, along with a very rapid and prolonged economic expansion, the deficits dwindled to $22 billion in 1997. Large budget surpluses occurred in 1999, 2000, and 2001. In 2001 the Congressional Budget Office projected that $5 trillion of annual budget surpluses would accumulate between 2000 and 2010.

7. In 2001 the Bush administration and Congress chose to reduce marginal tax rates and phase out the Federal estate tax. A recession occurred in 2001, the stock market crashed, and Federal spending for the war on terrorism rocketed. The Federal budget swung from a surplus of $127 billion in 2001 to a deficit of $158 billion in 2002. In 2003 the Bush administration and Congress accelerated the tax reductions scheduled under the 2001 tax law and cut tax rates on capital gains and dividends. The purposes were to stimulate a sluggish economy. In 2004 the budget deficit reached $413 billion. Although deficits declined through 2007, they are expected to grow for a time because of large tax rebates, permanent tax cuts, and increases in government spending, all designed to stimulate aggregate demand. The purpose is to help boost the economy out of the recession that began December 2007 and became severe in the last half of 2008.

8. The public debt is the total accumulation of the government's deficits (minus surpluses) over time and consists of Treasury bills, Treasury notes, Treasury bonds, and U.S. savings bonds. In 2007 the U.S. public debt was $9.01 trillion, or $29,987 per person. The public (which here includes banks and state and local governments) holds 47 percent of that Federal debt; the Federal Reserve and Federal agencies hold the other 53 percent. Foreigners hold 25 percent of the Federal debt. Interest payments as a percentage of GDP were about 1.7 percent in 2007. This is down from 3.2 percent in 1990.

9. The concern that a large public debt may bankrupt the government is a false worry because (a) the debt need only be refinanced rather than refunded and (b) the Federal government has the power to increase taxes to make interest payments on the debt.

10. In general, the public debt is not a vehicle for shifting economic burdens to future generations. Americans inherit not only most of the public debt (a liability) but also most of the U.S. securities (an asset) that finance the debt.

11. More substantive problems associated with public debt include the following: (a) Payment of interest on the debt may increase income inequality. (b) Interest payments on the debt require higher taxes, which may impair incentives. (c) Paying interest or principal on the portion of the debt held by foreigners means a transfer of real output to abroad. (d) Government borrowing to refinance or pay interest on the debt may increase interest rates and crowd out private investment spending, leaving future generations with a smaller stock of capital than they would have otherwise.

12. The increase in investment in public capital that may result from debt financing may partly or wholly offset the crowding-out effect of the public debt on private investment. Also, the added public investment may stimulate private investment, where the two are complements.

13. The Social Security system has a significant long-run funding problem. The number of Social Security beneficiaries is projected to significantly rise in future years, and those retirees, on average, are expected to live longer than current retirees. Meanwhile, the number of workers paying Social Security taxes will increase relatively slowly. So a large gap between Social Security revenues and payments will eventually arise. This problem has created calls for various kinds of Social Security reform.

Terms and Concepts

fiscal policy

Council of Economic Advisers (CEA)

expansionary fiscal policy

budget deficit

contractionary fiscal policy

budget surplus

built-in stabilizer

standardized budget

cyclical deficit

political business cycle

crowding-out effect

public debt

U.S. securities

external public debt

investment demand curve

public investments

Social Security trust fund

Study Questions

1. The Federal government establishes its budget to decide what programs to provide and how to pay for them. How does fiscal policy differ from this ordinary fiscal activity of budgeting? **LO1**

2. What are government's fiscal policy options for moving the economy out of a recession? Speculate on which of these fiscal options might be favored by (a) a person who wants to preserve the size of government and (b) a person who thinks the public sector is too large. How does the "ratchet effect" affect anti-inflationary fiscal policy? **LO1**

3. Explain how built-in (or automatic) stabilizers work. What are the differences between proportional, progressive, and regressive tax systems as they relate to an economy's built-in stability? **LO2**

4. Define the standardized budget, explain its significance, and state why it may differ from the actual budget. Suppose the full-employment, noninflationary level of real output is GDP$_3$ (not GDP$_2$) in the economy depicted in Figure 8.3. If the economy is operating at GDP$_2$, instead of GDP$_3$, what is the status of its standardized budget? The status of its current fiscal policy? What change in fiscal policy would you recommend? How would you accomplish that in terms of the G and T lines in the figure? **LO3**

5. How would you expect the Economic Stimulus Act of 2008 to affect the actual budget (as a percentage of GDP) and the standardized budget? The main feature of the act was a one-time tax rebate to households. How would the actual and standardized budgets be affected if those rebates became permanent tax policy and were distributed annually? **LO1**

6. Briefly state and evaluate the problem of time lags in enacting and applying fiscal policy. How might "politics" complicate fiscal policy? How might expectations of a near-term policy reversal weaken fiscal policy based on changes in tax rates? What is the crowding-out effect, and why might it be relevant to fiscal policy? **LO1**

7. Use Figure 8.4. to explain why the deliberate increase of the standardized budget deficit (resulting from the tax cut) will reduce the size of the actual budget deficit if the fiscal policy succeeds in pushing the economy to its full-employment output of GDP$_1$. In requesting a tax cut in the early 1960s,

President Kennedy said, "It is a paradoxical truth that tax rates are too high today and tax revenues are too low and the soundest way to raise tax revenues in the long run is to cut tax rates now." Relate this quotation to your previous answer in this question. **LO3**

8. Why did the budget deficits rise sharply in 1991 and 1992? What explains the large budget surpluses of the late 1990s and early 2000s? What caused the swing from the budget surpluses to the series of budget deficits beginning in 2002? **LO3**

9. Distinguish between the total U.S. debt and the debt held by the public. Why is the debt as a percentage of GDP more relevant than the total debt? Contrast the effects of paying off an internally held debt and paying off an externally held debt. **LO4**

10. True or false? If the statement is false, explain why: **LO4**
    a. An internally held public debt is like a debt of the left hand owed to the right hand.
    b. The Federal Reserve and Federal government agencies hold more than half the public debt.
    c. As a percentage of GDP, the Federal debt held by the public was smaller in 2007 than it was in 1990.

11. Why might economists be quite concerned if the annual interest payments on the debt sharply increased as a percentage of GDP? **LO4**

12. Trace the cause-and-effect chain through which financing and refinancing of the public debt might affect real interest rates, private investment, the stock of capital, and economic growth. How might investment in public capital and complementarities between public capital and private capital alter the outcome of the cause-effect chain? **LO4**

13. What do economists mean when they refer to Social Security as a pay-as-you-go plan? What is the Social Security trust fund? What is the nature of the long-run fiscal imbalance in the Social Security retirement system? What are the broad options for fixing the long-run problem? **LO5**

**FURTHER TEST YOUR KNOWLEDGE AT
www.mcconnellbriefmacro1e.com**

Web-Based Questions

At the text's Online Learning Center, **www.mcconnellbriefmacro 1e.com**, you will find a multiple-choice quiz on this chapter's content. We encourage you to take the quiz to see how you do.

Also, you will find one or more Web-based questions that require information from the Internet to answer.

PART FOUR

Money, Banking, and Monetary Policy

9

Money and Banking

Money is a fascinating aspect of the economy:

> Money bewitches people. They fret for it, and they sweat for it. They devise most ingenious ways to get it, and most ingenious ways to get rid of it. Money is the only commodity that is good for nothing but to be gotten rid of. It will not feed you, clothe you, shelter you, or amuse you unless you spend it or invest it. It imparts value only in parting. People will do almost anything for money, and money will do almost anything for people. Money is a captivating, circulating, masquerading puzzle.[1]

In this chapter and the next we want to unmask the critical role of money and the monetary system in the economy. When the monetary system is working properly, it provides the lifeblood of the circular flows of income and expenditure. A well-operating monetary system helps the economy achieve both full employment and the efficient use of resources. A malfunctioning monetary system distorts the allocation of resources and creates severe fluctuations in the economy's levels of output, employment, and prices.

---

[1]Federal Reserve Bank of Philadelphia, "Creeping Inflation," *Business Review,* August 1957, p. 3.

The Functions of Money

There is an old saying that "money *is* what money *does*." In a conceptual sense, anything that performs the functions of money *is* money. Here are those functions:

- *Medium of exchange*   First and foremost, money is a **medium of exchange** that is usable for buying and selling goods and services. A bakery worker does not want to be paid 200 bagels per week. Nor does the bakery owner want to receive, say, halibut in exchange for bagels. Money, however, is readily acceptable as payment. As we saw in Chapter 2, money is a social invention with which resource suppliers and producers can be paid and that can be used to buy any of the full range of items available in the marketplace. As a medium of exchange, money allows society to escape the complications of barter. And because it provides a convenient way of exchanging goods, money enables society to gain the advantages of geographic and human specialization.

- *Unit of account*   Money is also a **unit of account.** Society uses monetary units—dollars, in the United States—as a yardstick for measuring the relative worth of a wide variety of goods, services, and resources. Just as we measure distance in miles or kilometers, we gauge the value of goods in dollars. With money as an acceptable unit of account, the price of each item need be stated only in terms of the monetary unit. We need not state the price of cows in terms of corn, crayons, and cranberries. Money aids rational decision making by enabling buyers and sellers to easily compare the prices of various goods, services, and resources. It also permits us to define debt obligations, determine taxes owed, and calculate the nation's GDP.

- *Store of value*   Money also serves as a **store of value** that allows people to transfer purchasing power from the present to the future. People normally do not spend all their incomes on the day they receive them. In order to buy things later, they store some of their wealth as money. The money you place in a safe or a checking account will still be available to you a few weeks or months from now. When inflation is nonexistent or mild, holding money is a relatively risk-free way to store wealth for later use.

medium of exchange
An item that sellers generally accept and buyers generally use to pay for goods and services.

unit of account
A standard measurement unit in terms of which prices can be stated and the relative value of goods and services compared.

store of value
An asset set aside to purchase items in the future.

People can, of course, choose to hold some or all of their wealth in a wide variety of assets besides money. These include real estate, stocks, bonds, precious metals such as gold, and even collectible items like fine art or comic books. But a key advantage that money has over all other assets is that it has the most *liquidity*, or spendability.

An asset's **liquidity** is the ease with which it can be converted quickly into the most widely accepted and easily spent form of money, cash, with little or no loss of purchasing power. The more liquid an asset is, the more quickly it can be converted into cash and used either for purchases of goods and services or purchases of other assets.

Levels of liquidity vary radically. By definition, cash is perfectly liquid. By contrast, a house is highly illiquid for two reasons. First, it may take several months before a willing buyer can be found and a sale negotiated so that its value can be converted into cash. Second, there is a loss of purchasing power when the house is sold because numerous fees have to be paid to real estate agents and other individuals in order to complete the sale.

As we are about to discuss, our economy uses several different types of money including cash, coins, checking account deposits, savings account deposits, and even more exotic things like deposits in money market mutual funds. As we describe the various forms of money in detail, take the time to compare their relative levels of liquidity—both with each other and with other assets like stocks, bonds, and real estate. Cash is perfectly liquid. Other forms of money are highly liquid, but less liquid than cash.

liquidity
The ease with which an asset can be converted into cash.

The Components of the Money Supply

Money is a "stock" of some item or group of items (unlike income, for example, which is a "flow"). Societies have used many items as money, including whales' teeth, circular stones, elephant-tail bristles, gold coins, furs, and pieces of paper. Anything that is widely accepted as a medium of exchange can serve as money. In the United States, currency is not the only form of money. As you will see, certain debts of government and financial institutions are also used as money.

Money Definition: *M*1

M1
The most narrowly defined money supply, equal to currency (outside banks) plus the checkable deposits of commercial bank and thrift institutions.

The narrowest definition of the U.S. money supply is called **M1.** It consists of:

- Currency (coins and paper money) in the hands of the nonbank public.
- All checkable deposits (all deposits in commercial banks and "thrift" or savings institutions on which checks of any size can be drawn).[2]

Government and government agencies supply coins and paper money. Commercial banks and savings institutions provide checkable deposits.

Federal Reserve Notes
Paper bills issued by the Federal Reserve Banks.

Currency: Coins + Paper Money The currency of the United States consists of metal coins and paper money. The coins are issued by the United States Treasury while the paper money consists of **Federal Reserve Notes** issued by the Federal Reserve System (the U.S. central bank). Coins are minted by the United States Mint while the paper money is printed by the Bureau of Engraving and Printing. Both the U.S. Mint and the Bureau of Engraving and Printing are part of the U.S. Department of the Treasury.

token money
Currency that has a face value greater than the materials used to produce it.

As with the currencies of other countries, the currency of the United States is **token money**. This means that the face value of any piece of currency is unrelated to its *intrinsic value*—the value of the physical material (metal or paper and ink) out of which that currency is constructed. Governments make sure that face values exceed intrinsic values in order to discourage people from destroying coins and bills in order to resell the material that they are made out of. For instance, if 50-cent pieces each contained 75 cents' worth of metal, then it would be profitable to melt them down and sell the metal. Fifty-cent pieces would disappear from circulation very quickly!

Figure 9.1 shows that coins and paper money (currency) constitute 56 percent of the U.S. economy's *M*1 money supply.

checkable deposits
Deposits in banks or thrifts against which checks may be written.

Checkable Deposits The safety and convenience of checks has made checkable deposits a large component of the *M*1 money supply. You would not think of stuffing $4896 in bills in an envelope and dropping it in a mailbox to pay a debt. But writing and mailing a check for a large sum is commonplace. The person cashing a check must endorse it (sign it on the reverse side); the writer of the check subsequently receives a record of the cashed check as a receipt attesting to the fulfillment of the obligation. Similarly, because the writing of a check requires a signature, the theft or loss of your checkbook is not nearly as calamitous as losing an identical amount of currency. Finally, it is more convenient to write a check than to transport and count out a large sum of currency. For all these reasons, **checkable deposits** (checkbook money)

---

[2] In order to avoid a maze of details in the ensuing discussion, we do not discuss several of the quantitatively less significant components of the definitions of money. For example, traveler's checks are included in the *M*1 money supply. The statistical appendix of any recent *Federal Reserve Bulletin* provides more comprehensive definitions.

FIGURE 9.1 **Components of money supply *M*1 and money supply *M*2, in the United States.** *M*1 is a narrow definition of the money supply that includes currency (in circulation) and checkable deposits. *M*2 is a broader definition that includes *M*1 along with several other relatively liquid account balances.

* These categories include other, quantitatively smaller components such as traveler's checks.

Source: Federal Reserve System, **www.federalreserve.gov**. Data are for January 2008.

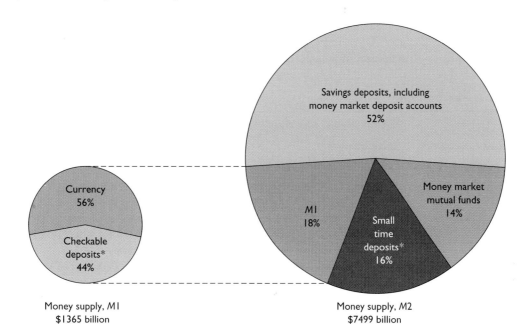

are a large component of the stock of money in the United States. About 44 percent of *M*1 is in the form of checkable deposits, on which checks can be drawn.

It might seem strange that checking account balances are regarded as part of the money supply. But the reason is clear: Checks are nothing more than a way to transfer the ownership of deposits in banks and other financial institutions and are generally acceptable as a medium of exchange. Although checks are less generally accepted than currency for small purchases, for major purchases most sellers willingly accept checks as payment. Moreover, people can convert checkable deposits into paper money and coins on demand; checks drawn on those deposits are thus the equivalent of currency.

To summarize:

$$\text{Money, } M1 = \text{Curency} + \text{Checkable Deposits}$$

Institutions That Offer Checkable Deposits
In the United States, a variety of financial institutions allow customers to write checks in any amount on the funds they have deposited. **Commercial banks** are the primary depository institutions. They accept the deposits of households and businesses, keep the money safe until it is demanded via checks, and in the meantime use it to make available a wide variety of loans. Commercial bank loans provide short-term financial capital to businesses, and they finance consumer purchases of automobiles and other durable goods.

Savings and loan associations (S&Ls), mutual savings banks, and credit unions supplement the commercial banks and are known collectively as savings or **thrift institutions,** or simply "thrifts." *Savings and loan associations* and *mutual savings banks*

commercial banks
Firms that engage in the business of banking (accepting deposits, offering checking accounts, and making loans).

thrift institutions
Savings and loan associations, mutual savings banks, or credit unions that offer savings and checking accounts.

accept the deposits of households and businesses and then use the funds to finance housing mortgages and to provide other loans. *Credit unions* accept deposits from and lend to "members," who usually are a group of people who work for the same company.

The checkable deposits of banks and thrifts are known variously as demand deposits, NOW (negotiable order of withdrawal) accounts, ATS (automatic transfer service) accounts, and share draft accounts. Their commonality is that depositors can write checks on them whenever, and in whatever amount, they choose.

Two Qualifications We must qualify our discussion in two important ways. First, currency held by the U.S. Treasury, the Federal Reserve Banks, commercial banks, and thrift institutions is *excluded* from $M1$ and other measures of the money supply. A paper dollar or four quarters in the billfold of, say, Emma Buck obviously constitutes just $1 of the money supply. But if we counted currency held by banks as part of the money supply, the same $1 would count for $2 of money supply when Emma deposited the currency into her checkable deposit in her bank. It would count for $1 of checkable deposit owned by Buck and also $1 of currency in the bank's cash drawer or vault. By excluding currency held by banks when determining the total supply of money, we avoid this problem of double counting.

Also *excluded* from the money supply are any checkable deposits of the government (specifically, the U.S. Treasury) or the Federal Reserve that are held by commercial banks or thrift institutions. This exclusion is designed to enable a better assessment of the amount of money available *to the private sector* for potential spending. The amount of money available to households and businesses is of keen interest to the Federal Reserve in conducting its monetary policy (a topic we cover in the next chapter).

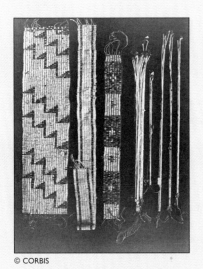
© CORBIS

© PhotoLink/Getty Images

© Getty Images

Photo Op Money: Then and Now

Items such as wampum belts were once used as money. Today, bills and coins, along with checkable deposits, constitute the *M*I money supply.

Money Definition: *M2*

A second and broader definition of money includes *M1* plus several near-monies. **Near-monies** are certain highly liquid financial assets that do not function directly or fully as a medium of exchange but can be readily converted into currency or checkable deposits. Three categories of near-monies owned by individuals are included in the *M2* definition of money:

- *Savings deposits, including money market deposit accounts* A depositor can withdraw funds from an interest-earning **savings account** at a bank or thrift or simply request that the funds be transferred to a checkable account. A person can also withdraw funds from a **money market deposit account (MMDA),** which is an interest-earning account containing interest-earning short-term securities. MMDAs, however, have a minimum-balance requirement and a limit on how often a person can withdraw funds.
- *Small (less than $100,000) time deposits* Funds from **time deposits** become available at their maturity. For example, a person can convert a 6-month time deposit ("certificate of deposit" or simply "CD") to currency without penalty 6 months or more after it has been deposited. In return for this withdrawal limitation, the financial institution pays a higher interest rate on such deposits than it does on its MMDAs. Also, a person can "cash in" a CD before its maturity but must pay a severe penalty.
- *Money market mutual funds* By making a telephone call, using the Internet, or writing a check for $500 or more, a depositor can redeem shares in a **money market mutual fund (MMMF)** offered by a mutual fund company. Such companies combine the funds of individual shareholders to buy interest-bearing short-term credit instruments such as certificates of deposit and U.S. government securities. Then they can offer interest on the MMMF accounts of the shareholders (depositors) who jointly own those financial assets.

All three categories of near-monies imply substantial liquidity. In summary, *M2* includes the immediate medium-of-exchange items (currency and checkable deposits) that constitute *M1* plus certain near-monies that can be easily converted into currency and checkable deposits. In Figure 9.1 we see that the addition of all these items yields an *M2* money supply that is about five times larger than the narrower *M1* money supply. Thus, to summarize in equation form,

$$\text{Money, } M2 = M1 + \text{savings deposits, including MMDAs} + \text{small}$$
$$(\text{less than } \$100,000) \text{ time deposits} + \text{MMMFs}$$

Actually, there is an entire spectrum of assets that vary slightly in terms of their liquidity or "moneyness" that are not included in *M1* or *M2*. Because the simple *M1* definition includes only items directly and immediately usable as a medium of exchange, it is often cited in discussions of the money supply. But, for some purposes economists prefer the broader *M2* definition. For example, *M2* is used as one of the 10 trend variables in the index of leading indicators (an economic forecasting tool). Still broader definitions of money are so inclusive that they have limited usefulness.

We will use the narrow *M1* definition of the money supply in our discussion and analysis, unless stated otherwise. The important principles we will develop relating to *M1* also apply to *M2* because *M1* is included in *M2*.

What "Backs" the Money Supply?

The money supply in the United States essentially is "backed" (guaranteed) by government's ability to keep the value of money relatively stable. Nothing more! Paper currency and checkable deposits have no intrinsic value. A $5 bill is just an inscribed piece of paper. A checkable deposit is merely a bookkeeping entry. And coins, we know, have less intrinsic value than their face value. Nor will government redeem the paper money you hold for anything tangible, such as gold.

near-monies
Financial assets that do not directly serve as a medium of exchange but readily can be converted into narrowly defined money (currency + checkable deposits).

M2
A more broadly defined money supply, equal to M1 plus noncheckable savings accounts (including money market deposit accounts), time deposits of less than $100,000, and individual money market mutual fund balances.

savings account
An interest-earning account (at a bank or thrift) from which funds normally can be withdrawn at any time.

money market deposit account (MMDA)
An interest-earning account (at a bank or thrift) consisting of short-term securities and on which a limited number of checks can be written each year.

time deposits
Interest-earning deposits (at a bank or thrift) such as certificates of deposit (CDs) that depositors can withdraw without penalty after the end of a specified period.

money market mutual fund (MMMF)
An interest-earning account at an investment company, which pools the funds of depositors to purchase short-term securities.

To many people, the fact that the government does not back the currency with anything tangible seems implausible and insecure. But the decision not to back the currency with anything tangible was made for a very good reason. If the government backed the currency with something tangible like gold, then the supply of money would vary with how much gold was available. By not backing the currency, the government avoids this constraint and indeed receives a key freedom—the ability to provide as much or as little money as needed to maintain the value of money and to best suit the economic needs of the country. In effect, by choosing not to back the currency, the government has chosen to give itself the ability to freely "manage" the nation's money supply. Its monetary authorities attempt to provide the amount of money needed for the particular volume of business activity that will promote full employment, price-level stability, and economic growth.

Nearly all today's economists agree that managing the money supply is more sensible than linking it to gold or to some other commodity whose supply might change arbitrarily and capriciously. For instance, if we used gold to back the money supply so that gold was redeemable for money, and *vice versa*, then a large increase in the nation's gold stock as the result of a new gold discovery might increase the money supply too rapidly and thereby trigger rapid inflation. Or a long-lasting decline in gold production might reduce the money supply to the point where recession and unemployment resulted.

In short, people cannot convert paper money into a fixed amount of gold or any other precious commodity. Money is exchangeable only for paper money. If you ask the government to redeem $5 of your paper money, it will swap one paper $5 bill for another bearing a different serial number. That is all you can get. Similarly, checkable deposits can be redeemed not for gold but only for paper money, which, as we have just seen, the government will not redeem for anything tangible.

Value of Money

So why are currency and checkable deposits money, whereas, say, Monopoly (the game) money is not? What gives a $20 bill or a $100 checking account entry its value? The answer to these questions has three parts.

Acceptability Currency and checkable deposits are money because people accept them as money. By virtue of long-standing business practice, currency and checkable deposits perform the basic function of money: They are acceptable as a medium of exchange. We accept paper money in exchange because we are confident it will be exchangeable for real goods, services, and resources when we spend it.

legal tender
A legal designation of a nation's official currency (bills and coins).

Legal Tender Our confidence in the acceptability of paper money undoubtedly is strengthened because government has designated currency as **legal tender.** Specifically, each bill contains the statement "This note is legal tender for all debts, public and private." That means paper money is a valid and legal means of payment of any debt that was contracted in dollars. (But private firms and government are not mandated to accept cash. It is not illegal for them to specify payment in noncash forms such as checks, cashier's checks, money orders, or credit cards.)

The general acceptance of paper currency as money is more important than the government's decree that money is legal tender, however. The government has never decreed checks to be legal tender, and yet they serve as such in many of the economy's exchanges of goods, services, and resources. But it is true that government agencies— the Federal Deposit Insurance Corporation (FDIC) and the National Credit Union

Administration (NCUA)—insure individual deposits of up to $250,000 at commercial banks and thrifts. That fact enhances our willingness to store money in checkable accounts and write checks on those accounts to buy goods, services, and resources.

ILLUSTRATING
THE
IDEA

Are Credit Cards Money?

You may wonder why we have ignored credit cards such as Visa and MasterCard in our discussion of the money supply. After all, credit cards are a convenient way to buy things and account for about 25 percent of the dollar value of all transactions in the United States. The answer is that a credit card is not money. Rather, it is a convenient means of obtaining a short-term loan from the financial institution that issued the card.

What happens when you purchase an item with a credit card? The bank that issued the card will reimburse the store, charging it a transaction fee, and later you will reimburse the bank. Rather than reduce your cash or checking account with each purchase, you bunch your payments once a month. You may have to pay an annual fee for the services provided, and if you pay the bank in installments, you will pay a sizable interest charge on the loan. Credit cards are merely a means of deferring or postponing payment for a short period. Your checking account balance used to pay your monthly credit card bill *is* money; the credit card is *not* money.*

Although credit cards are not money, they allow individuals and businesses to "economize" in the use of money. Credit cards enable people to hold less currency in their billfolds and have smaller checkable deposit balances (prior to the due date for paying the credit card bill) in their bank accounts. Credit cards also help people coordinate the timing of their expenditures with their receipt of income.

Question:
If credit cards are not money, why are they so popular?

*A bank debit card, however, is very similar to a blank check in your checkbook. Unlike a purchase with a credit card, a purchase with a debit card creates a direct "debit" (a subtraction) from your checking account balance. That checking account balance *is* money—it is part of *M*1.

Relative Scarcity The value of money, like the economic value of anything else, depends on its supply and demand. Money derives its value from its scarcity relative to its utility (its want-satisfying power). The utility of money lies in its capacity to be exchanged for goods and services, now or in the future. The economy's demand for money thus depends on the total dollar volume of transactions in any period plus the amount of money individuals and businesses want to hold for future transactions. With a reasonably constant demand for money, the supply of money provided by the monetary authorities will determine the value or "purchasing power" of the monetary unit (dollar, yen, peso, or whatever).

Money and Prices

The purchasing power of money is the amount of goods and services a unit of money will buy. When money rapidly loses its purchasing power, it loses its role as money.

The Purchasing Power of the Dollar

The amount a dollar will buy varies inversely with the price level, meaning a reciprocal relationship exists between the general price level and the purchasing power of the dollar. When the Consumer Price Index or "cost-of-living" index goes up, the purchasing power of the dollar goes down, and vice versa. Higher prices lower the purchasing power of the dollar, because more dollars are needed to buy a particular amount of goods, services, or resources. For example, if the price level doubles, the purchasing power of the dollar declines by one-half, or 50 percent.

Conversely, lower prices increase the purchasing power of the dollar, because fewer dollars are needed to obtain a specific quantity of goods and services. If the price level falls by, say, one-half, or 50 percent, the purchasing power of the dollar doubles.

Inflation and Acceptability

In Chapter 6 we noted situations in which a nation's currency became worthless and unacceptable in exchange. These instances of runaway inflation, or *hyperinflation*, happened when the government issued so many pieces of paper currency that the purchasing power of each of those units of money was almost totally undermined. The infamous post–World War I hyperinflation in Germany is an example. In December 1919 there were about 50 billion marks in circulation. Four years later there were 496,585,345,900 billion marks in circulation! The result? The German mark in 1923 was worth an infinitesimal fraction of its 1919 value.[3]

Runaway inflation may significantly depreciate the purchasing power of money between the time it is received and the time it is spent. Rapid declines in the purchasing power of a currency may cause it to cease being used as a medium of exchange. Businesses and households may refuse to accept paper money in exchange because they do not want to bear the loss in its value that will occur while it is in their possession. (All this despite the fact that the government says that paper currency is legal tender!) Without an acceptable domestic medium of exchange, the economy may simply revert to barter. Alternatively, more internally stable currencies such as the U.S. dollar may come into widespread use.

Similarly, people will use money as a store of value only as long as there is no sizable deterioration in the value of that money because of inflation. And an economy can effectively employ money as a unit of account only when its purchasing power is relatively stable. A monetary yardstick that no longer measures a yard (in terms of purchasing power) does not permit buyers and sellers to establish the terms of trade clearly. When the value of the dollar is declining rapidly, sellers do not know what to charge and buyers do not know what to pay.

---

[3] Frank G. Graham, *Exchange, Prices and Production in Hyperinflation Germany, 1920–1923* (Princeton, N.J.: Princeton University Press, 1930), p. 13.

The Federal Reserve and the Banking System

A key element of the U.S. banking system is the **Federal Reserve System** (the "Fed"). As shown in Figure 9.2, a Board of Governors directs the activities of 12 Federal Reserve Banks, which in turn control the lending activity of the nation's banks and thrift institutions. The Fed's major goal is to control the money supply. But since checkable deposits in banks are such a large part of the money supply, an important part of its duties involves assuring the stability of the banking system.

Board of Governors

The central authority of the U.S. money and banking system is the **Board of Governors** of the Federal Reserve System. The U.S. president, with the confirmation of the Senate, appoints the seven Board members. Terms are 14 years and staggered so that one member is replaced every 2 years. In addition, new members are appointed when resignations occur. The president selects the chairperson and vice-chairperson of the Board from among the members. Those officers serve 4-year terms and can be reappointed to new 4-year terms by the president. The long-term appointments provide the Board with continuity, experienced membership, and independence from political pressures that could result in inflation.

The 12 Federal Reserve Banks

The 12 **Federal Reserve Banks,** which blend private and public control, collectively serve as the nation's "central bank." These banks also serve as bankers' banks.

Central Banks Most nations have a single central bank—for example, Britain's Bank of England or Japan's Bank of Japan. The United States' central bank consists of 12 banks whose policies are coordinated by the Fed's Board of Governors. The

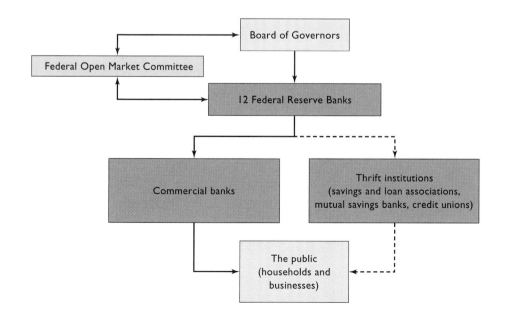

FIGURE 9.2 The framework of the Federal Reserve System and its relationship to the nonbank public. With the aid of the Federal Open Market Committee, the Board of Governors makes the basic policy decisions that provide monetary control of the U.S. money and banking system. The 12 Federal Reserve Banks implement these decisions.

12 Federal Reserve Banks accommodate the geographic size and economic diversity of the United States and the nation's large number of commercial banks and thrifts.

Figure 9.3 locates the 12 Federal Reserve Banks and indicates the district that each serves. These banks implement the basic policy of the Board of Governors.

Quasi-Public Banks

The 12 Federal Reserve Banks are quasi-public banks, which blend private ownership and public control. Each Federal Reserve Bank is owned by the private commercial banks in its district. (Federally chartered commercial banks are required to purchase shares of stock in the Federal Reserve Bank in their district.) But the Board of Governors is an independent, quasi-government body that sets the basic policies that the Federal Reserve Banks pursue.

Despite their private ownership, the Federal Reserve Banks are in practice public institutions. Unlike private firms, they are not motivated by profit. The policies they follow are designed by the Board of Governors to promote the well-being of the economy as a whole. Also, the Federal Reserve Banks do not compete with commercial banks. In general, they do not deal with the public; rather, they interact with the government and commercial banks and thrifts.

Bankers' Banks

The Federal Reserve Banks are "bankers' banks." They perform essentially the same functions for banks and thrifts as those institutions perform for the public. Just as banks and thrifts accept the deposits of and make loans to the public, so the central banks accept the deposits of and make loans to banks and thrifts. Normally, these loans average only about $150 million a day. But in emergency circumstances the Federal Reserve Banks become the "lender of last resort" to the banking system and can lend out as much as needed to ensure that banks and thrifts can meet their cash obligations. During the mortgage debt crisis of 2007–2008, the Fed loaned billions of dollars to banks and thrifts and also loaned funds to other financial institutions that were in severe financial distress.

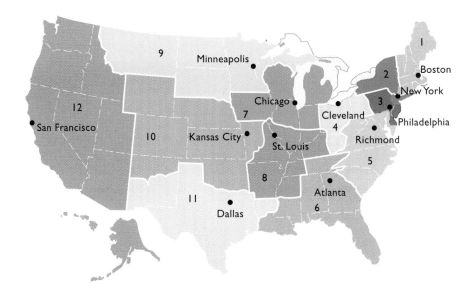

FIGURE 9.3 **The 12 Federal Reserve Districts.** The Federal Reserve System divides the United States into 12 districts, each having one central bank and in some instances one or more branches of the central bank. Hawaii and Alaska are included in the 12th district.
Source: *Federal Reserve Bulletin,*
www.federalreserve.gov/pubs/bulletin.

But the Federal Reserve Banks have a third function, which banks and thrifts do not perform: They issue currency. Congress has authorized the Federal Reserve Banks to put into circulation Federal Reserve Notes, which constitute the economy's paper money supply.

FOMC

The **Federal Open Market Committee (FOMC)** aids the Board of Governors in conducting monetary policy. The FOMC is made up of 12 individuals:

- The seven members of the Board of Governors.
- The president of the New York Federal Reserve Bank.
- Four of the remaining presidents of Federal Reserve Banks on a 1-year rotating basis.

The FOMC meets regularly to direct the purchase and sale of government securities (bills, notes, bonds) in the open market in which such securities are bought and sold on a daily basis. We will find in Chapter 10 that the purpose of these aptly named *open-market operations* is to control the nation's money supply and influence interest rates. The Federal Reserve Bank in New York City conducts most of the Fed's open-market operations.

Federal Open Market Committee (FOMC) The 12-member Federal Reserve group that determines the purchase and sale policies of the Federal Reserve Banks in the market for U.S. government securities.

Commercial Banks and Thrifts

There are about 7300 commercial banks. Roughly three-fourths are *state banks*, which are chartered (authorized) by individual states to operate within those states. The other one-fourth of all banks are *national banks*, chartered by the Federal government to operate nationally. Some of the U.S. national banks are very large, ranking among the world's largest financial institutions (see Global Snapshot 9.1). The 11,000 thrift institutions—the vast majority of which are credit unions—are regulated by agencies separate and apart from the Board of Governors and the Federal Reserve Banks. For example, the operations of savings and loan associations are regulated and monitored by the Treasury Department's Office of Thrift Supervision. But the thrifts *are* subject to monetary control by the Federal Reserve System. In particular, like the banks, thrifts are required to keep a certain percentage of their checkable deposits as reserves. In Figure 9.2 we use dashed arrows to indicate that the thrift institutions are partially subject to the control of the Board of Governors and the central banks. Decisions concerning monetary policy affect the thrifts along with the commercial banks.

Fed Functions and Responsibilities

The Fed performs several functions, some of which we have already mentioned. They and other functions are worth summarizing:

- *Issuing currency* The Federal Reserve Banks issue Federal Reserve Notes, the paper currency used in the U.S. monetary system. (The Federal Reserve Bank that issued a particular bill is identified in black in the upper left of the front of the newly designed bills. "A1," for example, identifies the Boston bank, "B2" the New York bank, and so on.)
- *Setting reserve requirements and holding reserves* The Fed sets legal reserve ratios, which are the fractions of checking account balances that banks must maintain as currency reserves. The central banks accept as deposits from the banks and thrifts any portion of their mandated reserves not held as vault cash.
- *Lending money to financial institutions* The Fed routinely lends money to banks and thrifts. Additionally, in times of national emergency, the Fed serves as a *lender of last resort* not only to banks and thrifts but also to other critical firms in the financial industry.

GLOBAL SNAPSHOT 9.1

The World's 12 Largest Financial Institutions

The world's 12 largest private sector financial institutions are headquartered in Europe, Japan, and the United States (2007 data).

Assets (billions of U.S. dollars)

Institution	Assets
Barclays (U.K.)	1,949
BNP Paribas (France)	1,898
Citigroup (U.S.)	1,884
HSBC (U.K.)	1,860
UBS (Switzerland)	1,776
Royal Bank of Scotland (U.K.)	1,705
ING Group (Netherlands)	1,615
Mitsubishi UFJ (Japan)	1,585
Deutsche Bank (Germany)	1,485
Bank of America (U.S.)	1,459
Allianz (Germany)	1,380
JP Morgan Chase (U.S.)	1,351

Source: Forbes Global 2000, **www.forbes.com**.

- *Providing for check collection*   The Fed provides the banking system with a means for collecting checks. If Sue writes a check on her Miami bank or thrift to Joe, who deposits it in his Dallas bank or thrift, how does the Dallas bank collect the money represented by the check drawn against the Miami bank? Answer: The Fed handles it in 2 or 3 days by adjusting the reserves (deposits) of the two banks.
- *Acting as fiscal agent*   The Fed acts as the fiscal agent (provider of financial services) for the Federal government. The government collects huge sums through taxation, spends equally large amounts, and sells and redeems bonds. To carry out these activities, the government uses the Fed's facilities as its bank.
- *Supervising banks*   The Fed supervises the operations of banks. It makes periodic examinations to assess bank profitability, to ascertain that banks perform in accordance with the many regulations to which they are subject, and to uncover questionable practices or fraud.[4]
- *Controlling the money supply*   Finally, the major task of the Fed is to manage the nation's money supply, and thus indirectly set interest rates, according to the needs of the economy. This involves making an amount of money available that is consistent with high and rising levels of output and employment *and* a relatively constant price level. While all the other functions of the Fed are routine activities or have a service nature, managing the

---

[4] The Fed is not alone in this task of supervision. The individual states supervise all banks that they charter. The Comptroller of the Currency supervises all national banks, and the Office of Thrift Supervision supervises all thrifts. Also, the Federal Deposit Insurance Corporation supervises all banks and thrifts whose deposits it insures.

nation's money supply requires making basic, but unique, policy decisions. (We discuss those decisions in detail in Chapter 10.)

Federal Reserve Independence

Congress purposely established the Fed as an independent agency of government. The objective was to protect the Fed from political pressures so that it could effectively control the money supply and interest rates in order to maintain price-level stability. Political pressures on Congress and the executive branch may at times result in inflationary fiscal policies, including tax cuts and special-interest spending. If Congress and the executive branch also controlled the nation's monetary policy, citizens and lobbying groups undoubtedly would pressure elected officials to keep interest rates low even though at times high interest rates are necessary to reduce aggregate demand and thus control inflation. An independent monetary authority (the Fed) can take actions to increase interest rates when higher rates are needed to stem inflation. Studies show that countries that have independent central banks like the Fed have lower rates of inflation, on average, than countries that have little or no central bank independence.

The Fractional Reserve System

We have seen that the $M1$ money supply consists of currency (coins and Federal Reserve Notes) and checkable deposits. The U.S. Mint creates the coins and the U.S. Bureau of Engraving creates the Federal Reserve Notes. So who creates the checkable deposits that make up about half the nation's $M1$ money supply? Surprisingly, it is loan officers at banks and thrifts!

The United States, like most other countries today, has a **fractional reserve banking system** in which only a portion (fraction) of the total money supply is held in reserve as currency. Our goal is to explain how commercial banks and thrifts can create checkable deposits by issuing loans. Our examples will involve commercial banks, but remember that thrift institutions also provide checkable deposits. So the analysis applies to banks and thrifts alike.

fractional reserve banking system A banking system in which banks and thrifts are required to hold less than 100 percent of their checkable-deposit liabilities as reserves.

ILLUSTRATING THE IDEA

The Goldsmiths

Here is the history behind the idea of the fractional reserve system.

When early traders began to use gold in making transactions, they soon realized that it was both unsafe and inconvenient to carry gold and to have it weighed and assayed (judged for purity) every time they negotiated a transaction. So by the 16th century they had begun to deposit their gold with goldsmiths, who would store it in vaults for a fee. On receiving a gold deposit, the goldsmith would issue a receipt to the depositor. Soon people were paying for goods with goldsmiths' receipts, which served as one of the first types of paper money.

At this point the goldsmiths—embryonic bankers—used a 100 percent reserve system; they backed their circulating paper money receipts fully with the gold that they held "in reserve" in their vaults. But because of the public's acceptance of the goldsmiths' receipts as paper money, the goldsmiths soon realized that owners rarely redeemed the gold they had in storage. In fact, the goldsmiths observed that the amount of gold being deposited with them in any week or month was likely to exceed the amount that was being withdrawn.

Then some clever goldsmith hit on the idea that paper "receipts" could be issued in excess of the amount of gold held. Goldsmiths would put these receipts, which were redeemable in gold, into circulation by making interest-earning loans to merchants, producers, and consumers. A borrower might, for instance, borrow $10,000 worth of gold receipts today with the promise to repay $10,500 worth of gold receipts in one year (a five percent interest rate). Borrowers were willing to accept loans in the form of gold receipts because the receipts were accepted as a medium of exchange in the marketplace.

This was the beginning of the fractional reserve system of banking, in which reserves in bank vaults are a fraction of the total money supply. If, for example, the goldsmith issued $1 million in receipts for actual gold in storage and another $1 million in receipts as loans, then the total value of paper money in circulation would be $2 million—twice the value of the gold. Gold reserves would be a fraction (one-half) of outstanding paper money.

Question:
Explain how the gold receipts issued by goldsmiths performed the three major functions of money.

The goldsmith story highlights two significant characteristics of fractional reserve banking. First, banks can create money through lending. In fact, goldsmiths created money when they made loans by giving borrowers paper money that was not fully backed by gold reserves. The quantity of such money goldsmiths could create depended on the amount of reserves they deemed prudent to have available. The smaller the amount of reserves thought necessary, the larger the amount of paper money the goldsmiths could create. Today, gold is no longer used as bank reserves. Instead, currency itself serves as bank reserves so that the creation of checkable-deposit money by banks (via their lending) is limited by the amount of *currency reserves* that the banks feel obligated, or are required by law, to keep.

A second reality is that banks operating on the basis of fractional reserves are vulnerable to "panics" or "runs." A goldsmith who issued paper money equal to twice the value of his gold reserves would be unable to convert all that paper money into gold in the event that all the holders of that money appeared at his door at the same time demanding their gold. In fact, many European and U.S. banks were once ruined by this unfortunate circumstance. However, a bank panic is highly unlikely if the banker's reserve and lending policies are prudent. Indeed, one reason why banking systems are highly regulated industries is to prevent runs on banks. This is also the reason why the United States has a system of deposit insurance.

A Single Commercial Bank

To illustrate the workings of the modern fractional reserve banking system, we need to examine a commercial bank's balance sheet.

balance sheet
A statement of the assets, liabilities, and net worth of a firm, individual, or institution at some time.

The **balance sheet** of a commercial bank (or thrift) is a statement of assets and claims on assets that summarizes the financial position of the bank at a certain time. Every balance sheet must balance; this means that the value of *assets* must equal the amount of claims against those assets. The claims shown on a balance sheet are divided into two groups: the claims of nonowners against the firm's assets, called *liabilities*, and the claims of the owners of the firm against the firm's assets, called *net worth*. A balance sheet is balanced because

$$\text{Assets} = \text{liabilities} + \text{net worth}$$

For every $1 change in assets, there must be an offsetting $1 change in liabilities + net worth. For every $1 change in liabilities + net worth, there must be an offsetting $1 change in assets.

Now let's work through a series of bank transactions involving balance sheets to establish how individual banks can create money.

Transaction 1: Creating a Bank

Suppose some farsighted citizens of the town of Somewhere decide their town needs a new commercial bank to provide banking services for that growing community. Once they have secured a state or national charter for their bank, they turn to the task of selling, say, $250,000 worth of stock certificates (equity shares) to buyers, both in and out of the community. Their efforts meet with success and the Bank of Somewhere comes into existence—at least on paper. What does its balance sheet look like at this stage?

The founders of the bank have sold $250,000 worth of shares of stock in the bank—some to themselves, some to other people. As a result, the bank now has $250,000 in cash on hand and $250,000 worth of stock certificates outstanding. The cash is an asset to the bank. Cash held by a bank is sometimes called *vault cash* or *till money*. The shares of stock outstanding constitute an equal amount of claims that the owners have against the bank's assets. Those shares of stock constitute the net worth of the bank. The bank's balance sheet reads:

Creating a Bank Balance Sheet 1: Somewhere Bank			
Assets		Liabilities and net worth	
Cash	$250,000	Stock shares	$250,000

Each item listed in a balance sheet such as this is called an *account*.

Transaction 2: Acquiring Property and Equipment

The board of directors (who represent the bank's owners) must now get the new bank off the drawing board and make it a reality. First, property and equipment must be acquired. Suppose the directors, confident of the success of their venture, purchase a building for $220,000 and pay $20,000 for office equipment. This simple transaction changes the composition of the bank's assets. The bank now has $240,000 less in cash and $240,000 of new property assets. Using blue to denote accounts affected by each transaction, we show that the bank's balance sheet at the end of transaction 2 appears as follows:

Acquiring Property and Equipment Balance Sheet 2: Somewhere Bank			
Assets		Liabilities and net worth	
Cash	$ 10,000	Stock shares	$250,000
Property	240,000		

Note that the balance sheet still balances, as it must.

Transaction 3: Accepting Deposits

Commercial banks have two basic functions: to accept deposits of money and to make loans. Now that the bank is operating, suppose that the citizens and businesses of Somewhere decide to deposit $100,000 in the Somewhere bank. What happens to the bank's balance sheet?

The bank receives cash, which is an asset to the bank. Suppose this money is deposited in the bank as checkable deposits (checking account entries), rather than as savings accounts or time deposits. These newly created *checkable deposits* constitute claims that the depositors have against the assets of the Somewhere bank and thus are a new liability account. The bank's balance sheet now looks like this:

Accepting Deposits			
Balance Sheet 3: Somewhere Bank			
Assets		Liabilities and net worth	
Cash	$110,000	Checkable deposits	$100,000
Property	240,000	Stock shares	250,000

There has been no change in the economy's total supply of money as a result of transaction 3, but a change has occurred in the composition of the money supply. Bank money, or checkable deposits, has increased by $100,000, and currency held by the public has decreased by $100,000. Currency held by a bank, you will recall, is not part of the economy's money supply.

A withdrawal of cash will reduce the bank's checkable-deposit liabilities and its holdings of cash by the amount of the withdrawal. This, too, changes the composition, but not the total supply, of money in the economy.

Transaction 4: Depositing Reserves in a Federal Reserve Bank

required reserves
The funds that banks and thrifts must deposit with the Federal Reserve Bank (or hold as vault cash) to meet the Fed's reserve requirement.

All commercial banks and thrift institutions that provide checkable deposits must by law keep **required reserves.** Required reserves are an amount of funds equal to a specified percentage of the bank's own deposit liabilities. A bank must keep these reserves on deposit with the Federal Reserve Bank in its district or as cash in the bank's vault. To simplify, we suppose the Bank of Somewhere keeps its required reserves entirely as deposits in the Federal Reserve Bank of its district. But remember that vault cash is counted as reserves and real-world banks keep a significant portion of their own reserves in their vaults.

reserve ratio
The legally required percentage of reserves for every $1 of a bank or thrift's checkable deposits.

The "specified percentage" of checkable-deposit liabilities that a commercial bank must keep as reserves is known as the **reserve ratio**—the ratio of the required reserves the commercial bank must keep to the bank's own outstanding checkable-deposit liabilities:

$$\text{Reserve ratio} = \frac{\text{commercial bank's required reserves}}{\text{commercial bank's checkable-deposit liabilities}}$$

If the reserve ratio is $\frac{1}{10}$, or 10 percent, the Somewhere bank, having accepted $100,000 in deposits from the public, would have to keep $10,000 as reserves. If the ratio is $\frac{1}{5}$, or 20 percent, $20,000 of reserves would be required. If $\frac{1}{2}$, or 50 percent, $50,000 would be required.

The Fed has the authority to establish and vary the reserve ratio within limits legislated by Congress. A 10 percent reserve is required on checkable deposits over $43.9 million, although the Fed can vary that percentage between 8 and 14 percent. Also, after consultation with appropriate congressional committees, the Fed for 180 days may impose reserve requirements outside the 8–14 percent range.

In order to simplify, we will suppose that the reserve ratio for checkable deposits in commercial banks is $\frac{1}{5}$, or 20 percent. Although 20 percent obviously is higher than the requirement really is, the figure is convenient for calculations. The main point is that reserve requirements are fractional, meaning that they are less than 100 percent.

By depositing $20,000 in the Federal Reserve Bank, the Somewhere bank will just be meeting the required 20 percent ratio between its reserves and its own deposit liabilities. We will use "reserves" to mean the funds commercial banks deposit in the Federal Reserve Banks, to distinguish those funds from the public's deposits in commercial banks.

But suppose the Somewhere bank anticipates that its holdings of checkable deposits will grow in the future. Then, instead of sending just the minimum amount, $20,000, it sends an extra $90,000, for a total of $110,000. In so doing, the bank will avoid the inconvenience of sending additional reserves to the Federal Reserve Bank each time its own checkable-deposit liabilities increase. And, as you will see, it is these extra reserves that enable banks to lend money and earn interest income.

Actually, a real-world bank would not deposit *all* its cash in the Federal Reserve Bank. However, because (1) banks as a rule hold vault cash only in the amount of $1\frac{1}{2}$ or 2.0 percent of their total assets and (2) vault cash can be counted as reserves, we will assume for simplicity that all of Somewhere's cash is deposited in the Federal Reserve Bank and therefore constitutes the commercial bank's actual reserves. By making this simplifying assumption, we do not need to bother adding two assets—"cash" and "deposits in the Federal Reserve Bank"—to determine reserves.

After the Somewhere bank deposits $110,000 of reserves at the Fed, its balance sheet becomes:

Depositing Reserves at the Fed
Balance Sheet 4: Somewhere Bank

Assets		Liabilities and net worth	
Cash	$ 0	Checkable	
Reserves	110,000	deposits	$100,000
Property	240,000	Stock shares	250,000

There are three things to note about this latest transaction.

Excess Reserves A bank's **excess reserves** are found by subtracting its *required reserves* (or legally required reserves) from its **actual reserves:**

Excess reserves = actual reserves − required reserves

In this case,

Actual reserves	$110,000
Required reserves	−20,000
Excess reserves	$ 90,000

excess reserves
Actual bank or thrift reserves minus legally required reserves.

actual reserves
The funds that a bank or thrift has on deposit at a Federal Reserve Bank or is holding as vault cash.

The only reliable way of computing excess reserves is to multiply the bank's checkable-deposit liabilities by the reserve ratio to obtain required reserves ($100,000 × 20 percent = $20,000) and then to subtract the required reserves from the actual reserves listed on the asset side of the bank's balance sheet.

To test your understanding, compute the bank's excess reserves from balance sheet 4, assuming that the reserve ratio is (1) 10 percent, (2) $33\frac{1}{3}$ percent, and (3) 50 percent.

We will soon demonstrate that the ability of a commercial bank to make loans depends on the existence of excess reserves. Understanding this concept is crucial in seeing how the banking system creates money.

Control You might think the basic purpose of reserves is to enhance the liquidity of a bank and protect commercial bank depositors from losses. Reserves would constitute a ready source of funds from which commercial banks could meet large, unexpected cash withdrawals by depositors.

But this reasoning breaks down under scrutiny. Although historically reserves have been seen as a source of liquidity and therefore as protection for depositors, a bank's required reserves are not great enough to meet sudden, massive cash withdrawals. If the banker's nightmare should materialize—everyone with checkable deposits appearing at once to demand those deposits in cash—the legal reserves held as vault cash or at the Federal Reserve Bank would be insufficient. The banker simply could not meet this "bank panic." Because reserves are fractional, checkable deposits are usually much greater than a bank's required reserves.

So commercial bank deposits must be protected by other means. Periodic bank examinations are one way of promoting prudent commercial banking practices. Furthermore, as we have mentioned, government-sponsored deposit insurance funds insure individual deposits in banks and thrifts up to $250,000.

If it is not the purpose of reserves to provide for commercial bank liquidity, then what is their function? *Control* is the answer. Required reserves help the Fed control the lending ability of commercial banks. The Fed can take certain actions that either increase or decrease commercial bank reserves and affect the ability of banks to grant credit. The objective is to prevent banks from overextending or underextending bank credit. To the degree that these policies successfully influence the volume of commercial bank credit, the Fed can help the economy avoid business fluctuations. Another function of reserves is to facilitate the collection or "clearing" of checks.

Transaction 5: Clearing a Check Drawn against the Bank

Assume that Fred Bradshaw, a Somewhere farmer, deposited a substantial portion of the $100,000 in checkable deposits that the Somewhere bank received in transaction 3. Now suppose that Fred buys $50,000 of farm machinery from the Ajax Farm Implement Company of Elsewhere. Bradshaw pays for this machinery by writing a $50,000 check against his deposit in the Somewhere bank. He gives the check to the Ajax Company. What are the results?

Ajax deposits the check in its account with the Elsewhere bank. The Elsewhere bank increases Ajax's checkable deposits by $50,000 when Ajax deposits the check. Ajax is now paid in full. Bradshaw is pleased with his new machinery.

Now the Elsewhere bank has Bradshaw's check. This check is simply a claim against the assets of the Somewhere bank. The Elsewhere bank will collect this claim by sending the check (along with checks drawn on other banks) to the regional Federal Reserve Bank. Here a clerk will clear, or collect, the check for the Elsewhere bank by increasing Elsewhere's reserve in the Federal Reserve Bank by $50,000 and decreasing the Somewhere bank's reserve by that same amount. The check is "collected" merely by making bookkeeping notations to the effect that Somewhere's claim against the Federal Reserve Bank is reduced by $50,000 and Elsewhere's claim is increased by $50,000.

Finally, the Federal Reserve Bank sends the cleared check back to the Somewhere bank, and for the first time the Somewhere bank discovers that one of its depositors has drawn a check for $50,000 against his checkable deposit. Accordingly, the Somewhere bank reduces Bradshaw's checkable deposit by $50,000 and notes that the collection of this check has caused a $50,000 decline in its reserves at the Federal Reserve Bank. All the balance sheets balance: The Somewhere bank has reduced both its assets (reserves) and its liabilities (checkable deposits) by $50,000. The Elsewhere bank has $50,000 more both assets (reserves) and liabilities (checkable deposits). Ownership of reserves at the Federal Reserve Bank has changed—with Somewhere owning $50,000 less and Elsewhere owning $50,000 more—but total reserves stay the same.

Whenever a check is drawn against one bank and deposited in another bank, collection of that check will reduce both the reserves and the checkable deposits of the bank on which the check is drawn. Conversely, if a bank receives a check drawn on another bank, the bank receiving the check will, in the process of collecting it, have its reserves and deposits increased by the amount of the check. In our example, the Somewhere bank loses $50,000 in both reserves and deposits to the Elsewhere bank. But there is no loss of reserves or deposits for the banking system as a whole. What one bank loses, another bank gains.

If we bring all the other assets and liabilities back into the picture, the Somewhere bank's balance sheet looks like this at the end of transaction 5:

Clearing a Check
Balance Sheet 5: Somewhere Bank

Assets		Liabilities and net worth	
Reserves	$ 60,000	Checkable deposits	$ 50,000
Property	240,000	Stock shares	250,000

Verify that with a 20 percent reserve requirement, the bank's excess reserves now stand at $50,000.

Transaction 6: Granting a Loan (Creating Money)

In addition to accepting deposits, commercial banks grant loans to borrowers. What effect does lending by a commercial bank have on its balance sheet?

Suppose the Gristly Meat Packing Company of Somewhere decides it is time to expand its facilities. Suppose, too, that the company needs exactly $50,000—which just happens to be equal to the Somewhere bank's excess reserves—to finance this project.

Gristly goes to the Somewhere bank and requests a loan for this amount. The Somewhere bank knows the Gristly Company's fine reputation and financial soundness and is convinced of its ability to repay the loan. So the loan is granted. In return, the president of Gristly hands a promissory note—a fancy IOU—to the Somewhere bank. Gristly wants the convenience and safety of paying its obligations by check. So, instead of receiving a bushel basket full of currency from the bank, Gristly gets a $50,000 increase in its checkable-deposit account in the Somewhere bank.

The Somewhere bank has acquired an interest-earning asset (the promissory note, which it files under "Loans") and has created checkable deposits (a liability) to "pay" for this asset. Gristly has swapped an IOU for the right to draw an additional $50,000 worth of checks against its checkable deposit in the Somewhere bank. Both parties are pleased.

At the moment the loan is completed, the Somewhere bank's position is shown by balance sheet 6a:

When a Loan Is Negotiated
Balance Sheet 6a: Somewhere Bank

Assets		Libabiliites and net worth	
Reserves	$ 60,000	Checkable	
Loans	50,000	deposits	$100,000
Property	240,000	Stock shares	250,000

All this looks simple enough. But a close examination of the Somewhere bank's balance statement reveals a startling fact: *When a bank makes loans, it creates money.* The president of Gristly went to the bank with something that is *not* money—her IOU—and walked out with something that *is* money—a checkable deposit.

Contrast transaction 6a with transaction 3, in which checkable deposits were created but only as a result of currency having been taken out of circulation. There was a change in the *composition* of the money supply in that situation but no change in the *total supply* of money. But when banks lend, they create checkable deposits that *are* money. By extending credit, the Somewhere bank has "monetized" an IOU. Gristly and the Somewhere bank have created and then swapped claims. The claim created by Gristly and given to the bank is not money; an individual's IOU is not acceptable as a medium of exchange. But the claim created by the bank and given to Gristly *is* money; checks drawn against a checkable deposit are acceptable as a medium of exchange.

Much of the money we use in our economy is created through the extension of credit by commercial banks. This checkable-deposit money may be thought of as "debts" of commercial banks and thrift institutions. Checkable deposits are bank debts in the sense that they are claims that banks and thrifts promise to pay "on demand."

But there are factors limiting the ability of a commercial bank to create checkable deposits ("bank money") by lending. The Somewhere bank can expect the newly created checkable deposit of $50,000 to be a very active account. Gristly would not borrow $50,000 at, say, 7, 10, or 12 percent interest for the sheer joy of knowing that funds were available if needed.

Assume that Gristly awards a $50,000 building contract to the Quickbuck Construction Company. Quickbuck, true to its name, completes the expansion promptly and is paid with a check for $50,000 drawn by Gristly against its checkable deposit in the Somewhere bank. Quickbuck does not deposit this check in the Somewhere bank but instead deposits it in the Elsewhere bank. Elsewhere now has a $50,000 claim against the Somewhere bank. The check is collected in the manner described in transaction 5. As a result, the Somewhere bank loses both reserves and deposits equal to the amount of the check; Elsewhere acquires $50,000 of reserves and deposits.

In summary, assuming a check is drawn by the borrower for the entire amount of the loan ($50,000) and is given to a firm that deposits it in some other bank, the Somewhere bank's balance sheet will read as follows *after the check has been cleared against it:*

After a Check Is Drawn on the Loan
Balance Sheet 6b: Somewhere Bank

Assets		Liabilities and net worth	
Reserves	$ 10,000	Checkable	
Loans	50,000	deposits	$ 50,000
Property	240,000	Stock shares	250,000

After the check has been collected, the Somewhere bank just meets the required reserve ratio of 20 percent (=$10,000/$50,000). The bank has *no* excess reserves. This poses a question: Could the Somewhere bank have lent more than $50,000—an amount greater than its excess reserves—and still have met the 20 percent reserve requirement when a check for the full amount of the loan was cleared against it? The answer is no; the bank is "fully loaned up."

Here is why: Suppose the Somewhere bank had lent $55,000 to the Gristly company and that the Gristly company had spent all of that money by writing a $55,000 check to Quickbuck Construction. Collection of the check against the Somewhere bank would have lowered its reserves to $5000 (=$60,000 − $55,000), and checkable deposits would once again stand at $50,000 (=$105,000 − $55,000). The ratio of actual reserves to checkable deposits would then be $5000/$50,000, or 10 percent, not the 20 percent required. So the Somewhere bank could not have lent $55,000.

By experimenting with other amounts over $50,000, you will find that the maximum amount the Somewhere bank could lend at the outset of transaction 6 is $50,000. This amount is identical to the amount of excess reserves the bank had available when the loan was negotiated. *A single commercial bank in a multibank banking system can lend only an amount equal to its initial preloan excess reserves.* When it lends, the lending bank faces the possibility that checks for the entire amount of the loan will be drawn and cleared against it. If that happens, the lending bank will lose (to other banks) reserves equal to the amount it lends. So, to be safe, it limits its lending to the amount of its excess reserves.

Bank creation of money raises an interesting question: If banks create checkable deposit money when they lend their excess reserves, is money destroyed when borrowers pay off their loans? The answer is yes. When loans are paid off the process just described works in reverse. Checkable deposits decline by the amount of the loan payment.

WORKED PROBLEMS

W 9.1

Single bank accounting

The Banking System: Multiple-Deposit Expansion

Thus far we have seen that a single bank in a banking system can lend one dollar for each dollar of its excess reserves. The situation is different for all commercial banks as a group. We will find that the commercial banking system can lend—that is, can create money—by a multiple of its excess reserves. This multiple lending is accomplished even though each bank in the system can lend only "dollar for dollar" with its excess reserves.

How do these seemingly paradoxical results come about? To answer this question succinctly, we will make three simplifying assumptions:

- The reserve ratio for all commercial banks is 20 percent.
- Initially all banks are meeting this 20 percent reserve requirement exactly. No excess reserves exist; or, in the parlance of banking, they are "loaned up" (or "loaned out") fully in terms of the reserve requirement.

- If any bank can increase its loans as a result of acquiring excess reserves, an amount equal to those excess reserves will be lent to one borrower, who will write a check for the entire amount of the loan and give it to someone else, who will deposit the check in another bank. This third assumption means that the worst thing possible happens to every lending bank—a check for the entire amount of the loan is drawn and cleared against it in favor of another bank.

The Banking System's Lending Potential

Suppose a junkyard owner finds a $100 bill while dismantling a car that has been on the lot for years. He deposits the $100 in bank A, which adds the $100 to its reserves. We will record only changes in the balance sheets of the various commercial banks. The deposit changes bank A's balance sheet as shown by entries (a_1):

Multiple-Deposit Expansion Process			
Balance Sheet: Commercial Bank A			
Assets		Liabilities and net worth	
Reserves	$+100 ($a_1$) − 80 ($a_3$)	Checkable deposits	$+100 ($a_1$) + 80 ($a_2$) − 80 ($a_3$)
Loans	+ 80 (a_2)		

Recall from transaction 3 that this $100 deposit of currency does not alter the money supply. While $100 of checkable-deposit money comes into being, it is offset by the $100 of currency no longer in the hands of the nonbank public (the junkyard owner). But bank A *has* acquired excess reserves of $80. Of the newly acquired $100 in currency, 20 percent, or $20, must be earmarked for the required reserves on the new $100 checkable deposit, and the remaining $80 goes to excess reserves. Remembering that a single commercial bank can lend only an amount equal to its excess reserves, we conclude that bank A can lend a maximum of $80. When a loan for this amount is made, bank A's loans increase by $80 and the borrower gets an $80 checkable deposit. We add these figures—entries (a_2)—to bank A's balance sheet.

But now we employ our third assumption: The borrower draws a check ($80) for the entire amount of the loan and gives it to someone who deposits it in bank B, a different bank. As we saw in transaction 6, bank A loses both reserves and deposits equal to the amount of the loan, as indicated in entries (a_3). The net result of these transactions is that bank A's reserves now stand at +$20 (=$100 − $80), loans at +$80, and checkable deposits at +$100 (=$100 + $80 − $80). When the dust has settled, bank A is just meeting the 20 percent reserve ratio.

Recalling our previous discussion, we know that bank B acquires both the reserves and the deposits that bank A has lost. Bank B's balance sheet is changed as shown in the entries (b_1) that follow.

Multiple-Deposit Expansion Process			
Balance Sheet: Commercial Bank B			
Assets		Liabilities and net worth	
Reserves	$+80 ($b_1$) −64 ($b_3$)	Checkable deposits	$+80 ($b_1$) +64 ($b_2$) −64 ($b_3$)
Loans	+64 (b_2)		

When the borrower's check is drawn and cleared, bank A loses $80 in reserves and deposits and bank B gains $80 in reserves and deposits. But 20 percent, or $16, of bank B's new reserves must be kept as required reserves against the new $80 in checkable deposits. This means that bank B has $64 (=$80 − $16) in excess reserves. It can therefore lend $64 [entries ($b_2$)]. When the new borrower draws a check for the entire amount and deposits it in bank C, the reserves and deposits of bank B both fall by $64 [entries ($b_3$)]. As a result of these transactions, bank B's reserves now stand at +$16 (=$80 − $64), loans at +$64, and checkable deposits at +$80 (=$80 + $64 − $64). After all this, bank B is just meeting the 20 percent reserve requirement.

We could go ahead with this procedure by bringing banks C, D, E, … , N and so on into the picture. In fact, the process will go on almost indefinitely, just as long as banks further down the line receive at least one penny in new reserves that they can use to back another round of lending and money creation. But that might be annoying! Instead, we summarize the entire analysis in Table 9.1. Our conclusion is startling: On the basis of only $80 in excess reserves (acquired by the banking system when someone deposited $100 of currency in bank A), the entire commercial banking system is able to lend $400, the sum of the amounts in column 4. The banking system can lend excess reserves by a multiple of 5 (=$400/$80) when the reserve ratio is 20 percent. Yet each single bank in the banking system is lending only an amount equal to its own excess reserves. How do we explain this? How can the banking system as a whole lend by a multiple of its excess reserves, when each individual bank can lend only dollar for dollar with its excess reserves?

The answer is that reserves lost by a single bank are not lost to the banking system as a whole. The reserves lost by bank A are acquired by bank B. Those lost by B are gained by C. C loses to D, D to E, E to F, and so forth. Although reserves can be, and are, lost by individual banks in the banking system, there is no loss of reserves for the banking system as a whole.

An individual bank can safely lend only an amount equal to its excess reserves, *but the commercial banking system can lend by a multiple of its collective excess reserves.* Commercial banks as a group can create money by lending in a manner very different from that of the individual banks in the group.

Bank	(1) Acquired Reserves and Deposits	(2) Required Reserves (Reserve Ratio = .2)	(3) Excess Reserves, (1) − (2)	(4) Amount Bank Can Lend; New Money Created = (3)
Bank A	$100.00 ($a_1$)	$20.00	**$80.00**	$80.00 ($a_2$)
Bank B	80.00 (a_3, b_1)	16.00	64.00	64.00 (b_2)
Bank C	64.00	12.80	51.20	51.20
Bank D	51.20	10.24	40.96	40.96
Bank E	40.96	8.19	32.77	32.77
Bank F	32.77	6.55	26.21	26.21
Bank G	26.21	5.24	20.97	20.97
Bank H	20.97	4.20	16.78	16.78
Bank I	16.78	3.36	13.42	13.42
Bank J	13.42	2.68	10.74	10.74
Bank K	10.74	2.15	8.59	8.59
Bank L	8.59	1.72	6.87	6.87
Bank M	6.87	1.37	5.50	5.50
Bank N	5.50	1.10	4.40	4.40
Other banks	21.99	4.40	17.59	17.59
Total amount of money created (sum of the amounts in column 4)				**$400.00**

TABLE 9.1
Expansion of the Money Supply by the Commercial Banking System

monetary multiplier
The multiple of its excess reserves by which the banking system can expand checkable deposits and thus the money supply by making new loans.

The Monetary Multiplier

The banking system magnifies any original excess reserves into a larger amount of newly created checkable-deposit money. The *checkable-deposit multiplier*, or **monetary multiplier**, exists because the reserves and deposits lost by one bank become reserves of another bank. It magnifies excess reserves into a larger creation of checkable-deposit money. The monetary multiplier m is the reciprocal of the required reserve ratio R (the leakage into required reserves that occurs at each step in the lending process). In short,

$$\text{Monetary multiplier} = \frac{1}{\text{required reserve ratio}}$$

or, in symbols,

$$m = \frac{1}{R}$$

WORKED PROBLEMS

W 9.2

Money creation

In this formula, m represents the maximum amount of new checkable-deposit money that can be created by a single dollar of excess reserves, given the value of R. By multiplying the excess reserves E by m, we can find the maximum amount of new checkable-deposit money, D, that can be created by the banking system. That is,

Maximum checkable-deposit creation = excess reserves × monetary multiplier or, more simply,

$$D = E \times m$$

In our example in Table 9.1, R is .20, so m is 5 (=1/.20). Then

$$D = \$80 \times 5 = \$400$$

Reversibility: The Multiple Destruction of Money

The process we have described is reversible. Just as money is created when banks make loans, money is destroyed when loans are paid off. Loan repayment, in effect, sets off a process of multiple destruction of money akin to the multiple creation process. Because loans are both made and paid off in any period, the direction of the money supply in a given period will depend on the net effect of the two processes. If the dollar amount of loans made in some period exceeds the dollar amount of loans paid off, checkable deposits will expand and the money supply will increase. In contrast, if the dollar amount of loans made in some period is less than the dollar amount of loans paid off, checkable deposits will contract and the money supply will decline.

APPLYING THE ANALYSIS

The Bank Panics of 1930 to 1933

In the early months of the Great Depression, before there was deposit insurance, several financially weak banks went out of business. As word spread that customers of those banks had lost their deposits, a general concern arose that something similar could happen at other banks. Depositors became frightened that their banks did not, in fact, still have all the money they had deposited. And, of course, that is a reality in a fractional reserve banking system. Acting on their fears, people en masse tried to "cash out" their bank accounts by withdrawing their money before it was all gone. This "run on the banks" caused many previously financially sound banks to declare bankruptcy. More than 9000 banks failed within 3 years.

The massive conversion of checkable deposits to currency during 1930 to 1933 reduced the nation's money supply. This might seem strange, since a check written for "cash" reduces checkable-deposit money and increases currency in the hands of the public by the same amount. So how does the money supply decline? Our discussion of the money-creation process provides the answer, but now the story becomes one of money destruction.

Suppose that people collectively cash out $10 billion from their checking accounts. As an immediate result, checkable-deposit money declines by $10 billion, while currency held by the public increases by $10 billion. But here is the catch: Assuming a reserve ratio of 20 percent, the $10 billion of currency in the banks had been supporting $50 billion of deposit money, the $10 billion of deposits plus $40 billion created through loans. The $10 billion withdrawal of currency forces banks to reduce loans (and thus checkable-deposit money) by $40 billion to continue to meet their reserve requirement. In short, a $40 billion destruction of deposit money occurs. This is the scenario that occurred in the early years of the 1930s.

Accompanying this multiple contraction of checkable deposits was the banks' "scramble for liquidity" to try to meet further withdrawals of currency. To obtain more currency, they sold many of their holdings of government securities to the public. A bank's sale of government securities to the public, like a reduction in loans, reduces the money supply. People write checks for the securities, reducing their checkable deposits, and the bank uses the currency it obtains to meet the ongoing bank run. In short, the loss of reserves from the banking system, in conjunction with the scramble for security, reduced the amount of checkable-deposit money by far more than the increase in currency in the hands of the public. Thus, the money supply collapsed.

In 1933, President Franklin Roosevelt ended the bank panic by declaring a "national bank holiday." This closed all national banks for 1 week so that government inspectors could have time to go over each bank's accounting records. Only healthy banks with plenty of reserves were allowed to reopen. This meant that when the holiday was over, people could trust in any bank that had been allowed to reopen. This policy along with the initiation of the federal deposit insurance program reassured depositors and ended the bank panics.

But before these policies could begin to turn things around, the nation's money supply had plummeted by 25–33 percent, depending on how narrowly or broadly the money supply is defined. This was the largest drop in the money supply in U.S. history. This decline contributed substantially to the nation's deepest and longest depression. Simply put, less money meant less spending on goods and services as well as fewer loans for businesses. Both effects exacerbated the Great Depression.

Today, a multiple contraction of the money supply of the 1930–1933 magnitude is unthinkable. FDIC deposit insurance has kept individual bank failures from becoming general panics. Also, while the Fed stood idly by during the bank panics of 1930 to 1933, today it would take immediate and dramatic actions to maintain the banking system's reserves and the nation's money supply. Those actions are the subject of Chapter 10.

Question:
Why do fractional reserve banking and deposit insurance closely accompany one another in modern banking systems?

Summary

1. Conceptually, money is any item that society accepts as (a) a medium of exchange, (b) a unit of monetary account, and (c) a store of value.

2. In the United States, two "official" definitions of money are *M*1, consisting of currency (outside banks) and checkable deposits, and *M*2, consisting of *M*1 plus savings deposits, including money market deposit accounts, small (less than $100,000) time deposits, and money market mutual fund balances.

3. Money has value because of the goods, services, and resources it will command in the market. Maintaining the purchasing power of money depends largely on the government's effectiveness in managing the money supply to prevent inflation.

4. The U.S. banking system consists of (a) the Board of Governors of the Federal Reserve System, (b) the 12 Federal Reserve Banks, and (c) some 7300 commercial banks and 11,000 thrift institutions (mainly credit unions). The Board of Governors is the basic policymaking body for the entire banking system. The directives of the Board and the Federal Open Market Committee (FOMC) are made effective through the 12 Federal Reserve Banks, which are simultaneously (a) central banks, (b) quasi-public banks, and (c) bankers' banks.

5. The major functions of the Fed are to (a) issue Federal Reserve Notes, (b) set reserve requirements and hold reserves deposited by banks and thrifts, (c) lend money to financial institutions, (d) provide for the rapid collection of checks, (e) act as the fiscal agent for the Federal government, (f) supervise the operations of the banks, and (g) control the supply of money in the best interests of the economy.

6. The Fed is essentially an independent institution, controlled neither by the president of the United States nor by Congress. This independence shields the Fed from political pressure and allows it to raise and lower interest rates (via changes in the money supply) as needed to promote full employment, price stability, and economic growth.

7. Modern banking systems are fractional reserve systems: Only a fraction of checkable deposits is backed by currency. Commercial banks keep required reserves on deposit in a Federal Reserve Bank or as vault cash. These required reserves are equal to a specified percentage of the commercial bank's checkable-deposit liabilities. Excess reserves are equal to actual reserves minus required reserves.

8. Commercial banks create money—checkable deposits, or checkable-deposit money—when they make loans. The ability of a single commercial bank to create money by lending depends on the size of its excess reserves. Generally, a commercial bank can lend only an amount equal to its excess reserves. Money creation is thus limited because, in all likelihood, checks drawn by borrowers will be deposited in other banks, causing a loss of reserves and deposits to the lending bank equal to the amount of money lent.

9. The commercial banking system as a whole can lend by a multiple of its excess reserves because the system as a whole cannot lose reserves. Individual banks, however, can lose reserves to other banks in the system. The multiple by which the banking system can lend on the basis of each dollar of excess reserves is the reciprocal of the reserve ratio.

10. The bank panics of 1930–1933 resulted in a significant contraction of the U.S. money supply, contributed to the Great Depression, and gave rise to Federal deposit insurance.

Terms and Concepts

medium of exchange

unit of account

store of value

liquidity

*M*1

Federal Reserve Notes

token money

checkable deposits

commercial banks

thrift institutions

near-monies

*M*2

savings account

money market deposit account (MMDA)

time deposits

money market mutual fund (MMMF)

legal tender

Federal Reserve System

Board of Governors

Federal Reserve Banks

Federal Open Market Committee (FOMC)

fractional reserve banking system

balance sheet

required reserves

reserve ratio

excess reserves

actual reserves

monetary multiplier

Study Questions ■ connect economics

1. What are the three basic functions of money? Describe how rapid inflation can undermine money's ability to perform each of the three functions. **LO1**

2. Which two of the following financial institutions offer checkable deposits included within the *M1* money supply: mutual fund companies; insurance companies; commercial banks; securities firms; thrift institutions? Which of the following is *not* included in either *M1* or *M2*: currency held by the public; checkable deposits; money market mutual fund balances; small (less than $100,000) time deposits; currency held by banks; savings deposits? **LO1**

3. What are the components of the *M1* money supply? What is the largest component? Which of the components of *M1* is *legal tender?* Why is the face value of a coin greater than its intrinsic value? What near-monies are included in the *M2* money supply? **LO1**

4. How does the purchasing power of the dollar relate to the nation's price level? **LO2**

5. Who selects the chairperson of the Federal Reserve System? Describe the relationship between the Board of Governors of the Federal Reserve System and the 12 Federal Reserve Banks. What is the composition and purpose of the Federal Open Market Committee (FOMC)? **LO3**

6. What is meant when economists say that the Federal Reserve Banks are central banks, quasi-public banks, and bankers' banks? What are the seven basic functions of the Federal Reserve System? **LO4**

7. Why must a balance sheet always balance? What are the major assets and claims on a commercial bank's balance sheet? **LO5**

8. Why does the Federal Reserve require that commercial banks have reserves? What are excess reserves? How do you calculate the amount of excess reserves held by a bank? What is the significance of excess reserves? **LO5**

9. "Whenever currency is deposited in a commercial bank, cash goes out of circulation and, as a result, the *M1* supply of money is reduced." Do you agree? Explain why or why not. **LO5**

10. Explain why a single commercial bank can safely lend only an amount equal to its excess reserves but the commercial banking system as a whole can lend by a multiple of its excess reserves. What is the monetary multiplier, and how does it relate to the reserve ratio? **LO5**

11. Suppose the National Bank of Commerce has excess reserves of $8000 and outstanding checkable deposits of $150,000. If the reserve ratio is 20 percent, what is the size of the bank's actual reserves? **LO5**

12. Suppose that Continental Bank has the simplified balance sheet shown below and that the reserve ratio is 20 percent: **LO5**
   a. What is the maximum amount of new loans that this bank can make? Show in column 1 how the bank's balance sheet will appear after the bank has lent this additional amount.
   b. By how much has the supply of money changed? Explain.
   c. How will the bank's balance sheet appear after checks drawn for the entire amount of the new loans have been cleared against the bank? Show the new balance sheet in column 2.

Assets		(1)	(2)	Liabilities and net worth		(1)	(2)
Reserves	$22,000	___	___	Checkable			
Securities	38,000	___	___	deposits	$100,000	___	___
Loans	40,000	___	___				

13. Suppose the simplified consolidated balance sheet shown below is for the entire commercial banking system. All figures are in billions. The reserve ratio is 25 percent. **LO5**
   a. What amount of excess reserves does the commercial banking system have? What is the maximum amount the banking system might lend? Show in column 1 how the consolidated balance sheet would look after this amount has been lent. What is the monetary multiplier?
   b. Answer the questions in part *a* assuming the reserve ratio is 20 percent. Explain the resulting difference in the lending ability of the commercial banking system.

Assets		(1)	Liabilities and net worth		(1)
Reserves	$ 52	___	Checkable		
Securities	48	___	deposits	$200	___
Loans	100	___			

FURTHER TEST YOUR KNOWLEDGE AT
www.mcconnellbriefmacro1e.com

Web-Based Questions

At the text's Online Learning Center, **www.mcconnellbriefmacro 1e.com**, you will find a multiple-choice quiz on this chapter's content. We encourage you to take the quiz to see how you do.

Also, you will find one or more Web-based questions that require information from the Internet to answer.

10

Interest Rates and Monetary Policy

Some newspaper commentators have stated that the chairperson of the Federal Reserve Board (previously Alan Greenspan and now Ben Bernanke) is the second most powerful person in the United States, after the U.S. president. That is undoubtedly an exaggeration because the chair has only a single vote on the 7-person Federal Reserve Board and 12-person Federal Open Market Committee. But there can be no doubt about the chair's influence, the overall importance of the Federal Reserve, and the **monetary policy** that it conducts. Such policy consists of deliberate changes in the money supply to influence interest rates and thus the total level of spending in the economy. The goal is to achieve and maintain price-level stability, full employment, and economic growth.

Interest Rates

Before we examine how the Federal Reserve can influence the money supply and interest rates, we need to better understand the market in which interest rates are established. As indicated in Table 10.1, there are many different interest rates that vary by purpose, size, risk, maturity, and taxability. (Global Snapshot 10.1 compares one interest rate—the percentage rate on 3-month loans—for several countries in a recent year.) But for simplicity economists often speak of a single interest rate. As we will see, the interest rate in the economy results from the interaction of money demand and money supply.

The Demand for Money

Why does the public want to hold some of its wealth as *money?* There are two main reasons: to make purchases with it and to hold it as an asset.

Transactions Demand, D_t People hold money because it is convenient for purchasing goods and services. Households usually are paid once a week, every 2 weeks, or monthly, whereas their expenditures are less predictable and typically more frequent. So households must have enough money on hand to buy groceries and pay mortgage and utility bills. Nor are businesses' revenues and expenditures simultaneous. Businesses need to have money available to pay for labor, materials, power, and other inputs. The demand for money as a medium of exchange is called the **transactions demand** for money.

The level of nominal GDP is the main determinant of the amount of money demanded for transactions. The larger the total money value of all goods and services exchanged in the economy, the larger the amount of money needed to negotiate those transactions. The transactions demand for money varies directly with nominal GDP. We specify *nominal* GDP because households and firms will want more money for transactions if prices rise or if real output increases. In both instances there will be a need for a larger dollar volume to accomplish the desired transactions.

TABLE 10.1
Selected U.S. Interest Rates, March 2008

Type of Interest Rate	Annual Percentage
20-year Treasury bond rate (interest rate on Federal government security used to finance the public debt)	4.39%
90-day Treasury bill rate (interest rate on Federal government security used to finance the public debt)	1.37
Prime interest rate (interest rate used as a reference point for a wide range of bank loans)	6.00
30-year mortgage rate (fixed-interest rate on loans for houses)	5.74
4-year automobile loan rate (interest rate for new autos by automobile finance companies)	6.80
Tax-exempt state and municipal bond rate (interest rate paid on a low-risk bond issued by a state or local government)	4.94
Federal funds rate (interest rate on overnight loans between banks)	2.25
Consumer credit card rate (interest rate charged for credit card purchases)	11.88

Source: Federal Reserve, **www.federalreserve.gov**, and Bankrate.com, **www.bankrate.com**.

GLOBAL SNAPSHOT 10.1

Short-Term Nominal Interest Rates, Selected Nations

These data show the short-term nominal interest rates (percentage rates on 3-month loans) in various countries in 2008. Because these are nominal rates, much of the variation reflects differences in rates of inflation. But differences in central bank monetary policies and in risk of default also explain the variations.

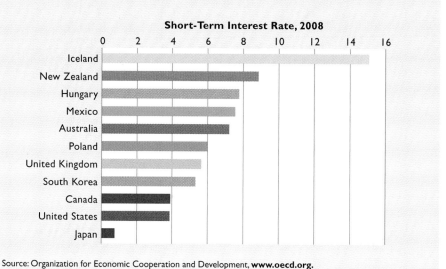

Short-Term Interest Rate, 2008

Source: Organization for Economic Cooperation and Development, **www.oecd.org.**

In Figure 10.1a we graph the quantity of money demanded for transactions against the interest rate. For simplicity, let's assume that the amount demanded depends exclusively on the level of nominal GDP and is independent of the real interest rate. (In reality, higher interest rates are associated with slightly lower volumes of money demanded for transactions.) Our simplifying assumption allows us to graph the transactions demand, D_t, as a vertical line. This demand curve is positioned at $100 billion, on the assumption that each dollar held for transactions purposes is spent an average of three times per year and that nominal GDP is $300 billion. Thus the public needs $100 billion (=$300 billion/3) to purchase that GDP.

Asset Demand, D_a

The second reason for holding money derives from money's function as a store of value. People may hold their financial assets in many forms, including corporate stocks, corporate or government bonds, or money. To the extent they want to hold money as an asset, there is an **asset demand** for money.

People like to hold some of their financial assets as money (apart from using it to buy goods and services) because money is the most liquid of all financial assets; it is immediately usable for purchasing other assets when opportunities arise. Money is also an attractive asset to hold when the prices of other assets such as bonds are expected to decline. For example, when the price of a bond falls, the bondholder who sells the bond prior to the payback date of the full principal will suffer a loss (called a *capital loss*). That loss will partially or fully offset the interest received on the bond. There is no such risk of capital loss in holding money.

The disadvantage of holding money as an asset is that it earns no or very little interest. Checkable deposits pay either no interest or lower interest rates than bonds. Currency itself earns no interest at all.

asset demand
The amount of money people want to hold as a store of value.

ORIGIN OF THE IDEA

O 10.1

Liquidity preference

FIGURE 10.1 **The demand for money, supply of money, and equilibrium interest rate.** The total demand for money, D_m, is determined by horizontally adding the asset demand for money, D_a, to the transactions demand, D_t. The transactions demand is vertical because it is assumed to depend solely on nominal GDP rather than on the interest rate. The asset demand varies inversely with the interest rate because of the opportunity cost involved in holding currency and checkable deposits that pay no interest or very low interest. Combining the money supply, S_m, with the total money demand, D_m, portrays the money market and determines the equilibrium interest rate, i_e.

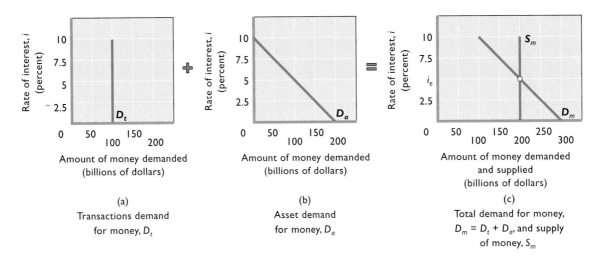

(a)
Transactions demand
for money, D_t

(b)
Asset demand
for money, D_a

(c)
Total demand for money,
$D_m = D_t + D_a$, and supply
of money, S_m

Knowing these advantages and disadvantages, the public must decide how much of its financial assets to hold as money, rather than other assets such as bonds. The answer depends primarily on the rate of interest. A household or a business incurs an opportunity cost when it holds money; in both cases, interest income is forgone or sacrificed. If a bond pays 6 percent interest, for example, it costs $6 per year of forgone income to hold $100 as cash or in a noninterest checkable account.

The amount of money demanded as an asset therefore varies inversely with the rate of interest (which is the opportunity cost of holding money as an asset). When the interest rate rises, it becomes more costly to be liquid and to avoid capital losses. The public reacts by reducing its holdings of money as an asset. When the interest rate falls, the cost of being liquid and avoiding capital losses also declines. The public therefore increases the amount of financial assets that it wants to hold as money. This inverse relationship just described is shown by D_a in Figure 10.1b.

Total Money Demand, D_m As shown in Figure 10.1, we find the **total demand for money,** D_m, by horizontally adding the asset demand to the transactions demand. The resulting downward-sloping line in Figure 10.1c represents the total amount of money the public wants to hold, both for transactions and as an asset, at each possible interest rate.

Recall that the transactions demand for money depends on the nominal GDP. A change in the nominal GDP—working through the transactions demand for money—will shift the total money demand curve. Specifically, an increase in nominal GDP means that the public wants to hold a larger amount of money for transactions, and that extra demand will shift the total money demand curve to the right. In contrast, a decline in the nominal GDP will shift the total money demand curve to the left. As an example, suppose nominal GDP increases from $300 billion to $450 billion and the average dollar held for transactions is still spent three times per year. Then the transactions demand curve will shift from $100 billion (=$300 billion/3) to $150 billion (=$450 billion/3). The total money demand curve will then lay $50 billion farther to the right at each possible interest rate.

total demand for money
The sum of the transactions demand and asset demand for money.

WORKED PROBLEMS

W 10.1

The demand for money

The Equilibrium Interest Rate

We can combine the demand for money with the supply of money to determine the equilibrium rate of interest. In Figure 10.1c the vertical line, S_m, represents the money supply. It is a vertical line because the monetary authorities and financial institutions have provided the economy with some particular stock of money. Here it is $200 billion.

Just as in a product market or a resource market, the intersection of demand and supply in the **money market** determines equilibrium price. Here, the equilibrium "price" is the *real* interest rate (i_e)—the inflation-adjusted price that is paid for the use of money over some time period.

INTERACTIVE GRAPHS

G 10.1

Equilibrium interest rate

money market
The market in which the demand for and the supply of money determine the interest rate (or series of interest rates) in the economy.

ILLUSTRATING THE IDEA

That Is Interest

Interest is needed to entice individuals to give up liquidity or sacrifice their present consumption, that is, to let someone else use their money for a period of time. The following story told by economist Irving Fisher (1867–1947) helps illustrate the idea of the "time value of money." The irony is that it was Fisher who had earlier formalized this exact idea in his theory of interest.

> In the process of a massage, a masseur informed Fisher that he was a socialist who believed that "interest is the basis of capitalism and is robbery." Following the massage, Fisher asked, "How much do l owe you?"
> The masseur replied, "Thirty dollars."
> "Very well," said Fisher, "I will give you a note payable a hundred years hence. I suppose you have no objections to taking this note without any interest. At the end of that time, you, or perhaps your grandchildren, can redeem it."
> "But I cannot afford to wait that long," said the masseur.
> "I thought you said that interest was robbery. If interest is robbery, you ought to be willing to wait indefinitely for the money. If you are willing to wait ten years, how much would you require?"
> "Well, I would have to get more than thirty dollars."
> His point now made, Fisher replied, "That is interest."*

Question:
Who benefits most from lending at interest: the lender or the borrower?

* Irving Fisher, as quoted in Irving Norton Fisher, *My Father Irving Fisher* (New York: Comet, 1956), p. 77.

Tools of Monetary Policy

We can now explore how the Federal Reserve (the "Fed") can change the supply of money in the economy and therefore alter the interest rate. The Fed has four tools of monetary control it can use to alter the money supply: open-market operations, the reserve ratio, the discount rate, and the term auction facility.

ORIGIN OF THE IDEA

O 10.2

Tools of monetary policy

Open-Market Operations

Bond markets are "open" to all buyers and sellers of corporate and government bonds (securities). The Federal Reserve is the largest single holder of U.S. government securities. The U.S. government, not the Fed, issued these Treasury bills (short-term securities), Treasury notes (mid-term securities), and Treasury bonds (long-term securities) to finance past budget deficits. Over the decades, the Fed has purchased these securities from major financial institutions that buy and sell government and corporate securities for themselves or their customers.

open-market operations
The buying and selling of U.S. government securities by the Fed for purposes of carrying out monetary policy.

The Fed's **open-market operations** consist of the buying of government bonds from, or the selling of government bonds to, commercial banks and the general public. (The Fed actually buys and sells the government bonds to commercial banks and the public through two-dozen or so large financial firms called *primary dealers*.) Open-market operations are the Fed's most important day-to-day instrument for influencing the money supply.

Buying Securities Suppose the Federal Open Market Committee (FOMC) directs the Federal Reserve Bank of New York to buy $100 million of government bonds. The Federal Reserve Bank indirectly purchases these bonds from commercial banks (or thrifts) or the public. In both cases the reserves of the commercial banks will increase.

When a Federal Reserve Bank buys government bonds from *commercial banks*, those banks send some of their holdings of securities to the Federal Reserve Bank. In paying for the securities, the Federal Reserve Bank in essence writes checks for $100 million to the commercial banks. The banks deposit the $100 million of checks in their own accounts. When the checks clear against the Federal Reserve Bank, $100 million of reserves flow to the commercial banks. Because there are no new checkable deposits, the entire $100 million of new reserves in the banking system are excess reserves.

We know from Chapter 9 that excess reserves allow the banking system to make loans (expand the money supply) by a multiple of excess reserves. Suppose the reserve requirement is 20 percent, so the monetary multiplier is 5. Then commercial banks can expand the $100 million of excess reserves to $500 million of new checkable deposit money.

The effect on commercial bank reserves is much the same when a Federal Reserve Bank purchases securities from the *general public* rather than directly from banks. The Federal Reserve Bank buys the $100 million of securities by issuing checks to the sellers, who deposit the checks in their checkable-deposit accounts at their commercial banks. When the checks clear, $100 million of new reserves flow from the Federal Reserve Bank to the commercial banks. Because the banks need only 20 percent of the new reserves for the $100 million of new checkable deposits, the commercial banks have excess reserves of $80 million (=$100 million of actual reserves − $20 million of required reserves). They lend out the excess reserves, expanding checkable deposits by $400 million (=5 × $80 million). When added to the original checkable deposits of $100 million, the $400 million of loan-created checkable deposits result in a total of $500 million of new money in the economy.

WORKED PROBLEMS

W 10.2

Open market operations

Selling Securities As you may suspect, when a Federal Reserve Bank sells government bonds, the reserves of commercial banks are reduced. Let's see why, this time dispensing with the math because it is the exact reverse of the prior examples.

When a Federal Reserve Bank sells securities in the open market to commercial banks, the Federal Reserve Bank gives up securities that the commercial banks acquire. To pay for those securities, the commercial banks in essence write checks payable to the Federal Reserve Bank. When the checks clear, reserves flow from the commercial banks to the Federal Reserve Bank. If all excess reserves are already lent out, this decline in commercial bank reserves produces a multiple decline in money created through lending. That is, the nation's money supply declines. This multiple decline in money will equal the decline in reserves times the monetary multiplier.

The outcome is the same when a Federal Reserve Bank sells securities to the public rather than directly to banks. The public pays for the securities with checks drawn on individuals' banks. When the checks clear, the commercial banks send reserves to the Federal Reserve Bank and reduce accordingly the checkable deposits of customers who wrote the checks. The lower reserves mean a multiple contraction of the money supply.

The Reserve Ratio

The Fed can also manipulate the reserve ratio in order to influence the ability of commercial banks to lend. Suppose a commercial bank's balance sheet shows that reserves are $5000 and checkable deposits are $20,000. If the reserve ratio is 20 percent (row 2, Table 10.2), the bank's required reserves are $4000. Since actual reserves are $5000, the excess reserves of this bank are $1000. On the basis of $1000 of excess reserves, this one bank can lend $1000; however, the banking system as a whole can create a maximum of $5000 of new checkable-deposit money by lending (column 7).

Raising the Reserve Ratio Now, what if the Fed raised the reserve ratio from 20 to 25 percent? (See row 3.) Required reserves would jump from $4000 to $5000, shrinking excess reserves from $1000 to zero. Raising the reserve ratio increases the amount of required reserves banks must keep. As a consequence, either the banks lose excess reserves, diminishing their ability to create money by lending, or they find their reserves deficient and are forced to contract checkable deposits and therefore the money supply. In the example in Table 10.2, excess reserves are transformed into required reserves, and the money-creating potential of our single bank is reduced from $1000 to zero (column 6). Moreover, the banking system's money-creating capacity declines from $5000 to zero (column 7).

What if the Fed increases the reserve requirement to 30 percent? (See row 4.) The commercial bank, to protect itself against the prospect of failing to meet this requirement, would be forced to lower its checkable deposits and at the same time increase its reserves. To reduce its checkable deposits, the bank could let outstanding loans mature and be repaid without extending new credit. This action would reduce the supply of money.

Lowering the Reserve Ratio What would happen if the Fed lowered the reserve ratio from the original 20 percent to 10 percent? (See row 1.) In this case, required

TABLE 10.2
The Effects of Changes in the Reserve Ratio on the Lending Ability of Commercial Banks

(1) Reserve Ratio, %	(2) Checkable Deposits	(3) Actual Reserves	(4) Required Reserves	(5) Excess Reserves, (3) − (4)	(6) Money-Creating Potential of Single Bank, = (5)	(7) Money-Creating Potential of Banking System
(1) 10	$20,000	$5000	$2000	$ 3000	$ 3000	$30,000
(2) 20	20,000	5000	4000	1000	1000	5,000
(3) 25	20,000	5000	5000	0	0	0
(4) 30	20,000	5000	6000	−1000	−1000	−3,333

reserves would decline from $4000 to $2000, and excess reserves would jump from $1000 to $3000. The single bank's lending (money-creating) ability would increase from $1000 to $3000 (column 6), and the banking system's money-creating potential would expand from $5000 to $30,000 (column 7). Lowering the reserve ratio transforms required reserves into excess reserves and enhances the ability of banks to create new money by lending.

The examples in Table 10.2 show that a change in the reserve ratio affects the money-creating ability of the *banking system* in two ways:

- It changes the amount of excess reserves.
- It changes the size of the monetary multiplier.

For example, when the legal reserve ratio is raised from 10 to 20 percent, excess reserves are reduced from $3000 to $1000 and the monetary multiplier is reduced from 10 to 5. The money-creating potential of the banking system declines from $30,000 (=$3000 × 10) to $5000 (=$1000 × 5). Raising the reserve ratio forces banks to reduce the amount of checkable deposits they create through lending.

The Discount Rate

One of the functions of a central bank is to be a "lender of last resort." Occasionally, commercial banks have unexpected and immediate needs for additional funds. In such cases, each Federal Reserve Bank will make short-term loans to commercial banks in its district.

When a commercial bank borrows, it gives the Federal Reserve Bank a promissory note (IOU) drawn against itself and secured by acceptable collateral—typically U.S. government securities. Just as commercial banks charge interest on the loans they make to their clients, so too Federal Reserve Banks charge interest on loans they grant to commercial banks. The interest rate they charge is called the **discount rate.**

discount rate
The interest rate the Federal Reserve Banks charge on the loans they make to commercial banks and thrifts.

In providing the loan, the Federal Reserve Bank increases the reserves of the borrowing commercial bank. Since no required reserves need be kept against loans from Federal Reserve Banks, all new reserves acquired by borrowing from Federal Reserve Banks are excess reserves. In short, borrowing from the Federal Reserve Banks by commercial banks increases the reserves of the commercial banks and enhances their ability to extend credit.

The Fed has the power to set the discount rate at which commercial banks borrow from Federal Reserve Banks. From the commercial banks' point of view, the discount rate is a cost of acquiring reserves. A lowering of the discount rate entices commercial banks to obtain additional reserves, if needed, by borrowing from Federal Reserve Banks. When the commercial banks lend new reserves to bank customers, the money supply increases.

An increase in the discount rate discourages commercial banks from obtaining additional reserves through borrowing from the Federal Reserve Banks. So the Fed may raise the discount rate when it wants to restrict the money supply.

Term Auction Facility

term auction facility
A monetary policy tool used by the Fed to expand reserves through auctioning off loans (reserves) anonymously to commercial banks.

The fourth Fed tool for altering bank reserves is its **term auction facility.** This tool was introduced in December 2007 in response to the mortgage debt crisis, in which tens of thousands of homeowners defaulted on mortgage loans when they experienced higher mortgage interest rates and falling home prices. Under the term auction facility, the Fed holds two auctions each month at which banks bid for the right to borrow reserves for 28-day periods. For instance, the Fed might auction off $20 billion in reserves. Banks that want to participate in the auction submit bids that include two pieces of information: how much they wish to borrow and the interest rate that they would be willing to pay. As an example, Somewhere bank might want to borrow $1 billion and offer to pay an annual interest rate of 4.35 percent.

These bids are submitted secretly. Once they are received, Fed officials arrange them from highest to lowest by interest rate. The limited pool of $20 billion goes to those banks that offer to pay the highest interest rates for the money that they desire to borrow. But the rate that all the auction winners actually pay is the same—it is the rate offered by the lowest bidder whose bid is accepted. For instance, suppose that 56 banks submit bids that total $36 billion. The Fed sorts these from highest to lowest based upon interest rates and then goes down the list to see how many banks can get their desired loan amounts before exhausting the $20 billion. Suppose that the top 23 banks together wish to borrow $18 billion and that the 24th bank wishes to borrow the remaining $2 billion. Since its request would exhaust the $20 billion that is being auctioned off, its interest rate is the one that all 24 of the auction-winning banks will have to pay.

Lending through the term auction facility guarantees that the amount of reserves that the Fed wishes to lend will be borrowed. This is true because the auction procedure for determining the interest rate on the loans serves to produce an equilibrium price (interest rate) at which the quantity demanded of loans exactly equals the quantity supplied of loans (the amount of reserves that the Fed is auctioning off). The Fed finds this to be very helpful when it wants to increase reserves by a specific amount because it can be sure that those reserves will in fact be borrowed, thereby increasing the overall level of reserves in the banking system. In contrast, lowering the discount rate may or may not produce the exact level of borrowing the Fed desires.

It was this particular aspect of the term auction facility that led the Fed to start using it in late 2007 during the mortgage debt crisis. Reserves fell dramatically during that crisis, and the Fed wanted to be sure to increase reserves so that banks would have the ability to keep making loans. By increasing or decreasing the amount of reserves provided at each auction, the Fed can affect the money supply.

Relative Importance

All four of the Fed's instruments of monetary control are useful in particular economic circumstances, but open-market operations are clearly the most important of the four tools over the course of the business cycle. The buying and selling of securities in the open market has the advantage of flexibility—government securities can be purchased or sold daily in large or small amounts—and the impact on bank reserves is prompt. And, compared with reserve-requirement changes, open-market operations work subtly and less directly. Furthermore, the ability of the Federal Reserve Banks to affect commercial bank reserves through the purchase and sale of bonds is virtually unquestionable. The Federal Reserve Banks have very large holdings of government securities ($713 billion in early 2008, for example). The sale of those securities could theoretically reduce commercial bank reserves to zero.

Changing the reserve requirement is a potentially powerful instrument of monetary control, but the Fed has used this technique only sparingly. Normally, it can accomplish its monetary goals more easily through open-market operations. The limited use of changes in the reserve ratio undoubtedly relates to the fact that reserves earn no interest. Indeed, when the Fed raises or lowers the reserve ratio, it has a substantial effect on bank profits because it implicitly changes the amount of money on which banks are forced to earn a zero percent rate of return. The last change in the reserve requirement was in 1992, when the Fed reduced the requirement from

12 percent to 10 percent. The main purpose was to shore up the profitability of banks and thrifts in the aftermath of the 1990-91 recession rather than to reduce interest rates by increasing reserves and expanding the money supply.

Until recently, the discount rate was mainly a passive tool of monetary control, with the Fed raising and lowering the rate simply to keep it in line with other interest rates. However, during the mortgage debt crisis the Fed aggressively lowered the discount rate independently of other interest rates in order to provide a cheap and plentiful source of reserves to banks whose reserves were being sharply reduced by unexpectedly high default rates on home mortgage loans. Banks borrowed billions at the lower discount rate. This allowed them to meet reserve requirements and thereby preserved their ability to keep extending loans.

As the mortgage debt crisis grew more severe, however, the Fed found that banks became increasingly reluctant to borrow at the discount rate for fear that such borrowing would be interpreted by their own lenders and stockholders as a sign of being in deep financial trouble. This prompted the Fed to create the term auction facility and, perhaps more importantly, to make it anonymous. When the Fed holds an auction of reserves using the term auction facility, banks submit their bids anonymously and auction winners are given their loans anonymously. This anonymity ensures that banks will participate in the auctions since they do not have to worry about being suspected of being in financially weak condition.

Easy Money and Tight Money

Suppose the economy faces recession and unemployment. The Fed decides that an increase in the supply of money is needed to increase aggregate demand so as to employ idle resources. To increase the supply of money, the Fed must increase the excess reserves of commercial banks. How can it do that?

- **Buy securities**   By purchasing securities in the open market, the Fed can increase commercial bank reserves. When the Fed's checks for the securities are cleared against it, the commercial banks discover that they have more reserves.
- **Lower the reserve ratio**   By lowering the reserve ratio, the Fed changes required reserves into excess reserves and increases the size of the monetary multiplier.
- **Lower the discount rate**   By lowering the discount rate, the Fed may entice commercial banks to borrow more reserves from the Fed.
- **Auction more reserves**   By auctioning more reserves to commercial banks through the term auction facility, the Fed can increase the amount of reserves in the banking system.

easy money policy
Fed actions designed to increase the money supply, lower interest rates, and expand real GDP.

These actions are called an **easy money policy** (or *expansionary monetary policy*). Its purpose is to make bank loans less expensive and more available and thereby increase aggregate demand, output, and employment.

Suppose, on the other hand, excessive spending is pushing the economy into an inflationary spiral. Then the Fed should try to reduce aggregate demand by limiting or contracting the supply of money. That means reducing the reserves of commercial banks. How is that done?

- **Sell securities**   By selling government bonds in the open market, the Federal Reserve Banks can reduce commercial bank reserves.
- **Increase the reserve ratio**   An increase in the reserve ratio will automatically strip commercial banks of their excess reserves and decrease the size of the monetary multiplier.
- **Raise the discount rate**   A boost in the discount rate will discourage commercial banks from borrowing from Federal Reserve Banks in order to build up their reserves.
- **Auction fewer reserves**   By auctioning fewer reserves to commercial banks through the term auction facility, the Fed can decrease the amount of reserves in the banking system.

These actions are called a **tight money policy** (or *restrictive monetary policy*). The objective is to tighten the supply of money in order to reduce spending and control inflation.

Monetary Policy, Real GDP, and the Price Level

So far we have explained only how the Fed can change the money supply. Now we need to link up the money supply, the interest rate, investment spending, and aggregate demand to see how monetary policy affects the economy. How does monetary policy work?

Cause-Effect Chain

The three diagrams in Figure 10.2 will help you understand how monetary policy works toward achieving its goals.

Market for Money   Figure 10.2a represents the market for money, in which the demand curve for money and the supply curve of money are brought together. Recall that the total demand for money is made up of the transactions and asset demands. The transactions demand is directly related to the nominal GDP. The asset demand is inversely related to the interest rate. The interest rate is the opportunity cost of holding money as an asset; the higher that cost, the smaller the amount of money the public wants to hold. The total demand for money, D_m, is thus inversely related to the interest rate, as is indicated in Figure 10.2a. Also, recall that an increase in nominal GDP will shift D_m to the right and a decline in nominal GDP will shift D_m to the left.

This figure also shows three potential money supply curves, S_{m1}, S_{m2}, and S_{m3}. In each case the money supply is shown as a vertical line representing some fixed amount of money determined by the Fed. While monetary policy (specifically, the supply of money) helps determine the interest rate, the interest rate does not determine the location of the money supply curve.

The equilibrium interest rate is the rate at which the amount of money demanded and the amount supplied are equal. With money demand D_m in Figure 10.2a, if the supply of money is $125 billion ($S_{m1}$), the equilibrium interest rate is 10 percent. With a money supply of $150 billion ($S_{m2}$), the equilibrium interest rate is 8 percent; with a money supply of $175 billion ($S_{m3}$), it is 6 percent.

Investment   These 10, 8, and 6 percent real interest rates are carried rightward to the investment demand curve in Figure 10.2b. This curve shows the inverse relationship between the interest rate—the cost of borrowing to invest—and the amount of investment spending. At the 10 percent interest rate it will be profitable for the nation's businesses to invest $15 billion; at 8 percent, $20 billion; at 6 percent, $25 billion.

Changes in the interest rate mainly affect the investment component of total spending, although they also affect spending on durable consumer goods (such as autos) that are purchased on credit. The impact of changing interest rates on investment spending is great because of the large cost and long-term nature of capital purchases. Manufacturing equipment, factory buildings, and warehouses are tremendously expensive. In absolute terms, interest charges on funds borrowed for these purchases are considerable.

Similarly, the interest cost on a house purchased on a long-term contract is very large: A percentage-point change in the interest rate would amount to thousands of dollars in the total cost of a typical home.

FIGURE 10.2 **Monetary policy and equilibrium GDP.** An easy money policy that shifts the money supply curve rightward from S_{m1} to S_{m2} lowers the interest rate from 10 to 8 percent. As a result, investment spending increases from $15 billion to $20 billion, shifting the aggregate demand curve rightward from AD_1 to AD_2, and real output rises from the recessionary level Q_1 to the full-employment level Q_F. A tight money policy that shifts the money supply curve leftward from S_{m3} to S_{m2} increases the interest rate from 6 to 8 percent. Investment spending thus falls from $25 billion to $20 billion, and the aggregate demand curve shifts leftward from AD_3 to AD_2, curtailing inflation.

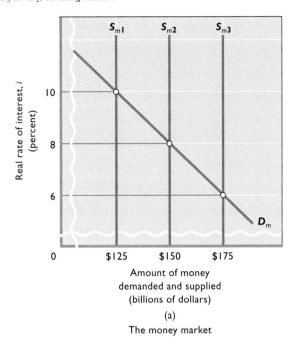

(a)
The money market

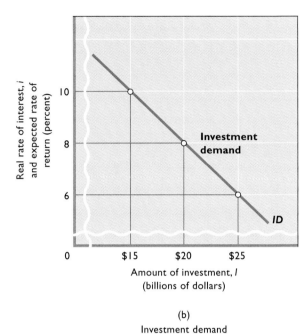

(b)
Investment demand

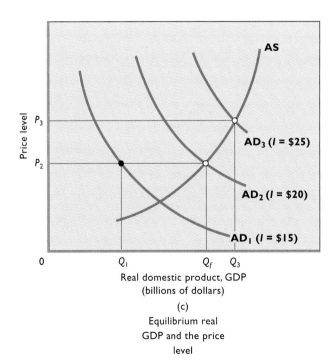

(c)
Equilibrium real
GDP and the price
level

Also, changes in the interest rate may affect investment spending by changing the relative attractiveness of purchases of capital equipment versus purchases of bonds. In purchasing capital goods, the interest rate is the cost of borrowing the funds to make the investment. In purchasing bonds, the interest rate is the return on the financial investment. If the interest rate increases, the cost of buying capital goods increases while the return on bonds increases. Businesses are then more inclined to use business savings to buy securities than to buy equipment. Conversely, a drop in the interest rate makes purchases of capital goods relatively more attractive than bond ownership.

In brief, the impact of changing interest rates is mainly on investment (and, through that, on aggregate demand, output, employment, and the price level). Moreover, as Figure 10.2b shows, investment spending varies inversely with the interest rate.

Equilibrium GDP Figure 10.2c shows the impact of our three interest rates and corresponding levels of investment spending on aggregate demand. As noted, aggregate demand curve AD_1 is associated with the $15 billion level of investment, AD_2 with investment of $20 billion, and AD_3 with investment of $25 billion. That is, investment spending is one of the determinants of aggregate demand. Other things equal, the greater the investment spending, the farther to the right lies the aggregate demand curve.

Suppose the money supply in Figure 10.2a is $150 billion ($S_{m2}$), producing an equilibrium interest rate of 8 percent. In Figure 10.2b we see that this 8 percent interest rate will bring forth $20 billion of investment spending. This $20 billion of investment spending joins with consumption spending, net exports, and government spending to yield aggregate demand curve AD_2 in Figure 10.2c. The equilibrium levels of real output and prices are Q_f and P_2, as determined by the intersection of AD_2 and the aggregate supply curve AS.

To test your understanding of these relationships, explain why each of the other two levels of money supply in Figure 10.2a results in a different interest rate, level of investment, aggregate demand curve, and equilibrium real output.

Effects of an Easy Money Policy

Next, suppose that the money supply is $125 billion ($S_{m1}$) in Figure 10.2a. Because the resulting real output Q_1 in Figure 10.2c is far below the full-employment output, Q_f, the economy must be experiencing recession and substantial unemployment. The Fed therefore should institute an easy money policy.

To increase the money supply, the Federal Reserve Banks will take some combination of the following actions: (1) Buy government securities from banks and the public in the open market, (2) lower the legal reserve ratio, (3) lower the discount rate, and (4) loan out additional reserves using the term auction facility. The intended outcome will be an increase in excess reserves in the commercial banking system. Because excess reserves are the basis on which commercial banks and thrifts can earn profit by lending and thus creating checkable-deposit money, the nation's money supply probably will rise. An increase in the money supply will lower the interest rate, increasing investment, aggregate demand, and equilibrium GDP.

For example, an increase in the money supply from $125 billion to $150 billion ($S_{m1}$ to S_{m2}) will reduce the interest rate from 10 to 8 percent, as indicated in Figure 10.2a, and will boost investment from $15 billion to $20 billion, as shown in Figure 10.2b. This $5 billion increase in investment will shift the aggregate demand curve rightward, as shown by the shift from AD_1 to AD_2 in Figure 10.2c. This rightward

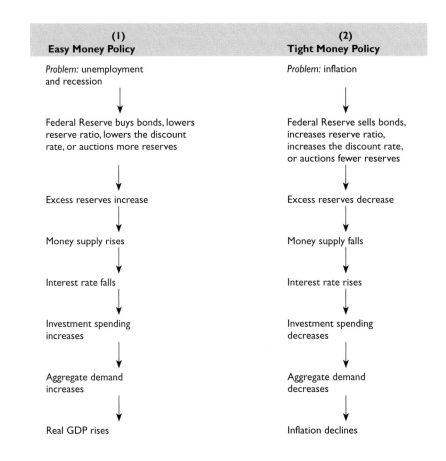

(1)	(2)
Easy Money Policy	**Tight Money Policy**
Problem: unemployment and recession	*Problem:* inflation
↓	↓
Federal Reserve buys bonds, lowers reserve ratio, lowers the discount rate, or auctions more reserves	Federal Reserve sells bonds, increases reserve ratio, increases the discount rate, or auctions fewer reserves
↓	↓
Excess reserves increase	Excess reserves decrease
↓	↓
Money supply rises	Money supply falls
↓	↓
Interest rate falls	Interest rate rises
↓	↓
Investment spending increases	Investment spending decreases
↓	↓
Aggregate demand increases	Aggregate demand decreases
↓	↓
Real GDP rises	Inflation declines

shift in the aggregate demand curve will eliminate the negative GDP gap by increasing GDP from Q_1 to the full-employment GDP of Q_f.[1]

Column 1 in Table 10.3 summarizes the chain of events associated with an easy money policy.

Effects of a Tight Money Policy

Now let's assume that the money supply is $175 billion ($Sm_3$) in Figure 10.2a. This results in an interest rate of 6 percent, investment spending of $25 billion, and aggregate demand AD_3. As you can see in Figure 10.2c, we have depicted a positive GDP gap of $Q_3 - Q_f$ and demand-pull inflation. Aggregate demand AD_3 is excessive relative to the economy's full-employment level of real output Q_f. To rein in spending, the Fed will institute a tight money policy.

The Federal Reserve Board will direct Federal Reserve Banks to undertake some combination of the following actions: (1) Sell government securities to banks and the public in the open market, (2) increase the legal reserve ratio, (3) increase the discount rate, and (4) auction off fewer reserves. Banks then will discover that their reserves are below those required. So they will need to reduce their checkable deposits

---

[1] For simplicity we assume that the increase in real GDP does not increase the demand for money. In reality, the transactions demand for money would rise, slightly dampening the decline in the interest rate shown in Figure 10.2a. We also assume that the price level was inflexible downward at P_2 when the economy entered the recession. So the easy money policy expands real GDP from Q_1 to Q_f without causing inflation.

by refraining from issuing new loans as old loans are paid back. This will shrink the money supply and increase the interest rate. The higher interest rate will discourage investment, lowering aggregate demand and restraining demand-pull inflation.

If the Fed reduces the money supply from $175 billion to $150 billion ($S_{m3}$ to S_{m2} in Figure 10.2a), the interest rate will rise from 6 to 8 percent and investment will decline from $25 billion to $20 billion (Figure 10.2b). This $5 billion decrease in investment will shift the aggregate demand curve leftward from AD_3 to AD_2 (Figure 10.2c). This leftward shift of the aggregate demand curve will eliminate the excessive spending and halt the demand-pull inflation. In the real world, of course, the goal will be to stop inflation—that is, to halt further increases in the price level—rather than to actually drive down the price level, which tends to be inflexible downward.[2] Given the downward inflexibility of prices, reducing the money supply to $150 billion would push the equilibrium GDP below its full employment level. To stop the inflation and restore output to its full employment level without causing a recession, a smaller monetary contraction would be necessary.

Column 2 in Table 10.3 summarizes the cause-effect chain of a tight money policy.

Monetary Policy in Action

We now turn from monetary policy in theory to monetary policy in action. Monetary policy has become the dominant component of U.S. national stabilization policy. It has two key advantages over fiscal policy:

- Speed and flexibility.
- Isolation from political pressure.

Compared with fiscal policy, monetary policy can be quickly altered. Recall that congressional deliberations may delay the application of fiscal policy for months. In contrast, the Fed can buy or sell securities from day to day and thus affect the money supply and interest rates almost immediately.

Also, because members of the Fed's Board of Governors are appointed and serve 14-year terms, they are relatively isolated from lobbying and need not worry about retaining their popularity with voters. Thus, the Board, more readily than Congress, can engage in politically unpopular policies (higher interest rates) that may be necessary for the long-term health of the economy. Moreover, monetary policy is a subtler and more politically neutral measure than fiscal policy. Changes in government spending directly affect the allocation of resources, and changes in taxes can have extensive political ramifications. Because monetary policy works more subtly, it is more politically palatable.

The Focus on the Federal Funds Rate

The Fed currently focuses monetary policy on altering the **Federal funds rate** as needed to stabilize the economy. Normal day-to-day flows of funds to banks rarely leave all banks with their exact levels of legally required reserves. Also, funds held at the Federal Reserve Banks are highly liquid, but they do not draw interest. Banks therefore lend these excess reserves to other banks on an overnight basis to earn interest without sacrificing long-term liquidity. Banks that borrow in this Federal funds market—the market for immediately available reserve balances at the Federal

Federal funds rate
The interest rate banks and thrifts charge one another on overnight loans made out of their excess reserves.

---

[2] Again, we assume for simplicity that the decrease in nominal GDP does not feed back to reduce the demand for money and thus the interest rate. In reality, this would occur, slightly dampening the increase in the interest rate shown in Figure 10.2a.

FIGURE 10.3 **The prime interest rate and the Federal funds rate in the United States.** The prime interest rate rises and falls with changes in the Federal funds rate.
Source: Federal Reserve data, **www.federalreserve. gov.**

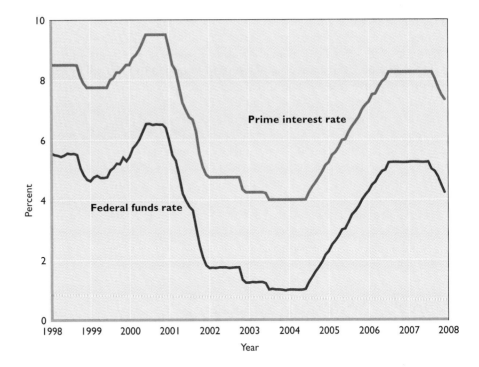

prime interest rate The benchmark interest rate that banks and thrifts use as a reference point for a wide range of loans to businesses and individuals.

Reserve—do so because they are temporarily short of required reserves. The interest rate paid on these overnight loans is called the *Federal funds rate.*

Because the Federal Reserve can control the supply of Federal funds—the supply of reserves in the banking system—it can control the Federal Funds interest rate. The Fed is a monopoly supplier of reserves. When it wants to increase the Federal funds rate, it sells securities in the open market to reduce (or withdraw) bank reserves. This is a "tighter" or "more restrictive" monetary policy. When it wants to reduce the Federal funds rate, it buys securities in the open market to increase (or inject) reserves. This is an "easier" or "more accommodating" monetary policy.

The Fed can target the Federal funds rate because it knows that interest rates in general typically rise and fall with that rate. For example, in Figure 10.3 observe that the **prime interest rate** generally parallels the Federal funds rate. The prime interest rate is the benchmark rate that banks use as a reference point for a wide range of interest rates on loans to businesses and individuals. By changing the Federal funds rate, the Fed in effect alters the economy's prime interest rate along with a wide array of other short-term interest rates.

Why the lockstep pattern between the Federal funds rate and the prime interest rate? Sales of securities by the Fed in the open market reduce excess reserves in the banking system, lessening the supply of excess reserves available for overnight loans in the Federal funds market. The decreased supply of excess reserves in that market increases the Federal funds rate. In addition, reduced excess reserves decrease the amount of bank lending and hence the amount of checkable-deposit money. Declines in the supply of money produce higher interest rates in general, including the prime interest rate.

Purchases of securities by the Fed in the open market increase the supply of reserves in the Federal funds market, reducing the Federal funds rate. The money supply rises because the increased supply of excess reserves leads to more lending and thus greater creation of checkable-deposit money. As a result, interest rates in general fall, including the prime interest rate.

Recent U.S. Monetary Policy

In the early 1990s, the Fed's easy money policy helped the economy recover from the 1990–1991 recession. The expansion of GDP that began in 1992 continued through the rest of the decade. By 2000 the U.S. unemployment rate had declined to 4 percent—the lowest rate in 30 years. To counter potential inflation during that strong expansion, in 1994 and 1995, and then again in early 1997, the Fed reduced reserves in the banking system to raise the interest rate. In 1998 the Fed temporarily reversed its course and moved to an easier monetary policy to ensure that the U.S. banking system had adequate liquidity during a severe financial crisis in southeast Asia. The economy continued to expand briskly, and in 1999 and 2000 the Fed, boosted interest rates to keep inflation under control.

Significant inflation did not occur in the late 1990s. But in the last quarter of 2000 the economy abruptly slowed. The Fed responded by cutting interest rates by a full percentage point in two increments in January 2001. Despite these rate cuts, the economy entered a recession in March 2001. Between March 20, 2001, and August 21, 2001, the Fed cut the Federal funds rate from 5 percent to 3.5 percent in a series of steps. In the 3 months following the terrorist attacks of September 11, 2001, it lowered the Federal funds rate from 3.5 to 1.75 percent, and it left the rate there until it lowered it to 1.25 percent in November 2002. Partly because of the Fed's actions, the prime interest rate dropped from 9.5 percent at the end of 2000 to 4.25 percent in December 2002.

Economists generally credit the Fed's adroit use of monetary policy as one of a number of factors that helped the U.S. economy achieve and maintain the rare combination of full employment, price stability, and strong economic growth that occurred between 1996 and 2000. The Fed also deserves high marks for helping to keep the recession of 2001 relatively mild, particularly in view of the adverse economic impacts of the terrorist attacks of September 11, 2001, and the steep stock market drop in 2001–2002.

In 2003 the Fed kept the Federal funds rate at historic lows. But as the economy began to expand more robustly in 2004, the Fed engineered a gradual series of rate hikes designed to boost the prime interest rates to make sure that aggregate demand continued to grow at a pace consistent with low inflation. By the summer of 2006, the Fed's targeted Federal funds rate had risen to 5.25 percent and the prime rate was 8.25 percent. With the economy enjoying robust, non-inflationary growth, the Fed held the Federal funds rate at 5.25 percent for over a year until the mortgage debt crisis battered the economy during the late summer of 2007.

In response to the crisis, the Fed took several actions. In August it lowered the discount rate by half a percentage point. Then, between September 2007 and April 2008, it lowered the target for the Federal funds rate from 5.25 percent to 2.00 percent. It also initiated the term auction facility in December 2007. All three actions helped to stabilize the banking sector and stabilize aggregate demand. Nevertheless, the economy badly stumbled again in the last half of 2008 and into 2009, prompting the Fed to lower the Federal funds rate in steps to less than 0.25 percent in January 2009.

Question:
What is the current monetary policy stance of the Fed? Has it been increasing interest rates, decreasing them, or leaving them unchanged in recent months? (Answer this question by going to the Federal Reserve's Web site, www.federalreserve.gov.)

Problems and Complications

Despite its recent successes in the United States, monetary policy has certain limitations and faces real-world complications.

Lags Recall that fiscal policy is hindered by three delays, or lags—a recognition lag, an administrative lag, and an operational lag. Monetary policy also faces a recognition lag and an operational lag, but because the Fed can decide and implement policy changes within days, it avoids the long administrative lag that hinders fiscal policy.

A recognition lag affects monetary policy because normal monthly variations in economic activity and the price level mean that the Fed may not be able to quickly recognize when the economy is truly starting to recede or when inflation is really starting to rise. Once the Fed acts, an operational lag of 3 to 6 months or more affects monetary policy because that much time is typically required for interest-rate changes to have their full impacts on investment, aggregate demand, real GDP, and the price level.

Cyclical Asymmetry Monetary policy may be highly effective in slowing expansions and controlling inflation but less reliable in pushing the economy from a severe recession. Economists say that monetary policy may suffer from **cyclical asymmetry.**

If pursued vigorously, a tight money policy could deplete commercial banking reserves to the point where banks would be forced to reduce the volume of loans. That would mean a contraction of the money supply, higher interest rates, and reduced aggregate demand. The Fed can turn down the monetary spigot and eventually achieve its goal.

But it cannot be certain of achieving its goal when it turns up the monetary spigot. An easy money policy suffers from a "You can lead a horse to water, but you cannot make it drink" problem. The Fed can create excess reserves, but it cannot guarantee that the banks will actually make the added loans and thus increase the supply of money. If commercial banks seek liquidity and are unwilling to lend, the efforts of the Fed will be of little avail. Similarly, businesses can frustrate the intentions of the Fed by not borrowing excess reserves. And when the Fed buys securities from the public, people may choose to pay off existing loans with the money received, rather than increasing their spending on goods and services.

Furthermore, a severe recession may so undermine business confidence that the investment demand curve shifts to the left and frustrates an easy money policy. That is what happened in Japan in the 1990s and early 2000s. Although its central bank drove the real interest rate to 0 percent, investment spending remained low and the Japanese economy stayed mired in recession. In fact, deflation—a fall in the price level—occurred. The Japanese experience reminds us that monetary policy is not an assured cure for the business cycle.

That fact became apparent in 2008 when the Fed's reductions of the target Federal funds rate to less than 1 percent failed to revive U.S. investment spending and expand aggregate demand. The Fed was said to be "pushing on a string."

cyclical asymmetry The potential problem of monetary policy successfully controlling inflation during the expansionary phase of the business cycle but failing to expand spending and real GDP during the recessionary phase of the cycle.

ILLUSTRATING THE IDEA

Pushing on a String

In the late 1990s and early 2000s, the central bank of Japan used an easy money policy to reduce real interest rates to zero. Even with "interest-free" loans available, most consumers and businesses did not borrow and spend more. Japan's economy continued to sputter in and out of recession.

The Japanese circumstance illustrates the possible *asymmetry* of monetary policy, which economists have likened to "pulling versus pushing on a string." A string may be effective at pulling something back to a desirable spot, but it is ineffective at pushing it toward a desired location. So it is with monetary policy, say some economists. Monetary policy can readily *pull* the aggregate demand curve to the left, reducing demand-pull inflation. There is no limit on how much a central bank can restrict a nation's money supply and hike interest rates. Eventually, a sufficiently tight money policy will reduce aggregate demand and inflation.

But during severe recession, participants in the economy may be highly pessimistic about the future. If so, an easy money policy may not be able to *push* the aggregate demand curve to the right, increasing real GDP. The central bank can produce excess reserves in the banking system by reducing the reserve ratio, lowering the discount rate, purchasing government securities, and auctioning off additional reserves. But commercial banks may not be able to find willing borrowers for those excess reserves, no matter how low interest rates fall. Instead of borrowing and spending, consumers and businesses may be more intent on reducing debt and increasing saving in preparation for expected worse times ahead. If so, monetary policy will be ineffective. Using it will be much like pushing on a string.

Question:
What levers does government have to push the economy from recession, if monetary policy fails?

APPLYING
THE
ANALYSIS

The Mortgage Debt Crisis: The Fed Responds

In 2007, a major wave of defaults on home mortgages threatened the health of any financial institution that had invested in home mortgages either directly or indirectly. A majority of these mortgage defaults were on *subprime mortgage loans*— high-interest rate loans to home buyers with higher-than-average credit risk. Crucially, several of the biggest indirect investors in these sub-prime loans had been banks. The banks had lent money to investment companies that had invested in mortgages. When the mortgages started to go bad, many investment funds "blew up" and couldn't repay the loans they had taken out from the banks. The banks had to "write off" (declare unrecoverable) the loans they had made to the investment funds. Doing so meant reducing the banks' reserves, which in turn limited their ability to generate new loans. This was a major threat to the economy since both consumers and businesses rely on loans to finance consumption and investment expenditures.

In the second half of 2007 and into early 2008, the Federal Reserve took several important steps to increase bank reserves and avert a financial crisis. In August, it fulfilled its important (but thankfully rarely needed) role as a "lender of last resort" by lowering the discount rate and encouraging banks to borrow reserves directly from the Fed. When many banks proved reluctant to borrow reserves at the discount rate (because they thought that doing so might make them appear to be in bad financial condition and in need of a quick loan from the Fed), the Fed introduced the anonymous term auction facility in December as an innovative new way of encouraging banks to borrow reserves and thereby preserve their ability to keep extending loans. In March 2008, the Fed announced the formation of the Primary Dealer Credit Facility (PDCF), another mechanism for loaning reserves to banks. The PDCF offers overnight loans, with borrowers using investment-grade securities (including mortgage debt) for collateral. The program was set to last as long as necessary to relieve the mortgage debt crisis.

Most important, the FOMC lowered the target for the Federal funds rate from 5.25 percent to 4.75 percent in September 2007, 4.50 percent in October, 4.25 percent in December, 3.00 percent in January 2008, and 2.00 percent in April. To accomplish these rate cuts, it bought bonds in the open market. This raised bank reserves and increased the ability of banks to expand their lending.

The lower Federal funds rate also resulted in lower interest rates in general, thereby bolstering aggregate demand. But the expansionary effects of the easy money policy were more than offset by further deterioration of aggregate demand resulting from additional shocks to the financial system. The recession that began in December 2007 worsened in the last half of 2008. At the start of 2009, the Fed faced a severely weakened financial system and a worsening recession. It clearly needed the help of fiscal policy.

Question:
Did the Fed's action (along with fiscal policies enacted during the same period) succeed in preventing recession?

Summary

1. There is a set of interest rates that vary by loan purpose, size, risk, maturity, and taxability. Nevertheless, economists often speak of a single interest rate in order to simplify their analysis.

2. The total demand for money consists of the transactions demand and asset demand for money. The amount of money demanded for transactions varies directly with the nominal GDP; the amount of money demanded as an asset varies inversely with the interest rate. The money market combines the total demand for money with the money supply to determine equilibrium interest rates.

3. The goal of monetary policy is to help the economy achieve price stability, full employment, and economic growth.

4. The four instruments of monetary policy are (a) open-market operations, (b) the reserve ratio, (c) the discount rate, and (d) the term auction facility.

5. The Fed's most often used monetary policy tool is its open-market operations. The Fed injects reserves into the banking system (and reduces interest rates) by buying securities from commercial banks and the general public. The Fed withdraws reserves from the banking system (and increases interest rates) by selling securities to commercial banks and the general public.

6. Monetary policy affects the economy through a complex cause-effect chain: (a) Policy decisions affect commercial bank reserves; (b) changes in reserves affect the money supply; (c) changes in the money supply alter the interest rate; (d) changes in the interest rate affect investment; (e) changes in investment affect aggregate demand; and (f) changes in aggregate demand affect the equilibrium real GDP and the price level. Table 10.3 draws together all the basic ideas relevant to the use of monetary policy.

7. The advantages of monetary policy include its flexibility and political acceptability. Recently, the Fed has targeted changes in the Federal funds rate as the immediate focus of its monetary policy. When it deems it necessary, the Fed uses open-market operations to change that rate, which is the interest rate banks charge one another on overnight loans of excess reserves. Interest rates in general, including the prime interest rate, rise and fall with the Federal funds rate. The prime interest rate is the benchmark rate that banks use as a reference rate for a wide range of interest rates on short-term loans to businesses and individuals.

8. In recent years, the Fed has used monetary policy to keep inflation low while helping to limit the depth of the recession of 2001, boost the economy as it recovered from that recession, and to help stabilize the banking sector in the wake of the mortgage debt crisis.

9. Monetary policy has two major limitations and potential problems: (a) Recognition and operation lags complicate the timing of monetary policy. (b) In a severe recession, the reluctance of firms to borrow and spend on capital goods may limit the effectiveness of an expansionary monetary policy.

Terms and Concepts

monetary policy	open-market operations	Federal funds rate
transactions demand	discount rate	prime interest rate
asset demand	term auction facility	cyclical asymmetry
total demand for money	easy money policy	
money market	tight money policy	

Study Questions

1. What is the basic determinant of (a) the strength of the transactions demand for money (the location of the transactions demand for money curve) and (b) the amount of money demanded for assets, given a particular asset demand for money curve? How is the equilibrium interest rate in the market for money determined? Use a graph to show the impact of an increase in the total demand for money on the equilibrium interest rate (no change in money supply). Use your general knowledge of equilibrium prices to explain why the previous interest rate is no longer sustainable. **LO1**

2. Assume that the following data characterize a hypothetical economy: money supply = $200 billion; quantity of money demanded for transactions = $150 billion; quantity of money demanded as an asset = $10 billion at 12 percent interest, increasing by $10 billion for each 2-percentage-point fall in the interest rate. **LO1**
   a. What is the equilibrium interest rate? Explain.
   b. At the equilibrium interest rate, what are the quantity of money supplied, the total quantity of money demanded, the amount of money demanded for transactions, and the amount of money demanded as an asset?

3. What is the basic objective of monetary policy? State the cause-effect chain through which monetary policy is made effective. What are the major strengths of monetary policy? **LO2**

4. What is the impact of each of the following transactions on commercial bank reserves? **LO2**
   a. The New York Federal Reserve Bank purchases government securities from private businesses and consumers.
   b. Commercial banks borrow from Federal Reserve Banks at the discount rate.
   c. The Fed reduces the reserve ratio.

   d. Commercial banks borrow from Federal Reserve Banks after winning an auction held as part of the term auction facility.

5. Why do changes in bank reserves resulting from open-market operations by the Fed produce *multiple* changes in checkable deposits (and therefore money) in the economy? **LO3**

6. Suppose that you are a member of the Board of Governors of the Federal Reserve System. The economy is experiencing a sharp and prolonged inflationary trend. What changes in (a) the reserve ratio, (b) the discount rate, (c) open-market operations, and (d) the amount of reserves offered at the term auction facility would you recommend? Explain in each case how the change you advocate would affect commercial bank reserves, the money supply, interest rates, and aggregate demand. **LO3**

7. Why is monetary policy easier to undertake than fiscal policy in a highly divided national political environment? **LO4**

8. What do economists mean when they say that monetary policy can exhibit cyclical asymmetry? Why is this possibility significant to policymakers? **LO4**

9. Distinguish between the Federal funds rate and the prime interest rate. Which of these two rates does the Fed explicitly target in undertaking its monetary policy? In 2004 and 2005 the Fed used open-market operations to significantly increase the Federal funds rate. What was the logic of those actions? What was the effect on the prime interest rate? **LO5**

10. What actions did the Fed take in the second half of 2007 and early 2008? What motivated these actions? **LO5**

FURTHER TEST YOUR KNOWLEDGE AT
www.mcconnellbriefmacro1e.com

Web-Based Questions

At the text's Online Learning Center, **www.mcconnellbriefmacro 1e.com,** you will find a multiple-choice quiz on this chapter's content. We encourage you to take the quiz to see how you do.

Also, you will find one or more Web-based questions that require information from the Internet to answer.

PART FIVE

Long-Run Considerations and International Economics

IN THIS CHAPTER YOU WILL LEARN:

1 About the relationship between short-run aggregate supply and long-run aggregate supply.

2 How to apply the long-run AD-AS model to inflation, recessions, and economic growth.

3 About the short-run trade-off between inflation and unemployment (the Phillips Curve).

4 Why there is no long-run trade-off between inflation and unemployment.

5 The relationship between tax rates, tax revenues, and long-run aggregate supply.

11

Long-Run Aggregate Supply and Aggregate Demand

During the early years of the Great Depression, many economists suggested that the economy would correct itself in the long run without government intervention. To this line of thinking, economist John Maynard Keynes remarked, "In the long run we are all dead!"

For several decades following the Great Depression, macroeconomic economists understandably focused on refining fiscal and monetary policy to smooth business cycles and address the problems of unemployment and inflation. The main emphasis was on the short-run problems and policies associated with the business cycle.

But over people's lifetimes, and from generation to generation, the long run is tremendously important for economic well-being. For that reason, macroeconomists have refocused attention on long-run macroeconomic adjustments, processes, and outcomes. The renewed emphasis on the long run has produced significant insights about aggregate supply and economic growth.

In Chapter 5 we discussed economic growth. Our goals in this chapter are to develop the long-run model of aggregate supply and aggregate demand, examine the inflation-unemployment relationship, and evaluate the effect of taxes on aggregate supply. The latter is a key concern of so-called *supply-side economics*.

From Short Run to Long Run

In Chapter 7, we noted that in macroeconomics the difference between the **short run** and the **long run** has to do with the flexibility of input prices, particularly wages and salaries. Input prices are inflexible or even totally fixed in the short run but fully flexible in the long run. By contrast, output prices are assumed under these definitions to be flexible in both the short run and the long run. (They are fixed only in the immediate short run.)

The assumption that input prices are flexible only in the long run leads to large differences in the shape and position of the short-run aggregate supply curve and the long-run aggregate supply curve. As explained in Chapter 7, the short-run aggregate supply curve is an upward sloping line, whereas the long-run aggregate supply curve is a vertical line situated directly above the economy's full-employment output level, Q_f.

Short-Run Aggregate Supply

Our first objective is to demonstrate the *relationship* between short-run aggregate supply and long-run aggregate supply. We begin by briefly reviewing short-run aggregate supply.

Consider the short-run aggregate supply curve AS_1 in Figure 11.1a. This curve is based on three assumptions: (1) The initial price level is P_1, (2) firms and workers have established nominal wages on the expectation that this price level will persist, and (3) the price level is flexible both upward and downward. Observe from point a_1 that at price level P_1 the economy is operating at its full-employment output Q_f. This output is the real production forthcoming when the economy is operating at its natural rate of unemployment (or potential output).

Now let's review the short-run effects of changes in the price level, say, from P_1 to P_2 in Figure 11.1a. The higher prices associated with price level P_2 increase firms' revenues, and because their nominal wages and other input prices remain unchanged, their profits rise. Those higher profits lead firms to increase their output from Q_f to Q_2, and the economy moves from a_1 to a_2 on aggregate supply AS_1. At output Q_2 the economy is operating beyond its full-employment output. The firms make this possible by extending the work hours of part-time and full-time workers, enticing new workers such as homemakers and retirees into the labor force, and hiring and training the structurally unemployed. Thus, the nation's unemployment rate declines below its natural rate.

How will the firms respond when the price level *falls*, say, from P_1 to P_3 in Figure 11.1a? Because the prices they receive for their products are lower while the nominal wages they pay workers remain unchanged, firms discover that their revenues and profits have diminished or disappeared. So they reduce their production and employment, and, as shown by the movement from a_1 to a_3, real output falls to Q_3. Increased

FIGURE 11.1 **Short-run and long-run aggregate supply.** (a) In the short run, nominal wages and other input prices are unresponsive to price-level changes and based on the expectation that price level P_1 will continue. An increase in the price level from P_1 to P_2 increases profits and output, moving the economy from a_1 to a_2; a decrease in the price level from P_1 to P_3 reduces profits and real output, moving the economy from a_1 to a_3. The short-run aggregate supply curve therefore slopes upward. (b) In the long run, a rise in the price level results in higher nominal wages and other input prices and thus shifts the short-run aggregate supply curve to the left. Conversely, a decrease in the price level reduces nominal wages and shifts the short-run aggregate supply curve to the right. After such adjustments, the economy obtains equilibrium of points such as b_1 and c_1. Thus, the long-run aggregate supply curve is vertical at the full-employment output.

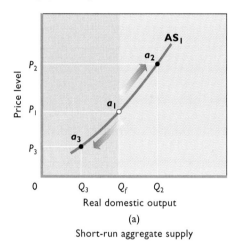
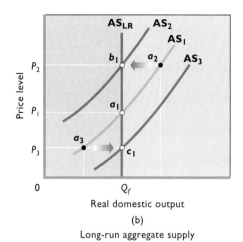

(a)
Short-run aggregate supply

(b)
Long-run aggregate supply

unemployment and a higher unemployment rate accompany the decline in real output. At output Q_3 the unemployment rate is greater than the natural rate of unemployment associated with output Q_f.

Long-Run Aggregate Supply

The outcomes are different in the long run. To see why, we need to extend the analysis of aggregate supply to account for changes in nominal wages that occur *in response to changes in the price level*. That will enable us to derive the economy's long-run aggregate supply curve.

We illustrate the implications for aggregate supply in Figure 11.1b. Again, suppose that the economy is initially at point a_1 (P_1 and Q_f). As we just demonstrated, an increase in the price level from P_1 to P_2 will move the economy from point a_1 to a_2 along the short-run aggregate supply curve AS_1. At a_2, the economy is producing at more than its potential output. This implies very high demand for productive inputs, so input prices will begin to rise. In particular this high demand for labor will drive up nominal wages. Because nominal wages are one of the determinants of aggregate supply (see Figure 7.6), the short-run supply curve then shifts leftward from AS_1 to AS_2, which now reflects the higher price level P_2 and the new expectation that P_2, not P_1, will continue. The leftward shift in the short-run aggregate supply curve to AS_2 moves the economy from a_2 to b_1. Real output falls to its full-employment level Q_f, and the unemployment rate rises to its natural rate.

What is the long-run outcome of a *decrease* in the price level? *Assuming eventual downward wage flexibility*, a decline in the price level, as from P_1 to P_3 in Figure 11.1b, works in the opposite way from a price-level increase. At first the economy moves from point a_1 to a_3 on AS_1. Profits are squeezed or eliminated because prices have fallen and nominal wages have not. But this movement along AS_1 is the short-run supply response that results only while input prices remain constant. As time passes, input prices will begin to fall because the economy is producing less than its full-employment output. With so little output being produced, the demand for inputs will be weak and their product prices will begin to decline. In particular, the low demand for labor will drive down nominal wages. Lower nominal wages shift the short-run aggregate supply curve rightward from AS_1 to AS_3, and real output returns to its full-employment level of Q_f at point c_1.

By tracing a line between the long-run equilibrium points b_1, a_1, and c_1, we obtain a long-run aggregate supply curve. Observe that it is vertical at the full-employment level of real GDP. After long-run adjustments in nominal wages and other input prices, real output is Q_f regardless of the specific price level.

Long-Run Equilibrium in the AD-AS Model

long-run AD-AS model
A model in which the equilibrium price level and level of real GDP are determined by the intersection of the AD curve and the vertical long-run AS curve.

Figure 11.2 helps us understand the equilibrium in the **long-run AD-AS model,** which includes the distinction between short-run and long-run aggregate supply. In the long-run AD-AS model, the price level, the wage rate, and the prices of other inputs are all flexible. The equilibrium price level and level of real GDP are determined by the intersection of the AD curve and the vertical long-run AS curve.

In the short-run, equilibrium occurs wherever the downsloping aggregate demand curve and upsloping short-run aggregate supply curve intersect. This can be at any level of output, not simply the full-employment level. Either a negative GDP gap or a positive GDP gap is possible in the short-run.

But in the long run, the short-run aggregate supply curve adjusts as we have just described. After those adjustments, long-run equilibrium occurs where the aggregate demand curve, vertical long-run aggregate supply curve, and short-run aggregate supply curve all intersect. Figure 11.2 shows the long-run outcome. Equilibrium occurs at point a, where AD_1 intersects both AS_{LR} and AS_1, and the economy achieves its full-employment (or potential) output, Q_f. At long-run equilibrium price level P_1 and output level Q_f, neither a negative GDP gap nor a positive GDP gap occurs.

INTERACTIVE GRAPHS

G 11.1

Long-run AD-AS model

FIGURE 11.2 **The long-run AD-AS model.** The equilibrium price level P_1 and level of real output Q_f occur at the intersection of the aggregate demand curve AD_1, the long-run aggregate supply curve AS_{LR}, and the short-run aggregate supply curve AS_1. At this equilibrium price-output combination, neither a positive GDP gap nor a negative GDP gap occurs. The economy achieves it full-employment level of real GDP.

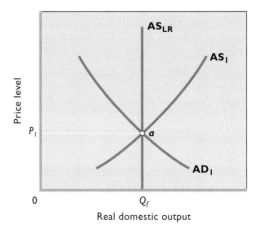

Demand-Pull Inflation in the Long-Run AD-AS Model

The long-run AD-AS model provides added understanding of demand-pull inflation. Recall that demand-pull inflation occurs when an increase in aggregate demand pulls up the price level. Previously, we depicted this inflation by shifting an aggregate demand curve rightward along a stable aggregate supply curve (Figure 7.8)—and that was the end of the matter.

In our more complex version of aggregate supply, however, an increase in the price level will eventually lead to a "catch-up" increase in nominal wages and thus a leftward shift of the short-run aggregate supply curve. This is shown in Figure 11.3, where we initially suppose the price level is P_1 at the intersection of aggregate demand curve AD_1, short-run supply curve AS_1, and long-run aggregate supply curve AS_{LR}. Observe that the economy is achieving its full-employment real output Q_f at point a.

Now consider the effects of an unexpected increase in aggregate demand as represented by the rightward shift from AD_1 to AD_2. This shift might result from any one of a number of factors, including an increase in investment spending or a rise in net exports. Whatever its cause, the increase in aggregate demand boosts the price level from P_1 to P_2 and expands real output from Q_f to Q_2 at point b. There, a positive GDP gap of Q_2-Q_f occurs.

So far, none of this is new to you. But now the distinction between short-run aggregate supply and long-run aggregate supply becomes important. With the economy producing above potential output, inputs will be in high demand. Input prices, including nominal wages, therefore will rise. As they do, the short-run aggregate supply curve will ultimately shift leftward such that it intersects long-run aggregate supply at point c. There, the economy has reestablished long-run equilibrium, with the price level and real output now P_3 and Q_f, respectively. Only at point c does the new aggregate demand curve AD_2 intersect both the short-run aggregate supply curve AS_2 and the long-run aggregate supply curve AS_{LR}.

In the short run, demand-pull inflation drives up the price level and increases real output; in the long run, only the price level rises. In the long run, the initial increase in aggregate demand moves the economy along its vertical aggregate supply curve AS_{LR}. For a while, an economy can operate beyond its full-employment

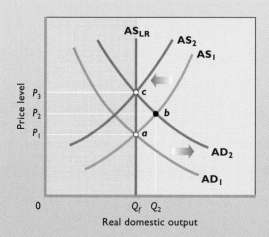

FIGURE 11.3 Demand-pull inflation in the long-run AD-AS model. An increase in aggregate demand from AD_1 to AD_2 drives up the price level and increases real output in the short run. But in the long run, nominal wages rise and the short-run aggregate supply curve shifts leftward, as from AS_1 to AS_2. Real output then returns to its prior level, and the price level rises even more. In this scenario, the economy moves from a to b and then eventually to c.

249

level of output. But the demand-pull inflation eventually causes adjustments of nominal wages that return the economy to its full-employment output Q_f.

The analysis provides a major insight: What sometimes appears to be cost-push inflation because nominal wages, natural resource prices, and other input prices are rising rapidly is often simply a facet of demand-pull inflation. Higher product prices caused by increasing aggregate demand eventually pull up input prices through the adjustment process that we have just described.

Question:
How do long-term contracts between resource suppliers and resource buyers affect the length of the time it takes for the economy to move from *b* to *c* in Figure 11.3?

APPLYING
THE
ANALYSIS

Cost-Push Inflation in the Long-Run AD-AS Model

The long-run model also clarifies a policy dilemma relating to cost-push inflation. Recall that this kind of inflation arises from factors that increase the cost of production at each price level, shifting the aggregate supply curve leftward and raising the equilibrium price level. Previously (Figure 7.9), we considered cost-push inflation using only the short-run aggregate supply curve. Now we want to analyze that type of inflation in its long-run context.

Look at Figure 11.4, in which we again assume that the economy is initially operating at price level P_1 and output level Q_f (point *a*). Suppose that an unanticipated international crisis causes a boost in the price of oil by, for example, 100 percent, in a very short period of time. As a result, the per-unit production cost of producing and transporting goods and services rises substantially in the economy represented by Figure 11.4. This increase in per-unit production costs shifts the short-run aggregate supply curve to the left, as from AS_1 to AS_2, and the price level rises from P_1 to P_2 (as seen by comparing points *a* and *b*). In this case, the leftward shift of the short-run aggregate supply curve is *not a response* to a price-

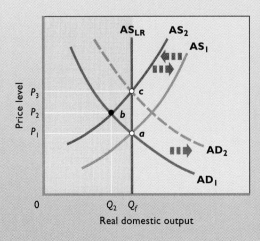

FIGURE 11.4 Cost-push inflation in the long-run AD-AS model. Cost-push inflation occurs when the short-run aggregate supply curve shifts leftward, as from AS_1 to AS_2. If government counters the decline in real output by increasing aggregate demand to the broken line, the price level rises even more. That is, the economy moves in steps from *a* to *b* to *c*. In contrast, if government allows a recession to occur, nominal wages eventually fall and the aggregate supply curve shifts back rightward to its original location. The economy moves from *a* to *b* and eventually back to *a*.

level increase, as it was in our previous discussions of demand-pull inflation; it is the *initiating cause* of the price-level increase.

Cost-push inflation creates a dilemma for policymakers. Without some expansionary stabilization policy, aggregate demand in Figure 11.4 remains in place at AD_1 and real output declines from Q_f to Q_2. Government can counter this recession, negative GDP gap, and the attendant high unemployment by using fiscal policy and monetary policy to increase aggregate demand to AD_2. But there is a potential policy trap here: An increase in aggregate demand to AD_2 will further raise inflation by increasing the price level from P_2 to P_3 (a move from point b to point c).

Suppose the government recognizes this policy trap and decides not to increase aggregate demand from AD_1 to AD_2 (you can now disregard the dashed AD_2 curve) and instead decides to allow a cost-push-caused recession to run its course. How will that happen? Widespread layoffs, plant shutdowns, and business failures eventually occur. At some point the demand for oil, labor, and other inputs will decline so much that oil prices and nominal wages will decline. When that happens, the initial leftward shift of the short-run aggregate supply curve will reverse itself. That is, the declining per-unit production costs caused by the recession will shift the short-run aggregate supply curve rightward from AS_2 to AS_1. The price level will return to P_1, and the full-employment level of output will be restored at Q_f (point a on the long-run aggregate supply curve AS_{LR}).

This analysis yields two generalizations:

• If the government attempts to maintain full employment when cost-push inflation occurs, even more inflation will occur.

• If the government takes a hands-off approach to cost-push inflation, the recession will linger. Although falling input prices will eventually undo the initial rise in per-unit production costs, the economy in the meantime will experience high unemployment and a loss of real output.

Question:
Why do you think it is so difficult politically for Congress or even the Federal Reserve to let cost-push inflation burn itself out for lack of aggregate demand fuel?

Recession in the Long-Run AD-AS Model

What does the long-run AD-AS model inform us about recession (or depression)? Will recessions caused by decreases in aggregate demand eventually self-correct?

Suppose in Figure 11.5 that aggregate demand initially is AD_1 and that the short-run and long-run aggregate supply curves are AS_1 and AS_{LR}, respectively. Therefore, as shown by point a, the price level is P_1 and output is Q_f. Now suppose that investment spending declines dramatically, reducing aggregate demand to AD_2. Observe that real output declines from Q_f to Q_1, indicating that a recession has occurred. But if we make the controversial assumption that

FIGURE 11.5 **Recession in the long-run AD-AS model.** A recession occurs when aggregate demand shifts leftward, as from AD_1 to AD_2. If prices and wages are downwardly flexible, the price level falls from P_1 to P_2 as the economy moves from point a to point b. With the economy in recession at point b, wages eventually fall, shifting the short-run aggregate supply curve from AS_1 to AS_2. The price level declines to P_3, and real output returns to Q_f. The economy moves in steps from point a to b to c.

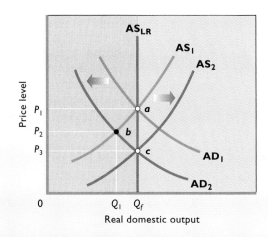

prices and wages are flexible downward, the price level falls from P_1 to P_2. With the economy producing below potential output at point b, demand for inputs will be weak. Eventually, nominal wages themselves fall to restore the previous real wage; when that happens, the short-run aggregate supply curve shifts rightward from AS_1 to AS_2. The negative GDP gap evaporates without the need for expansionary fiscal or monetary policy, since real output expands from Q_1 (point b) back to full-employment real output Q_f (point c). The economy is again located on its long-run aggregate supply curve AS_{LR}, but now at the lower price level P_3.

There is considerable disagreement as to whether this hypothetical scenario bears any resemblance to reality. The key point of dispute resolves around the degree to which both input and output prices are downwardly flexible and how long it would take in the actual economy for the necessary downward price and wage adjustments to occur to regain the full-employment level of output. Most economists believe that if such adjustments are forthcoming, they will occur only after the economy has experienced a relatively long-lasting recession with its accompanying high unemployment and large loss of output. Also, they point out that it is better to use fiscal and monetary policy to try to halt the decline in real GDP and increase in unemployment than simply to wait and hope that the hypothesized adjustments in the long-run AD-AS model are actually forthcoming. Following such advice, the Federal government and Federal Reserve used aggressive fiscal and monetary policy to try to halt and reverse the decline in aggregate demand occurring during the recessionary year 2008. A second, more massive dose of fiscal policy was prescribed for 2009.

Question:
Why are wages so sticky downward, even during recessions?

Economic Growth and Ongoing Inflation

In our analysis so far, we have demonstrated how demand and supply shocks can cause, respectively, demand-pull inflation and cost-push inflation. But in all the cases analyzed up to now, the extent of the inflation was *finite* because the size of the initial movement in either the AD curve or the AS curve was *limited*. For instance, in Figure 11.3, the aggregate demand curve shifts right by a limited amount, from AD_1 to AD_2. As the economy's equilibrium moves from a to b to c, the price level rises from P_1 to P_2

to P_3. During this transition, inflation obviously occurs since the price level is rising. But once the economy reaches its new equilibrium at point c, the price level remains constant at P_3 and there is no further inflation. That is, the limited movement in aggregate demand causes a limited amount of inflation that ends when the economy returns to full employment.

This fact is crucial to understanding why modern economies experience positive and ongoing rates of inflation. Simply put, ongoing shifts in either the aggregate demand or aggregate supply curves must be occurring since any single, finite shift in either curve will only cause an inflation of limited duration.

In this section, we explore this idea, pointing out the following facts:

- Ongoing economic growth causes continuous rightward shifts of the aggregate supply curve that, by themselves, would tend to cause a perpetual deflation.
- Simultaneously, central banks engineer ongoing increases in the money supply in order to cause continuous rightward shifts of the aggregate demand curve. Taken alone, these rightward shifts in aggregate demand are inflationary.
- Because the Fed purposely causes the inflationary rightward shifts of the aggregate demand curve to proceed slightly faster than the growth-caused deflationary rightward shifts of the aggregate supply curve, the net effect is (usually) a small positive rate of inflation. (We say "usually" because unexpected shocks to either aggregate demand or aggregate supply may cause inflation to be either a bit higher or a bit lower than the small positive rate that the central banks are attempting to engineer.)

As discussed in Chapter 5, economic growth is driven by supply factors such as improved technologies and access to more or better resources. We can illustrate economic growth either as an outward shift of the economy's production possibilities curve or as a rightward shift of its long-run aggregate supply curve. Observe Figure 11.6, in which the outward shift of the production possibilities curve from AB to CD in graph (a) is equivalent to the rightward shift of the economy's long-run aggregate supply curve from AS_{LR1} to AS_{LR2} in graph (b). Keeping this shift in

FIGURE 11.6 Production possibilities and long-run aggregate supply (a) Economic growth driven by supply factors (such as improved technologies or the use of more or better resources) shifts an economy's production possibilities outward, as from AB to CD. (b) The same factors shift the economy's long-run aggregate supply curve to the right, as from AS_{LR1} to AS_{LR2}.

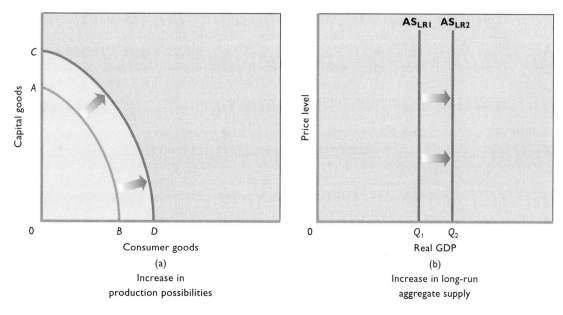

(a)
Increase in
production possibilities

(b)
Increase in long-run
aggregate supply

FIGURE 11.7 **Depicting U.S. growth via the long-run AD-AS model** Long-run aggregate supply and short-run aggregate supply have increased over time, as from AS_{LR1} to AS_{LR2} and AS_1 to AS_2. Simultaneously, aggregate demand has shifted rightward, as from AD_1 to AD_2. The actual outcome of these combined shifts in the United States has been economic growth, shown as the increase in real GDP from Q_1 to Q_2, accompanied by mild inflation, shown as the rise in the price level from P_1 to P_2.

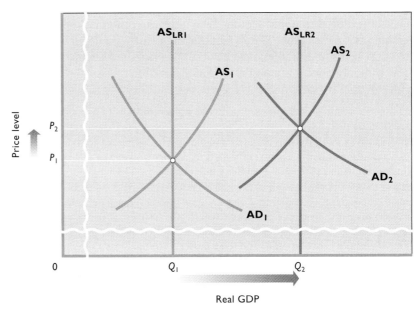

long-run aggregate supply clearly in mind, let's quickly move our attention to Figure 11.7. There, we show how the long-run aggregate demand–aggregate supply model can depict the economic growth process.

Suppose that an economy's aggregate demand curve, long-run aggregate supply curve, and short-run aggregate supply curve initially are AD_1, AS_{LR1}, and AS_1, as shown. The equilibrium price level and level of real output are P_1 and Q_1.

Now let's assume that economic growth driven by the changes in the supply factors (quantity and quality of resources and technology) shifts the long-run aggregate supply curve rightward from AS_{LR1} to AS_{LR2}. The economy's potential output has increased, as reflected by the expansion of available real output from Q_1 to Q_2.

With no change in aggregate demand, the increase in long-run aggregate supply from AS_{LR1} to AS_{LR2} in Figure 11.7 would expand real GDP and lower the price level. Put plainly, economic growth is deflationary, other things equal. But declines in the price level are not a part of the U.S. growth experience. Why not? The Federal Reserve has expanded the nation's money supply over the years such that increases in aggregate demand have more than matched the increases in aggregate supply. We depict this increase of aggregate demand as the rightward shift from AD_1 to AD_2.

The increases of aggregate supply and aggregate demand in Figure 11.7 have increased real output from Q_1 to Q_2 and have boosted the price level from P_1 to P_2. At the higher price level P_2, the economy confronts a new short-run aggregate supply curve AS_2. The changes shown in Figure 11.7 describe the actual U.S. experience: economic growth, accompanied by mild inflation.

In brief, economic growth causes increases in aggregate supply and aggregate demand. Whether zero, mild, or rapid inflation accompanies economic growth depends on the extent to which aggregate demand increases relative to aggregate supply. Over long periods, any inflation that occurs is the result of the growth of aggregate demand. It is not the result of the growth of real GDP.

The Inflation-Unemployment Relationship

We have just seen that the Fed can determine how much inflation occurs in the economy by how much it causes aggregate demand to shift relative to long-run aggregate supply. Given that low inflation and low unemployment rates are the Fed's major goals, its ability to control inflation brings up at least two interesting policy questions: Are low unemployment and low inflation compatible goals or conflicting goals? What explains situations in which high unemployment and high inflation coexist?

The long-run AD-AS model supports three significant generalizations relating to these questions:

- Under normal circumstances, a short-run trade-off exists between the rate of inflation and the rate of unemployment.
- Aggregate supply shocks can cause both higher rates of inflation and higher rates of unemployment.
- No significant trade-off exists between inflation and unemployment over long periods of time.

Let's examine each of these three important points.

Short-Run Trade-Off: The Phillips Curve

Let's view the short-run aggregate supply curve in Figure 11.8 and perform a simple mental experiment. Suppose that in some period aggregate demand expands from AD_0 to AD_2, either because firms decided to buy more capital goods or the government decided to increase its expenditures. Whatever the cause, in the short run the price level rises from P_0 to P_2 and real output rises from Q_0 to Q_2. As real output rises, the unemployment rate falls.

Now let's compare what would have happened if the increase in aggregate demand had been larger, say, from AD_0 to AD_3. The new equilibrium tells us that the amount of inflation and the growth of real output would both have been greater (and the unemployment rate would have been lower). Similarly, suppose aggregate demand during the year had increased only modestly, from AD_0 to AD_1.

Compared with our shift from AD_0 to AD_2, the amount of inflation and the growth of real output would have been smaller (and the unemployment rate higher).

FIGURE 11.8 The effect of changes in aggregate demand on real output and the price level. Comparing the effects of various possible increases in aggregate demand leads to the conclusion that the larger the increase in aggregate demand, the higher the rate of inflation and the greater the increase in real output. Because real output and the unemployment rate move in opposite directions, we can generalize that, given short-run aggregate supply, high rates of inflation should be accompanied by low rates of unemployment.

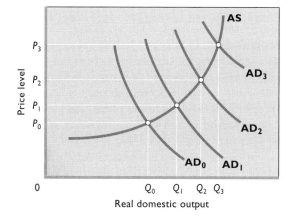

FIGURE 11.9 **The Phillips Curve.** The Phillips Curve (here, stylized) relates annual rates of inflation and annual rates of unemployment for a series of years. Because this is an inverse relationship, a trade-off presumably exists between unemployment and inflation.

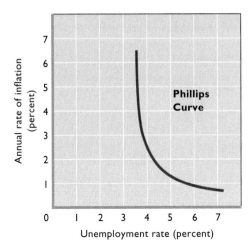

The generalization we draw from this mental experiment is this: *Assuming a constant short-run aggregate supply curve,* high rates of inflation are accompanied by low rates of unemployment, and low rates of inflation are accompanied by high rates of unemployment.

We can demonstrate this short-run trade-off between the rate of inflation and the rate of unemployment through the **Phillips Curve.** This curve is named after economist A. W. Phillips, who developed the idea by plotting data points for inflation rates and unemployment rates for each year on a graph. Generalized in Figure 11.9, the Phillips Curve suggests an inverse relationship between the rate of inflation and the rate of unemployment. Lower unemployment rates (measured as leftward movements on the horizontal axis) are associated with higher rates of inflation (measured as upward movements on the vertical axis).

The facts for the United States in the 1960s nicely fit the theory and approximate the curve Phillips Curve drawn in Figure 11.9. Unemployment rates above 4 percent were associated with inflation rates below 2 percent; unemployment rates below 4 percent were associated with inflation rates from 2 to 6 percent. On the basis of that evidence and evidence from other countries, most economists at that time concluded that a stable, predictable trade-off existed between unemployment and inflation.

Moreover, U.S. economic policy was built on that supposed trade-off. According to this thinking, it was impossible to achieve "full employment without inflation." Manipulation of aggregate demand through fiscal and monetary measures would simply move the economy along the Phillips Curve. An expansionary fiscal and monetary policy that boosted aggregate demand and lowered the unemployment rate would simultaneously increase inflation. A restrictive fiscal and monetary policy could be used to reduce the rate of inflation but only at the cost of a higher unemployment rate and more forgone production. Society had to choose between the incompatible goals of price stability and full employment; it had to decide where to locate on its Phillips Curve.

For reasons we will soon see, today's economists reject the idea of a stable, predictable Phillips Curve. Nevertheless, they agree there is a short-run trade-off between unemployment and inflation. Given aggregate supply, increases in aggregate demand increase real output and reduce the unemployment rate. As the

Phillips Curve
A curve showing the relationship between the unemployment rate and the rate of inflation.

ORIGIN OF THE IDEA

O 11.1

Phillips Curve

unemployment rate falls and dips below the natural rate, the excessive spending produces demand-pull inflation. Conversely, when a recession sets in and the unemployment rate jumps, the weak aggregate demand that caused the recession also leads to lower inflation rates.

Aggregate Supply Shocks and Shifts of the Phillips Curve

The unemployment-inflation experience of the 1970s and early 1980s demolished the idea of an always-stable Phillips Curve. In most of the years of the 1970s and early 1980s, the economy experienced both higher inflation rates *and* higher unemployment rates than it did in the 1960s. For example, in 1975 the unemployment rate was 8.5 percent and the inflation rate (December-to-December) was 6.9 percent. In 1981, the unemployment rate was 7.6 percent and the inflation rate was 8.9 percent.

In fact, inflation and unemployment rose simultaneously in some years. This condition is called **stagflation**—a media term that combines the words "stagnation" and "inflation." If any such thing as a Phillips Curve still existed, it had clearly shifted outward. We would show such changes, in a generalized way, as upward and outward shifts of curve PC in Figure 11.9. The shifts in the 1970 and early 1980s would place the curve at some location off the graph!

The unemployment rates and inflation rates in the 1970s and early 1980s support our second generalization: Aggregate supply shocks can cause both higher rates of inflation and higher rates of unemployment. A series of adverse **aggregate supply shocks**—sudden, large increases in resource costs that jolt an economy's short-run aggregate supply curve leftward—hit the economy in the 1970s and early 1980s. The most significant of these shocks was a quadrupling of oil prices by the Organization of Petroleum Exporting Countries (OPEC). Consequently, the cost of producing and distributing virtually every product and service rose rapidly. (Other factors working to increase U.S. costs during this period included major agricultural shortfalls, a greatly depreciated dollar, wage hikes previously held down by wage-price controls, and slower rates of productivity growth.)

These shocks shifted the short-run aggregate supply curve to the left and distorted the usual inflation-unemployment relationship. Remember that we derived the inverse relationship between the rate of inflation and the unemployment rate shown in Figure 11.9 by shifting the aggregate demand curve along a stable short-run aggregate supply curve (Figure 11.8). But the cost-push inflation model shown in Figure 11.4 tells us that a *leftward shift* of the short-run aggregate supply curve increases the price level and reduces real output (and increases the unemployment rate). This, say most economists, is what happened in two periods in the 1970s. The U.S. unemployment rate shot up from 4.9 percent in 1973 to 8.5 percent in 1975, contributing to a significant decline in real GDP. In the same period, the U.S. price level rose by 21 percent. The stagflation scenario recurred in 1978, when OPEC increased oil prices by more than 100 percent. The U.S. price level rose by 26 percent between 1978 and 1980, while unemployment increased from 6.1 to 7.1 percent.

The stagflation of the 1970 and early 1980s ended in the 1980s, and by 1989 the lingering effects of the early period had subsided. One precursor to this favorable trend was the deep recession of 1981–1982, largely caused by a tight money policy aimed at reducing double-digit inflation. The recession upped the unemployment rate to 9.5 percent in 1982. With so many workers unemployed, those who were working accepted smaller increases in their nominal wages—or, in some cases, wage reductions—in order to preserve their jobs. Firms, in turn, restrained their price increases to try to retain their relative shares of a greatly diminished market.

stagflation
Simultaneous increases in the price level and the unemployment rate.

aggregate supply shocks
Sudden unanticipated large changes in resource costs that shift an economy's aggregate supply curve.

GLOBAL SNAPSHOT 11.1

The Misery Index, Selected Nations, 1997–2007

The misery index adds together a nation's unemployment rate and its inflation rate to get a measure of national economic discomfort. For example, a nation with a 5 percent rate of unemployment and a 5 percent inflation rate would have a misery index number of 10, as would a nation with an 8 percent unemployment rate and a 2 percent inflation rate.

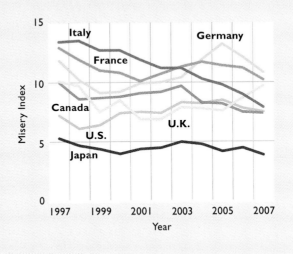

Source: Bureau of Labor Statistics, **www.bls.gov.**

Other factors were at work. Foreign competition throughout this period held down wage and price hikes in several basic industries such as automobiles and steel. Deregulation of the airline and trucking industries also resulted in wage reductions or so-called wage givebacks. A significant decline in OPEC's monopoly power and a greatly reduced reliance on oil in the production process produced a stunning fall in the price of oil and its derivative products, such as gasoline.

All these factors combined to reduce per-unit production costs and shift the short-run aggregate supply curve rightward. Employment and output expanded, and the unemployment rate fell from 9.6 percent in 1983 to 5.3 percent in 1989. Since 1990 inflation-unemployment points have settled back to closer to the points associated with the Phillips Curve of the 1960s. The points for 1997–2007, in fact, are very close to points on the 1960s curve. (The very low inflation and unemployment rates in this later period produced a low value of the so-called *misery index*, as shown in Global Snapshot 11.1.)

No Long-Run Inflation-Unemployment Trade-Off

The historical record supports our third generalization relating to the inflation-unemployment relationship: No apparent *long-run* trade-off exists between inflation and unemployment. Economists point out that when decades as opposed to a few years are considered, any rate of inflation is consistent with the natural rate of unemployment prevailing at that time. We know from Chapter 6 that the natural rate of unemployment is the unemployment rate that occurs when cyclical unemployment is zero; it is the full-employment rate of unemployment or the rate of unemployment when the economy achieves it potential output.

FIGURE 11.10 **The long-run vertical Phillips Curve.** Increases in aggregate demand beyond those consistent with full-employment output may temporarily boost profits, output, and employment (as from a_1 to b_1). But nominal wages eventually will catch up so as to sustain real wages. When they do, profits will fall, negating the previous short-run stimulus to production and employment (the economy now moves from b_1 to a_2). Consequently, there is no trade-off between the rates of inflation and unemployment in the long run; that is, the long-run Phillips Curve is roughly a vertical line at the economy's natural rate of unemployment.

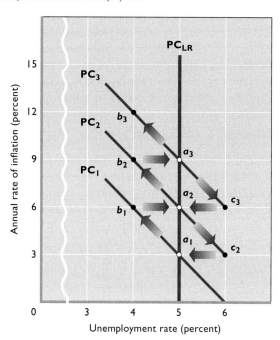

How can there be a short-run inflation-unemployment trade-off but not a long-run trade-off? Figure 11.10 provides the answer. Consider Phillips Curve PC_1. Suppose that the economy initially is experiencing a 3 percent rate of inflation and a 5 percent natural rate of unemployment. Such short-term curves as PC_1, PC_2, and PC_3 (drawn as straight lines for simplicity) exist because the actual rate of inflation is not always the same as the expected rate.

Establishing an additional point on Phillips Curve PC_1 will clarify this. We begin at a_1, where we assume nominal wages are set on the assumption that the 3 percent rate of inflation will continue. That is, because workers expect output prices to rise by 3 percent per year, they agreed to wage contracts that feature a 3 percent per year increases in nominal wages so that these nominal wage increases will exactly offset the expected rises in prices and thereby keep their real wages the same.

But suppose that the rate of inflation rises to 6 percent, perhaps because the Fed has decided to increase aggregate demand even faster than it had before. With a nominal wage rate set on the expectation that the 3 percent rate of inflation will continue, the higher product prices raise business profits. Firms respond to the higher profits by hiring more workers and increasing output. In the short run, the economy moves to b_1, which, in contrast to a_1, involves a lower rate of unemployment (4 percent) and a higher rate of inflation (6 percent). The move from a_1 to b_1 is consistent both with an upsloping aggregate supply curve and with the inflation-unemployment trade-off implied by the Phillips Curve analysis. But this short-run Phillips Curve simply is a manifestation of the following principle: *When the actual rate of inflation is higher than expected, profits temporarily rise and the unemployment rate temporarily falls.*

But point b_1 is not a stable equilibrium. Workers will recognize that their nominal wages have not increased as fast as inflation and will therefore obtain nominal wage increases to restore their lost purchasing power. But as nominal wages rise to restore the level of real wages that previously existed at a_1, business profits will fall to their prior level. The reduction in profits means that the original motivation to employ more workers and increase output has disappeared.

Unemployment then returns to its natural level at point a_2. Note, however, that the economy now faces a higher actual and expected rate of inflation—6 percent rather than 3 percent. This happens because the new labor contracts feature 6 percent per year increases in wage rates to make up for the 6 percent per year inflation rate. Because wages are a production cost, this faster increase in wages will imply faster future increases in output prices as firms are forced to raise prices more rapidly to make up for the faster future rate of wage growth. Stated a bit differently, the initial increase in inflation will become persistent because it leads to renegotiated labor contracts that will perpetuate the higher rate of inflation. In addition, because the new labor contracts are public, it will also be the case that the higher rates of inflation that they will cause will be expected by everyone rather than being a surprise.

In view of the higher 6 percent expected rate of inflation, the short-run Phillips Curve shifts upward from PC_1 to PC_2 in Figure 11.10. An "along-the-Phillips-Curve" kind of move from a_1 to b_1 on PC_1 is merely a short-run or transient occurrence. In the long run, after nominal wage contracts catch up with increases in the inflation rate, unemployment returns to its natural rate at a_2, and there is a new short-run Phillips Curve PC_2 at the higher expected rate of inflation.

The scenario repeats if aggregate demand continues to increase. Prices rise momentarily ahead of nominal wages, profits expand, and employment and output increase (as implied by the move from a_2 to b_2). But, in time, nominal wages increase so as to restore real wages. Profits then fall to their original level, pushing employment back to the normal rate at a_3. The economy's "reward" for lowering the unemployment rate below the natural rate is a still higher (9 percent) rate of inflation.

Movements along the short-run Phillips curve (a_1 to b_1 on PC_1) cause the curve to shift to a less favorable position (PC_2, then PC_3, and so on). A stable Phillips Curve with the dependable series of unemployment-rate–inflation-rate trade-offs simply does not exist in the long run. The economy is characterized by a **long-run vertical Phillips Curve.**

The vertical line through a_1, a_2, and a_3 shows the long-run relationship between unemployment and inflation. Any rate of inflation is consistent with the 5 percent natural rate of unemployment. So, society ought to choose a low rate of inflation rather than a high one.

The distinction between the short-run Phillips Curve and the long-run Phillips Curve also helps explain **disinflation**—reductions in the inflation rate from year to year. Suppose in Figure 11.10 that the economy is at a_3, where the inflation rate is 9 percent. And suppose that the pace of the nation's economic activity slows (as happened during the 1981–1982 recession), such that inflation falls below the 9 percent expected rate to, say, 6 percent. Business profits fall because prices are rising less rapidly than wages. The nominal wage increases, remember, were set on the assumption that the 9 percent rate of inflation would continue. In response to the decline in profits, firms reduce their employment and consequently the unemployment rate rises. The economy temporarily slides downward from point a_3 to c_3 along the short-run Phillips Curve PC_3. *When the actual rate of inflation is lower than the expected rate, profits temporarily fall and the unemployment rate temporarily rises.*

Firms and workers eventually adjust their expectations to the new 6 percent rate of inflation, and thus newly negotiated wage increases decline. Profits are restored,

long-run vertical Phillips Curve
A Phillips Curve showing that over long periods of time there is no trade-off between inflation rates and the unemployment rates.

disinflation
A decline in the annual rate of inflation from the previous year.

ORIGIN OF THE IDEA

O 11.2

Long-Run Vertical Phillips Curve

employment rises, and the unemployment rate falls back to its natural rate of 5 percent at a_2. Because the expected rate of inflation is now 6 percent, the short-run Phillips Curve PC_3 shifts leftward to PC_2.

If there is a further decline in the rate at which aggregate demand shifts to the right faster than aggregate supply, the scenario will continue. Inflation declines from 6 percent to, say, 3 percent, moving the economy from a_2 to c_2 along PC_2. The lower-than-expected rate of inflation (lower prices) squeezes profits and reduces employment. But, in the long run, firms respond to the lower profits by reducing their nominal wage increases. Profits are restored and unemployment returns to its natural rate at a_1 as the short-run Phillips Curve moves from PC_2 to PC_1. Once again, the long-run Phillips Curve is vertical at the 5 percent natural rate of unemployment.

Taxation and Aggregate Supply

A final topic in our discussion of aggregate supply is taxation, a key aspect of **supply-side economics.** "Supply-side economists" or "supply-siders" stress that changes in aggregate supply are an active force in determining the levels of inflation, unemployment, and economic growth. Government policies can either impede or promote rightward shifts of long-run aggregate supply curves such as those shown in Figure 11.7. One such policy is taxation.

These economists say that the enlargement of the U.S. tax system has impaired incentives to work, save, and invest. In this view, high tax rates impede productivity growth and hence slow the expansion of long-run aggregate supply. By reducing the after-tax rewards of workers and producers, high tax rates reduce the financial attractiveness of working, saving, and investing.

Supply-siders focus their attention on *marginal tax rates*—the rates on extra dollars of income—because those rates affect the benefits from working, saving, or investing more. In 2008 the marginal tax rates varied from 10 to 35 percent in the United States.

Supply-siders believe that how long and how hard people work depends on the amounts of additional after-tax earnings they derive from their efforts. They say that lower marginal tax rates on earned incomes induce more work, and therefore increase aggregate inputs of labor. Lower marginal tax rates increase the after-tax wage rate and make leisure more expensive and work more attractive. The higher opportunity cost of leisure encourages people to substitute work for leisure. This increase in productive effort is achieved in many ways: by increasing the number of hours worked per day or week, by encouraging workers to postpone retirement, by inducing more people to enter the labor force, by motivating people to work harder, and by avoiding long periods of unemployment.

High marginal tax rates also reduce the rewards for saving and investing. For example, suppose that Tony saves $10,000 at 8 percent interest, bringing him $800 of interest per year. If his marginal tax rate is 40 percent, his after-tax interest earnings will be $480, not $800, and his after-tax interest rate will fall to 4.8 percent. While Tony might be willing to save (forgo current consumption) for an 8 percent return on his saving, he might rather consume when the return is only 4.8 percent.

Saving, remember, is the prerequisite of investment. Thus, supply-side economists recommend lower marginal tax rates on interest earned from saving. They also call for lower taxes on income from capital to ensure that there are ready investment outlets for the economy's enhanced pool of saving. A critical determinant of investment spending is the expected *after-tax* return on that spending.

To summarize: Lower marginal tax rates encourage saving and investing. Workers therefore find themselves equipped with more and technologically superior machinery

supply-side economics
A view of macroeconomics that emphasizes the role of marginal tax rates and other factors that affect long-run aggregate supply and therefore affect inflation, unemployment, and economic growth.

FIGURE 11.11 **The Laffer Curve.** The Laffer Curve suggests that up to point *m* higher tax rates will result in larger tax revenues. But higher tax rates will adversely affect incentives to work and produce, reducing the size of the tax base (output and income) to the extent that tax revenues will decline. It follows that if tax rates are above *m*, reductions in tax rates will produce increases in tax revenues.

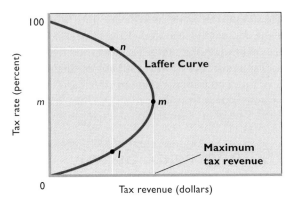

and equipment. Labor productivity rises, and that expands long-run aggregate supply and economic growth, which in turn helps keeps unemployment rates and inflation low.

The Laffer Curve

In the supply-side view, reductions in marginal tax rates increase the nation's aggregate supply and can leave the nation's tax revenues unchanged or even enlarge them. Thus, supply-side tax cuts need not produce Federal budget deficits.

Laffer Curve
A curve relating tax rates and tax revenues.

This idea is based on the **Laffer Curve,** named after Arthur Laffer, who popularized it. As Figure 11.11 shows, the Laffer Curve depicts the relationship between tax rates and tax revenues. As tax rates increase from 0 to 100 percent, tax revenues increase from zero to some maximum level (at *m*) and then fall to zero. Tax revenues decline beyond some point because higher tax rates discourage economic activity, thereby shrinking the tax base (domestic output and income). This is easiest to see at the extreme, where the tax rate is 100 percent. Tax revenues here are, in theory, reduced to zero because the 100 percent confiscatory tax rate has halted production. A 100 percent tax rate applied to a tax base of zero yields no revenue.

In the early 1980s Laffer suggested that the United States was at a point such as *n* on the curve in Figure 11.11. There, tax rates are so high that production is discouraged to the extent that tax revenues are below the maximum at *m*. If the economy is at *n*, then lower tax rates can either increase tax revenues or leave them unchanged. For example, lowering the tax rate from point *n* to point *l* would bolster the economy such that the government would bring in the same total amount of tax revenue as before.

Laffer's reasoning was that lower tax rates stimulate incentives to work, save and invest, innovate, and accept business risks, thus triggering an expansion of real output and income. That enlarged tax base sustains tax revenues even though tax rates are lowered. Indeed, between *n* and *m* lower tax rates result in *increased* tax revenue.

Also, when taxes are lowered, tax avoidance (which is legal) and tax evasion (which is not) decline. High marginal tax rates prompt taxpayers to avoid taxes through various tax shelters, such as buying municipal bonds, on which the interest earned is tax-free. High rates also encourage some taxpayers to conceal income from the Internal Revenue Service. Lower tax rates reduce the inclination to engage in either tax avoidance or tax evasion.

Sherwood Forest

The popularization of the idea that tax-rate reductions will increase tax revenues owed much to Arthur Laffer's ability to present his ideas simply. In explaining his thoughts to a *Wall Street Journal* editor over lunch, Laffer reportedly took out his pen and drew the curve on a napkin. The editor retained the napkin and later reproduced the curve in an editorial in *The Wall Street Journal*. The Laffer Curve was born. The idea it portrayed became the centerpiece of economic policy under the Reagan administration (1981–1989), which cut tax rates on personal income by 25 percent over a 3-year period.

Laffer illustrated his supply-side views with a story relating to Robin Hood, who, you may recall, stole from the rich to give to the poor. Laffer likened people traveling through Sherwood Forest to taxpayers, whereas Robin Hood and his band of merry men were government. As taxpayers passed through the forest, Robin Hood and his men intercepted them and forced them to hand over a large portion of their money. Laffer asked audiences, "Do you think that travelers continued to go through Sherwood Forest?"

The answer he sought and got, of course, was "no." Taxpayers will avoid Sherwood Forest to the greatest extent possible. They will lower their taxable income by reducing work hours, retiring earlier, saving less, and engaging in tax avoidance and tax evasion activities. Robin Hood and his men may end up with less revenue than if they collected a relatively small "tax" from each traveler for passage through the forest.

Question:
Have you ever changed some buying behavior because the price of some product got too high? If so, relate your change in behavior to how people might respond to increases in marginal tax rates.

Criticisms, Rebuttals, and Assessment

The Laffer Curve and its supply-side implications have been subject to major criticism. A fundamental criticism relates to the degree to which economic incentives are sensitive to changes in tax rates. Skeptics say there is ample empirical evidence showing that the impact of a tax cut on incentives is small, of uncertain direction, and relatively slow to emerge. For example, with respect to work incentives, studies indicate that decreases in tax rates lead some people to work more but others to work less. Those who work more are enticed by the higher after-tax pay; they substitute work for leisure because the opportunity cost of leisure has increased. But other people work less because the higher after-tax pay enables them to "buy more leisure." With the tax cut, they can earn the same level of after-tax income as before with fewer work hours.

Most economists think that the demand-side effects of a tax cut are more immediate and certain than the supply-side effects. Thus, tax cuts undertaken when the economy is at or near full employment may produce increases in aggregate demand that overwhelm any increase in aggregate supply. The likely result is inflation or a tight monetary policy to prevent it. If the latter, real interest rates will rise and investment will decline.

Skeptics say that the Laffer Curve is merely a logical proposition and assert that there must be some level of tax rates between 0 and 100 percent at which tax revenues will be at their maximum. Economists of all persuasions can agree with this. But the issue of where a particular economy is located on its Laffer Curve is an empirical question. If we assume that we are at point *n* in Figure 11.11, then tax cuts will increase tax revenues. But if the economy is at any point below *m* on the curve, tax-rate reductions will reduce tax revenues.

Supply-side advocates respond to the skeptics by contending that the Reagan tax cuts in the 1980s worked as Laffer predicted. Although the top marginal income tax rates on earned income were cut from 50 to 28 percent in that decade, real GDP and tax revenues were substantially higher at the end of the 1990s than at the beginning.

But the general view among economists is that the Reagan tax cuts, coming at a time of severe recession, helped boost aggregate demand and return real GDP to its full-employment output and trend-line growth path. As the economy expanded, so did tax revenues, despite the lower tax rates. The rise in tax revenues caused by economic growth swamped the declines in revenues from lower tax rates. That is, the Laffer Curve stretched rightward, increasing net tax revenues. But the tax-rate cuts did not produce extraordinary rightward shifts of the long-run aggregate supply curve. Indeed, saving fell as a percentage of personal income during the period, productivity growth was sluggish, and real GDP growth (although strong) was not extraordinary.

Because government expenditures rose more rapidly than tax revenues in the 1980s, large budget deficits occurred. In 1993 the Clinton administration increased the top marginal tax rates from 31 to 39.6 percent to address these deficits. The economy boomed in the last half of the 1990s, and by the end of the decade, tax revenues were so high relative to government expenditures that budget surpluses emerged. In 2001, the Bush administration reduced marginal tax rates over a series of years "to return excess revenues to taxpayers." In 2003 the top marginal tax rate fell to 35 percent. Also, the income tax rates on capital gains and dividends were reduced to 15 percent. Economists generally agree that the Bush tax cuts, along with highly expansionary monetary policy, helped revive and expand the economy following the recession of 2001. Strong growth of income in 2004 and 2005 produced large increases in tax revenues, although large deficits remained because Federal spending also increased rapidly. The 2004 deficit was $413 billion, and the 2005 deficit was $318 billion. The deficit fell over the next two years to $162 billion in 2007, but with the economy slowing in late 2007 and threatening to slip into recession in 2008, official forecasts predicted budget deficits of over $400 billion for both 2008 and 2009.

Today, there is general agreement that the U.S. economy is operating at a point below *m*—rather than above *m*—on the Laffer Curve in Figure 11.11. In this zone, the overall effect is that personal tax-rate increases expand tax revenues while personal tax-rate decreases reduce tax revenues. But at the same time, economists recognize that, other things equal, cuts in tax rates reduce tax revenues in percentage terms by less than the tax-rate reductions. Similarly, tax-rate increases do not raise tax revenues by as much in percentage terms as the tax-rate increases. This is true because changes in marginal tax rates *do* alter taxpayer behavior and thus affect taxable income. Although these effects are relatively modest, they need to be considered in designing tax policy—and, in fact, the Federal government's Office of Tax Policy created a special division in 2007 devoted to estimating the magnitude of such effects when it comes to proposed changes in U.S. tax laws. Thus, supply-side economics has contributed to how economists and policymakers design and implement fiscal policy.

Summary

1. In macroeconomics, the short run is a period in which nominal wages do not change in response to changes in the price level. In contrast, the long run is a period in which nominal wages are fully responsive to changes in the price level.

2. The short-run aggregate supply curve is upward-sloping. Because nominal wages are unresponsive to price-level changes, increases in the price level (prices received by firms) increase profits and real output. Conversely, decreases in the price level reduce profits and real output. However, the long-run aggregate supply curve is vertical. With sufficient time for adjustment, nominal wages rise and fall with the price level, moving the economy along a vertical aggregate supply curve at the economy's full-employment output.

3. In the short run, demand-pull inflation raises the price level and real output. Once nominal wages rise to match the increase in the price level, the temporary increase in real output is reversed.

4. In the short run, cost-push inflation raises the price level and lowers real output. Unless the government expands aggregate demand, nominal wages eventually will decline under conditions of recession, and the short-run aggregate supply curve will shift back to its initial location. Prices and real output will eventually return to their original levels.

5. If prices and wages are flexible downward, a decline in aggregate demand will lower output and the price level. The decline in the price level will eventually lower nominal wages and shift the short-run aggregate supply curve rightward. Full-employment output will thus be restored.

6. One-time shifts in the AD and AS curves can only cause limited bouts of inflation. Ongoing inflation, of the kind experienced in the United States, is caused by the Fed purposely shifting AD to the right slightly faster than the AS curve shifts to the right (due to economic growth).

7. Assuming a stable, upsloping aggregate supply curve, rightward shifts of the aggregate demand curve of various sizes yield the generalization that high rates of inflation are associated with low rates of unemployment, and vice versa. This inverse relationship is known as the Phillips Curve, and empirical data for the 1960s seemed to be consistent with it.

8. In the 1970s and early 1980s the Phillips Curve apparently shifted rightward, reflecting stagflation—simultaneously rising inflation rates and unemployment rates. The higher unemployment rates and inflation rates resulted mainly from huge oil price increases that caused large leftward shifts in the short-run aggregate supply curve (so-called aggregate supply shocks). The Phillips Curve shifted inward toward its original position in the 1980s. By 1989 stagflation had subsided, and the data points for the late 1990s and early 2000s were similar to those of the 1960s.

9. Although a short-run trade-off exists between inflation and unemployment, there is no long-run trade-off. Workers will adapt their expectations to new inflation realities, and when they do, the unemployment rate will return to the natural rate. So the long-run Phillips Curve is vertical at the natural rate, meaning that higher rates of inflation do not permanently "buy" the economy less unemployment.

10. Supply-side economists focus attention on government policies such as high taxation that impede the expansion of aggregate supply. The Laffer Curve relates tax rates to levels of tax revenue and suggests that, under some circumstances, cuts in tax rates will expand the tax base (output and income) and increase tax revenues. Most economists, however, believe that the United States is currently operating in the range of the Laffer Curve where tax rates and tax revenues move in the same, not opposite, directions.

11. Today's economists recognize the importance of considering supply-side effects of taxes in designing optimal tax structures and fiscal policy.

Terms and Concepts

short run

long run

long-run AD-AS model

Phillips Curve

stagflation

aggregate supply shocks

long-run vertical Phillips Curve

disinflation

supply-side economics

Laffer Curve

Study Questions

1. Distinguish between the short run and the long run as they relate to macroeconomics. Why is the distinction important? **LO1**

2. Which of the following statements are true? Which are false? Explain why the false statements are untrue. **LO1**

a. Short-run aggregate supply curves reflect an inverse relationship between the price level and the level of real output.

b. The long-run aggregate supply curve assumes that nominal wages are fixed.

c. In the long run, an increase in the price level will result in an increase in nominal wages.

3. Suppose the full-employment level of real output (Q) for a hypothetical economy is $250 and the price level (P) initially is 100. Use the short-run aggregate supply schedules below to answer the questions that follow: **LO1**

AS (P_{100})		AS (P_{125})		AS (P_{75})	
P	Q	P	Q	P	Q
125	$280	125	$250	125	$310
100	250	100	220	100	280
75	220	75	190	75	250

a. What will be the level of real output in the short run if the price level unexpectedly rises from 100 to 125 because of an increase in aggregate demand? What if the price level unexpectedly falls from 100 to 75 because of a decrease in aggregate demand? Explain each situation, using figures from the table.

b. What will be the level of real output in the long run when the price level rises from 100 to 125? When it falls from 100 to 75? Explain each situation.

c. Show the circumstances described in parts *a* and *b* on graph paper, and derive the long-run aggregate supply curve.

4. Use graphical analysis to show how each of the following would affect the economy first in the short run and then in the long run. Assume that the United States is initially operating at its full-employment level of output, that prices and wages are eventually flexible both upward and downward, and that there is no counteracting fiscal or monetary policy. **LO2**

a. Because of a war abroad, the oil supply to the United States is disrupted, sending oil prices rocketing upward.

b. Construction spending on new homes rises dramatically, greatly increasing total U.S. investment spending.

c. Economic recession occurs abroad, significantly reducing U.S. exports.

5. Between 1990 and 2007, the GDP price level rose by about 47 percent while real GDP increased by about 63 percent.

Use the long-run aggregate demand–aggregate supply model to illustrate these outcomes graphically. **LO2**

6. Assume there is a particular short-run aggregate supply curve for an economy and the curve is relevant for several years. Use the AD-AS analysis to show graphically why higher rates of inflation over this period would be associated with lower rates of unemployment, and vice versa. What is this inverse relationship called? **LO3**

7. Suppose that the U.S. inflation rate and unemployment rate both increased relative to previous years for several years in a row. What might explain this, and what could you conclude about the location of the short-run Phillips Curve? **LO3**

8. Suppose the government misjudges the natural rate of unemployment to be much lower than it actually is and thus undertakes expansionary fiscal and monetary policies to try to achieve the lower rate. Use the concept of the short-run Phillips Curve to explain why these policies might at first succeed. Use the concept of the long-run Phillips Curve to explain the long-run outcome of these policies. **LO4**

9. What do the distinctions between short-run aggregate supply and long-run aggregate supply have in common with the distinction between the short-run Phillips Curve and the long-run Phillips Curve? Explain. **LO4**

10. What is the Laffer Curve, and how does it relate to supply-side economics? Why is determining the economy's location on the curve so important in assessing tax policy? **LO5**

11. Why might one person work more, earn more, and pay more income tax when his or her tax rate is cut, while another person will work less, earn less, and pay less income tax under the same circumstance? **LO5**

12. The capital gains tax is the tax on the income realized when someone sells an asset for more than its purchase price. Why might tax revenues from this tax source actually decline for awhile if the tax rate on capital gains increases? **LO5**

FURTHER TEST YOUR KNOWLEDGE AT
www.mcconnellbriefmacro1e.com

Web-Based Questions

At the text's Online Learning Center, **www.mcconnellbriefmacro 1e.com,** you will find a multiple-choice quiz on this chapter's content. We encourage you to take the quiz to see how you do.

Also, you will find one or more Web-based questions that require information from the Internet to answer.

IN THIS CHAPTER YOU WILL LEARN:

1 Some key facts about U.S. international trade.

2 About comparative advantage, specialization, and international trade.

3 How exchange rates are determined in currency markets.

4 The rebuttals to common arguments for protectionism.

5 The role played by free-trade zones and the World Trade Organization (WTO) in promoting international trade.

International Trade and Exchange Rates

Backpackers in the wilderness like to think they are "leaving the world behind," but, like Atlas, they carry the world on their shoulders. Much of their equipment is imported—knives from Switzerland, rain gear from South Korea, cameras from Japan, aluminum pots from England, sleeping bags from China, and compasses from Finland. Moreover, they may have driven to the trailheads in Japanese-made Toyotas or German-made BMWs, sipping coffee from Brazil or snacking on bananas from Honduras.

International trade and the global economy affect all of us daily, whether we are hiking in the wilderness, driving our cars, listening to music, or working at our jobs. We cannot "leave the world behind." We are enmeshed in a global web of economic relationships—trading of goods and services, multinational corporations, cooperative ventures among the world's firms, and ties among the world's financial markets.

Trade Facts

The following facts provide an "executive summary" of U.S. international trade:

- A *trade deficit* occurs when imports exceed exports. The United States has a trade deficit in goods. In 2007, U.S. imports of goods exceeded U.S. exports of goods by $816 billion.
- A *trade surplus* occurs when exports exceed imports. The United States has a trade surplus in services (such as air transportation services and financial services). In 2007, U.S. exports of services exceeded U.S. imports of services by $107 billion.
- Principal U.S. exports include chemicals, agricultural products, consumer durables, semiconductors, and aircraft; principal imports include petroleum, automobiles, metals, household appliances, and computers.
- Canada is the United States' most important trading partner quantitatively. In 2007, 22 percent of U.S. exported goods were sold to Canadians, who in turn provided 16 percent of the U.S. imports of goods.
- The United States has a sizable trade deficit with China. In 2007, U.S. imports of goods from China exceeded exports of goods to China by $257 billion.
- The U.S. dependence on foreign oil is reflected in its trade with members of OPEC. In 2007, the United States imported $174 billion of goods (mainly oil) from OPEC members, while exporting $49 billion of goods to those countries.
- The United States leads the world in the combined volume of exports and imports, as measured in dollars. Germany, the United States, China, Japan, and France are the top five exporters by dollar volume (see Global Snapshot 12.1). Currently, the United States provides about 9 percent of the world's exports.

GLOBAL SNAPSHOT 12.1

Comparative Exports

Germany, the United States, and China are the world's largest exporters

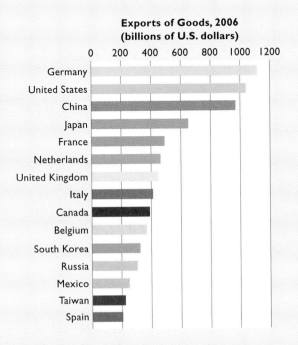

Exports of Goods, 2006
(billions of U.S. dollars)

Source: World Trade Organization, **www.wto.org.**

- Exports of goods and services make up about 10 percent of total U.S. output. That percentage is much lower than the percentage in many other nations, including Canada, Italy, France, and the United Kingdom (see Global Snapshot 12.2).
- China has become a major international trader, with an estimated $1.2 trillion billion of exports in 2007. Other Asian economies—including South Korea, Taiwan, and Singapore—are also active in international trade. Their combined exports exceed those of France, Britain, or Italy.
- International trade and finance are often at the center of economic policy.

With this information in mind, let's look more closely at the economics of international trade.

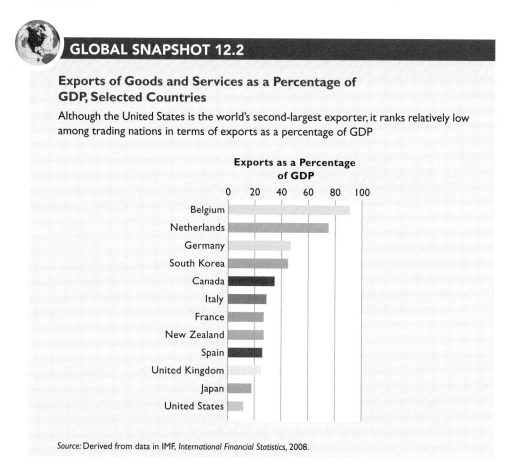

GLOBAL SNAPSHOT 12.2

Exports of Goods and Services as a Percentage of GDP, Selected Countries

Although the United States is the world's second-largest exporter, it ranks relatively low among trading nations in terms of exports as a percentage of GDP

Source: Derived from data in IMF, *International Financial Statistics*, 2008.

Comparative Advantage and Specialization

Given the presence of an *open economy*—one that includes the international sector—the United States produces more of certain goods (exports) and fewer of other goods (imports) than it would otherwise. Thus U.S. labor and other resources are shifted toward export industries and away from import industries. For example, the United States uses more resources to make computers and to grow wheat and less to make sporting goods and clothing. So we ask: "Do shifts of resources like these make economic sense? Do they enhance U.S. total output and thus the U.S. standard of living?"

The answers are affirmative. Specialization and international trade increase the productivity of a nation's resources and allow for greater total output than would otherwise be possible. This idea is not new. Adam Smith had this to say in 1776:

It is the maxim of every prudent master of a family, never to attempt to make at home what it will cost him more to make than to buy. The taylor does not attempt to make his own shoes, but buys them of the shoemaker. The shoemaker does not attempt to make his own clothes, but employs a taylor. The farmer attempts to make neither the one nor the other, but employs those different artificers. . . .

What is prudence in the conduct of every private family, can scarce be folly in that of a great kingdom. If a foreign country can supply us with a commodity cheaper than we can make it, better buy it of them with some part of the produce of our own industry, employed in a way in which we have some advantage.[1]

Nations specialize and trade for the same reasons that individuals do: Specialization and exchange result in greater overall output and income. In the early 1800s British economist David Ricardo expanded on Smith's idea by observing that it pays for a person or a country to specialize and trade even if a nation is more productive than a potential trading partner in *all* economic activities. We demonstrate Ricardo's principle in the examples that follow.

ILLUSTRATING
THE
IDEA

A CPA and a House Painter

Consider the certified public accountant (CPA) who is also a skilled house painter. Suppose the CPA is a swifter painter than the professional painter she is thinking of hiring. Also suppose that she can earn $50 per hour as an accountant but would have to pay the painter $15 per hour. And say it would take the accountant 30 hours to paint her house but the painter would take 40 hours.

Should the CPA take time from her accounting to paint her own house, or should she hire the painter? The CPA's opportunity cost of painting her house is $1500 (=30 hours of sacrificed CPA time × $50 per CPA hour). The cost of hiring the painter is only $600 (=40 hours of painting × $15 per hour of painting). Although the CPA is better at both accounting and painting, she will get her house painted at lower cost by specializing in accounting and using some of her earnings from accounting to hire a house painter.

Similarly, the house painter can reduce his cost of obtaining accounting services by specializing in painting and using some of his income to hire the CPA to prepare his income tax forms. Suppose it would take the painter 10 hours to prepare his tax return, while the CPA could handle the task in 2 hours. The house painter would sacrifice $150 of income (=10 hours of painting time × $15 per hour) to do something he could hire the CPA to do for $100 (=2 hours of CPA time × $50 per CPA hour). By using the CPA to prepare his tax return, the painter lowers the cost of getting his tax return prepared.

What is true for our CPA and house painter is also true for nations. Specializing enables nations to reduce the cost of obtaining the goods and services they desire.

Question:
How might the specialization described above change once the CPA retires? What generalization about the permanency of a particular pattern of specialization can you draw from your answer?

---

[1] Adam Smith, *The Wealth of Nations* (New York: Modern Library, 1937), p. 424. (Originally published in 1776.)

Comparative Advantage: Production Possibilities Analysis

Our simple example shows that the reason specialization is economically desirable is that it results in more efficient production. Now let's put specialization into the context of trading nations and use the familiar concept of the production possibilities table for our analysis.

Assumptions and Comparative Costs

Suppose the production possibilities for one product in Mexico and for one product in the United States are as shown in Tables 12.1 and 12.2. Both tables reflect constant costs. Each country must give up a constant amount of one product to secure a certain increment of the other product. (This assumption simplifies our discussion without impairing the validity of our conclusions. Later we will allow for increasing costs.)

Also for simplicity, suppose that the labor forces in the United States and Mexico are of equal size. The data then tell us that the United States has an *absolute advantage* in producing both products. If the United States and Mexico use their entire (equal-size) labor forces to produce avocados, the United States can produce 90 tons compared with Mexico's 60 tons. Similarly, the United States can produce 30 tons of soybeans compared to Mexico's 15 tons. There are greater production possibilities in the United States, using the same number of workers as in Mexico. So labor productivity (output per worker) in the United States exceeds that in Mexico in producing both products.

Although the United States has an absolute advantage in producing both goods, gains from specialization and trade are possible. Specialization and trade are mutually beneficial or "profitable" to the two nations if the *comparative* costs of producing the two products within the two nations differ. What are the comparative costs of avocados and soybeans in Mexico? By comparing production alternatives A and B in Table 12.1, we see that Mexico must sacrifice 5 tons of soybeans (=15 − 10) to produce 20 tons of avocados (=20 − 0). Or, more simply, in Mexico it costs 1 ton of soybeans (S) to produce 4 tons of avocados (A); that is, $1S \equiv 4A$. (The "$\equiv$" sign simply means "equivalent to.") Because we assumed constant costs, this domestic opportunity cost will not change as Mexico expands the output of either product. This is evident from production possibilities B and C, where we see that 4 more tons of avocados (=24 − 20) cost 1 unit of soybeans (=10 − 9).

Similarly, in Table 12.2, comparing U.S. production alternatives R and S reveals that in the United States it costs 10 tons of soybeans (=30 − 20) to obtain 30 tons of

Product	Production Alternatives				
	A	**B**	**C**	**D**	**E**
Avocados	0	20	24	40	60
Soybeans	15	10	9	5	0

TABLE 12.1 **Mexico's Production Possibilities Table (in Tons)**

Product	Production Alternatives				
	R	**S**	**T**	**U**	**V**
Avocados	0	30	33	60	90
Soybeans	30	20	19	10	0

TABLE 12.2 **U.S. Production Possibilities Table (in Tons)**

avocados ($=30 - 0$). That is, the domestic (internal) comparative-cost ratio for the two products in the United States is $1S \equiv 3A$. Comparing production alternatives S and T reinforces this conclusion: an extra 3 tons of avocados ($=33 - 30$) comes at the sacrifice of 1 ton of soybeans ($=20 - 19$).

The comparative costs of the two products within the two nations are obviously different. Economists say that the United States has a **comparative advantage** over Mexico in soybeans. The United States must forgo only 3 tons of avocados to get 1 ton of soybeans, but Mexico must forgo 4 tons of avocados to get 1 ton of soybeans. In terms of opportunity costs, soybeans are relatively cheaper in the United States. *A nation has a comparative advantage in some product when it can produce that product at a lower opportunity cost than can a potential trading partner.* Mexico, in contrast, has a comparative advantage in avocados. While 1 ton of avocados costs $\frac{1}{3}$ ton of soybeans in the United States, it costs only $\frac{1}{4}$ ton of soybeans in Mexico. Comparatively speaking, avocados are cheaper in Mexico. We summarize the situation in Table 12.3. Be sure to give it a close look.

Because of these differences in comparative costs, Mexico should produce avocados and the United States should produce soybeans. If both nations specialize according to their comparative advantages, each can achieve a larger total output with the same total input of resources. Together they will be using their scarce resources more efficiently.

Terms of Trade
The United States can shift production between soybeans and avocados at the rate of 1S for 3A. Thus, the United States would specialize in soybeans only if it could obtain *more than* 3 tons of avocados for 1 ton of soybeans by trading with Mexico. Similarly, Mexico can shift production at the rate of 4A for 1S. So it would be advantageous to Mexico to specialize in avocados if it could get 1 ton of soybeans for *less than* 4 tons of avocados.

Suppose that through negotiation the two nations agree on an exchange rate of 1 ton of soybeans for $3\frac{1}{2}$ tons of avocados. These **terms of trade** are mutually beneficial to both countries, since each can "do better" through such trade than through domestic production alone. The United States can get $3\frac{1}{2}$ tons of avocados by sending 1 ton of soybeans to Mexico, while it can get only 3 tons of avocados by shifting its own resources domestically from soybeans to avocados. Mexico can obtain 1 ton of soybeans at a lower cost of $3\frac{1}{2}$ tons of avocados through trade with the United States, compared to the cost of 4 tons if Mexico produced the 1 ton of soybeans itself.

Gains from Specialization and Trade
Let's pinpoint the gains in total output from specialization and trade. Suppose that, before specialization and trade, production alternative C in Table 12.1 and alternative T in Table 12.2 were the optimal product mixes for the two countries. That is, Mexico preferred 24 tons of avocados

TABLE 12.3 **Comparative-Advantage Example: A Summary**

Soybeans	Avocados
Mexico: Must give up 4 tons of avocados to get 1 ton of soybeans	**Mexico:** Must give up $\frac{1}{4}$ ton of soybeans to get 1 ton of avocados
United States: Must give up 3 tons of avocados to get 1 ton of soybeans	**United States:** Must give up $\frac{1}{3}$ ton of soybeans to get 1 ton of avocados
Comparative advantage: United States	**Comparative advantage:** Mexico

and 9 tons of soybeans (Table 12.1) and the United States preferred 33 tons of avocados and 19 tons of soybeans (Table 12.2) to all other available domestic alternatives. These outputs are shown in column 1 in Table 12.4.

Now assume that both nations specialize according to their comparative advantages, with Mexico producing 60 tons of avocados and no soybeans (alternative E) and the United States producing no avocados and 30 tons of soybeans (alternative R). These outputs are shown in column 2 in Table 12.4. Using our $1S \equiv 3\frac{1}{2}A$ terms of trade, assume that Mexico exchanges 35 tons of avocados for 10 tons of U.S. soybeans. Column 3 in Table 12.4 shows the quantities exchanged in this trade, with a minus sign indicating exports and a plus sign indicating imports. As shown in column 4, after the trade Mexico has 25 tons of avocados and 10 tons of soybeans, while the United States has 35 tons of avocados and 20 tons of soybeans. Compared with their optimal product mixes before specialization and trade (column 1), *both* nations now enjoy more avocados and more soybeans! Specifically, Mexico has gained 1 ton of avocados and 1 ton of soybeans. The United States has gained 2 tons of avocados and 1 ton of soybeans. These gains are shown in column 5.

Specialization based on comparative advantage improves global resource allocation. The same total inputs of world resources and technology result in a larger global output. If Mexico and the United States allocate all their resources to avocados and soybeans, respectively, the same total inputs of resources can produce more output between them, indicating that resources are being allocated more efficiently.

Through specialization and international trade a nation can overcome the production constraints imposed by its domestic production possibilities table and curve. Our discussion of Tables 12.1, 12.2, and 12.4 has shown just how this is done. The domestic production possibilities data (Tables 12.1 and 12.2) of the two countries have not changed, meaning that neither nation's production possibilities curve has shifted. But specialization and trade mean that citizens of both countries can enjoy increased consumption (column 5 of Table 12.4).

WORKED PROBLEMS

W 12.1

Gains from specialization

Trade with Increasing Costs

To explain the basic principles underlying international trade, we simplified our analysis in several ways. For example, we limited discussion to two products and two nations. But multiproduct and multinational analysis yields the same conclusions. We also assumed constant opportunity costs, which is a more substantive simplification. Let's consider the effect of allowing increasing opportunity costs to enter the picture.

TABLE 12.4 **Specialization According to Comparative Advantage and the Gains from Trade (in Tons)**

Country	(1) Outputs before Specialization	(2) Outputs after Specialization	(3) Amounts Traded	(4) Outputs Available after Trade	(5) Gains from Specialization and Trade (4) − (1)
Mexico	24 avocados	60 avocados	−35 avocados	25 avocados	1 avocados
	9 soybeans	0 soybeans	+10 soybeans	10 soybeans	1 soybeans
United States	33 avocados	0 avocados	+35 avocados	35 avocados	2 avocados
	19 soybeans	30 soybeans	−10 soybeans	20 soybeans	1 soybeans

As before, suppose that comparative advantage indicates that the United States should specialize in soybeans and Mexico in avocados. But now, as the United States begins to expand soybean production, its cost of soybeans will rise. It will eventually have to sacrifice more than 3 tons of avocados to get 1 additional ton of soybeans. Resources are no longer perfectly substitutable between alternative uses, as our constant-cost assumption implied. Resources less and less suitable to soybean production must be allocated to the U.S. soybean industry in expanding soybean output, and that means increasing costs—the sacrifice of larger and larger amounts of avocados for each additional ton of soybeans.

© Getty Images

Photo Op The Fruits of Free Trade*

Because of specialization and exchange, fruits from all over the world appear in our grocery stores. For example, apples may be from New Zealand; bananas, from Ecuador; coconuts, from the Philippines; pineapples, from Costa Rica; raspberries, from Mexico; plums, from Chile; and grapes, from Peru

* This example is from "The Fruits of Free Trade," Federal Reserve Bank of Dallas, Annual Report 2002, p. 3.

Similarly, Mexico will find that its cost of producing an additional ton of avocados will rise beyond 4 tons of soybeans as it produces more avocados. Resources transferred from soybean to avocado production will eventually be less suitable to avocado production.

At some point the differing domestic cost ratios that underlie comparative advantage will disappear, and further specialization will become uneconomical. And, most importantly, this point of equal cost ratios may be reached while the United States is still producing some avocados along with its soybeans and Mexico is producing some soybeans along with its avocados. The primary effect of increasing opportunity costs is less-than-complete specialization. For this reason we often find domestically produced products competing directly against identical or similar imported products within a particular economy.

The Foreign Exchange Market

Buyers and sellers (whether individuals, firms, or nations) use money to buy products or to pay for the use of resources. Within the domestic economy, prices are stated in terms of the domestic currency and buyers use that currency to purchase domestic products. In Mexico, for example, buyers have pesos, and that is what sellers want.

International markets are different. Sellers set their prices in terms of their domestic currencies, but buyers often possess entirely different currencies. How many dollars does it take to buy a truckload of Mexican avocados selling for 3000 pesos, a German automobile selling for 50,000 euros, or a Japanese motorcycle priced at 300,000 yen? Producers in Mexico, Germany, and Japan want payment in pesos, euros, and yen, respectively, so that they can pay their wages, rent, interest, dividends, and taxes.

A **foreign exchange market,** a market in which various national currencies are exchanged for one another, serves this need. The equilibrium prices in such currency markets are called **exchange rates.** An exchange rate is the rate at which the currency of one nation can be exchanged for the currency of another nation. (See Global Snapshot 12.3.)

foreign exchange market
A market in which foreign currencies are exchanged and relative currency prices are established.

exchange rates
The rates at which national currencies trade for one another.

GLOBAL SNAPSHOT 12.3

Exchange Rates: Foreign Currency per U.S. Dollar

The amount of foreign currency that a dollar will buy varies greatly from nation to nation and fluctuates in response to supply and demand changes in the foreign exchange market. The amounts shown here are for March 2008.

$1 Will Buy

40.33 Indian rupees
.50 British pounds
1.01 Canadian dollars
10.72 Mexican pesos
.997 Swiss francs
.64 European euros
98.7 Japanese yen
1010 South Korean won
6.01 Swedish kronors
2.14 Venezuelan bolivares fuertes

© PhotoLink/Getty Images/DIL

Photo Op Foreign Currencies

The world is awash with hundreds of national currencies. Currency markets determine the rates of exchange between them.

The market price or exchange rate of a nation's currency is an unusual price; it links all domestic prices with all foreign prices. Exchange rates enable consumers in one country to translate prices of foreign goods into units of their own currency: They need only multiply the foreign product price by the exchange rate. If the U.S. dollar–yen exchange rate is $.01 (1 cent) per yen, a Sony television set priced at ¥20,000 will cost $200 (=20,000 × $.01) in the United States. If the exchange rate rises to $.02 (2 cents) per yen, the television will cost $400 (=20,000 × $.02) in the United States. Similarly, all other Japanese products would double in price to U.S. buyers in response to the altered exchange rate.

Exchange Rates

INTERACTIVE GRAPHS

G 12.1

Exchange rates

Let's examine the rate, or price, at which U.S. dollars might be exchanged for British pounds. In Figure 12.1 we show the dollar price of 1 pound on the vertical axis and the quantity of pounds on the horizontal axis. The demand for pounds is D_1 and the supply of pounds is S_1 in this market for British pounds.

The *demand-for-pounds curve* is downward-sloping because all British goods and services will be cheaper to the United States if pounds become less expensive to the United States. That is, at lower dollar prices for pounds, the United States can obtain more pounds for each dollar and therefore buy more British goods and services per dollar. To buy those cheaper British goods, U.S. consumers will increase the quantity of pounds they demand.

FIGURE 12.1 **The market for foreign currency (pounds)** The intersection of the demand-for-pounds curve D_1 and the supply-of-pounds curve S_1 determines the equilibrium dollar price of pounds, here, $2. That means that the exchange rate is $2 = £1. The upward blue arrow is a reminder that a higher dollar price of pounds (say, $3 = £1, caused by a shift in either the demand or the supply curve) means that the dollar has depreciated (the pound has appreciated). The downward blue arrow tells us that a lower dollar price of pounds (say, $1 = £1, again caused by a shift in either the demand or the supply curve) means that the dollar has appreciated (the pound has depreciated).

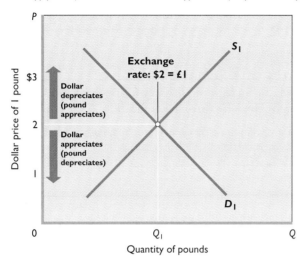

The *supply-of-pounds curve* slopes upward because the British will purchase more U.S. goods when the dollar price of pounds rises (that is, as the pound price of dollars falls). When the British buy more U.S. goods, they supply a greater quantity of pounds to the foreign exchange market. In other words, they must exchange pounds for dollars to purchase U.S. goods. So, when the dollar price of pounds rises, the quantity of pounds supplied goes up.

The intersection of the supply curve and the demand curve will determine the dollar price of pounds. In Figure 12.1, that price (exchange rate) is $2 for £1.

Depreciation and Appreciation

An exchange rate determined by market forces can, and often does, change daily like stock and bond prices. These price changes result from changes in the supply of, or demand for, a particular currency. When the dollar price of pounds *rises*, for example, from $2 = £1 to $3 = £1, the dollar has *depreciated* relative to the pound (and the pound has appreciated relative to the dollar). A **depreciation** of a currency means that more units of it (dollars) are needed to buy a single unit of some other currency (a pound).

When the dollar price of pounds *falls*, for example, from $2 = £1 to $1 = £1, the dollar has *appreciated* relative to the pound. An **appreciation** of a currency means that it takes fewer units of it (dollars) to buy a single unit of some other currency (a pound). For example, the dollar price of pounds might decline from $2 to $1. Each British product becomes less expensive in terms of dollars, so people in the United States purchase more British goods. In general, U.S. imports from the United Kingdom rise. Meanwhile, because it takes more pounds to get a dollar, U.S. exports to the United Kingdom fall.

The central point is this: When the dollar depreciates (dollar price of foreign currencies rises), U.S. exports rise and U.S. imports fall; when the dollar appreciates (dollar price of foreign currencies falls), U.S. exports fall and U.S. imports rise.

depreciation (of a currency)
A decrease in the value of a currency relative to another currency.

appreciation (of a currency)
An increase in the value of a currency relative to another currency.

In our U.S.-Britain illustrations, depreciation of the dollar means an appreciation of the pound, and vice versa. When the dollar price of a pound jumps from $2 = £1 to $3 = £1, the pound has appreciated relative to the dollar because it takes fewer pounds to buy $1. At $2 = £1, it took £1/2 to buy $1; at $3 = £1, it takes only £1/3 to buy $1. Conversely, when the dollar appreciates relative to the pound, the pound depreciates relative to the dollar. More pounds are needed to buy a U.S. dollar.

Determinants of Exchange Rates

What factors would cause a nation's currency to appreciate or depreciate in the market for foreign exchange? Here are three generalizations (other things equal):

- If the demand for a nation's currency increases, that currency will appreciate; if the demand declines, that currency will depreciate.
- If the supply of a nation's currency increases, that currency will depreciate; if the supply decreases, that currency will appreciate.
- If a nation's currency appreciates, some foreign currency depreciates relative to it.

With these generalizations in mind, let's examine the determinants of exchange rates—the factors that shift the demand or supply curve for a certain currency. As we do so, keep in mind that the other-things-equal assumption is always in force. Also note that we are discussing factors *that change the exchange rate*, not things that change *as a result of* a change in the exchange rate.

Tastes   Any change in consumer tastes or preferences for the products of a foreign country may alter the demand for that nation's currency and change its exchange rate. If technological advances in U.S. MP3 players make them more attractive to British consumers and businesses, then the British will supply more pounds in the exchange market in order to purchase more U.S. MP3 players. The supply-of-pounds curve will shift to the right, causing the pound to depreciate and the dollar to appreciate.

In contrast, the U.S. demand-for-pounds curve will shift to the right if British woolen apparel becomes more fashionable in the United States. So the pound will appreciate and the dollar will depreciate.

Relative Income   A nation's currency is likely to depreciate if its growth of national income is more rapid than that of other countries. Here's why: A country's imports vary directly with its income level. As total income rises in the United States, people there buy both more domestic goods and more foreign goods. If the U.S. economy is expanding rapidly and the British economy is stagnant, U.S. imports of British goods, and therefore U.S. demands for pounds, will increase. The dollar price of pounds will rise, so the dollar will depreciate.

Relative Price Levels   Changes in the relative price levels of two nations may change the demand for and supply of currencies and alter the exchange rate between the two nations' currencies. If, for example, the domestic price level rises rapidly in the United States and remains constant in Great Britain, U.S. consumers will seek out low-priced British goods, increasing the demand for pounds. The British will purchase fewer U.S. goods, reducing the supply of pounds. This combination of demand and supply changes will cause the pound to appreciate and the dollar to depreciate.

Relative Interest Rates Changes in relative interest rates between two countries may alter their exchange rate. Suppose that real interest rates rise in the United States but stay constant in Great Britain. British citizens will then find the United States a more attractive place in which to loan money directly or loan money indirectly by buying bonds. To make these loans, they will have to supply pounds in the foreign exchange market to obtain dollars. The increase in the supply of pounds results in depreciation of the pound and appreciation of the dollar.

Changes in Relative Expected Returns on Stocks, Real Estate, and Production Facilities International investing extends beyond buying foreign bonds. It includes international investments in stocks and real estate as well as foreign purchases of factories and production facilities. Other things equal, the extent of this foreign investment depends on relative expected returns. To make the investments, investors in one country must sell their currencies to purchase the foreign currencies needed for the foreign investments.

For instance, suppose that investing in England suddenly becomes more popular due to a more positive outlook regarding expected returns on stocks, real estate, and production facilities there. U.S. investors therefore will sell U.S. assets to buy more assets in England. The U.S. assets will be sold for dollars, which will then be brought to the foreign exchange market and exchanged for pounds, which will in turn be used to purchase British assets. The increased demand for pounds in the foreign exchange market will cause the pound to appreciate and the dollar to depreciate.

Speculation Currency speculators are people who buy and sell currencies with an eye toward reselling or repurchasing them at a profit. Suppose that, as a group, speculators anticipate that the pound will appreciate and the dollar will depreciate. Speculators holding dollars will therefore try to convert them into pounds. This effort will increase the demand for pounds and cause the dollar price of pounds to rise (that is, cause the dollar to depreciate). A self-fulfilling prophecy occurs: The pound appreciates and the dollar depreciates because speculators act on the belief that these changes will in fact take place. In this way, speculation can cause changes in exchange rates.

Government and Trade

If people and nations benefit from specialization and international exchange, why do governments sometimes try to restrict the free flow of imports or encourage exports? What kinds of world trade barriers can governments erect, and why would they do so?

Trade Protections and Subsidies

Trade interventions by government take several forms. Excise taxes on imported goods are called **tariffs.** A *protective tariff* is designed to shield domestic producers from foreign competition. Such tariffs impede free trade by causing a rise in the prices of imported goods, thereby shifting demand toward domestic products. An excise tax on imported shoes, for example, would make domestically produced shoes more attractive to consumers. Although protective tariffs are usually not high enough to stop the importation of foreign goods, they put foreign producers at a competitive disadvantage in selling in domestic markets.

tariffs
Taxes imposed by a nation on imported goods.

import quotas
Limits imposed by nations on the quantities (or total values) of goods that may be imported during some period of time.

nontariff barriers (NTBs)
All impediments other than protective tariffs that nations establish to impede imports, including import quotas, licensing requirements, unreasonable product-quality standards, and unnecessary bureaucratic detail in customs procedures.

voluntary export restriction (VER)
An agreement by countries or foreign firms to limit their exports to a certain foreign nation to avoid enactment of formal trade barriers by that nation.

export subsidies
Government payments to domestic producers to enable them to reduce the price of a product to foreign buyers.

ORIGIN OF THE IDEA

O 12.2
Mercantilism

Import quotas are limits on the quantities or total value of specific items that may be imported. Once a quota is "filled," further imports of that product are choked off. Import quotas are more effective than tariffs in retarding international commerce. With a tariff, a product can go on being imported in large quantities; with an import quota, however, all imports are prohibited once the quota is filled.

Nontariff barriers (NTBs) include onerous licensing requirements, unreasonable standards pertaining to product quality, or excessive bureaucratic hurdles and delays in customs procedures. Some nations require that importers of foreign goods obtain licenses. By restricting the issuance of licenses, imports can be restricted. Although many nations carefully inspect imported agricultural products to prevent the introduction of potentially harmful insects, some countries use lengthy inspections to impede imports.

A **voluntary export restriction (VER)** is a trade barrier by which foreign firms "voluntarily" limit the amount of their exports to a particular country. Exporters agree to a VER, which has the effect of an import quota, to avoid more stringent trade barriers. In the late 1990s, for example, Canadian producers of softwood lumber (fir, spruce, cedar, pine) agreed to a VER on exports to the United States under the threat of a permanently higher U.S. tariff.

Export subsidies consist of government payments to domestic producers of export goods. By reducing production costs, the subsidies enable producers to charge lower prices and thus to sell more exports in world markets. Example: The United States and other nations have subsidized domestic farmers to boost the domestic food supply. Such subsidies have lowered the market price of agricultural commodities and have artificially lowered their export prices.

Economic Impact of Tariffs

Tariffs, quotas, and other trade restrictions have a series of economic effects predicted by supply and demand analysis and observed in reality. These effects vary somewhat by type of trade protection. So to keep things simple, we will focus on the effects of tariffs.

Direct Effects Because tariffs raise the price of goods imported to the United States, U.S. consumption of those goods declines. Higher prices reduce quantity demanded, as indicated by the law of demand. A tariff prompts consumers to buy fewer of the imported goods and reallocate a portion of their expenditures to less desired substitute products. U.S. consumers are clearly injured by the tariff.

U.S. producers—who are not subject to the tariff—receive the higher price (pretariff foreign price + tariff) on the imported product. Because this new price is higher than before, the domestic producers respond by producing more. Higher prices increase quantity supplied, as indicated by the law of supply. So domestic producers increase their output. They therefore enjoy both a higher price and expanded sales; this explains why domestic producers lobby for protective tariffs. But from a social point of view, the greater domestic production means the tariff allows domestic producers to bid resources away from other, more efficient, U.S. industries.

Foreign producers are hurt by tariffs. Although the sales price of the imported good is higher, that higher amount accrues to the U.S. government as tariff revenues, not to foreign producers. The after-tariff price, or the per-unit revenue to foreign producers, remains as before, but the volume of U.S. imports (foreign exports) falls.

Government gains revenue from tariffs. This revenue is a transfer of income from consumers to government and does not represent any net change in the nation's economic well-being. The result is that government gains a portion of what consumers lose by paying more for imported goods.

Indirect Effects   Tariffs have a subtle effect beyond those just mentioned. They also hurt domestic firms that use the protected goods as inputs in their production process. For example, a tariff on imported steel boosts the price of steel girders, thus hurting firms that build bridges and office towers. Also, tariffs reduce competition in the protected industries. With less competition from foreign producers, domestic firms may be slow to design and implement cost-saving production methods and introduce new products.

Because foreigners sell fewer imported goods in the United States, they earn fewer dollars and so must buy fewer U.S. exports. U.S. export industries must then cut production and release resources. These are highly efficient industries, as we know from their comparative advantage and their ability to sell goods in world markets.

Tariffs directly promote the expansion of inefficient industries that do not have a comparative advantage; they also indirectly cause the contraction of relatively efficient industries that do have a comparative advantage. Put bluntly, tariffs cause resources to be shifted in the wrong direction—and that is not surprising. We know that specialization and world trade lead to more efficient use of world resources and greater world output. But protective tariffs reduce world trade. Therefore, tariffs also reduce efficiency and the world's real output.

Net Costs of Tariffs

Tariffs impose costs on domestic consumers but provide gains to domestic producers and revenue to the Federal government. The consumer costs of trade restrictions are calculated by determining the effect the restrictions have on consumer prices. Protection raises the price of a product in three ways: (1) The price of the imported product goes up; (2) the higher price of imports causes some consumers to shift their purchases to higher-priced domestically produced goods; and (3) the prices of domestically produced goods rise because import competition has declined.

Study after study finds that the costs to consumers substantially exceed the gains to producers and government. A sizable net cost or efficiency loss to society arises from trade protection. Furthermore, industries employ large amounts of economic resources to influence Congress to pass and retain protectionist laws. Because these efforts divert resources away from more socially desirable purposes, trade restrictions also impose that cost on society.

Conclusion: The gains that U.S. trade barriers produce for protected industries and their workers come at the expense of much greater losses for the entire economy. The result is economic inefficiency, reduced consumption, and lower standards of living.

So Why Government Trade Protections?

In view of the benefits of free trade, what accounts for the impulse to impede imports and boost exports through government policy? There are several reasons—some legitimate, most not.

Misunderstanding the Gains from Trade   It is a commonly accepted myth that the greatest benefit to be derived from international trade is greater domestic sales and employment in the export sector. This suggests that exports are "good" because they increase domestic sales and employment, whereas imports are "bad" because they reduce domestic sales and deprive people of jobs at home. Actually, the true benefit created by international trade is the extra output obtained from abroad—the imports obtained for a lower opportunity cost than if they were produced at home.

A recent study suggests that the elimination of trade barriers since the Second World War has increased the income of the average U.S. household by at least $7000 and perhaps by as much as $13,000. These income gains are recurring; they happen year after year.[2]

Political Considerations

While a nation as a whole gains from trade, trade may harm particular domestic industries and particular groups of resource suppliers. In our earlier comparative-advantage example, specialization and trade adversely affected the U.S. avocado industry and the Mexican soybean industry. Understandably, those industries might seek to preserve their economic positions by persuading their respective governments to protect them from imports—perhaps through tariffs.

Those who directly benefit from import protection are relatively few in number but have much at stake. Thus, they have a strong incentive to pursue political activity to achieve their aims. Moreover, because the costs of import protection are buried in the price of goods and spread out over millions of citizens, the cost borne by each individual citizen is quite small. However, the full cost of tariffs and quotas typically greatly exceeds the benefits. It is not uncommon to find that it costs the public $250,000 or more a year to protect a domestic job that pays less than one-fourth that amount.

In the political arena, the voice of the relatively few producers and unions demanding *protectionism* is loud and constant, whereas the voice of those footing the bill is soft or nonexistent. When political deal making is added in—"You back tariffs for the apparel industry in my state, and I'll back tariffs for the steel industry in your state"—the outcome can be a network of protective tariffs.

ILLUSTRATING THE IDEA

Buy American?

Will "buying American" make Americans better off? No, says Dallas Federal Reserve economist W. Michael Cox:

> A common myth is that it is better for Americans to spend their money at home than abroad. The best way to expose the fallacy of this argument is to take it to its logical extreme. If it is better for me to spend my money here than abroad, then it is even better yet to buy in Texas than in New York, better yet to buy in Dallas than in Houston . . . in my own neighborhood . . . within my own family . . . to consume only what I can produce. Alone and poor.*

* "The Fruits of Free Trade," Federal Reserve Bank of Dallas, Annual Report 2002, p. 16.

---

[2] Scott C. Bradford, Paul L.E. Grieco, and Gary C. Hufbauer, "The Payoff to America from Globalization," *The World Economy,* July 2006, pp. 893–916.

Three Arguments for Protection

Arguments for trade protection are many and diverse. Some—such as tariffs to protect "infant industries" or to create "military self-sufficiency"—have some legitimacy. But other arguments break down under close scrutiny. Three protectionist arguments, in particular, have persisted decade after decade in the United States.

Increased Domestic Employment Argument

Arguing for a tariff to "save U.S. jobs" becomes fashionable when the economy encounters a recession or experiences slow job growth during a recovery (as in the early 2000s in the United States). In an economy that engages in international trade, exports involve spending on domestic output and imports reflect spending to obtain part of another nation's output. So, in this argument, reducing imports will divert spending on another nation's output to spending on domestic output. Thus domestic output and employment will rise. But this argument has several shortcomings.

While imports may eliminate some U.S. jobs, they create others. Imports may have eliminated the jobs of some U.S. steel and textile workers in recent years, but other workers have gained jobs unloading ships, flying imported aircraft, and selling imported electronic equipment. Import restrictions alter the composition of employment, but they may have little or no effect on the volume of employment.

The *fallacy of composition*—the false idea that what is true for the part is necessarily true for the whole—is also present in this rationale for tariffs. All nations cannot simultaneously succeed in restricting imports while maintaining their exports; what is true for one nation is not true for all nations. The exports of one nation must be the imports of another nation. To the extent that one country is able to expand its economy through an excess of exports over imports, the resulting excess of imports over exports worsens another economy's unemployment problem. It is no wonder that tariffs and import quotas meant to achieve domestic full employment are called "beggar my neighbor" policies: They achieve short-run domestic goals by making trading partners poorer.

Moreover, nations adversely affected by tariffs and quotas are likely to retaliate, causing a "trade-barrier war" that will choke off trade and make all nations worse off. The **Smoot-Hawley Tariff Act** of 1930 is a classic example. Although that act was meant to reduce imports and stimulate U.S. production, the high tariffs it authorized prompted adversely affected nations to retaliate with tariffs equally high. International trade fell, lowering the output and income of all nations. Economic historians generally agree that the Smoot-Hawley Tariff Act was a contributing cause of the Great Depression.

Finally, forcing an excess of exports over imports cannot succeed in raising domestic employment over the long run. It is through U.S. imports that foreign nations earn dollars for buying U.S. exports. In the long run a nation must import in order to export. The long-run impact of tariffs is not an increase in domestic employment but, at best, a reallocation of workers away from export industries and to protected domestic industries. This shift implies a less efficient allocation of resources.

Smoot-Hawley Tariff Act
Legislation passed in 1930 that established very high U.S. tariffs designed to reduce imports and stimulate the domestic economy. Instead, the law resulted only in retaliatory tariffs by other nations and a decline in trade worldwide.

Cheap Foreign Labor Argument

The cheap foreign labor argument says that government must shield domestic firms and workers from the ruinous competition of countries where wages are low. If protection is not provided, cheap imports will flood U.S. markets and the prices of U.S. goods—along with the wages of U.S. workers—will be pulled down. That is, the domestic living standards in the United States will be reduced.

This argument can be rebutted at several levels. The logic of the argument suggests that it is not mutually beneficial for rich and poor persons to trade with one another. However, that is not the case. A relatively low-income mechanic may fix the Mercedes owned by a wealthy lawyer, and both may benefit from the transaction. And both U.S. consumers and Chinese workers gain when they "trade" a pair of athletic shoes priced at $30 as opposed to U.S. consumers being restricted to a similar shoe made in the U.S. for $60.

Also, recall that gains from trade are based on comparative advantage, not on absolute advantage. Again, think back to our U.S.-Mexico (soybean-avocado) example in which the United States had greater labor productivity than Mexico in producing both soybeans and avocados. Because of that greater productivity, wages and living standards will be higher for U.S. labor. Mexico's less productive labor will receive lower wages.

The cheap foreign labor argument suggests that, to maintain American living standards, the United States should not trade with low-wage Mexico. Suppose it forgoes trade with Mexico. Will wages and living standards rise in the United States as a result? Absolutely not! To obtain avocados, the United States will have to reallocate a portion of its labor from its relatively efficient soybean industry to its relatively inefficient avocado industry. As a result, the average productivity of U.S. labor will fall, as will real wages and living standards for American workers. The labor forces of both countries will have diminished standards of living because without specialization and trade they will have less output available to them. Compare column 4 with column 1 in Table 12.4 to confirm this point.

Protection-against-Dumping Argument

The protection-against dumping argument contends that tariffs are needed to protect domestic firms from "dumping" by foreign producers. **Dumping** is the sale of a product in a foreign country at prices either below cost or below the prices commonly charged at home.

dumping
The sale of products in a foreign country at prices either below costs or below the prices charged at home.

Economists cite two plausible reasons for this behavior. First, with regard to below-cost dumping, firms in country A may dump goods at below cost into country B in an attempt to drive their competitors in country B out of business. If the firms in country A succeed in driving their competitors in country B out of business, they will enjoy monopoly power and monopoly prices and profits on the goods they subsequently sell in country B. Their hope is that the longer-term monopoly profits will more than offset the losses from below-cost sales that must take place while they are attempting to drive their competitors in country B out of business.

Second, dumping that involves selling abroad at a price that is below the price commonly charged in the home country (but which is still at or above production costs) may be a form of price discrimination, which is charging different prices to different customers. As an example, a foreign seller that has a monopoly in its home market may find that it can maximize its overall profit by charging a high price in its monopolized domestic market while charging a lower price in the United States, where it must compete with U.S. producers. Curiously, it may pursue this strategy even if it makes no profit at all from its sales in the United States, where it must charge the competitive price. So why bother selling in the United States? Because the increase in overall production that comes about by exporting to the United States may allow the firm to obtain the per unit cost savings often associated with large-scale production. These cost savings imply even higher profits in the monopolized domestic market.

Because dumping is an "unfair trade practice," most nations prohibit it. For example, where dumping is shown to injure U.S. firms, the Federal government imposes tariffs called *antidumping duties* on the goods in question. But relatively few documented cases of dumping occur each year, and specific instances of unfair trade do not justify widespread, permanent tariffs. Moreover, antidumping duties can be abused. Often, what appears to be dumping is simply comparative advantage at work.

Trade Adjustment Assistance

A nation's comparative advantage in the production of a certain product is not forever fixed. As national economies evolve, the size and quality of their labor forces may change, the volume and composition of their capital stocks may shift, new technologies may develop, and even the quality of land and the quantity of natural resources may be altered. As these changes take place, the relative efficiency with which a nation can produce specific goods will also change. Also, new trade agreements can suddenly leave formerly protected industries highly vulnerable to major disruption or even collapse.

Shifts in patterns of comparative advantage and removal of trade protection can hurt specific groups of workers. For example, the erosion of the United States' once strong comparative advantage in steel has caused production plant shutdowns and layoffs in the U.S. steel industry. The textile and apparel industries in the United States face similar difficulties. Clearly, not everyone wins from free trade (or freer trade). Some workers lose.

The **Trade Adjustment Assistance Act** of 2002 introduced some new, novel elements to help those hurt by shifts in international trade patterns. The law provides cash assistance (beyond unemployment insurance) for up to 78 weeks for workers displaced by imports or plant relocations abroad. To obtain the assistance, workers must participate in job searches, training programs, or remedial education. There also are relocation allowances to help displaced workers move geographically to new jobs within the United States. Refundable tax credits for health insurance serve as payments to help workers maintain their insurance coverage during the retraining and job search period. Also, workers who are 50 years of age or older are eligible for "wage insurance," which replaces some of the difference in pay (if any) between their old and new jobs.

Many economists support trade adjustment assistance because it not only helps workers hurt by international trade but also helps create the political support necessary to reduce trade barriers and export subsidies.

But not all economists are keen on trade adjustment assistance. Loss of jobs from imports or plant relocations abroad is only a small fraction (about 4 percent in recent years) of total job loss in the economy each year. Many workers also lose their jobs because of changing patterns of demand, changing technology, bad management, and other dynamic aspects of a market economy. Some critics ask, "What makes losing one's job to international trade worthy of such special treatment, compared to losing one's job to, say, technological change or domestic competition?" There is no totally satisfying answer.

Trade Adjustment Assistance Act
A U.S. law passed in 2002 that provides cash assistance, education and training benefits, health care subsidies, and wage subsidies (for persons age 50 or more) to workers displaced by imports or plant relocations abroad.

Is Offshoring of Jobs Bad?

offshoring
The practice of shifting work previously done by American workers to workers located in other nations.

In recent years U.S. firms have found it increasingly profitable to outsource work abroad. Economists call this business activity **offshoring:** shifting work previously done by American workers to workers located in other nations. Offshoring is not a new practice but traditionally has involved components for U.S. manufacturing goods. For example, Boeing has long offshored the production of major airplane parts for its "American" aircraft.

Recent advances in computer and communications technology have enabled U.S. firms to offshore service jobs such as data entry, book composition, software coding, call-center operations, medical transcription, and claims processing to countries such as India. Where offshoring occurs, some of the value added in the production process occurs in foreign countries rather than the United States. So part of the income generated from the production of U.S. goods is paid to foreigners, not to American workers.

Offshoring is obviously costly to Americans who lose their jobs, but it is not generally bad for the economy. Offshoring simply reflects a growing international trade in services, or, more descriptively, "tasks." That trade has been made possible by recent trade agreements and new information and communication technologies. As with trade in goods, trade in services reflects comparative advantage and is beneficial to both trading parties. Moreover, the United States has a sizable trade surplus with other nations in services. The United States gains by specializing in high-valued services such as transportation services, accounting services, legal services, and advertising services, where it still has a comparative advantage. It then "trades" to obtain lower-valued services such as call-center and data entry work, for which comparative advantage has gone abroad.

Offshoring also increases the demand for complementary jobs in the United States. Jobs that are close substitutes for existing U.S. jobs are lost, but complementary jobs in the United States are expanded. For example, the lower price of offshore maintenance of aircraft and reservation centers reduces the price of airline tickets. That means more domestic and international flights by American carriers, which in turn means more jobs for U.S.-based pilots, flight attendants, baggage handlers, and check-in personnel. Moreover, offshoring encourages domestic investment and expansion of firms in the United States by reducing their production costs and keeping them competitive worldwide. Some observers equate "offshoring jobs" to "importing competitiveness."

Question:
What has enabled white-collar labor services to become the world's newest export and import commodity even though such labor itself remains in place?

Multilateral Trade Agreements and Free-Trade Zones

Being aware of the overall benefits of free trade, nations have worked to lower tariffs worldwide. Their pursuit of free trade has been aided by the growing power of free-trade interest groups: Exporters of goods and services, importers of foreign

CHAPTER 12 **287**
International Trade and Exchange Rates

components used in "domestic" products, and domestic sellers of imported products all strongly support lower tariffs. And, in fact, tariffs have generally declined during the past half-century.

General Agreement on Tariffs and Trade

Following the Second World War, the major nations of the world set upon a general course of liberalizing trade. In 1947 some 23 nations, including the United States, signed the **General Agreement on Tariffs and Trade (GATT).** GATT was based on the principles of equal, nondiscriminatory trade treatment for all member nations and the reduction of tariffs and quotas by multilateral negotiation. Basically, GATT provided a continuing forum for the negotiation of reduced trade barriers on a multilateral basis among nations.

Since 1947, member nations have completed eight "rounds" of GATT negotiations to reduce trade barriers. The *Uruguay Round* agreement of 1993 phased in trade liberalizations between 1995 and 2005.

World Trade Organization

The Uruguay Round of 1993 established the **World Trade Organization (WTO)** as GATT's successor. In 2008, 153 nations belonged to the WTO, which oversees trade agreements and rules on disputes relating to them. It also provides forums for further rounds of trade negotiations. The ninth and latest round of negotiations—the **Doha Round**—was launched in Doha, Qatar, in late 2001. (The trade rounds occur over several years in several geographic venues but are named after the city or country of origination.) The negotiations are aimed at further reducing tariffs and quotas, as well as agricultural subsidies that distort trade. One of this chapter's questions asks you to update the progress of the Doha Round via an Internet search.

GATT and the WTO have been positive forces in the trend toward liberalized world trade. The trade rules agreed upon by the member nations provide a strong and necessary bulwark against the protectionism called for by the special-interest groups in the various nations. For that reason and because current WTO agreements lack strong labor standards and environmental protections, the WTO is controversial.

European Union

Countries have also sought to reduce tariffs by creating regional *free-trade zones*—also called *trade blocs*. The most dramatic example is the **European Union (EU).** In 2007, the addition of Bulgaria and Romania expanded the EU to 27 nations.[3]

The EU has abolished tariffs and import quotas on nearly all products traded among the participating nations and established a common system of tariffs applicable to all goods received from nations outside the EU. It has also liberalized the movement of capital and labor within the EU and has created common policies in other economic matters of joint concern, such as agriculture, transportation, and business

General Agreement on Tariffs and Trade (GATT)
An international accord reached in 1947 in which 23 nations agreed to give equal and nondiscriminatory treatment to one another, to reduce tariffs through multinational negotiations, and to eliminate import quotas.

World Trade Organization (WTO)
An organization of 153 nations (as of 2008) that oversees the provisions of the current world trade agreement, resolves disputes stemming from it, and holds forums for further rounds of trade negotiations.

Doha Round
The latest, uncompleted (as of 2008) sequence of trade negotiations by members of the World Trade Organization; named after Doha, Qatar, where the set of negotiations began.

European Union (EU)
An association of 27 European nations that has eliminated tariffs and quotas among them, established common tariffs for imported goods from outside the member nations, reduced barriers to the free movement of capital, and created other common economic policies.

---

[3] The other 25 are France, Germany, United Kingdom, Italy, Belgium, the Netherlands, Luxembourg, Denmark, Ireland, Greece, Spain, Portugal, Austria, Finland, Sweden, Poland, Hungary, Czech Republic, Slovakia, Lithuania, Latvia, Estonia, Slovenia, Malta, and Cyprus.

trade bloc
A group of nations that lower or abolish trade barriers among themselves.

euro
The common currency unit used by 15 (as of 2008) European nations in the European Union.

practices. The EU is now a strong **trade bloc:** a group of countries having common identity, economic interests, and trade rules. Of the 27 EU countries, 15 used the **euro** as a common currency in 2008.

EU integration has achieved for Europe what the U.S. constitutional prohibition on tariffs by individual states has achieved for the United States: increased regional specialization, greater productivity, greater output, and faster economic growth. The free flow of goods and services has created large markets for EU industries. The resulting economies of large-scale production have enabled those industries to achieve much lower costs than they could have achieved in their small, single-nation markets.

North American Free Trade Agreement

North American Free Trade Agreement (NAFTA)
A 1993 agreement establishing, over a 15-year period, a free-trade zone composed of Canada, Mexico, and the United States.

In 1993 Canada, Mexico, and the United States formed a major trade bloc. The **North American Free Trade Agreement (NAFTA)** established a free-trade zone that has about the same combined output as the EU but encompasses a much larger geographic area. NAFTA has eliminated tariffs and other trade barriers between Canada, Mexico, and the United States for most goods and services.

Critics of NAFTA feared that it would cause a massive loss of U.S. jobs as firms moved to Mexico to take advantage of lower wages and weaker regulations on pollution and workplace safety. Also, there was concern that Japan and South Korea would build plants in Mexico and transport goods tariff-free to the United States, further hurting U.S. firms and workers.

In retrospect, critics were much too pessimistic. Since the passage of NAFTA in 1993, employment in the United States rose by more than 22 million workers and the unemployment rate fell from 6.9 percent to 4.7 percent. Increased trade between Canada, Mexico, and the United States has enhanced the standard of living in all three countries.

Not all aspects of trade blocs are positive. By giving preferences to countries within their free-trade zones, trade blocs such as the EU and NAFTA tend to reduce their members' trade with non-bloc members. Thus, the world loses some of the benefits of a completely open global trading system. Eliminating that disadvantage has been one of the motivations for liberalizing global trade through the World Trade Organization. Its liberalizations apply equally to all 153 nations that belong to the WTO.

U.S. Trade Deficits

As indicated in Figure 12.2, the United States has experienced large and persistent trade deficits over the past several years. These deficits climbed steeply between 1994 and 2000, fell slightly in the recessionary year 2001, and rose again between 2002 and 2007. In 2007 the trade deficit on goods was $816 billion and the trade deficit on goods and services was $709 billion. Large trade deficits are expected to continue for many years.

Causes of the Trade Deficits

There are several reasons for these large trade deficits. First, over recent years the U.S. economy has grown more rapidly than the economies of several of its major trading partners. The strong growth of U.S. income that accompanies economic growth has enabled Americans to buy more imported goods. In contrast, Japan and some European nations have either suffered recession or experienced slow income growth. So their

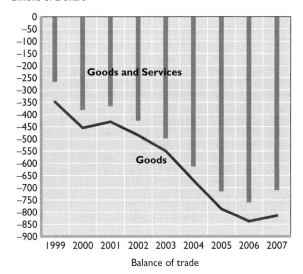

Billions of Dollars

FIGURE 12.2 U.S. trade deficits, 1999–2007. The United States experienced large deficits in goods and in goods and services between 1999 and 2007. These deficits have steadily increased, dipping only slightly in 2001 and 2007. They are expected to continue at least throughout the current decade. Source: U.S. Census Bureau, Foreign Trade Division, **www.census.gov/foreign-trade/ statistics.**

purchases of U.S. exports have not kept pace with the growing U.S. imports. Large trade deficits with Japan and Germany have been particularly noteworthy in this regard.

Second, large trade deficits with China have emerged, reaching $257 billion in 2007. This is even greater than the U.S. trade imbalance with Japan ($85 billion in 2007) or OPEC countries ($125 billion in 2007). The United States is China's largest export market, and although China has increased its imports from the United States, its standard of living has not yet increased enough for its citizens to afford large quantities of U.S. goods and services.

Finally, a declining U.S. saving rate (=saving/total income) undoubtedly has also contributed to U.S. trade deficits. Over the last 10 years, the saving rate has diminished while the investment rate (=investment/total income) has remained stable or increased. The gap between saving and investment has been met through foreign purchases of U.S. real and financial assets. Because foreign savers are willingly financing a larger part of U.S. investment, Americans are able to save less than otherwise and consume more. Part of that added consumption spending is on imported goods. That is, the inflow of funds from abroad may be one cause of the trade deficits, not just a result of those deficits.

The U.S. recession of 2001 temporarily lowered income and reduced U.S. imports and trade deficits. But the general trend toward higher trade deficits quickly reemerged in 2002 and ballooned until 2007, when they dipped slightly (though still remaining high).

Implications of U.S. Trade Deficits

There is disagreement on whether the large trade deficits should be of major policy concern for the United States. Most economists see both benefits and costs to trade deficits but are increasingly anxious about the size of these deficits.

Increased Current Consumption
At the time a trade deficit is occurring, American consumers benefit. A trade deficit means that the United States is receiving

more goods and services as imports from abroad than it is sending out as exports. Taken alone, a trade deficit augments the domestic standard of living. But there is a catch: The gain in present consumption may come at the expense of reduced future consumption.

Increased U.S. Indebtedness

A trade deficit is considered "unfavorable" because it must be financed by borrowing from the rest of the world, selling off assets, or dipping into foreign currency reserves. Trade deficits are financed primarily by net inpayments of foreign currencies to the United States. When U.S. exports are insufficient to finance U.S. imports, the United States increases both its debt to people abroad and the value of foreign claims against assets in the United States. Financing of the U.S. trade deficit has resulted in a larger foreign accumulation of claims against U.S. financial and real assets than the U.S. claim against foreign assets. In 2006, foreigners owned about $2.5 trillion more of U.S. assets (corporations, land, stocks, bonds, loan notes) than U.S. citizens and institutions owned of foreign assets.

If the United States wants to regain ownership of these domestic assets, at some future time it will have to export more than it imports. At that time, domestic consumption will be lower because the United States will need to send more of its output abroad than it receives as imports. Therefore, the current consumption gains delivered by U.S. current account deficits may mean permanent debt, permanent foreign ownership, or large sacrifices of future consumption.

We say "may mean" above because the foreign lending to U.S. firms and foreign investment in the United States increase the stock of American capital. U.S. production capacity might increase more rapidly than otherwise because of a large inflow of funds to offset the trade deficits. We know that faster increases in production capacity and real GDP enhance the economy's ability to service foreign debt and buy back real capital, if that is desired.

Downward Pressure on the Dollar

Finally, the large U.S. trade deficits place downward pressure on the exchange value of the U.S. dollar. The surge of imports requires the United States to supply dollars in the currency market in order to obtain the foreign currencies required for purchasing the imported goods. That flood of dollars into the currency market causes the dollar to depreciate relative to other currencies. Between 2002 and 2008, the dollar depreciated against most other currencies, including 43 percent against the European euro, 27 percent against the British pound, 37 percent against the Canadian dollar, 15 percent against the Chinese yuan, and 25 percent against the Japanese yen. Some of this depreciation was fueled by the expansionary monetary policy (reduced real interest rates) undertaken by the Fed beginning in 2007 and carrying into 2008 (discussed in Chapter 10). Economists feared that the decline in the dollar would contribute to inflation as imports became more expensive to Americans in dollar terms. Traditionally the Fed would need to react to that inflation with a tight monetary policy that raises real interest rates in the United States. In 2008, however, the U.S. economy severely receded, largely as a result of spillover damage from the mortgage debt crisis and the decline in housing demand. The Fed chose to aggressively reduce interest rates, hoping to halt the downturn in the economy. In effect, it gambled that its actions would not ignite inflation because of the dampening effect of the severe economic recession on rising prices.

Summary

1. The United States leads the world in the volume of international trade, but trade is much larger as a percentage of GDP in many other nations.

2. Mutually advantageous specialization and trade are possible between any two nations if they have different domestic opportunity-cost ratios for any two products. By specializing on the basis of comparative advantage, nations can obtain larger real incomes with fixed amounts of resources. The terms of trade determine how this increase in world output is shared by the trading nations. Increasing costs lead to less-than-complete specialization for many tradable goods.

3. The foreign exchange market establishes exchange rates between currencies. Each nation's purchases from abroad create a supply of its own currency and a demand for foreign currencies. The resulting supply-demand equilibrium sets the exchange rate that links the currencies of all nations. Depreciation of a nation's currency reduces its imports and increases its exports; appreciation increases its imports and reduces its exports.

4. Currencies will depreciate or appreciate as a result of changes in their supply or demand, which in turn depend on changes in tastes for foreign goods, relative changes in national incomes, changes in relative price levels, changes in interest rates, and the extent and direction of currency speculation.

5. Trade barriers and subsidies take the form of protective tariffs, quotas, nontariff barriers, voluntary export restrictions, and export subsidies. Protective tariffs increase the prices and reduce the quantities demanded of the affected goods. Sales by foreign exporters diminish; domestic producers, however, gain higher prices and enlarged sales. Consumer losses from trade restrictions greatly exceed producer and government gains, creating an efficiency loss to society.

6. Three recurring arguments for free trade—increased domestic employment, cheap foreign labor, and protection against dumping—are either fallacies or overstatements that do not hold up under careful economic analysis.

7. Not everyone benefits from free (or freer) trade. The Trade Adjustment Assistance Act of 2002 provides cash assistance, education and training benefits, health care subsidies, and wage subsidies (for persons 50 years old or more) to workers who are displaced by imports or plant relocations abroad. But less than 4 percent of all job losses in the United States each year result from imports, plant relocations, or the offshoring of service jobs.

8. In 2008 the World Trade Organization (WTO) consisted of 153 member nations. The WTO oversees trade agreements among the members, resolves disputes over the rules, and periodically meets to discuss and negotiate further trade liberalization. In 2001 the WTO initiated a new round of trade negotiations in Doha, Qatar. The Doha Round (named after its place of initiation) will continue over the next several years.

9. Free-trade zones (trade blocs) liberalize trade within regions but may at the same time impede trade with non-bloc members. Two examples of free-trade arrangements are the 27-member European Union (EU) and the North American Free Trade Agreement (NAFTA), comprising Canada, Mexico, and the United States. Fifteen of the EU nations (as of 2008) have abandoned their national currencies for a common currency called the euro.

10. U.S. trade deficits have produced current increases in the livings standards of U.S. consumers. But the deficits have also increased U.S. debt to the rest of the world and increased foreign ownership of assets in the United States. This greater foreign investment in the United States, however, has undoubtedly increased U.S. production possibilities. The trade deficits also place extreme downward pressure on the international value of the U.S. dollar.

Terms and Concepts

comparative advantage

terms of trade

foreign exchange market

exchange rates

depreciation

appreciation

tariffs

import quotas

nontariff barriers (NTBs)

voluntary export restriction (VER)

export subsidies

Smoot-Hawley Tariff Act

dumping

Trade Adjustment Assistance Act

offshoring

General Agreement on Tariffs and Trade (GATT)

World Trade Organization (WTO)

Doha Round

European Union (EU)

trade bloc

euro

North American Free Trade Agreement (NAFTA)

Study Questions ⬛ connect™
economics

1. Quantitatively, how important is international trade to the United States relative to its importance to other nations? What country is the United States' most important trading partner, quantitatively? With what country does the United States have the largest current trade deficit? **LO1**

2. Below are hypothetical production possibilities tables for New Zealand and Spain. Each country can produce apples and plums. **LO2**

New Zealand's Production Possibilities Table
(Millions of Bushels)

	Production Alternatives			
Product	A	B	C	D
Apples	0	20	40	60
Plums	15	10	5	0

Spain's Production Possibilities Table
(Millions of Bushels)

	Production Alternatives			
Product	R	S	T	U
Apples	0	20	40	60
Plums	60	40	20	0

Referring to the tables, answer the following:

a. What is each country's cost ratio of producing plums and apples?

b. Which nation should specialize in which product?

c. Suppose the optimal product mixes before specialization and trade are alternative B in New Zealand and alternative S in Spain and the actual terms of trade are 1 plum for 2 apples. What will be the gains from specialization and trade?

3. The following are production possibilities tables for South Korea and the United States. Assume that before specialization and trade the optimal product mix for South Korea is alternative B and for the United States is alternative U. **LO2**

South Korea Production Possibilities

Product	A	B	C	D	E	F
LCD displays (in thousands)	30	24	18	12	6	0
Chemicals (in tons)	0	6	12	18	24	30

U.S. Production Possibilities

Product	R	S	T	U	V	W
LCD displays (in thousands)	10	8	6	4	2	0
Chemicals (in tons)	0	4	8	12	16	20

a. Are comparative-cost conditions such that the two areas should specialize? If so, which product should each produce?

b. What is the total gain in LCD displays and chemical output that would result from such specialization?

c. What are the limits of the terms of trade? Suppose actual terms of trade are $1\frac{1}{2}$ unit of LCD displays for units of chemicals and that 4 units of LCD displays are exchanged for 6 units of chemicals. What are the gains from specialization and trade for each nation?

d. Explain why this illustration allows you to conclude that specialization according to comparative advantage results in a more efficient use of world resources.

4. What effect do rising costs (rather than constant costs) have on the extent of specialization and trade? Explain. **LO2**

5. What is offshoring of white-collar service jobs, and how does it relate to international trade? Why has it recently increased? Why do you think more than half of all offshored jobs have gone to India? Give an example (other than that in the textbook) of how offshoring can eliminate some U.S. jobs while creating other U.S. jobs. **LO2**

6. Explain why the U.S. demand for Mexican pesos is downward-sloping and the supply of pesos to Americans is upward-sloping. Indicate whether each of the following would cause the Mexican peso to appreciate or depreciate: **LO3**

a. The United States unilaterally reduces tariffs on Mexican products.

b. Mexico encounters severe inflation.

c. Deteriorating political relations reduce American tourism in Mexico.

d. The U.S. economy moves into a severe recession.

e. The United States engages in a high-interest-rate monetary policy.

f. Mexican products become more fashionable to U.S. consumers.

g. The Mexican government encourages U.S. firms to invest in Mexican oil fields.

7. Explain why you agree or disagree with the following statements: **LO3**

a. A country that grows faster than its major trading partners can expect the international value of its currency to depreciate.

b. A nation whose interest rate is rising more rapidly than interest rates in other nations can expect the international value of its currency to appreciate.

c. A country's currency will appreciate if its inflation rate is less than that of the rest of the world.

8. If the European euro were to depreciate relative to the U.S. dollar in the foreign exchange market, would it be easier or harder for the French to sell their wine in the United States? Suppose you were planning a trip to Paris. How would depreciation of the euro change the dollar cost of your trip? **LO3**

9. What measures do governments take to promote exports and restrict imports? Who benefits and who loses from protectionist policies? What is the net outcome for society? **LO4**

10. Speculate as to why some U.S. firms strongly support trade liberalization while other U.S. firms favor protectionism. Speculate as to why some U.S. labor unions strongly support trade liberalization while other U.S. labor unions strongly oppose it. **LO4**

11. Explain: "Free-trade zones such as the EU and NAFTA lead a double life: They can promote free trade among members, but they pose serious trade obstacles for nonmembers." Do you think the net effects of trade blocs are good or bad for world trade? Why? How do the efforts of the WTO relate to these trade blocs? **LO5**

12. What is the WTO, and how does it affect international trade? How many nations belong to the WTO? (Update the number given in this book at **www.wto.org**.) Is the Doha Round (or Doha Agenda) still in progress, or has it been concluded with an agreement (again, use the WTO Website)? If the former, when and where was the latest ministerial meeting? If the latter, what are the main features of the agreement? **LO5**

**FURTHER TEST YOUR KNOWLEDGE AT
www.mcconnellbriefmacro1e.com**

Web-Based Questions

At the text's Online Learning Center, **www.mcconnellbriefmacro 1e.com**, you will find a multiple-choice quiz on this chapter's content. We encourage you to take the quiz to see how you do.

Also, you will find one or more Web-based questions that require information from the Internet to answer.

Glossary

ability-to-pay principle The idea that those who have greater income (or wealth) should pay a greater proportion of it as taxes than those who have less income (or wealth).

actual reserves The funds that a bank has on deposit at the Federal Reserve Bank of its district (plus its vault cash).

aggregate A collection of specific economic units treated as if they were one. For example, all prices of individual goods and services are combined into a price level, or all the units of output are aggregated into gross domestic product.

aggregate demand A schedule or curve that shows the total quantity of goods and services demanded (purchased) at different price levels.

aggregate demand–aggregate supply model The macroeconomic model that uses aggregate demand and aggregate supply to determine and explain the price level and the real domestic output.

aggregate supply A schedule or curve showing the total quantity of goods and services supplied (produced) at different price levels.

aggregate supply shocks Sudden unanticipated large changes in resource costs that shift an economy's aggregate supply curve.

allocative efficiency The apportionment of resources among firms and industries to obtain the production of the products most wanted by society (consumers); the output of each product at which its marginal cost and price or marginal benefit are equal.

anticipated inflation Increases in the price level (inflation) that occur at the expected rate.

appreciation (of the dollar) An increase in the value of the dollar relative to the currency of another nation, so a dollar buys a larger amount of the foreign currency and thus of foreign goods.

asset Anything of monetary value owned by a firm or individual.

asset demand for money The amount of money people want to hold as a store of value; this amount varies inversely with the interest rate.

average tax rate Total tax paid divided by total (taxable) income, as a percentage.

balance sheet A statement of the assets, liabilities, and net worth of a firm or individual at some given time.

bank deposits The deposits that individuals or firms have at banks (or thrifts) or that banks have at the Federal Reserve Banks.

bankers' bank A bank that accepts the deposits of and makes loans to depository institutions; in the United States, a Federal Reserve Bank.

bank reserves The deposits of commercial banks and thrifts at Federal Reserve Banks plus bank and thrift vault cash.

barter The exchange of one good or service for another good or service.

base year The year with which other years are compared when an index is constructed; for example, the base year for a price index.

benefits-received principle The idea that those who receive the benefits of goods and services provided by government should pay the taxes required to finance them.

Board of Governors The seven-member group that supervises and controls the money and banking system of the United States; also called the *Board of Governors of the Federal Reserve System* and the *Federal Reserve Board*.

bond A financial device through which a borrower (a firm or government) is obligated to pay the principal and interest on a loan at a specific date in the future.

budget constraint The limit that the size of a consumer's income (and the prices that must be paid for goods and services) imposes on the ability of that consumer to obtain goods and services.

budget deficit The amount by which the expenditures of the Federal government exceed its revenues in any year.

budget line A line that shows the different combinations of two products a consumer can purchase with a specific money income, given the products' prices.

budget surplus The amount by which the revenues of the Federal government exceed its expenditures in any year.

built-in stabilizer A mechanism that increases government's budget deficit (or reduces its surplus) during a recession and increases government's budget surplus (or reduces its deficit) during expansion without any action by policymakers. The tax system is one such mechanism.

Bureau of Economic Analysis (BEA) An agency of the U.S. Department of Commerce that compiles the national income and product accounts.

business cycles Recurring increases and decreases in the level of economic activity over periods of years; a cycle consists of peak, recession, trough, and expansion phases.

business firm (See **firm.**)

capital Human-made resources (buildings, machinery, and equipment) used to produce goods and services; goods that do not directly satisfy human wants; also called *capital goods* and *investment goods*.

capital gain The gain realized when securities or properties are sold for a price greater than the price paid for them.

capital goods   (See **capital.**)

capitalism   An economic system in which property resources are privately owned and markets and prices are used to direct and coordinate economic activities.

capital stock   The total available capital in a nation.

cartel   A formal agreement among firms (or countries) in an industry to set the price of a product and establish the outputs of the individual firms (or countries) or to divide the market for the product geographically.

ceiling price   (See **price ceiling.**)

central bank   A bank whose chief function is the control of the nation's money supply; in the United States, the Federal Reserve System.

central economic planning   Government determination of the objectives of the economy and how resources will be directed to attain those goals.

ceteris paribus **assumption**   (See **other-things-equal assumption.**)

change in demand   A change in the quantity demanded of a good or service at every price; a shift of the demand curve to the left or right.

change in quantity demanded   A change in the amount of a product that consumers are willing and able to purchase because of a change in the product's price; a movement from one point to another on a fixed demand curve.

change in quantity supplied   A change in the amount of a product that producers offer for sale because of a change in the product's price.

change in supply   A change in the quantity supplied of a good or service at every price; a shift of the supply curve to the left or right.

checkable deposit   Any deposit in a commercial bank or thrift institution against which a check may be written.

check clearing   The process by which funds are transferred from the checking accounts of the writers of checks to the checking accounts of the recipients of the checks.

checking account   A checkable deposit in a commercial bank or thrift institution.

circular flow diagram   The flow of resources from households to firms and of products from firms to households. These flows are accompanied by reverse flows of money from firms to households and from households to firms.

Coase theorem   The idea, first stated by economist Ronald Coase, that externality problems may be resolved through private negotiations of the affected parties.

coincidence of wants   A situation in which the good or service that one trader desires to obtain is the same as that which another trader desires to give up and an item that the second trader wishes to acquire is the same as that which the first trader desires to surrender.

command system   A method of organizing an economy in which property resources are publicly owned and government uses central economic planning to direct and coordinate economic activities; command economy; communism.

commercial bank   A firm that engages in the business of banking (accepts deposits, offers checking accounts, and makes loans).

commercial banking system   All commercial banks and thrift institutions as a group.

communism   (See **command system.**)

comparative advantage   A situation in which a person or country can produce a specific product at a lower opportunity cost than some other person or country; the basis for specialization and trade.

compensation of employees   Wages and salaries plus wage and salary supplements paid by employers to workers.

competition   The presence in a market of independent buyers and sellers competing with one another along with the freedom of buyers and sellers to enter and leave the market.

complementary goods   Products and services that-are used together. When the price of one falls, the demand for the other increases (and conversely).

constant opportunity cost   An opportunity cost that remains the same for each additional unit as a consumer (or society) shifts purchases (production) from one product to another along a straight-line budget line (production possibilities curve).

consumer goods   Products and services that satisfy human wants directly.

Consumer Price Index (CPI)   An index that measures the prices of a fixed "market basket" of some 300 goods and services bought by a "typical" consumer.

consumer sovereignty   Determination by consumers of the types and quantities of goods and services that will be produced with the scarce resources of the economy; consumers' direction of production through their dollar votes.

contractionary fiscal policy   A decrease in government purchases for goods and services, an increase in net taxes, or some combination of the two, for the purpose of decreasing aggregate demand and thus controlling inflation.

corporate income tax   A tax levied on the net income (accounting profit) of corporations.

corporation   A legal entity ("person") chartered by a state or the Federal government that is distinct and separate from the individuals who own it.

cost-benefit analysis   A comparison of the marginal costs of a government project or program with the marginal benefits to decide whether or not to employ resources in that project or program and to what extent.

cost-of-living adjustment (COLA)   An automatic increase in the incomes (wages) of workers when inflation occurs; guaranteed by a collective bargaining contract between firms and workers.

cost-push inflation   Increases in the price level (inflation) resulting from an increase in resource costs (for example, raw-material prices) and hence in per-unit production costs; inflation caused by reductions in aggregate supply.

Council of Economic Advisers (CEA) A group of three persons that advises and assists the president of the United States on economic matters (including the preparation of the annual *Economic Report of the President*).

creative destruction The hypothesis that the creation of new products and production methods simultaneously destroys the market power of existing monopolies.

credit union An association of persons who have a common tie (such as being employees of the same firm or members of the same labor union) that sells shares to (accepts deposits from) its members and makes loans to them.

crowding-out effect A rise in interest rates and a resulting decrease in investment caused by the Federal government's increased borrowing to finance budget deficits or debt.

currency Coins and paper money.

cyclical asymmetry The potential problem of monetary policy successfully controlling inflation during the expansionary phase of the business cycle but failing to expand spending and real GDP during the recessionary phase of the cycle.

cyclical deficit A Federal budget deficit that is caused by a recession and the consequent decline in tax revenues.

cyclical unemployment A type of unemployment caused by insufficient total spending (or by insufficient aggregate demand).

deflating Finding the real gross domestic product by decreasing the dollar value of the GDP for a year in which prices were higher than in the base year.

deflation A decline in the economy's price level.

demand A schedule showing the amounts of a good or service that buyers (or a buyer) wish to purchase at various prices during some time period.

demand curve A curve illustrating demand.

demand-pull inflation Increases in the price level (inflation) resulting from an excess of demand over output at the existing price level, caused by an increase in aggregate demand.

demand shocks Sudden, unexpected change in demand.

dependent variable A variable that changes as a consequence of a change in some other (independent) variable; the "effect" or outcome.

depository institutions Firms that accept deposits of money from the public (businesses and persons); commercial banks, savings and loan associations, mutual savings banks, and credit unions.

depreciation (of the dollar) A decrease in the value of the dollar relative to another currency, so a dollar buys a smaller amount of the foreign currency and therefore of foreign goods.

determinants of aggregate demand Factors such as consumption spending, investment, government spending, and net exports that, if they change, shift the aggregate demand curve.

determinants of aggregate supply Factors such as-input prices, productivity, and the legal-institutional environment that, if they change, shift the aggregate supply curve.

determinants of demand Factors other than price that locate the position of the demand curve.

determinants of supply Factors other than price that locate the position of the supply curve.

developing countries Many countries of Africa, Asia, and Latin America that are characterized by lack of capital goods, use of nonadvanced technologies, low literacy rates, high unemployment, rapid population growth, and labor forces heavily committed to agriculture.

direct relationship The relationship between two variables that change in the same direction, for example, product price and quantity supplied.

discount rate The interest rate that the Federal Reserve Banks charge on the loans they make to commercial banks and thrift institutions.

discretionary fiscal policy Deliberate changes in taxes (tax rates) and government spending by Congress to promote full employment, price stability, and economic growth.

discrimination The practice of according individuals or groups inferior treatment in hiring, occupational access, education and training, promotion, wage rates, or working conditions even though they have the same abilities, education, skills, and work experience as other workers.

disinflation A decline in the annual rate of inflation from the previous year.

dividends Payments by a corporation of all or part of its profit to its stockholders (the corporate owners).

division of labor The separation of the work required to produce a product into a number of different tasks that are performed by different workers; specialization of workers.

Doha Round The latest, uncompleted (as of 2008) sequence of trade negotiations by members of the World Trade Organization; named after Doha, Qatar, where the set of negotiations began.

dollar votes The "votes" that consumers and entrepreneurs cast for the production of consumer and capital goods, respectively, when they purchase those goods in product and resource markets.

dumping The sale of products in a foreign country at prices either below costs or below the prices charged at home.

durable good A consumer good with an expected life (use) of 3 or more years.

easy money policy Federal Reserve System actions to increase the money supply to lower interest rates and expand real GDP.

economic cost A payment that must be made to obtain and retain the services of a resource; the income a firm must provide to a resource supplier to attract the resource away from an alternative use; equal to the quantity of other products that cannot be produced when resources are instead used to make a particular product.

economic efficiency The use of the minimum necessary resources to obtain the socially optimal amounts of goods and services; entails both productive efficiency and allocative efficiency.

economic growth (1) An outward shift in the production possibilities curve that results from an increase in resource supplies or quality or an improvement in technology; (2) an increase of real output (gross domestic product) or real output per capita.

economic law An economic principle that has been tested and retested and has stood the test of time.

economic model A simplified picture of economic reality; an abstract generalization.

economic perspective A viewpoint that envisions individuals and institutions making rational decisions by comparing the marginal benefits and marginal costs associated with their actions.

economic policy A course of action intended to correct or avoid a problem.

economic principle A widely accepted generalization about the economic behavior of individuals or institutions.

economic problem The choices necessitated because society's economic wants for goods and services are unlimited but the resources available to satisfy these wants are limited (scarce).

economic profit The total revenue of a firm less its economic costs (which include both explicit costs and implicit costs); also called *pure profit* and *above-normal profit*.

economic resources The land, labor, capital, and entrepreneurial ability that are used in the production of goods and services; productive agents; factors of production.

economics The study of how people, institutions, and society make economic choices under conditions of scarcity.

economic system A particular set of institutional arrangements and a coordinating mechanism for solving the economizing problem; a method of organizing an economy, of which the market system and the command system are the two general types.

economic theory A statement of a cause-effect relationship; when accepted by nearly all economists, an economic principle.

economies of scale Reductions in the average total cost of producing a product as the firm expands the size of plant (its output) in the long run; the economies of mass production.

efficient allocation of resources That allocation of an economy's resources among the production of different products that leads to the maximum satisfaction of consumers' wants, thus producing the socially optimal mix of output with society's scarce resources.

entrepreneurial ability The human resource that combines the other resources to produce a product, makes nonroutine decisions, innovates, and bears risks.

equilibrium price The price in a competitive market at which the quantity demanded and the quantity supplied are equal, there is neither a shortage nor a surplus, and there is no tendency for price to rise or fall.

equilibrium price level The price level at which the aggregate demand curve intersects the aggregate supply curve.

equilibrium quantity The quantity demanded and supplied at the equilibrium price in a competitive market.

equilibrium real output The gross domestic product at which the total quantity of final goods and services purchased (aggregate expenditures) is equal to the total quantity of final goods and services produced (the real domestic output); the real domestic output at which the aggregate demand curve intersects the aggregate supplycurve.

euro The common currency unit used by 15 European nations as of 2008 (Austria, Belgium, Cyprus, Finland, France, Germany, Greece, Ireland, Italy, Luxembourg, Malta, the Netherlands, Portugal, Slovenia, and Spain).

European Union (EU) An association of 27 European nations (as of 2008) that has eliminated tariffs and quotas among them, established common tariffs for imported goods from outside the member nations, eliminated barriers to the free movement of capital, and created other common economic policies.

excess reserves The amount by which a bank's or thrift's actual reserves exceed its required reserves; actual reserves minus required reserves.

exchange rate The rate of exchange of one nation's currency for another nation's currency.

exchange-rate appreciation An increase in the value of a nation's currency in foreign exchange markets; an increase in the rate of exchange for foreign currencies.

exchange-rate depreciation A decrease in the value of a nation's currency in foreign exchange markets; a decrease in the rate of exchange for foreign currencies.

excise tax A tax levied on the production of a specific product or on the quantity of the product purchased.

expansion The phase of the business cycle in which output, income, and business activity rise.

expansionary fiscal policy An increase in government purchases of goods and services, a decrease in net taxes, or some combination of the two, for the purpose of increasing aggregate demand and expanding real output.

expectations The anticipations of consumers, firms, and others about future economic conditions.

expected rate of return The increase in profit a firm anticipates it will obtain by purchasing capital (or engaging in research and development); expressed as a percentage of the total cost of the investment (or R&D) activity.

exports Goods and services produced in a nation and sold to buyers in other nations.

export subsidies Government payments to domestic producers to enable them to reduce the price of a good or service to foreign buyers.

external benefit A benefit obtained without compensation by third parties from the production or consumption of sellers or buyers. Example: A beekeeper benefits when a neighboring farmer plants clover.

external cost A cost imposed without compensation on third parties by the production or consumption of sellers or buyers. Example: A manufacturer dumps toxic chemicals into a river, killing the fish sought by sport fishers.

externality A benefit or cost from production or consumption, accruing without compensation to nonbuyers and nonsellers of the product (see **external benefit** and **external cost**).

external public debt Public debt owed to foreign citizens, firms, and institutions.

factors of production Economic resources: land, capital, labor, and entrepreneurial ability.

fallacy of composition The false idea that what is true for the individual (or part) is necessarily true for the group (or whole).

Federal Deposit Insurance Corporation (FDIC) The federally chartered corporation that insures deposit liabilities (up to $250,000 per account) of commercial banks and thrift institutions (excluding credit unions, whose deposits are insured by the National Credit Union Administration).

Federal funds rate The interest rate banks and other depository institutions charge one another on overnight loans made out of their excess reserves.

Federal government The government of the United States, as distinct from the state and local governments.

Federal Open Market Committee (FOMC) The 12-member group that determines the purchase and sale policies of the Federal Reserve Banks in the market for U.S. government securities.

Federal Reserve Banks The 12 banks chartered by the U.S. government to control the money supply and perform other functions. (See **central bank, quasi-public bank,** and **bankers' bank.**)

Federal Reserve Note Paper money issued by the Federal Reserve Banks.

Federal Reserve System A central component of the U.S. banking system, consisting of the Board of Governors of the Federal Reserve and 12 regional Federal Reserve Banks.

final goods and services Goods and services that have been purchased for final use and not for resale or further processing or manufacturing.

financial capital Money available to purchase capital; simply money, as defined by economists.

firm An organization that employs resources to produce a good or service for profit and owns and operates one or more plants.

fiscal policy Changes in government spending and-tax collections designed to achieve a full-employment and noninflationary domestic output; also called *discretionary fiscal policy.*

flexible prices Product prices that freely move upward or downward when product demand or supply changes.

foreign exchange market A market in which the money (currency) of one nation can be used to purchase (can be exchanged for) the money of another nation.

foreign exchange rate (See **exchange rate.**)

fractional reserve A reserve requirement that is less than 100 percent of the checkable-deposit liabilities of a commercial bank or thrift institution.

fractional reserve banking system A banking system in which banks and thrifts are required to hold less than 100 percent of their checkable-deposit liabilities as reserves.

freedom of choice The freedom of owners of property resources to employ or dispose of them as they see fit, of workers to enter any line of work for which they are qualified, and of consumers to spend their incomes in a manner that they think is appropriate.

freedom of enterprise The freedom of firms to obtain economic resources, to use those resources to produce products of the firm's own choosing, and to sell their products in markets of their choice.

free-rider problem The inability of a firm to profitably provide a good because everyone, including nonpayers, can obtain the benefit.

free trade The absence of artificial (government–imposed) barriers to trade among individuals and firms in different nations.

frictional unemployment A type of unemployment caused by workers voluntarily changing jobs and by temporary layoffs; unemployed workers between jobs.

full employment (1) The use of all available resources to produce want-satisfying goods and services; (2) the situation in which the unemployment rate is equal to the full-employment unemployment rate and where frictional and structural unemployment occur but not cyclical unemployment (and the real GDP of the economy equals potential output).

full-employment unemployment rate The unemployment rate at which there is no cyclical unemployment of the labor force; equal to between 4 and 5 percent in the United States because some frictional and structural unemployment is unavoidable.

gains from trade The extra output that trading partners obtain through specialization of production and exchange of goods and services.

GDP (See **gross domestic product.**)

GDP gap Actual gross domestic product minus potential output; may be either a positive amount (a positive GDP gap) or a negative amount (a negative GDP gap).

General Agreement on Tariffs and Trade (GATT) The international agreement reached in 1947 in which 23 nations agreed to give equal and nondiscriminatory treatment to one another, to reduce tariff rates by multinational negotiations, and to eliminate import quotas. It now includes most nations and has become the World Trade Organization.

government purchases Expenditures by government for goods and services that government consumes in providing public goods and for public capital that has a long lifetime; the expenditures of all governments in the economy for those final goods and services.

government transfer payment   The disbursement of money (or goods and services) by government for which government receives no currently produced good or service in return.

gross domestic product (GDP)   The total market value of all final goods and services produced annually within the boundaries of the United States, whether by U.S.- or foreign-supplied resources.

gross private domestic investment   Expenditures for newly produced capital goods (such as machinery, equipment, tools, and buildings) and for additions to inventories.

growth accounting   The bookkeeping of the supply-side elements that contribute to changes in real GDP over some specific time period.

household   An economic unit (of one or more persons) that provides the economy with resources and uses the income received to purchase goods and services that satisfy economic wants.

human capital   The accumulation of knowledge and skills that make a worker productive.

human capital investment   Any expenditure undertaken to improve the education, skills, health, or mobility of workers, with an expectation of greater productivity and thus a positive return on the investment.

hyperinflation   A very rapid rise in the price level; an extremely high rate of inflation.

hypothesis   A tentative explanation of cause and effect that requires testing.

immediate short-run aggregate supply curve   An aggregate supply curve for which real output, but not the price level, changes when the aggregate demand curves shifts; a horizontal aggregate supply curve that implies an inflexible price level.

import quota   A limit imposed by a nation on the quantity (or total value) of a good that may be imported during some period of time.

imports   Spending by individuals, firms, and governments for goods and services produced in foreign nations.

income   A flow of dollars (or purchasing power) per unit of time derived from the use of human or property resources.

increase in demand   An increase in the quantity demanded of a good or service at every price; a shift of the demand curve to the right.

increasing returns   An increase in a firm's output by a larger percentage than the percentage increase in its inputs.

increase in supply   An increase in the quantity supplied of a good or service at every price; a shift of the supply curve to the right.

independent goods   Products or services for which there is little or no relationship between the price of one and the demand for the other. When the price of one rises or falls, the demand for the other tends to remain constant.

independent variable   The variable causing a change in some other (dependent) variable.

industry   A group of (one or more) firms that produce identical or similar products.

inferior good   A good or service whose consumption declines when income rises, prices held constant.

inflation   A rise in the general level of prices in an economy.

inflationary expectations   The belief of workers, firms, and consumers about future rates of inflation.

inflation premium   The component of the nominal interest rate that reflects anticipated inflation.

inflationary output gap   see *positive GDP gap.*

inflexible prices   Product prices that remain in place (at least for a while) even though supply or demand has changed; stuck prices or sticky prices.

information technology   New and more efficient methods of delivering and receiving information through use of computers, fax machines, wireless phones, and the Internet.

infrastructure   The capital goods usually provided by the public sector for the use of its citizens and firms (for example, highways, bridges, transit systems, wastewater treatment facilities, municipal water systems, and airports).

interest   The payment made for the use of money (of borrowed funds).

interest rate   The annual rate at which interest is paid; a percentage of the borrowed amount.

intermediate goods   Products that are purchased for resale or further processing or manufacturing.

internally held public debt   Public debt owed to citizens, firms, and institutions of the same nation that issued the debt.

inventories   Goods that have been produced but remain unsold.

inverse relationship   The relationship between two variables that change in opposite directions, for example, product price and quantity demanded.

investment   Spending for the production and accumulation of capital and additions to inventories.

investment demand curve   A curve that shows the amounts of investment demanded by an economy at a series of real interest rates.

investment goods   (See **capital.**)

investment in human capital   (See **human capital investment.**)

"invisible hand"   The tendency of firms and resource suppliers that seek to further their own self-interests in competitive markets to also promote the interest of society.

labor   People's physical and mental talents and efforts that are used to help produce goods and services.

labor force   Persons 16 years of age and older who are not in institutions and who are employed or are unemployed and seeking work.

labor-force participation rate   The percentage of the working-age population that is actually in the labor force.

labor productivity   Total output divided by the quantity of labor employed to produce it; the average product of labor or output per hour of work.

labor union   A group of workers organized to advance the interests of the group (to increase wages, shorten the hours worked, improve working conditions, and so on).

Laffer Curve   A curve relating tax rates and tax revenues and on which a particular tax rate (between zero and 100 percent) maximizes tax revenues.

land   Natural resources ("free gifts of nature") used to produce goods and services.

law of demand   The principle that, other things equal, an increase in a product's price will reduce the quantity of it demanded, and conversely for a decrease in price.

law of increasing opportunity costs   The principle that as the production of a good increases, the opportunity cost of producing an additional unit rises.

law of supply   The principle that, other things equal, as price rises, the quantity supplied rises, and as price falls, the quantity supplied falls.

learning by doing   Achieving greater productivity and lower average total cost through gains in knowledge and skill that accompany repetition of a task; a source of economies of scale.

legal tender   A legal designation of a nation's official currency (bills and coins). Payment of debts must be accepted in this monetary unit, but creditors can specify the form of payment, for example, "cash only" or "check or credit card only."

liability   A debt with a monetary value; an amount owed by a firm or an individual.

limited liability   Restriction of the maximum loss to a predetermined amount for the owners (stockholders) of a corporation. The maximum loss is the amount they paid for their shares of stock.

liquidity   The ease with which an asset can be converted quickly into cash with little or no loss of purchasing power. Money is said to be perfectly liquid, whereas other assets have a lesser degree of liquidity.

long run   In macroeconomics, a period in which output prices, wages, and other input prices are all flexible.

long-run AD-AS model   A model in which the equilibrium price level and level of real GDP are determined by the intersection of the AD curve and the vertical long-run AS curve.

long-run aggregate supply curve   The aggregate supply curve associated with a time period in which input prices (especially nominal wages) are fully responsive to changes in the price level.

long-run vertical Phillips Curve   The Phillips Curve after all nominal wages and other input prices have adjusted to changes in the rate of inflation; a line emanating straight upward at the economy's natural rate of unemployment, indicating that over long periods of time there is no trade-off between inflation rates and unemployment rates.

M1   The most narrowly defined money supply, equal to currency in the hands of the public and the checkable deposits of commercial banks and thrift institutions.

M2   A more broadly defined money supply, equal to $M1$ plus noncheckable savings accounts (including money market deposit accounts), small time deposits (deposits of less than \$100,000), and individual money market mutual fund balances.

macroeconomics   The part of economics concerned with the economy as a whole; with such major aggregates as the household, business, and government sectors; and with measures of the total economy.

marginal analysis   The comparison of marginal ("extra" or "additional") benefits and marginal costs, usually for decision making.

marginal benefit   The extra (additional) benefit of consuming 1 more unit of some good or service; the change in total benefit when 1 more unit is consumed.

marginal cost   The extra (additional) cost of producing 1 more unit of output; equal to the change in total cost divided by the change in output (and, in the short run, to the change in total variable cost divided by the change in output).

marginal tax rate   The tax rate paid on an additional dollar of income.

market   Any institution or mechanism that brings together buyers (demanders) and sellers (suppliers) of a particular good or service.

market economy   An economy in which only the private decisions of consumers, resource suppliers, and firms determine how resources are allocated; the market system.

market failure   The inability of a market to bring about the allocation of resources that best satisfies the wants of society; in particular, the overallocation or underallocation of resources to the production of a particular good or service because of spillovers or informational problems or because markets do not provide desired public goods.

market for externality rights   A market in which firms can buy rights to discharge pollutants. The price of such rights is determined by the demand for the right to discharge pollutants and a perfectly inelastic supply of such rights (the latter determined by the quantity of discharges that the environment can assimilate).

market system   All the product and resource markets of a market economy and the relationships among them; a method that allows the prices determined in those markets to allocate the economy's scarce resources and to communicate and coordinate the decisions made by consumers, firms, and resource suppliers.

Medicare A Federal program that is financed by payroll taxes and provides for (1) compulsory hospital insurance for senior citizens, (2) low-cost voluntary insurance to help older Americans pay physicians' fees, and (3) subsidized insurance to buy prescription drugs.

medium of exchange Any item sellers generally accept and buyers generally use to pay for a good or service; money; a convenient means of exchanging goods and services without engaging in barter.

microeconomics The part of economics concerned with such individual units as a household, a firm, or an industry and with individual markets, specific goods and services, and product and resource prices.

minimum wage The lowest wage employers may legally pay for an hour of work.

monetary multiplier The multiple of its excess reserves by which the banking system can expand checkable deposits and thus the money supply by making new loans (or buying securities); equal to 1 divided by the reserve requirement.

monetary policy A central bank's changing of the money supply to influence interest rates and assist the economy in achieving price stability, full employment, and economic growth.

money Any item that is generally acceptable to sellers in exchange for goods and services.

money income (See **nominal income.**)

money market The market in which the demand for and the supply of money determine the interest rate (or the level of interest rates) in the economy.

money market deposit account (MMDA) An interest–earning account (at a bank or thrift) consisting of short-term securities and on which a limited number of checks may be written each year.

money market mutual funds (MMMFs) Interest-bearing accounts offered by investment companies, which pool depositors' funds for the purchase of short-term securities. Depositors may write checks in minimum amounts or more against their accounts.

money supply Narrowly defined, $M1$; more broadly defined, $M2$. (See $M1$, $M2$.)

monopoly A market structure in which the number of sellers is so small that each seller is able to influence the total supply and the price of the good or service.

mortgage debt crisis The period beginning in late 2007 when thousands of homeowners defaulted on mortgage loans when they experienced a combination of higher mortgage interest rates and falling home prices.

multiple counting Wrongly including the value of intermediate goods in the gross domestic product; counting the same good or service more than once.

multiplier The ratio of a change in the equilibrium GDP to the change in *investment* or in any other component of *aggregate expenditures* or *aggregate demand*; the number by which a change in any such component must be multiplied to find the resulting change in the equilibrium GDP.

multiplier effect The effect on equilibrium GDP of a change in *aggregate expenditures* or *aggregate demand* (caused by a change in the *consumption schedule*, *investment*, government expenditures, or *net exports*).

national bank A commercial bank authorized to operate by the U.S. government.

National Credit Union Administration (NCUA) The federally chartered agency that insures deposit liabilities (up to $100,000 per account) in credit unions.

national income Total income earned by resource suppliers for their contributions to gross domestic product (plus taxes on production and imports); the sum of wages and salaries, rent, interest, profit, and proprietor's income.

national income accounting The techniques used to measure the overall production of the economy and other related variables for the nation as a whole.

national income and product accounts The national accounts that measure overall production and income of the economy and other related aggregates for the nation as a whole.

natural rate of unemployment The full-employment unemployment rate; the unemployment rate occurring when there is no cyclical unemployment and the economy is achieving its potential output; the unemployment rate at which actual inflation equals expected inflation.

near-money Financial assets, the most important of which are noncheckable savings accounts, time deposits, and U.S. short-term securities and savings bonds, which are not a medium of exchange but can be readily converted into money.

negative externalities A cost imposed without compensation on third parties by the production or consumption of sellers or buyers. Example: A manufacturer dumps toxic chemicals into a river, killing the fish sought by sports fishers; an external cost or a spillover cost.

negative GDP gap A situation in which actual gross domestic product is less than *potential output*. Also known as a recessionary output gap.

negative relationship (See **inverse relationship.**)

net exports Exports minus imports.

net taxes The taxes collected by government less government transfer payments.

network effects Increases in the value of a product to each user, including existing users, as the total number of users rises.

net worth The total assets less the total liabilities of a firm or an individual; for a firm, the claims of the owners against the firm's total assets; for an individual, his or her wealth.

nominal GDP Gross domestic product measured in terms of the price level at the time of the measurement; GDP that is unadjusted for inflation.

nominal income   The number of dollars received by an individual or group for supplying resources during some period of time; income that is not adjusted for inflation.

nominal interest rate   The interest rate expressed in terms of annual amounts currently charged for interest and not adjusted for inflation.

nominal wage   The amount of money received by a worker per unit of time (hour, day, etc.); money wage that is not adjusted for inflation.

nondiscretionary fiscal policy   (See **built-in stabilizer.**)

nondurable good   A consumer good with an expected life (use) of less than 3 years.

nonexcludability   The inability to keep nonpayers (free riders) from obtaining benefits from a certain good; a public goods characteristic.

nonmarket transactions   The value of the goods and services not included in the measurement of the gross domestic product because they are not bought and sold.

nonproduction transaction   The purchase and sale of any item that is not a currently produced good or service.

nonrivalry   The idea that one person's benefit from a certain good does not reduce the benefit available to others; a public goods characteristic.

nontariff barriers   All barriers other than protective tariffs that nations erect to impede international trade, including import quotas, licensing requirements, unreasonable product-quality standards, and unnecessary bureaucratic detail in customs procedures.

normal good   A good or service whose consumption increases when income increases and falls when income decreases, price remaining constant.

North American Free Trade Agreement (NAFTA)   A 1993 agreement establishing, over a 15-year period, a free-trade zone composed of Canada, Mexico, and the United States.

offshoring   The practice of shifting work previously done by American workers to workers located abroad.

OPEC   (See **Organization of Petroleum Exporting Countries.**)

open-market operations   The buying and selling of U.S. government securities by the Federal Reserve Banks for purposes of carrying out monetary policy.

opportunity cost   The value of the good, service, or time forgone to obtain something else.

Organization of Petroleum Exporting Countries (OPEC)   A cartel of oil-producing countries (Algeria, Angola, Ecuador, Indonesia, Iran, Iraq, Kuwait, Libya, Nigeria, Qatar, Saudi Arabia, Venezuela, and the UAE) that attempts to control the quantity and price of crude oil exported by its members and that accounts for 60 percent of the world's export of oil.

other-things-equal assumption   The assumption that factors other than those being considered are held constant; *ceteris paribus* assumption.

partnership   An unincorporated firm owned and operated by two or more persons.

patent   An exclusive right given to inventors to produce and sell a new product or machine for 20 years from the time of patent application.

payroll tax   A tax levied on employers of labor equal to a percentage of all or part of the wages and salaries paid by them and on employees equal to a percentage of all or part of the wages and salaries received by them.

per capita GDP   Gross domestic product (GDP) per person; the average GDP of a population.

per capita income   A nation's total income per person; the average income of a population.

personal consumption expenditures   The expenditures of households for durable and nondurable consumer goods and services.

personal income tax   A tax levied on the taxable income of individuals, households, and unincorporated firms.

per-unit production cost   The average production cost of a particular level of output; total input cost divided by units of output.

Phillips Curve   A curve showing the relationship between the unemployment rate (on the horizontal axis) and the inflation rate (on the vertical axis).

political business cycle   The alleged tendency of Congress to destabilize the economy by reducing taxes and increasing government expenditures before elections, and by raising taxes and reducing expenditures after elections.

positive GDP gap   A situation in which actual gross domestic product exceeds *potential output*. Also known as an inflationary output gap.

positive relationship   A direct relationship between two variables.

potential output   The real output (GDP) an economy can produce when it fully employs its available resources.

poverty   A situation in which the basic needs of an individual or family exceed the means to satisfy them.

poverty rate   The percentage of the population with incomes below the official poverty income levels that are established by the Federal government.

price   The amount of money needed to buy a particular good, service, or resource.

price ceiling   A legally established maximum price for a good or service.

price floor   A legally determined price above the equilibrium price.

price index An index number that shows how the weighted-average price of a "market basket" of goods changes over time.

price level The weighted average of the prices of all the final goods and services produced in an economy.

price-level stability A steadiness of the price level from one period to the next; zero or low annual inflation; also called *price stability*.

price support A minimum price that government allows sellers to receive for a good or service; a legally established or maintained minimum price.

price war Successive and continued decreases in the prices charged by firms in an oligopolistic industry. Each firm lowers its price below rivals' prices, hoping to increase its sales and revenues at its rivals' expense.

prime interest rate The benchmark interest rate that banks use as a reference point for a wide range of loans to businesses and individuals.

principal-agent problem A conflict of interest that occurs when agents (workers or managers) pursue their own objectives to the detriment of the principals' (stockholders') goals.

principles Statements about economic behavior that enable predictions of the probably effects of certain actions.

private good A good or service that is individually consumed and that can be profitably provided by privately owned firms because they can exclude nonpayers from receiving the benefits.

private property The right of private persons and firms to obtain, own, control, employ, dispose of, and bequeath land, capital, and other property.

private sector The households and business firms of the economy.

production possibilities curve A curve showing the different combinations of two goods or services that can be produced in a full-employment, full-production economy where the available supplies of resources and technology are fixed.

productive efficiency The production of a good in the least costly way; occurs when production takes place at the output at which average total cost is a minimum and marginal product per dollar's worth of input is the same for all inputs.

productivity A measure of average output or real output per unit of input. For example, the productivity of labor is determined by dividing real output by hours of work.

productivity growth The increase in productivity from one period to another.

product market A market in which products are sold by firms and bought by households.

progressive tax A tax whose average tax rate increases as the taxpayer's income increases and decreases as the taxpayer's income decreases.

property tax A tax on the value of property (capital, land, stocks and bonds, and other assets) owned by firms and households.

proportional tax A tax whose average tax rate remains constant as the taxpayer's income increases or decreases.

proprietor's income The net income of the owners of unincorporated firms (proprietorships and partnerships).

protective tariff A tariff designed to shield domestic producers of a good or service from the competition of foreign producers.

public debt The total amount owed by the Federal government to the owners of government securities; equal to the sum of past government budget deficits less government budget surpluses.

public good A good or service that is characterized by nonrivalry and nonexcludability; a good or service with these characteristics provided by government.

public investments Government expenditures on public capital (such as roads, highways, bridges, mass-transit systems, and electric power facilities) and on human capital (such as education, training, and health).

public sector The part of the economy that contains all government entities; government.

purchasing power The amount of goods and services that a monetary unit of income can buy.

quantity demanded The amount of a good or service that buyers (or a buyer) desire to purchase at a particular price during some period.

quantity supplied The amount of a good or service that producers (or a producer) offer to sell at a particular price during some period.

quasi-public bank A bank that is privately owned but governmentally (publicly) controlled; each of the U.S. Federal Reserve Banks.

quasi-public good A good or service to which excludability could apply but that has such a large spillover benefit that government sponsors its production to prevent an underallocation of resources.

rate of return The gain in net revenue divided by the cost of an investment or an R&D expenditure; expressed as a percentage.

rational behavior Human behavior based on comparison of marginal costs and marginal benefits; behavior designed to maximize total utility.

real capital (See **capital**.)

real GDP (See **real gross domestic product**.)

real GDP per capita Real output (GDP) divided by population.

real gross domestic product (GDP) Gross domestic product adjusted for inflation; gross domestic product in a year divided by the GDP price index for that year, the index expressed as a decimal.

real income The amount of goods and services that can be purchased with nominal income during some period of time; nominal income adjusted for inflation.

real interest rate The interest rate expressed in dollars of constant value (adjusted for inflation) and equal to the nominal interest rate less the expected rate of inflation.

recession A period of declining real GDP, accompanied by lower real income and higher unemployment.

recessionary output gap *see negative GDP gap.*

refinancing the public debt Selling new government securities to owners of expiring securities or paying them money gained from the sales of new securities to others.

regressive tax A tax whose average tax rate decreases as the taxpayer's income increases and increases as the taxpayer's income decreases.

required reserves The funds that banks and thrifts must deposit with the Federal Reserve Bank (or hold as vault cash) to meet the legal reserve requirement; a fixed percentage of the bank's or thrift's checkable deposits.

reserve ratio The specified minimum percentage of its checkable deposits that a bank or thrift must keep on deposit at the Federal Reserve Bank in its district or hold as vault cash.

resource A natural, human, or manufactured item that helps produce goods and services; a productive agent or factor of production.

resource market A market in which households sell and firms buy resources or the services of resources.

rule of 70 A method for determining the number of years it will take for some measure to double, given its annual percentage increase. Example: To determine the number of years it will take for the price level to double, divide 70 by the annual rate of inflation.

sales tax A tax levied on the cost (at retail) of a broad group of products.

saving Disposable income not spent for consumer goods; equal to disposable income minus personal consumption expenditures.

savings account A deposit that is interest-bearing and that the depositor can normally withdraw at any time.

savings institution (See **thrift institution**.)

scarce resources The limited quantities of land, capital, labor, and entrepreneurial ability that are never sufficient to satisfy people's virtually unlimited economic wants.

scientific method The procedure for the systematic pursuit of knowledge involving the observation of facts and the formulation and testing of hypotheses to obtain theories, principles, and laws.

secular trend A long-term tendency; a change in some variable over a very long period of years.

self-interest The most-advantageous outcome as viewed by each firm, property owner, worker, or consumer.

service An (intangible) act or use for which a consumer, firm, or government is willing to pay.

shocks Sudden, unexpected changes in *demand* (or *aggregate demand*) or *supply (or aggregate supply)*.

shortage The amount by which the quantity demanded of a product exceeds the quantity supplied at a particular (below-equilibrium) price.

short run In macroeconomics, a period in which prices of output are flexible but wages and other input prices are inflexible.

short-run aggregate supply curve An aggregate supply curve relevant to a time period in which input prices (particularly nominal wages) do not change in response to changes in the price level.

simultaneous consumption A product's ability to satisfy a large number of consumers at the same time.

slope of a line The ratio of the vertical change (the rise or fall) to the horizontal change (the run) between any two points on a line. The slope of an upward-sloping line is positive, reflecting a direct relationship between two variables; the slope of a downward-sloping line is negative, reflecting an inverse relationship between two variables.

Smoot-Hawley Tariff Act Legislation passed in 1930 that established very high tariffs. Its objective was to reduce imports and stimulate the domestic economy, but it resulted only in retaliatory tariffs by other nations.

Social Security The Federal program, financed by compulsory payroll taxes, that partially replaces earnings lost when workers retire, become disabled, or die.

Social Security trust fund A Federal fund that saves excessive Social Security tax revenues received in one year to meet Social Security benefit obligations that exceed Social Security tax revenues in some subsequent year.

sole proprietorship An unincorporated firm owned and operated by one person.

specialization The use of the resources of an individual, a firm, a region, or a nation to concentrate production on one or a small number of goods and services.

speculation The activity of buying or selling with the motive of later reselling or rebuying for profit.

standardized budget A measure of what the Federal budget deficit or budget surplus would be with the existing tax and government spending programs if the economy had achieved full-employment GDP in the year.

stagflation Inflation accompanied by stagnation in the rate of growth of output and an increase in unemployment in the economy; simultaneous increases in the inflation rate and the unemployment rate.

start-up (firm) A new firm focused on creating and introducing a particular new product or employing a specific new production or distribution method.

sticky prices (See *inflexible prices*)

stock (corporate) An ownership share in a corporation.

store of value An asset set aside for future use; one of the three functions of money.

structural unemployment Unemployment of workers whose skills are not demanded by employers, who lack sufficient skill to obtain employment, or who cannot easily move to locations where jobs are available.

subsidy A payment of funds (or goods and services) by a government, firm, or household for which it receives no good or service in return. When made by a government, it is a government transfer payment.

substitute goods Products or services that can be used in place of each other. When the price of one falls, the demand for the other product falls; conversely, when the price of one product rises, the demand for the other product rises.

supply A schedule showing the amounts of a good or service that sellers (or a seller) will offer at various prices during some period.

supply-side economics A view of macroeconomics that emphasizes the role of marginal tax rates and other factors that affect long-rung aggregate supply and therefore affect inflation, unemployment, and economic growth.

supply curve A curve illustrating the direct relationship between the price of a product and the quantity of it supplied, other things equal.

supply shocks Sudden, unexpected changes in *aggregate supply*

surplus The amount by which the quantity supplied of a product exceeds the quantity demanded at a specific (above-equilibrium) price.

tariff A tax imposed by a nation on an imported good.

tax An involuntary payment of money (or goods and services) to a government by a household or firm for which the household or firm receives no good or service directly in return.

tax incidence The person or group that ends up paying a tax.

technological advance New and better goods and services and new and better ways of producing or distributing them.

technology The body of knowledge and techniques that can be used to combine economic resources to produce goods and services.

term auction facility The *monetary policy* procedure used by the Federal Reserve, in which commercial banks anonymously bid to obtain loans being made available by the Fed as a way to expand reserves in the banking system.

terms of trade The rate at which units of one product can be exchanged for units of another product; the price of a good or service; the amount of one good or service that must be given up to obtain 1-unit of another good or service.

thrift institution A savings and loan association, mutual savings bank, or credit union.

tight money policy Federal Reserve System actions that contract, or restrict, the growth of the nation's money supply for the purpose of reducing or eliminating inflation.

time deposit An interest-earning deposit in a commercial bank or thrift institution that the depositor can withdraw without penalty after the end of a specified period.

token money Bills or coins for which the amount printed on the *currency* bears no relationship to the value of the paper or metal embodied within it; for currency still circulating, money for which the face value exceeds the commodity value.

total cost The total expense to a firm of producing a particular lever of output.

total demand for money The sum of the transactions demand for money and the asset demand for money.

total revenue The total number of dollars received by a firm (or firms) from the sale of a product; equal to the total expenditures for the product produced by the firm (or firms); equal to the quantity sold (demanded) multiplied by the price at which it is sold.

Trade Adjustment Assistance Act A U.S. law passed in 2002 that provides cash assistance, education and training benefits, health care subsidies, and wage subsidies (for persons age 50 or more) to workers displaced by imports or plant relocations abroad.

trade balance The export of goods (or goods and services) of a nation less its imports of goods (or goods and services).

trade bloc A group of nations that lower or abolish trade barriers among members. Examples include the European Union and the nations of the North American Free Trade Agreement.

trade deficit The amount by which a nation's imports of goods (or goods and services) exceed its exports of goods (or goods and services).

trademark A legal protection that gives the originators of a product an exclusive right to use the brand name.

trade-off The sacrifice of some or all of one economic goal, good, or service to achieve some other goal, good, or service.

trade surplus The amount by which a nation's exports of goods (or goods and services) exceed its imports of goods (or goods and services).

transactions demand for money The amount of money people want to hold for use as a medium of exchange (to make payments); varies directly with nominal GDP.

transfer payment A payment of money (or goods and services) by a government to a household or firm for which the payer receives no good or service directly in return.

unanticipated inflation Increases in the price level (inflation) at a rate greater than expected.

unemployment The failure to use all available economic resources to produce desired goods and services; the failure of the economy to fully employ its labor force.

unemployment compensation (See **unemployment insurance.**)

unemployment insurance The social insurance program that in the United States is financed by state payroll taxes on employers and makes income available to workers who become unemployed and are unable to find jobs.

unemployment rate The percentage of the labor force unemployed at any time.

unfulfilled expectations Situations in which households and businesses were expecting one thing to happen but instead find that something else has happened; unrealized anticipations or plans relating to future economic conditions and outcomes.

unit of account A standard unit in which prices can be stated and the value of goods and services can be compared; one of the three functions of money.

unlimited wants The insatiable desire of consumers for goods and services that will give them satisfaction or utility.

U.S. securities Treasury bills, Treasury notes, Treasury bonds, and U.S. savings bonds issued by the Federal government to finance expenditures that exceed tax revenues.

utility The want-satisfying power of a good or service; the satisfaction or pleasure a consumer obtains from the consumption of a good or service (or from the consumption of a collection of goods and services).

value of money The quantity of goods and services for which a unit of money (a dollar) can be exchanged; the purchasing power of a unit of money; the reciprocal of the price index.

vault cash The currency a bank has in its vault and cash drawers.

voluntary export restrictions Voluntary limitations by countries or firms of their exports to a particular foreign nation to avoid enactment of formal trade barriers by that nation.

wage (or wage rate) The price paid for the use or services of labor per unit of time (per hour, per day, and so on).

wealth Anything that has value because it produces income or could produce income. Wealth is a stock; income is a flow. Assets less liabilities; net worth.

wealth effect The tendency for people to increase their consumption spending when the value of their financial and real assets rises and to decrease their consumption spending when the value of those assets falls.

World Trade Organization (WTO) An organization of 153 nations (as of 2008) that oversees the provisions of the current world trade agreement, resolves trade disputes stemming from it, and holds forums for further rounds of trade negotiations.

Page numbers followed by n refer to notes.